The Origins of Health and Disease

Michael E. Hyland

D0002577

CAMBRIDGE
UNIVERSITY PRESS

CAMBRIDGE UNIVERSITY PRESS
Cambridge, New York, Melbourne, Madrid, Cape Town,
Singapore, São Paulo, Delhi, Tokyo, Mexico City

Cambridge University Press
The Edinburgh Building, Cambridge CB2 8RU, UK

Published in the United States of America by Cambridge University Press,
New York

www.cambridge.org
Information on this title: www.cambridge.org/9780521719704

First published 2011

Printed in the United Kingdom at the University Press, Cambridge

A catalogue record for this publication is available from the British Library

Library of Congress Cataloguing in Publication data
Hyland, Michael.
  The origins of health and disease / Michael E. Hyland.
    p. ; cm.
  Includes bibliographical references and index.
  ISBN 978-0-521-89539-2 (hardback) – ISBN 978-0-521-71970-4 (pbk.)
  1. Psychoneuroimmunology. I. Title.
  [DNLM: 1. Psychoneuroimmunology. 2. Cumulative Trauma
  Disorders–etiology. 3. Fatigue Syndrome, Chronic–etiology.
  4. Irritable Bowel Syndrome–etiology. 5. Neuroimmunomodulation.
  WL 103.7]
  QP356.47.H95 2011
  616.07′9–dc22
  2010052185

ISBN 978-0-521-89539-2 Hardback
ISBN 978-0-521-71970-4 Paperback

To my wife

Contents

Figures

Tables

Boxes

Acknowledgements

New ideas do not come out of a vacuum, but it is often difficult to tell how they have arisen. I would like to thank those academic colleagues in the UK and elsewhere as well as my research students, who, through discussion, have encouraged and helped me to develop these ideas. I will not embarrass them by name but they will know who they are.

1 The two philosophies: health, disease, medicine and psychotherapy

What is this book about?

During the last 50 years modern science has provided explanations for many previously unexplained phenomena. Of those that remain unexplained, four are particularly pertinent to this book. First, up to a third of patients who attend their general practitioner (GP) have 'medically unexplained symptoms'. The term 'medically unexplained symptoms' is self-explanatory. Such patients report symptoms in the absence of any diagnosed disease, which, more importantly, cannot be explained in terms of an underlying physiological abnormality – called pathophysiology. In addition, there are so-called *functional diseases* that cannot be explained in terms of pathophysiology, including chronic fatigue syndrome, irritable bowel syndrome and repetitive strain injury.

Second, for diseases that *are* understood in terms of their pathophysiology, it remains unclear how those diseases originate in the first place. We know that diseases such as cancer, heart disease and asthma arise out of a combination of genetics and lifestyle factors. In many cases the environment 'switches on' disease-causing genes that are otherwise inactive. In addition, research shows that events that occur in the womb and in early childhood can influence disease onset decades later. We do not know what exactly it is that is being 'programmed' by these early events to cause later disease. We do not know why or how environmental factors switch on disease-causing genes so that they express the biochemical changes that lead to disease.

Third, there is no adequate explanation for the effectiveness of psychological effects on mental or physical disease. There are two parts to any therapy: the part that the therapist has been trained to deliver and that is believed to be the cause of therapeutic outcome, and what might be labelled 'the other part'. The 'other part' is known by a variety of names. In medicine it is called 'the art of medicine'. Good communication is believed to be an important part of this art of medicine. In psychotherapy the 'other part' involves the therapeutic

1

bond, therapist effect and expectancy, namely common factors of all therapies that together form the contextual model. In complementary medicine there is recognition that some therapists have that little bit of extra something that provides better outcome compared with their peers. Additionally, the 'other part' of therapy appears in topics such as the placebo effect, the non-specific effect and the human effect. The 'other part' of therapy can be defined as the part that contributes to improvement in psychological and physiological outcome, but without being the primary intent of the psychological or medical intervention.

From a clinical perspective, the 'other part' of therapy can be important. The 'other part' explains at least 80% of the improvement that occurs when patients take antidepressants; it accounts for about 90% of improvement from psychotherapy (some suggest even more); and in the case of complementary and alternative medicine it accounts for between 80% and 100% depending on the therapy and controversial conclusions of those working in this field. Despite its importance, the 'other part' is neglected. Any understanding of therapy is based on the logic that therapy is correcting something that is wrong. The intended parts of all therapies do just that: they are based on the rationale that something is wrong and the therapy corrects that something. However, in the case of the 'other part' of therapy there is no clear science of 'that which is wrong'. For example, in the placebo effect, what is wrong that is being corrected? Without an understanding of the mechanism on which the 'other part' is operating, there can be no great advance in our ability to exploit what may be an important therapeutic mechanism.

The fourth phenomenon for which there is no clear explanation is how some of the body's control systems work. The body's control systems consist of two kinds: those where the reference criterion or set point is fixed and those where the reference criterion or set point varies. Those control systems with fixed reference criteria (called homeostatic control systems) are easy to understand. The genome specifies what the set point should be. The control systems with varying reference criteria (called homeodynamic control systems) are not easy to understand. *Something* must be controlling the reference criteria. Something, for example, controls the level of inflammatory biochemicals in the body, increasing and decreasing these levels on the basis of external threat or relaxation. In addition, for many diseases the reference criterion of a control loop is set at an incorrect level – for example, too much inflammation. There *must* be something that controls the body's control systems.

This book sets out a theory that provides an explanation for all four of the above unexplained phenomena. There is something that controls the body's homeodynamic reference criteria and that simultaneously manages the many different and sometimes competing control systems. This something can become dysregulated and, when it becomes dysregulated, the dysregulation leads to medically unexplained symptoms and functional diseases as well as acting as a precursor to the diseases with known pathophysiology. Finally, this something is influenced by psychological inputs, and it is here that the 'other part' of therapy has its effects. In addition to explaining the four phenomenon above, the theory explains why there is a correlation between mental states such as depression, fatigue and anxiety, why these mental states correlate with the immune system, and why there is limited specificity between mental states and either immune parameters or neurotransmitters. The theory explains why repeated acute or chronic stress leads to the physiological and psychological changes, provides a rationale for psychologically mediated therapeutic effects, including placebo effects, and provides a rationale for the effect of psychological aspects of lifestyle on health. Finally, the theory provides a rationale for the cause and management of several diseases or conditions whose treatment is controversial or problematic: repetitive strain injury, attention-deficit/hyperactivity disorder, chronic fatigue syndrome, depression and food intolerance.

Any new theoretical idea must be consistent with existing data. This book contains a review of data from a variety of areas of research; taken together they provide evidence for the theory that is being presented. However, a new theory cannot be corroborated only on the basis of existing data. A primary aim of this book is to stimulate new, theory-driven, empirical research.

The book has the following structure. This chapter deals with underlying assumptions and the basic ideas of the theory. Chapters 2 and 3 develop the theory by focusing on mind–body interactions – research on psychoneuroimmunology, and the relationship between personality/mood and disease is reviewed. Chapter 4 provides an account of network theory. Chapters 5, 6 and 7 provide an account of the origins of poor health and disease. Chapter 8 reviews research on psychologically mediated effects on health, and Chapter 9 examines mechanisms for these effects. Chapter 10 examines lifestyle and health and shows how patterns of living can contribute to better or worse health. Chapter 11 provides a brief evaluation of the theory.

Two philosophies

This first chapter concerns a basic assumption about how the body works. Two different philosophies underpin all therapeutic interactions and, historically, these two philosophies have been antagonistic to each other. One of the philosophies treats the body as an active, self-healing system that heals itself under the right conditions. The other treats it as a passive system that is healed only by the intervention of an active therapist. Of course, there may be a compromise: that the body is both an active and a passive system.

Until a few hundred years ago, all medical and health treatments in the world were guided by one of several *traditional medical systems*, of which the most influential were:

- hippocratic medicine (i.e. the medicine that developed from the writings of the ancient Greek Hippocrates, and which formed the basis of medicine in the West and near East for the following two thousand years);
- traditional Chinese medicine (developed in ancient China and formalised about 2,100 years ago); and
- ayurvedic medicine (developed in India about 3,500 years ago).

In the last couple of hundred years, an entirely new form of medicine, modern Western medicine, was developed that had a fundamentally different philosophy. Modern Western medicine gradually replaced the traditional medicines and is now the dominant form of medicine in all developed countries and most developing countries. It is the dominant form, even in those countries where a traditional medicine is practised alongside modern Western medicine. The term complementary and alternative medicine (CAM) is used to include all traditional medical systems, as well as more recent ones (such as homeopathy and chiropractic). CAMs provide the contemporary alternative to modern Western medicine.

Although modern Western medicine has, in the main, been very successful, several recent, parallel, scientific developments suggest that some of the ideas in these traditional medicines – or at least a modern variant on those ideas – have something important to offer to our modern understanding of human health. In brief, the philosophy of modern Western medicine is that therapy corrects that which is wrong. The new philosophy (or old philosophy of traditional medicine), is that the body is capable of healing by itself and so therapists should focus on enhancing that self-healing process. If both philosophies have some value and both apply to one and the same body, this raises an obvious question: how can the two philosophies be integrated?

The mechanical analogy

Where to start? An obvious way to start is with the earlier traditional medicines, but there is a very good reason for not doing this. The reason is that the 'scientific mind' and hence the modern mind is far more sympathetic to modern Western medicine. This chapter therefore starts by examining the assumptions of modern Western medicine, and then contrasting this philosophy with that of traditional medicine.

The philosophy of modern Western medicine can be traced back to Aristotle's ideas of causality. The idea of cause and effect, of one billiard ball hitting another and causing it roll, has been central to the development of Western science. However, although there are many contributors to modern medicine, it is often not philosophy but advances in technology that contribute to new ways of thinking. Modern medicine owes something to the development of clockwork and the subsequent mechanical revolution. The earliest medieval clocks were made by village blacksmiths. They were crude, but they worked. Gradually the technology of clock making improved so that during the Renaissance skilled clock makers developed the art of clockwork to a high degree of sophistication, including the construction of mechanical automata – mechanically constructed clockwork toys that looked like humans and animals and were able to move their arms and legs. Clockwork is an example of a mechanical device. Weaving machines and steam engines are all mechanical devices of one sort or another, and they were part of the mechanical revolution that occurred throughout Europe.

The mechanical devices and machines did not just change the physical world in which people lived; they also changed the way people thought about the world. People used mechanics as a way of understanding the world, and soon mechanical principles were applied by scientists to a range of problems. Galileo Galilei (1564–1642) applied mechanical principles to the movement of the planets round the sun. God is the celestial clockmaker, who makes the planets work according to mechanical principles. Isaac Newton (1642/3–1727) developed the mathematics of mechanics and so made precise predictions about the way mechanical systems work, both for the planets in the heavens and for machines on this earth. (Newton was born in 1642 by the Julian calendar in use at the time, but in 1643 by the Gregorian calendar that we use now.)

It was inevitable that the idea of mechanics would also be applied to the body. The mechanical interpretation of the body was prompted in part by the developing practice of dissection whereby the body could be understood as a physical rather than metaphysical entity. William Harvey (1578–1657) was a member of the Royal College of Physicians of London who made the daring suggestion that the heart pumped blood round the body. Harvey provided a mechanical interpretation of an organ once considered the seat of emotions. Like Galileo, who was forced to recant, Harvey received considerable criticism (see Box 1.1). Harvey's idea of applying mechanics to living animals was revolutionary and at odds with other ideas at the time.

Although Harvey was criticised, his ideas gained support over time, and the idea of the body as a mechanical system gained credibility. Over a century later, an Italian anatomist, Giovanni Morgagni (1682–1771), was able to establish that disease was due to pathology – i.e., some structural difference between the healthy and diseased body. Morgagni's ideas were developed further by several others to suggest that the pathology could be identified by abnormalities of tissues. The English physician James Smyth (1741–1821) published a fifty-page essay in 1790 entitled *Of the different Species of Inflammation, and of the Cause to*

Box 1.1 Theoretical assumptions determine the way we perceive health and disease

The following is a quotation from the Venetian physician Parisano. It is included here in part because it provides an example of how scientists do not see (or hear) things that are inconsistent with their underlying theories. Harvey was criticised by Parisano, who believed in the philosophy of Hippocratic medicine.

We have no problem to admit that, if the horse swallows water, we can perceive a movement and we can hear a sound. But that a pulse should arise in the breast that can be heard, when the blood is transported from the veins to the arteries, this we certainly can't perceive and we do not believe that this will ever happen, except Harvey lends us his hearing aid. But above all, we do not admit such a transport of the blood ... If blood is transported from the veins of the lung ... into the branches of the arteries, how could a pulse be felt in the breast, how a sound? I am completely innocent of such subtle speculations. Above all, Harvey has it that a pulse should arise from the movement of the blood from the heart into the aorta – no matter from which ventricle. He also claims that this movement produces a pulse, and, moreover, a sound: that sound, however, we deaf people cannot hear, and there is no one in Venice who can. If he can in London, we wish him all the best. But we are writing in Venice *which these Differences are to be ascribed.* The idea of tissue inflammation was developed in France by Philippe Pinel (1745–1826) and later by Xavier Bichat (1771–1802). In each case, these early researchers were able to show that there was a specific relationship between pathology and disease. That is, particular diseases were associated with particular (i.e., specific) forms of physiological abnormality.

The idea of specificity of disease gradually became accepted and, by the middle of the nineteenth century, the German pathologist Rudolph Virchow (1821–1902) was able to show how abnormality could be identified at the level of the cell, confirming that disease was due to abnormalities at a micro-level that then led to the grosser abnormalities that were observable to the naked eye. Virchow's dictum that there is no non-specific disease was a direct challenge to those who were using Hippocratic medicine: every disease had its own individual form of pathology.

By the latter part of the nineteenth century, the specificity argument had been won. Like a clock, the body is made of parts, and the parts together make up the completely functioning organism/clock. Each part exists independently, just in the way that the cogs of a clock each have an independent existence. Each body has a heart, lungs, stomach and so on, which through dissection can be separated from each other. Each is a 'module' that is linked to the others but has an independent existence. Parts of the body or parts of the clock sometimes go wrong, and when they go wrong they need to be repaired. The repairs are *specific* to the part that has gone wrong. For example, if a clock has a broken cog, then it is the broken cog that needs repair, not the spring. If the spring is broken, then it is the spring that needs repair rather than the cog. Similarly, errors in the body are *specific*. If the heart has a faulty heart valve, then it is the heart valve that needs repair or replacement, rather than the bones of the foot. This approach to the body is modular: disease occurs in specific modules.

Modern medicine is based on one fundamental principle: that diseases are caused by specific problems where the physiology has 'gone wrong' – the technical term used is pathophysiology. Pathophysiology consists of error in the body machine, that is, failure of a part to operate correctly. Some of these failures are catastrophic (e.g., if the heart stops beating) whereas others are an inconvenience (e.g., a broken leg). However, in all cases, a specific problem or group of specific problems exists. The problem may be widespread throughout the body, as in the case of blood poisoning, but still the principle of specific cause remains. In sum, each disease is associated with a unique pathophysiology, and the aim of medical science is to discover the pathophysiology.

Once the pathophysiology of a disease has been discovered, then the next challenge is to find a treatment that corrects the pathophysiology. Modern medicine treats specific pathophysiologies with specific treatments. Modern medicine treats the body like a broken clock: find out what is wrong and make it right. Treatment is specific to the pathophysiology. Pathophysiology requires specific therapy to put it right.

The idea of specificity is absolutely crucial to modern medicine, and was used in the nineteenth century for of distinguishing 'true' medicine from quackery. In the nineteenth century purveyors of 'snake oil' would sell often innocuous though sometimes harmful substances that were purported to cure all illnesses – from cancer to leprosy. The idea of a 'cure-all' therapy goes against the principle of specificity, and so cure-alls are treated with a good deal of scepticism by the medical community.

The idea of specificity also leads to an important development in the way medicine is practised. Specificity implies medical specialities. Nowadays some medical doctors specialise in particular parts of the body or particular systems that could exhibit pathology. So, for example, cardiologists specialise in the heart, pulmonologists in the lungs and endocrinologists in the endocrine system. In each case the specialist specialises in a particular part or 'module' of the body, as the underlying assumption is that, although the different modules are connected, each can be treated as an independent entity. Modern medicine is based on a *modular approach* to the body. If the GP cannot be certain of a diagnosis, he or she will refer on to a specialist (called the consultant), and the specialist will then decide whether the particular part or system specialised in is at fault – and if so treat it.

Where does this leave the general practitioner? The GP is a generalist who knows a little about all the specialties but refers on to the specialist when that little is not enough to treat the patient effectively. This 'broad but not very deep' view is not very flattering to the GP, and there have been several attempts to carve out a 'specialist' domain for the GP, including that involving good quality communication. Of course, all medical doctors can practise the art of medicine and use good communication. The problem is that the GP is taught the science of modern medicine, but many of the patients seen by the GP do not fit the model of modern medicine. Between 15% and 30% of patients seeing their GP have medically unexplained symptoms (MUS) (Kirmayer *et al.*, 2004), and although treatment appears to have no effect, good communication leads to a reduction in symptoms (Thomas, 1987). Although MUS patients do not fit the assumptions of modern medicine, they are treatable, but by the art or 'other part' of medicine, not the science of modern medicine.

In sum, the mechanical analogy gives rise to the idea of specific pathology, of modularity, of specific treatments for those specific pathologies and of clinicians, some of whom specialise in the treatment of different specific pathologists.

There is one further point we need to cover about modern medicine. The science of modern medicine is based on *analysis*. Imagine that the cog of a clock is faulty. It is possible to be more specific and identify the precise part of the cog that is faulty – it may be a worn spindle or a broken tooth, but it will be some specific part of the cog. Analysis means taking things apart examining something at a 'micro-level', i.e., seeing what the smallest parts are doing. In the same way, the science of modern medicine is based on the idea that finding out about the smallest parts provides the key to understanding how the system as a whole works. Notice that in the history of medicine, the idea of pathology starts with anatomical abnormality, then progresses to the idea of tissue abnormality, and finally to cellular abnormality. The human genome project and the search for genetic abnormality provide a final step in this story of looking at smaller and smaller parts. Analysis is also referred to as *micro-analysis*, which means that the smaller you go, the more you understand the function of a system. In the case of the human genome project, the hope is that by understanding human genes, the smallest part of information in a cell, it will be possible to understand how those cells develop pathology – and how to cure that pathology. The reasoning behind this is that the body is controlled by its genes, and if the genes can be controlled by a therapy, then it will also be possible to control disease.

The ecological analogy

The traditional medicines are based on an analogy derived from ecology. Ecological systems are self-regulating – they are systems in balance. For example, consider the relationship between foxes and rabbits. Foxes eat rabbits. Any increase in the rabbit population leads to the foxes having a more readily available source of food, so this will lead to the fox population increasing. As the fox population increases, the rabbits find it more difficult to escape from a fox, so then the rabbit population decreases. As the number of rabbits decrease, so the foxes go hungry and they breed less. The fox and rabbit populations 'balance' each other.

This principle of balance was well known to the philosophers who developed traditional medical systems two to four thousand years ago and they used this principle as the basis for understanding health. The body is a system in balance. Certain things put the body out of balance, and the lack of balance then causes disease. Restoring health involves getting the system back into balance again.

The three main traditional medicines (Hippocratic, Chinese, Ayurvedic) differ concerning what exactly it is that is in or out of balance, but in all cases there is no one-to-one relationship between particular diseases and a particular kind of imbalance. Instead, a group of diseases may be associated with an imbalance, but even within that group a disease may be caused by some other imbalance. The result is that there is no specificity between the underlying cause and its consequence of disease. So, for example, lack of liver Qi in traditional Chinese medicine may lead to stomach complaints but equally it may lead to respiratory complaints and fatigue. The cause of disease is non-modular.

Although there is no specificity between imbalance and disease in traditional medicines, there is an important relationship between people and imbalance. All traditional medicines suggest that certain types of people are more prone to particular types of imbalance than others, so the underlying treatment principle is to treat the person not the disease. In sum, modern medicines can be said to treat the disease; traditional medicines to treat the person.

Modern medicine is based on the principle of analysis. By contrast, traditional medicines can be said to use the principle of *synthesis*. Rather than trying to understand the body at the micro-level, the traditional medicines examine how the whole system works together in relation to its environment. Instead of examining the parts of the system, traditional medicines try to gain an understanding of the system as a whole. Of course, there can be problems in this holistic understanding because, at the very least, the different traditional medical systems suggest different kinds of holistic system.

The concept of *emergentism* is commonly associated with both synthesis and holistic understanding. The basic idea behind emergentism is this. Micro-analysis shows how the individual parts of a system work, but it does not show how the system operates as a whole. It sometimes happens that when all the parts function together, new properties 'emerge' that cannot be deduced from the properties of the parts in isolation. For example, the parts of a car each have their own properties, but the property of movement is something that occurs only when the parts are put together. The idea of emergentism is often cited in defence of the synthetic approach – and to provide a counterargument to the micro-analytic approach that has been so successful in modern science (the idea of emergentism is explained in more detail in Chapter 4).

The lack of disease specificity of traditional medicines coupled with the emphasis on synthesis rather than analysis leads to a number of differences compared with modern Western medicine. One obvious difference is that traditional medical systems do not generate therapists who specialise. There are no specialisms, either in terms of disease, part of the body, type of imbalance or cause of imbalance. An acupuncturist is an acupuncturist – he or she does not specialise in particular types of disease or treatment. However, there is another more interesting difference between the two philosophies which concerns the issue of preventive medicine.

Treatment and prevention from the perspective of the two philosophies

'Treatment' refers to therapies that are applied to existing disease. 'Prevention' refers to therapies that aim to prevent the occurrence of a disease. Both traditional and modern medicines have an interest in prevention of disease. In practice, there is a greater focus (or resourcing) of prevention in traditional compared with Western medicine. In traditional China, a person visits and pays the acupuncturist on a regular basis when they are well – not just when they are ill. Indeed, there is a tradition of paying for treatment when well, but not paying even though continuing treatment when ill. The rationale is that acupuncturist should prevent disease, and if he (typically it is a he) hasn't prevented disease, then it hasn't worked and the acupuncturist shouldn't be paid. Of course, modern Western medicine also has a preventive aspect. One of the most successful developments in this history of medicine (in terms of lives saved) is the preventive medicine of inoculation. Even so, comparatively little money is spent by health services on prevention compared with treatment – the UK's National Health Service has been criticised as an illness service rather than a health service.

Apart from the greater emphasis given by traditional medical systems to prevention, there is also a fundamental difference in how prevention is practised. In the case of modern Western medicine, prevention and treatment involve different types of therapy. So, for example, the bacterial infection of tetanus can be prevented by inoculation, but if an infection occurs then it is treated by antibiotics as well as other treatments that neutralise the tetanus toxins. The prevention (inoculation) and treatment (antibiotics) are different. By contrast, in the case of traditional medicines, the treatment and prevention are often the same. For example, an acupuncturist may insert a needle in the ankle to prevent a cold developing; but once the cold has started, the same point is used to cure it. The modern rationale given by the acupuncturist is that the needle insertion improves the immune system and is helpful whether or not there is an infection. So, just as modern medicine is specific in terms of disease and therapy, it is also specific with respect to treatment and prevention. In traditional medicines, the prevention and treatment are often the same.

The therapies of traditional medicine – which are usually the same for prevention and treatment – fall into two categories: interventions and lifestyle advice. First, there are therapies that involve some 'medical intervention', e.g., in Hippocratic medicine taking blood, in Chinese medicine giving acupuncture and herbs and in Ayurvedic medicine giving herbs. Second, there are therapies that involve lifestyle advice. Because of the Westernisation of traditional medicine, it is common to focus on the medical interventions of traditional medicines rather than the lifestyle advice. Careful reading of original texts suggests that lifestyle interventions are considered at least as important as medical interventions, if not more so. For example, in Ayurvedic medicine, meditation is considered the 'best' form of therapy. Chinese medicine involves Qi Kung, which has a similar effect of mental relaxation. Hippocrates believed in the healing power of rest. All these lifestyle interventions are based on one basic principle that is shared by all traditional medicines: that the body is self-healing when exposed to the right conditions. Hippocrates refers to the 'healing power of nature' or, in its Latin form *vis medicatrix naturae*. Taoism, a Chinese philosophy that was developed about 2,600 years ago, includes the idea that living in 'the right way' promotes health and lengthens life.

The idea of a self-healing body is inconsistent with the philosophy of modern Western medicine. Clocks do not repair themselves. They need to be repaired by a clockmaker. In the same way, a faulty heart valve is not going to get better by itself, nor will the body start producing insulin once its insulin-producing cells have died. Modern medicine is based on the principle that interventions are needed to put things right. By contrast, traditional medicines adopt a philosophy of restoring balance so that the body can self-heal and encouraging lifestyles that promote self-healing or prevent disease. Modern medicine, while recognising the importance of healthy living in the prevention of disease, with few exceptions treats disease, once it has occurred, not by lifestyle advice but by medical interventions wherein the doctor 'makes' the patient better. It is the doctor who does the making better rather than the patient. Indeed, some patients prefer this passive role of the doctor 'making you better'. Some people will prefer to take a pill rather than

Table 1.1 *A brief history of modern medicine*

Traditional medicines	Modern medicine
Based on an ecological analogy, of a body in or out of balance	Based on a mechanical analogy, of a body with or without error
Diseases do not have specific causes	Diseases have specific causes
Not modular	Modular
Synthesis	Analysis
No medical specialists	Medical specialists
Treating the person not the disease	Treating the disease
No disease-specific treatments	Disease-specific treatments
The same therapy can both prevent and treat	Therapies that are preventive are different from those that treat
The body is naturally self-healing	The body needs to be treated by an external agent

alter their lifestyle so as to improve health. Taking a pill is a relatively easy form of ritual to perform. Taking exercise is not.

Is the body actually self-healing? The answer is both yes and no. If you cut yourself, the wound will heal and, if the cut was not too bad, the healing will be so complete that there is no scar. However, if you develop blood poisoning, you will not get better without antibiotics. The reality is that the body does have some capacity to self-heal, but there are limits to that self-healing. Current knowledge of the extent to which the body is self-healing is also limited, and practitioners of conventional versus other medical systems have differing opinions about this capacity.

In sum, there are several differences in the assumptions of the two different philosophies of medicine, and these are summarized in Table 1.1.

Hippocratic medicine was gradually replaced by modern Western medicine over the period from about 1700 to 1900 (see above). Treatments such as bloodletting (which originated before Hippocrates in ancient Egypt) were popular at the beginning of the nineteenth century but had died out by the end of that century. However, the real success of modern Western medicine comes from the middle of the twentieth century when really important therapeutic advances were made. Before that date, and with the exception of inoculation, modern medicine was comparatively ineffective but was certainly less harmful than Hippocratic techniques such as bloodletting and emetics. In the early part of the twentieth century, modern Western medicine was accepted in part because it seemed a rational way of treating diseases, which was consistent with modern science.

Since the mid twentieth century, the techniques of modern medicine have become increasingly sophisticated and successful. However, the success of modern medicine has been patchy. For some diseases it has been extremely successful, for some moderately successful and for some not at all successful. A good common-sense way of identifying the strengths and weakness of modern medicine is to compare the problem caused by the disease or health problem in the eighteenth and nineteenth centuries with that in the twenty-first century.

Success   Smallpox used to kill thousands of people. It is now eradicated through the technique of inoculation, a technique that continues to protect the population against infectious diseases. Tuberculosis (TB) wards and clinics were once commonplace. Although TB still exists, it is no longer the killer disease it once was. The development of antibiotics led to a revolution in the success of infection control. Although resistant strains of bacteria exist, the reality is that infection is very well controlled compared with 100 years ago. Infection control is a success story. A second area of success is that of surgery. Techniques such as hip replacement or heart valve replacement were unthinkable 100 years ago. A final area of success is trauma management. The chance of survival following a life-threatening accident is many times greater now than before. The areas where modern medicine has been successful are those where there is an easily defined pathophysiology and where there is an attainable solution to correcting that pathophysiology. Smallpox is caused by the smallpox virus. No smallpox virus, no smallpox.

Moderate success   There is a group of diseases in which there is some dysregulation such that the body turns on itself and makes itself 'go wrong'. For example, asthma is a disease in which the body's own immune system creates inflammation in the lungs. This inflammation can (in almost all cases) be successfully controlled by the use of anti-inflammatory drugs (typically inhaled corticosteroids), but the disease is not cured by this treatment. In the case of other diseases in which the immune system attacks the body, treatment is less successful. Steroids and other drugs exist for suppressing the inflammatory action of the immune system, but the ability to target only the inflammatory tissue is more difficult to achieve. For example, in the case of multiple sclerosis the immune system attacks the nerves, but there is no successful way of reversing this process once it has started, and the disease leads to increasing disability and eventually death. Cancer and heart disease are also diseases in whose aetiology inflammation plays a role. Survival for some cancers (e.g., breast cancer) has improved considerably through modern techniques. Unfortunately, the outcome come for others cancers (e.g., lung cancer) is more bleak. Heart disease remains the most common cause of death in the Western world – followed by cancer.

The pathophysiology of these different inflammatory diseases is well understood, except for one thing. In all cases the distal cause of these diseases – i.e., the origin of the disease – is uncertain. The pathophysiology can be understood as a causal sequence of events. What causes that sequence is unclear, other than the fact that genetics and environment both play a role.

Box 1.2 Distal versus proximal causes

A distal cause is the cause at the beginning of a sequence. The proximal cause is the cause just prior to the event being explained.

Poor success Modern medicine has been less successful in treating diseases where there is no clearly defined pathophysiology. Irritable bowel syndrome (IBS) affects 1 in 10 people over the age of 50 years and involves pain as well as other symptoms such as diarrhoea, constipation and bloating, but there is no identifiable pathophysiology of the gut. The gut behaves in an abnormal way (hence the label 'functional disease'), but careful micro-analysis of the gut fails to identify any abnormality. There is no easy treatment for IBS, though lifestyle (including diet) can improve symptoms. Chronic fatigue syndrome (CFS) is another disease that poses a challenge for modern Western medicine and which, depending on the method of classification, affects between 0.3% and 1% of the population (Bates *et al.*, 1993). CFS involves extreme feelings of tiredness, malaise and a large and variable group of other symptoms. Although there are often disturbances in physiology, none of these disturbances is sufficiently consistent to define the disease, and in any case the disturbances are not sufficiently extreme to explain the debilitating levels of symptoms.

In addition to IBS and CFS, there is a group of patients who have a wide range of medically unexplained symptoms. Like CFS and IBS, patients with medically unexplained symptoms have no specific pathophysiology associated with their symptoms. Patients with medically unexplained symptoms comprise a surprisingly large group. Depending on the survey, between 15% and 30% of GP visits involve patients who cannot be given a diagnosis and therefore are labelled medically unexplained (Kirmayer, *et al.*, 2004). A survey of patients attending specialist clinics (i.e., patients who would have been referred by their GP) found that just over 50% of patients had medically unexplained symptoms (Nimnuan *et al.*, 2001). Over half of patients attending a specialist neurology clinic who had medically unexplained symptoms had not improved 8 months later (Carson *et al.*, 2003). However, there is evidence that the quality of communication by the doctor leads to a reduction in medically unexplained symptoms (Thomas, 1987), so clearly this group can be treated – though perhaps in a different way from that normally understood as treatment in medicine.

Where is modern medicine going?

Historians of medicine (Porter, 1996) have pointed out that most of the advances of modern medicine occurred in the thirty years after the Second World War – i.e., from the middle of the century to the mid 1970s. It was in this time that the miracle medical breakthroughs occurred – penicillin and the later antibiotics, the corticosteroids that were to be so successful in controlling inflammation, the polio vaccine, and chlorpromazine for the treatment of psychosis were all developed in this period. In the late 1940s and 1950s, medical advances were made in large strides. As time has gone on, these strides have become shorter and shorter. Current drug development typically involves very small improvements on existing drugs. Where new classes of drugs are discovered, they act as a small improvement on other existing classes of drugs. The big strides are all in the past. This is not to say, of course, that there is nothing to be solved. On the contrary, as shown in the section above, although the big strides have solved many problems, other problems remain. Porter (1996) and others (e.g., Le Fanu, 1999) suggest that modern medicine is going through a period of crisis.

In a paper entitled 'Why is modern medicine stuck in a rut?', Mittra (2009) suggests that one reason for the failure for modern medicine to advance is an over-reliance on the biomedical model – i.e., understanding of medicine in terms of biochemistry. Criticism of the biomedical model is not new. Some forty years ago, Engel (1977) proposed the bio-psychosocial model. Although many accept the biopsychosocial model, it has not produced any great shift in medical practice (Fava and Sonino 2008). More importantly, where it is applied the biopsychosocial model often means taking psychological factors into account as well as bio-logical factors. There is no theoretical development: no mechanism that explains how it is that psychological and biological factors are integrated. This lack of a theory is evident in a version of the biopsychosocial model that has the label psychoneuroimmunology (Ader *et al.*, 1995). There is no mechanism to explain how, and more importantly *why*, psychological mechanisms interact with the immune system (see Chapter 2). Neither the biopsychosocial model nor psychoneuroimmunology has provided the answer for the crisis identified by historians of medicine (Le Fanu, 1999; Mittra, 2009; Porter, 1996)

When the biomedical model is incapable of explaining a disease or symptoms, one possible response is to suggest that the philosophy of specific pathophysiology is correct but that scientists just need longer to get it right. For example, it is possible to argue that once the genetics of IBS and CFS are properly understood and genetic treatments have been developed then these diseases will no longer pose the challenge they do today, and that medically unexplained symptoms will be explained by some pathology as yet unnoticed. An alternative response is to suggest that the assumption of specific pathophysiology may not always be correct and that a new paradigm is needed. Given the above, it seems reasonable that any such new paradigm must not only include psychological factors, but more importantly must provide a rationale for how psychological factors and biochemistry are integrated. Simply reiterating the biopsychosocial model is unlikely to produce any great advance.

A brief history of psychological therapies

Towards the end of the nineteenth century there were two distinctly different approaches to treating mental illness: the mental hygiene approach and the medical approach. The mental hygiene approach was advocated by non-medical philanthropists, mainly from a religious background, who saw mental illness as a moral problem. They believed that if mentally ill people were placed in the care of a morally upright person, then guidance from such a person would effect a cure. Those advocating this approach donated money to build the large 'Victorian' mental asylums of the time, and they helped introduce a far more humane approach to mental illness than had gone before. Their techniques were not successful, however – or at least success was very limited.

The medical approach was based on the idea that mental illness was due to a specific pathology of the brain – just as other disease is a specific pathology of some or other part of the body. Researchers examined brains of people with and without mental illness, and with just one exception failed to find a difference. That one exception is the disease named after its discoverer, Alois Alzheimer, and for which there was then, as now, no cure. To cut a long story short, by the end of the nineteenth century, neither the mental hygiene approach nor the medical approach had provided any effective solution to mental illness.

Sigmund Freud started publishing at the end of the nineteenth century. At the start of his career he investigated hysteria from a biological, specific-pathology perspective, but he abandoned this earlier scientific approach to develop a psychological interpretation of mental illness. Freud's psychological perspective had an immense impact on psychiatry in the first part of the twentieth century. In part this was because he had (or at least claimed) success in treating patients, but also because his approach brought hope to patients and their families whom the earlier, biological perspective had labelled as having 'nervous degeneration' brought about by a hereditary weakness. In fact, Freud was successful only with a limited type of psychological problem, but he provided a much more optimistic view of mental illness.

Freud was a psychiatrist, rather than a psychologist, and was trained in the modern medical belief of specific pathology. However, rather than suggesting a physiological pathology, Freud suggested a psychological pathology. Broadly speaking, Freud believed that mental illness was caused by a specific psychological problem, namely that of repressed memories. He invented a therapy – 'the talking cure' – that involved talking to patients and that purported to cure patients by bringing these repressed memories into consciousness (Freud, 1910). Freud's specific pathology has been criticised, but his therapy had some success. Engaging in any therapy typically creates therapeutic benefit compared with doing nothing at all (Wampold, 2001). Most people nowadays believe that the talking cure worked not for the reason Freud believed but for reasons covered in later chapters of this book. Nevertheless, Freud had identified a specific pathology, although of a psychological rather than a physiological nature, and a way of overcoming this specific pathology. His approach therefore was consistent with the medical philosophy of specificity. It is worth noting in parentheses that later psychiatrists, who have now returned to a specific physiological interpretation of mental illness, often think Freud's approach was a wasteful detour of scientific endeavour.

The early psychologists were not greatly influenced by Freud: psychoanalysis influenced psychiatrists – i.e., people whose original training was in medicine. By the first quarter of the twentieth century psychologists had developed an alternative psychological interpretation of mental illness. This other interpretation was based on the then dominant paradigm of psychology, namely behaviourism. Using behaviourist principles, psychologists suggested, like Freud, that mental illness was caused by a specific psychological pathology. Behaviourists believed that mental illness was caused by 'wrong' forms of reinforcement, and they suggested alternative forms of reinforcement to overcome the patterns of learning created by these 'wrong' forms of reinforcement. Although behaviourist therapies were based on providing patients with new types of reinforcement, these therapies also involved talking to patients, and hence the 'other part' of therapy. Behaviourist principles began to be applied to patients in the late 1940s and early 1950s (Lindsley *et al.*, 1953).

More recently, the behaviourist approach has been replaced by a cognitive-behavioural approach in which the pathology of mental illness is attributed to incorrect cognitions (Beck, 1967). Cognitive behaviour therapies (which also involve talking) are designed to correct these incorrect cognitions. Like the other therapies, cognitive behaviour therapy, or CBT, has been demonstrated to be effective compared with doing nothing. Thus, over the last hundred years there have been three different broad types of psychological explanation and treatment for mental illness (psychoanalytic, behavioural and cognitive-behavioural) that suggest that a specific pathology is responsible for the problem, which is then treated by therapies designed to remedy that specific pathology. All of these three types of psychological treatment of mental illness adopt the medical principle of specific pathology. Sixty years ago, Freud's theories were accepted by the medical community. Nowadays it is CBT that is well accepted by the medical community. After all, CBT identifies a specific pathology, and then treats that specific pathology, in the same way that medicine identifies and treats specific pathologies. Furthermore, CBT produces impressive results.

During the 1930s, 1940s and 1950s, a group of psychologists suggested an alternative approach to psychological therapy: it was an alternative to the Freudian or psychoanalytic approach and behaviourist approaches. This rather different type of therapy has been variously labelled humanistic, phenomenological or existential psychology. Carl Rogers was one of the most influential of these humanistic psychologists, at least in terms of clinical practice. Rogers started from the assumption that humans are naturally capable of self-healing (Rogers, 1951). So, in the case of mental illness the aim was *not* to find and change the pathology but simply to help people to self-heal. Rogers believed that the therapist should try to create the conditions that promote self-healing. These healing conditions were brought about not by a specific skill that the therapist applied to the patient but by a healing attitude that involved unconditional positive regard. The idea that it is the healing attitude that is important has been adopted by later authors under the heading of the contextual model of psychotherapy (see Chapter 6). The contextual model suggests that psychotherapies work not because of the specific factors suggested by the various psychotherapies but by factors that are common to all psychotherapies, namely the interaction with a caring therapist.

There is an obvious parallel between Rogers' approach to psychotherapy (which like the other therapies involves talking) and the philosophy of traditional medical systems. In both cases there is an assumption that the body/person is self-healing. In both cases the therapy aims to promote self-healing rather than identify a specific pathology. In both cases, the emphasis is on helping people achieve a state that is 'good' for the whole person rather correcting a part that is 'bad'. Finally, the existential psychologists, along with traditional medicines, believe that what may be good for one person may not be good for another, so that treatment needs to be individualised for the person not for the disease (Yalom, 1980).

In sum, the one hundred years of history of psychological therapies shows that most have conformed to the modern medical philosophy of identifying a specific pathology that is then treated. However, one approach, the humanistic/existential approach, has adopted the traditional medicine philosophy of promoting self-healing without attention to the specific pathology.

Psychologists adopting the Rogerian approach have never been accepted in the same way that other specific psychological therapies have been and are accepted. Freudian theory was accepted in medicine for 50 years, and the current dominant psychological approach of CBT was first proposed half a century ago. Why should this be? The Rogerian therapist is not 'in charge' of the patient. The therapist is merely a facilitator of healing. The patient is in charge of the patient, and it is the patient who discovers the patient's route to recovery. By contrast, CBT shares with medicine the assumption that a scientific authority figure should be in charge and take control of the patient. The authority figure knows what is wrong and is able to help correct those things that are wrong. Medicine and CBT confer prestige, power and control for the practitioners. Rogerian therapy does not. Currently, CBT therapists have higher status than counsellors. The specific approach to illness, in addition to being plausible from the perspective of specific pathology, can be attractive to psychological practitioners as it provides a clear sense of worth and importance.

Where is psychotherapy going?

Modern medicine is now advancing in very small strides. What about psychotherapy? The answer is that the strides are even smaller. It is clear that psychotherapy is and always has been effective for many patients. CBT was developed in the late 1960s. Since then CBT has been developed in a number of ways, but these do not provide an entirely novel approach to psychotherapy. For example, one such development is dialectical behaviour therapy (DBT), which includes some elements associated with Rogerian therapy (Swenson *et al.*, 2001). Even with such developments there is an important problem. Although the main focus of current psychotherapy research is to demonstrate that one technique is better than another, the evidence for the superiority of one technique over another is weak. If there are differences in the effectiveness between therapies, that difference is small. Some argue that there is actually no difference in the effectiveness of different psychotherapies (Wampold, 2001), a controversy that will be covered in Chapter 8. Whatever one's view on this controversy, there is an inescapable conclusion that the crisis in psychotherapy development is even more acute than it is for medical development.

The problem of living organisms

Modern Western medicine is the type of medicine consistent with and supported by science. However, there is one small problem. The mechanical analogy on which modern Western medicine is based provides a poor analogy for living organisms. Quite simply, living systems are very different from mechanical systems. They differ in two ways: (a) observable behaviour and (b) the laws of physics.

The behaviour of living systems

If a human body is a kind of mechanism, then the human body should behave in the same way that mechanisms behave. To put it the other way round, if humans are a kind of machine, it should be possible to simulate humans through machines. The simulation of life by machines is limited, however. Living organisms reproduce, they grow and they are capable of healing themselves when damaged. Mechanical systems have none of these properties. Big jumbo jets do not seed baby jumbo jets, they do not grow from baby jumbo jets and they do not repair themselves when damaged.

Analogies are useful to the extent that they account for the behaviour of that which is to be explained. The mathematician Alan Turing proposed a way of testing analogies or simulations in a slightly different context, namely simulations of human intelligence. Simulations or analogies are a kind of explanation, and like all explanations can be tested by data. The Turing test states that a machine is a good simulator of a human if, when questioned, the machine responds in a way that is indistinguishable from that of a real human. Turing's test applies to artificial intelligence and the simulation of verbal behaviour, but the same logic can be applied to the use of the machine analogy for living organisms. To be a good simulator of the living human organism, the behaviour of the machine must be indistinguishable from *all the behaviour* of humans. The reality is that most people are aware whether something is a living organism or a machine (growth, reproduction, etc.). Machines fail the Turing test as simulators of living organisms – at least they do outside the realm of science fiction.

The problem of using machines as analogies for living organisms is nothing new, and various solutions have been proposed. Seventy years ago, the psychologist William McDougall provided a useful overview of some of these solutions in his book *The Riddle of Life* (McDougall, 1938). The several solutions fall into two categories, *vitalism* and *organisation*. The vitalist view is that there is something special, some 'vital principle', that makes living organisms live. The idea of vitalism appears in a variety of forms, but an early version appears in the novel *Frankenstein* by Mary Shelley. In this novel, Frankenstein makes his monster by assembling parts of dead bodies and then zapping the dead body with the (at that time) mysterious force of electricity, brought down from a thunderstorm. The basic idea is that dead bodies + vital energy = life. Electricity was the then mysterious force that could confer life. Other mysterious forces have been suggested.

The main problem with vitalism is not so much that a vital force has not been observed in nature – it may be that we don't know how to measure it – but that the concept amounts to an explanatory fiction. The term 'explanatory fiction' was introduced by B.F. Skinner (Skinner, 1971) as a criticism of theoretical terms in psychology. Explanatory fictions are explanations that appear, to the unwary, to explain but in reality do nothing of the sort. An explanatory fiction is a theoretical term – or some other type of theoretical argument – that purports to explain something but is really just a redescription in fancy language of that which is to be explained. The idea of an explanatory fiction, the idea of using words cleverly to give the appearance of knowledge, is not new. In Molière's book *The Imaginary Invalid*, the final scene involves a student doctor being examined. The question asked of the student is 'Why do sleeping draughts make people go to sleep?' to which the student gives the correct answer 'because they contain a dormative principle'. The term *dormative* derives from Latin, and means that it induces sleep. So, why do sleeping draughts make people go to sleep? Because they contain something that makes people go to sleep. Molière was poking fun at doctors and the way they used fancy language to give the appearance of superior knowledge. Returning now to vital principles or vital energy, 'Why are people alive?' 'Because they contain something which makes them alive'. Vitalism is an explanatory fiction. At least, vitalism is an explanatory fiction unless vital forces can be predicted and shown to have properties other than those of providing life. Theoretical terms are no longer explanatory fictions once they provide additional predictions (Hyland, 1981).

The alternative type of solution to the problem of life, *organisation*, proposes that living organisms are organised in some fundamentally different ways from non-living machines. This kind of view was proposed, for example, by Lowenthal, who suggested in 1934 that bodies were organised like 'supercells' (McDougall, 1938); that is, that cells of the body were organised together as a single entity. However, assertions that there was some organisational difference between living organisms and machines failed to provide a precise account of the *way* in which living organisms were organised differently from inanimate objects.

The term 'system' refers to a collection of smaller units that are organised in some way. Rather obviously, organisation plays a role in the way a system behaves – the behaviour of a jumbo jet depends on whether the parts are put together correctly. Systems have 'emergent properties'. Emergent properties are properties that cannot be predicted from the parts in isolation, they are properties that emerge because of the way the smaller units are arranged. For example, a jumbo jet is a system with a particular type of organisation. The jumbo jet has an emergent property – it can fly. A naive observer looking at the parts in isolation would never believe that they would fly. A jumbo jet is a complex system, but for all its complexity remains unable to repair itself. It is not enough just to say that life is an emergent property of organisation. One needs to be able to say what kind of organisation it is that confers those difficult-to-explain properties of living organisms – growth, reproduction and self-healing.

The laws of physics

Over time, all machines develop faults and stop working. This feature of machines is predicted by one of the fundamental laws of nature: the second law of thermodynamics. The second law of thermodynamics states that entropy – i.e., disorganisation – increases over time. All physical systems become more disorganised over time. Cars break down, computers break down and sewing machines break down. Over time, all machines and all physical objects approach thermodynamic equilibrium – unless, of course, there is some external agency (e.g., a human) imposing organisation. The problem with living systems is that they do not become less organised, and indeed can become more organised when they grow. Living matter therefore appears to break the second law. It is as though entropy is working backwards.

The quantum physicist Erwin Schrödinger suggested that organisms are able to break the second law because they extract order – i.e., negative entropy – from their surroundings. As a result, the second law is not broken for the total organism plus environment system, just for the organism bit. An example will illustrate how this happens. Glucose is a relatively complex molecule involving six carbon atoms. Living systems are able to break down the glucose molecule, by combining it with oxygen to form small molecules of carbon dioxide and water. The carbon dioxide molecule has only one carbon atom. So the six-carbon glucose has been converted into six one-carbon carbon dioxide molecules, thereby creating more entropy, but in so doing the living organism is able to extract negative entropy so as to create more order in the organism. Of course, central heating boilers will also create more entropy, when they burn fuel. However, the fuel burnt in a central heating boiler does not create negative entropy in the boiler. Central heating boilers do not repair themselves!

Schrödinger was well aware that the current theory could not explain how organisms were able to extract order from their environment. His conclusion was that there must be other laws of physics, currently unknown, that living matter exploits.

It is an inescapable fact that living matter must be subject to the second law of thermodynamics. If living matter can 'resist' the effects of that second law, then it follows that living matter can only function as living matter *if* it has a self-healing mechanism. Thus, living matter must necessarily be capable of self-healing.

Critics might point out that living organisms do die eventually. You and I will eventually die despite our best efforts. However, the reason is not that the second law wins in the end, but that our bodies are designed in such a way that they have built-in senescence. Most living systems are designed to die at a particular age. Life can achieve its escape from the second law over the long term through its ability to create new life. Dying is part of the mechanism that living systems have evolved to preserve life. We live on in our children.

A central thesis of this book is that the self-healing system is crucial to understanding those parts of medicine that have resisted conventional explanation. Dysregulation in the self-healing system creates health problems: the 'other part' of therapy remedies that dysregulation.

The discovery of parallel processing systems

Systems can be organised in two ways, one sequential and one parallel. Sequential processing or sequential causality is the kind of causality that is familiar. It is the kind of causality found in mechanical systems, such as a clock. The first cog causes the second cog to rotate, the second cog causes the third, and so on right up to the sixth cog or escapement cog that is controlled by the pendulum. The same sort of causality or processing occurs in a computer. One calculation is done and then another. Sequential causality is the kind of causality that is easy to understand. There is, however, another form of causality, a parallel processing form of causality. A parallel processing system consists of a network of many different nodes where the nodes of the network are massively connected to each other and have simultaneous causal effects. These parallel processing networks can be understood through the mathematics of complex systems and are modelled by sequential processing computers that now run so fast that they can pretend they are really parallel processing systems (real parallel processing machines are still at an elementary stage). Research shows that parallel processing systems operate very differently from sequential processing systems, and one of their many differences is that they have the capacity to self-organise. Self-organisation means that the system can change itself so as to self-regulate itself more effectively. Self-organisation is an emergent property of a parallel processing system because it is a property that cannot be predicted from the parts in isolation. Self-organisation and other properties of parallel processing systems will be described in Chapter 4. Parallel processing systems are fundamentally different from the mechanical systems that form an analogy for modern medicine. This other type of system is variously called a complex system, a network system, a parallel processing system and a connectionist system.

The discovery that parallel processing systems can have the property of self-organisation means that there is now a rationale for how living systems can learn and adapt in an environment, and do what machines cannot do – heal themselves. The idea of a self-healing system is no longer the implausible idea that it was once. Schrödinger's undiscovered physical laws may be emergent properties of parallel processing systems. Although current machines do not self-heal, it is certainly theoretically possible that robots can be made that will do their own self-maintenance. Thus, the idea of a self-healing system, which is an assumption of traditional medicines, is no longer implausible.

Parallel processing systems provide a possible rationale for life – i.e., an explanation why living things appear to break the second law of thermodynamics (Bedau, 1998; Larson-Freeman, 1997). It is fanciful to say that parallel processing systems explain life. Life still remains a mystery. However, it seems that the difference between living organisms and dead machines is not that the former have a vital force but that the two are organised in different ways.

Basic features of the theory

This book sets out a theory that the body functions in two ways. It functions as a sequential processing system in which error in that sequential processing system leads to the pathophysiology familiar to modern medicine. It also functions as a parallel processing system that is capable of self-healing. The components of the body (e.g., biochemicals) can function simultaneously within the sequential and parallel processing systems. The prima facie evidence for this theory comes from two observations. First, modern medicine is successful at treating diseases where there is an identifiable pathophysiology. Second, living systems are different from mechanical systems. Living systems are capable of breaking the second law of thermodynamics at a local level because they are self-healing. (Note: the second law is not broken if the organism is considered part of a total system that includes its environment.) This distinctive feature of life is believed to occur (Bedau, 1998; Larson-Freeman, 1997) because organisms have a parallel processing structure.

According to the theory proposed here, error in the specific system leads to pathophysiology with the consequent specific relationship between pathophysiology and disease. The sequential processing system is the system on which the biology of medicine is currently based, and will be referred to as the *specific system* because diseases and pathology are specific – just as Virchow and others suggested many years ago. Diseases within this system will be referred to as *specific diseases*. The parallel process system is a hypothesised system that will be the focus of this book. Error in the parallel processing system can be described as dysregulation. Dysregulation of the parallel processing system leads to *dysregulatory diseases*, namely those diseases do not have a specific pathology. In addition, dysregulation of the parallel processing system can act as a precursor to specific diseases.

The parallel processing system is a network system that extends through the neurological, endocrine and immune systems. This psychoneuroimmunoendocrine network is not separate from the specific system. Instead, elements of the neurological, endocrine and immune systems function both within the specific system and within the biopsychosocial information network. For example, cytokines (a class of immune communicator) have a role within the psychoneorimmunoendocrine network but also act to create systemic inflammation (i.e., non-specific inflammation) within the specific processing system.

The network system can be described in two ways. First, it can be described in terms of its underlying biology. For reasons that will be described later in the book, this form of description is likely to be very difficult. A second way of understanding the network system is in terms of its meaning. An analogy with computing may be useful at this point. A computer program exists as a physical object in terms of magnetised components on a hard drive. However, if you wish to understand a computer program, it makes little sense to take the computer to pieces and examine the hard drive under a microscope. The sensible way to understand the computer program is in terms of *meaning*. The theory being presented is that the body contains meaning, in just the same way that a computer program contains meaning. The parallel processing system is a psychoneuroimmunoendocrine information network.

The infornet

Neologisms should be avoided wherever possible. However, the term psychoneuroimmunoendocrine information network is rather a mouthful, and so I shall abbreviate it to the infornet. The term infornet emphasises the network (complex) structure of the system, and that it is an information processing system. Both biological information and psychological information are relevant to the infornet.

Health versus disease

The theory presented in this book will show *how* the infornet can become dysregulated or 'unbalanced' owing to a lifestyle events. The dysregulated infornet causes *dysregulatory diseases* (e.g., medically unexplained symptoms and functional diseases such as chronic fatigue syndrome and irritable bowel syndrome) and acts as a precursor to *specific diseases* (e.g., cancer, heart disease, asthma). The distinction between dysregulation and the onset of specific diseases provides a useful way of representing the difference between health and disease.

Figure 1.1 The two systems. The causal relationship between the parallel processing infornet and the sequential processing specific system

There is a common assumption that health is something more than simply the absence of disease. The World Health Organization (WHO) definition of health, which has not been amended since 1948 is that:

Health is a state of complete physical, mental and social well-being and not merely the absence of disease or infirmity. (WHO, 1948)

Despite the acceptance of this definition, there has always been a problem in understanding exactly what 'complete physical, mental and social well-being' means in practice. Mental well-being is well understood, but in what sense is mental well-being not the reverse of mental disease? The WHO definition and others suggest that health and disease are different dimensions, not simply opposite ends of the same dimension. The theory presented in this book, i.e., infornet theory, provides a way of representing these two dimensions. Disease occurs due to pathology in the specific system. By contrast, health is a state of optimal self-regulation in the infornet. Poor health occurs when the infornet is dysregulated, and poor health can contribute to disease. But poor health can occur without disease. It is possible to be unhealthy and to have no disease, i.e., no diagnosable pathophysiology. Medically unexplained symptoms and functional diseases can, according to this disease–health distinction, be considered states of very poor health.

Figure 1.1 provides a schematic representation of the relationship between the infornet and the specific system. The infornet influences the specific system. However, there is also a causal link in the other direction by which specific pathology can have a dysregulatory effect on the infornet. The difference in thickness of the two arrows indicates that the infornet's influence on the specific system is the greater.

Table 1.2 provides a summary of some of the features of the infornet and specific systems. Note the similarities between Tables 1.1 and 1.2.

The infornet is the self-healing system of the body, a self-healing system that can go wrong when it is dysregulated. This book not only shows *how* the infornet becomes dysregulated, but also *how* the infornet

Table 1.2 *Characteristics of the infornet and specific systems*

	Infornet Variation in health	Specific system Variation in disease
What goes wrong?	Dysregulation of a complex system	Specific pathology
What causes it?	Lifestyle, in particular psychological aspects of lifestyle and genetics	Dysregulation of the infornet coupled with biological environmental factors and genetics
Prevention?	A healthy lifestyle	Limited prevention but includes inoculation and other biological techniques to prevent infection (e.g., antimalaria medication)
Treatment?	Psychological aspects of therapy, lifestyle modification. Treatment is not tailored to diseases	Biological and specific forms of treatment for each pathophysiology
Why does treatment work?	The infornet self-organises to produce a well-regulated infornet under the right circumstances. Therapy is all about getting those circumstances right	The therapist intervenes and corrects that which is wrong

can become better regulated (well-regulated) through therapy and other lifestyle interventions. Of course, it is important to emphasise one point at the outset. Specific diseases need treatments that affect the specific system. Dysregulatory diseases need treatments that affect the infornet. Both types of treatment are needed. The paradigm of specific pathophysiology has been immensely successful – one must not lose sight of this fact. Infornet theory is an addition to, not a replacement for modern Western medicine.

2   The body's mind: psychoneuroimmunology, stress and adaptive response

Introduction

The effect of mind on body is sometimes considered puzzling. It is only a puzzle if one makes incorrect assumptions about the nature of the relationship between mind and body, namely that the mind and body are separate entities. This chapter examines how the mind acts as a signal in the body's information system and in particular how the mind relates to the immune system. The chapter starts with a brief overview of assumptions about the mind.

The mind as an emergent property of the body

The influence of Cartesian dualism

The naive view of the relationship between mind and body is consistent with an interpretation that was suggested some 350 years ago by the philosopher René Descartes – an interpretation called Cartesian dualism. This naive view is very influential and many people subscribe to it without being fully aware of doing so.

According to Cartesian dualism, there is 'body stuff' and 'mind stuff' – i.e., two different sorts of 'stuff' that exist in the world. Furthermore, the mind stuff is able to influence the body stuff, as represented in Figure 2.1.

The naive view can be updated with the modern understanding that the brain is important to mental function. Because the mind is commonly assumed to be located in that part of the body called the brain, this dualistic view of psychosomatics can also be represented as shown in Figure 2.2.

Figure 2.2 corresponds to common-sense notions about the way thought influences the brain and body, and so can be linked to modern brain science. You decide, in your mind, to move your finger, and so the brain then tells you finger to move. The above picture also represents a common view of sensation wherein the causal direction would be reversed: pain in your finger is transmitted to the brain and ends up

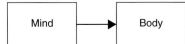

Figure 2.1 Cartesian dualism

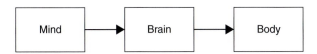

Figure 2.2 Cartesian dualism plus neuroscience

in your mind. Despite its intuitive appeal, there are several logical problems with the Cartesian view of minds, brains and bodies. This naive view has had immense impact, including the notion of psychosomatics. The naive (and common) view of psychosomatics is that events that occur in the mind (the psyche) can influence events that occur in the body (the soma). That is, there are two separate systems that interact.

This naive view is incorrect in several ways. One way in which it is wrong is the assumption that mind is located in the brain. Imagine that you cut your finger. Where is the pain? The pain feels as though it is in your finger – and if you didn't have a finger you wouldn't be able to have cut it. Certainly, it is true to say that the brain is an important part of the perception of pain, but it is not the only part that is relevant to that experience. The brain, the finger, the nerves in the finger and the nerves in the spinal cord are all parts of a system that is involved in the experience of pain. The same applies to movement. When you move your finger, the action is not only in the muscles of the finger, but also in the nerves that supply those muscles, the nerves in the spinal cord and events in the brain. Movement, just like sensation, involves a system that is distributed throughout the body. These examples show that mind is a property of parts of the body that extend beyond the brain. I shall show later in this chapter that the extension of the mind into the body includes the immune system and the gut.

A second, and possibly more important way in which Cartesian dualism is incorrect is in the assumption of a 'mind stuff'. This assumption is by no means trivial because it underlies the common distinction between mental and physical illness. Classifications of illness distinguish the mental (e.g., depression, schizophrenia) from the physical (e.g., cancer, heart disease). A moment's thought will show that this distinction between mental and physical illness cannot be based on the ontological status of the illness (i.e., whether the illness is an illness of mind stuff or body stuff). An illness cannot be mental and not physical – you cannot be ill if you do not have a body. Minds do not exist without bodies. Of course, it is possible to reframe the mental versus physical illness distinction in terms of 'brain illness' versus 'other parts of the body illness'. The distinction of brain illness versus other parts of the body illness is consistent with assumption of the specificity of modern Western medicine, and makes perfect sense in terms of the specific system. However, if the distinction is between brain illness and other parts of the body illness, then it would be less misleading to talk of brain illness rather than mental illness – and perhaps it would lead to less prejudice against the so-called mental illnesses. The term 'mental illness' carries the connotation that it is not a 'proper' illness because it is not physical. Of course, a possible reason why the term 'mental illness' is used in contrast to 'brain illness' is that the search for specific pathology in the brain has had limited success. For many so-called mental diseases, the search for specific pathologies has been controversial: abnormalities can be observed, but specificity can be weak (see Chapter 8).

The idea of brain illness is central to modern psychiatry, where disease is conceptualised as a problem of a specific part of the body (see the previous chapter). One of the differences between psychiatry and clinical psychology is that the former is more likely to treat the brain with drugs, whereas the latter is more likely to treat the mind with talking therapy, so the distinction between 'brain illness' and 'mental illness' does have implications for treatment. Nevertheless, the principle of biological disease specificity apples to both and is well established, so it makes perfect sense within the conceptual framework of disease specificity for diseases to be located solely in the brain.

In the previous chapter I suggested that the aetiology of specific diseases may involve a distributed initial cause, namely dysregulation of the infornet. Although brain diseases may involve some kind of pathology in the brain, it is also possible that the distal cause of that disease has a systemic or distributed component. For example, schizophrenia is normally thought of as mental illness – i.e., a brain illness. However, schizophrenia is statistically associated with diseases of the gut. The reason for this association is unclear but leads to suggestions that the gut is implicated in the aetiology of schizophrenia – though exactly how is not established. Similarly, depression is associated with marked changes in the immune system, and the immune system has been implicated in the cause of depression. Not only are so-called mental illnesses linked to physiological events outside the brain, but in addition so-called physical illnesses are linked to psychological states. Such relationships will be described in the next chapter, but for the moment it is sufficient to note that the simple distinction between mental and physical illness, whether or not conceptualised as brain versus non-brain illness, may be more complex than originally thought.

What is this thing called mind?

Although the mind may not be located in the brain, the question remains about the nature of this thing called the mind. No evidence has ever been presented for the existence of 'mind stuff'. On the contrary, the conventionally accepted materialist view is that 'mind stuff' does not exist (the question of 'spirit stuff' will not be discussed here). According to the materialist perspective, the only 'stuff' that exists is that of the material world. However, although mind is not 'stuff' in the sense of material 'stuff', this *does not mean* that mind does not exist. The *existence* of this experience of mind is uncontroversial, and has been explored by novelists, poets and artists. However, the *usefulness* of this experience of mind for scientific purposes, namely for prediction and explanation, has been highly controversial.

Is the concept of mind useful for prediction and explanation? The answer is that it depends on what is being predicted or explained.

Box 2.1 Prediction versus explanation

Prediction means being able to anticipate future events (i.e., observations) on the basis of present and past information (i.e., past and present observations). The accuracy of prediction can be represented mathematically or statistically in terms of the relation between the predicted event (i.e., the past and present observations that are expected to happen) and the observed event (i.e., the past and present observations that do happen). Explanation is a more complex concept, in that it involves something additional to prediction. Explanation is prediction *plus* something else.

Explanation involves a psychological judgement – we feel that something is explained by something else. Whereas the concept of prediction is relatively straightforward, the concept of explanation is more complex. The complexity arises over what kind of thing constitutes that 'something else'. Typically, the explanation of a set of observations involves a description *at some other level* than the observations themselves. So, for example, the observable action of one chemical on another is explained by describing how the molecules of the two chemicals interact. The action of the molecules cannot be seen, but their description provides a description that explains the chemical agents – which can be seen. In the case of health and behaviour, the issue of explanation is made yet more complex because people have preferences for different kinds of the 'some other level' that is used to do the explaining, with some people accepting mental content as a form of description that provides an explanation whereas others prefer physiological or molecular descriptions to do the explaining. For some people the only 'true' explanation is to find the physiological part that is causing the mental state. For others a 'true' explanation is based not on physiology but on detailed mental description.

Psychological research over the last hundred years has shown that introspection is not particularly useful for explaining processes that give rise to mental experiences. That is, we cannot find out about the underlying mechanisms of thought through introspection. Research shows, for example, that the explanations people give for their decisions are inconsistent with the decisions they actually make, suggesting that people do not have insight into how they form decisions (Evans, 2007). People make judgements but without proper awareness of how those judgements are formed.

However, once those judgements have been formed, then those judgements can influence behaviour. Mental events have an effect on behaviour, even if we cannot introspect where those mental events come from. Carl Rogers (see Chapter 1) was one of the founders of the American Humanistic Psychology society. The therapeutic approach taken by Rogers and other humanistic therapists is to encourage people gain insight into their experience and feelings (Rogers, 1951). By gaining such insight, people are able to make choices that then have therapeutic benefit. The mind is useful because it can be used to alter behaviour. To return to an earlier analogy, the mind is not useful for explaining how the sensation of pain arises, but it is useful for explaining the consequences of pain and how it can be avoided. The mind is a signal to which the person or animal responds, and hence is useful for predicting and explaining that response. By contrast, the mind is less useful for explaining itself – i.e., how the signal arises.

Methodological complementarity and emergentism

So if the Cartesian framework for understanding the mind is not correct, what is? There are several different interpretations of the mind–body relationship that are based on an underlying materialist philosophy – i.e., that the only stuff is that of the physical world. One type of interpretation is materialist and reductionist. Another type is materialist and non-reductionist.

Reduction is a technical term and can be defined as follows:

A secondary science is reduced to a primary science when the laws and assumptions of the secondary science are shown to be the logical consequence of the laws and assumptions of the primary science.

The question whether psychology can be reduced to physiology is controversial. Nevertheless, there are several reasons (beyond the scope of this book) why it seems unlikely that mental events will ever be reduced to physiological description (Kirsch and Hyland, 1987; Hyland

and Kirsch, 1988). It is certainly the case at the moment that the laws of psychology cannot be logically inferred from the laws of physiology, even though parallels are found between mental states and physiological states. An account of the intricacies of poetry and art cannot be represented in a one-to-one fashion with brain states, even though general mood states can be linked to activity in particular parts of the brain. So although there is no 'mind stuff', we still need the mental to fully describe the 'body stuff'. The physiological description of mental events is very crude.

Methodological complementarity is one of the non-reductionist, materialist interpretations of the mind–body relationship. Complementarity is a philosophical idea, first developed by Niels Bohr in the context of quantum mechanics. The principle of complementarity is that in order to fully describe a phenomenon it is necessary to have more than one *mutually incompatible* form of description. The physiological and mental are complementary descriptions of the mind–body system (Hyland, 1985; Kirsch and Hyland, 1987; Hyland and Kirsch, 1988).

According to methodological complementarity, the mental and physiological are parallel descriptions of the same event (see Figure 2.3). The technical term is that the mental and physiological descriptions are *identified* because they are both descriptions of the same event. That is, mind does not cause physiology, and physiological events do not cause mind. The mind and physiology *are one and the same thing*.

There are two important features of this approach to the mind–body problem. The first is that there are some physiological events that do not have a mental parallel. Much of the physiology of the body passes unnoticed at the mental level. The mind provides a signal of only certain events. The second is that the mind is an *emergent property* of the body and therefore mental description cannot be reduced to the physiological. Emergent properties are those that cannot be understood from the parts of the system in isolation. The output from a parallel processing system is a good example of an emergent property.

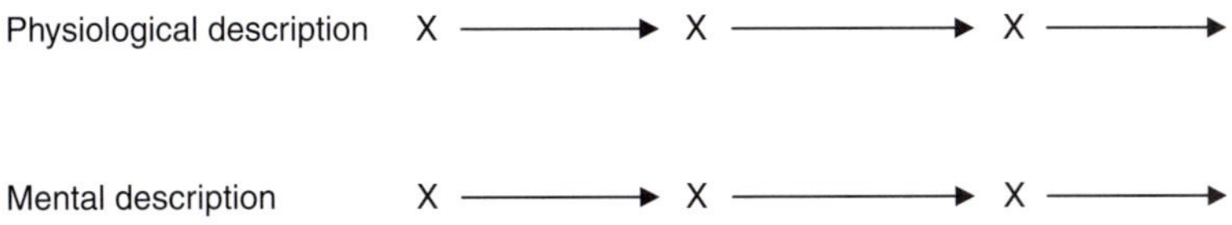

Physiological description   X ⟶ X ⟶ X ⟶

Mental description   X ⟶ X ⟶ X ⟶

Figure 2.3 Methodological complementarity

The idea of specificity in medicine was introduced in Chapter 1. According to modern Western medicine, each disease has a specific cause. The idea of specificity also occurs in terms of mind–body relationships, but it is a lopsided form of specificity. Any particular mental state can be identified with one or more different physiological states. So, for example, the mental state of depression may be indentified with a particular physiological state; but then again, depression may be identified with several different physiological states. However, if there are two different mental states, they *cannot* be identified with a single physiological state. Each different mental state *must* be associated with one or more different physiological states – otherwise a fundamental assumption of materialism is broken. This may appear an abstruse point, but there is an important message to come. Research has shown that depression and fatigue are both correlated with events in the immune system. However, because these different mental states are correlated with the same immune events, the mental states cannot be identified with the immune events. The mental events must be identified with something else. This book sets out the theory that the mental events are identified with a pattern of the infornet, not with the particular biochemicals whose abnormality is detected in the specific system.

In sum, the theory presented in this book is based on the assumptions that (a) the mind is an emergent property of the body and cannot be reduced to physiological description, (b) the mind does not exist independently of the body, and (c) the mind is useful for prediction and explanation in some contexts but not others. Note that the mind is an emergent property of the body, not an emergent property of the brain. The brain is very important for the emergence of mental phenomena, but it is not necessarily the only part of the body involved.

It this book I shall refer to the mind on many occasions. In each case, the use of the term 'mind' does not imply 'not body'. Instead it simply means that the mind provides a more convenient or more complete account of what is happening in the mind–body system. The terms *psychological input* and *mental state* can be defined as follows:

Psychological input means an input to the body that is mediated via the sense organs and interpreted by the brain/mind. The psychological input is an interpretation of external events, is described in terms of the meaning of those external events, and, although the effect is biological, cannot be described fully in biological terms.

Mental state means a signal from the body that cannot be described fully in biological terms but can be described in terms of meaning or feeling.

Why do living organisms need a mind? Why did it evolve?

As a general rule, characteristics of organisms evolve because they have a function. Why did the mind or consciousness evolve? The answer can be understood in terms of the functions of living organisms. All animals – humans, rats, jellyfish and single-celled organisms – need to control their internal environment, i.e., they need to keep the physiology of the body working sensibly so that all the various biochemicals are in their right places and at their correct levels. In addition, some animals control their external environment and this control of the external environment is normally achieved through behaviour. The control of the external environment tends to become more important with evolutionary development. Simple organisms do not control their environment much – jellyfish, for example, simply swim about in the sea, they don't change the sea. More complex animals modify their environment – or at least, they modify their position in the environment. A rat will search for food rather than wait for it to appear. Rats build nests. Humans are particularly adept at modifying the external environment – houses, cars and aeroplanes are all examples of the way humans control the external environment

The mind evolved as part of the ability to manage the external environment. Let us consider some ways in which the mind plays an adaptive role.

If you see a tiger approaching, you know that the sensible behaviour is to move away or defend yourself in some way. The mind provides an interpretation of the external world (psychological input) that allows action to be coordinated in a way which helps manage that external world. The use of the mind to manage the external environment can be represented by the flow diagram shown in Figure 2.4.

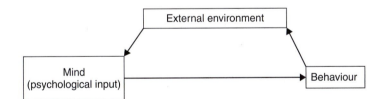

Figure 2.4 The mind helps people change their behaviour in response to events in the external environment. Note that there is a feedback system because once the mind has altered the external environment through behaviour, the external environment has changed and this can lead to a different signal in the mind. Once you have escaped from the tiger (through the behaviour of running away) then there is no tiger in the external environment.

However, the mind has a second function that is equally important. Once an animal starts controlling its external environment, it also needs to be able to alter its internal environment to meet the needs of the external environment. For example, when escaping from a tiger, the escaping animal needs to maximise resources to running rather than digestion. In brief, the animal needs to coordinate the internal and external environments. The reason for this need is less obvious than the need to control the external environment, but it is based on a general principle about the way the body is designed. The body is designed to be efficient. Efficiency requires coordination.

The body has evolved to use its resources efficiently through temporal specialisation. Temporal specialisation means doing one function at one time and another function at another time. A moment's reflection will show that the body is not designed to hunt mammoths and eat mammoths at the same time. When the body is in a relaxed state ready for eating, it is not in a state of preparedness for dealing with a mammoth. And when you are hunting mammoths, the last thing on your mind is how to cook a tasty mammoth pie. The body is not designed to do everything at once, but rather to do particular things at particular times.

Principle 1. The principle of efficiency states that the body conserves its resources by carrying out specific functions at specific times, so resources can be mobilised at those times to maximise the performance of those functions.

The coordination of internal and external environmental control is one of many examples of the principle of efficiency. This coordination involves the mind in two distinct roles: the mind as a signal of what is happening in the external environment and the mind as a signal of what is happening in the internal environment.

The mind as a signal of the internal environment

First, consider how the requirements of the internal environment lead to changes in the external environment that are mediated via behaviour.

Box 2.2 Internal versus external environment

The distinction between internal and external environment is used throughout this chapter. The concept is treated simplistically: the external environment is everything outside the organism's skin. The internal environment is everything within the skin. There are small areas of interpretation that can differ, for example whether the contents of the gut are part of the internal or external environment (technically, they are outside the skin), but these are not important to the main thrust of the arguments presented.

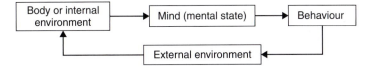

Figure 2.5 The mind provides a signal of the state of the internal environment. As with Figure 2.4, this figure is also a feedback system: people change their behaviour as a consequence of the mental signal that provides information about the internal environment

Lack of nutrition in the internal environment leads to the experience of hunger, and the mental state of hunger motivates a person to search for food. The eating of food increases nutrition in the internal environment. The experience of pain when putting a finger over a flame leads to the finger being withdrawn so that damage to the internal environment is minimised. Both are examples of the mind (mental state) controlling behaviour in order to improve the state of the internal environment.

Principle 2. The mind is a signal of the state of the internal environment of the organism, and enables the organism to change the external environment through behaviour so as to improve the functioning of the internal environment.

This second principle can be represented by the flow diagram shown in Figure 2.5.

The mind as a signal of the external environment

A second function of the mind is to alter the internal environment to make the internal environment more for suited for dealing with the external environment. The mind provides an interpretation of the external environment (i.e., psychological input). We sense the external environment through the five senses of touch, sight, taste, smell and hearing – as well as other senses such as pain, temperature and balance. The sense organs provide signals about the external environment, the signals are interpreted in the brain and this interpretation produces mental representations. These mental representations or interpretations have two functions. As stated above, they help in the control of the external environment – it helps people respond to tigers. The second function is that the mental events influence the internal environment to enable the body to cope better with the external environment. The most cited response of this kind is the fight or flight response. When you see a tiger, not only do you move away or prepare to fight, but your body modifies itself so it is better able to run or away from or fight

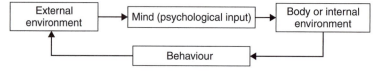

Figure 2.6 The mind is a signal from the external environment that alters the internal environment

the tiger. The internal environment is modified to suit the behaviour needed to deal with the external environment (see Figure 2.6).

Principle 3. The mind is a signal of the state of the external environment of the organism, and enables the organism to change the internal environment so as to improve the functioning within that external environment.

When taken together, Figures 2.5 and 2.6 show that there is a two-way flow of information between external and internal environments and that the mind is an intermediary between the two. The mind is an emergent property of the whole body. The brain is part of the body and plays an important part in the interpretation of signals from the external and internal environments, but the whole body is part of this reciprocal process of coordination between the internal and external environments. The next two sections provide more detail about this coordination. Two systems of the body will be considered to illustrate how the mind acts in an intermediary role in two systems of the body: the immune system and the gut.

At this point it is necessary to emphasise an important conclusion:

- Some mental states provide an interpretation of the external environment.
- Some mental states provide an interpretation of the internal environment or the body.

There are different *kinds* of mental state relating to the internal and external environments and they have different functions. The mental states providing an interpretation of the internal environment are called *mood states*; those providing an interpretation of the external environment are called *emotions* – also sometimes called *specific emotions*.

The immune system and the mind

Introduction to the immune system

The function of the immune system is to protect the organism from pathogens or any type of foreign matter. The immune system is immensely complex. It consists of a variety of different types of white blood cell as well as biochemicals that assist the action of those white cells and help the different parts of the immune system to communicate. Little of this detail will be described here, but the general principles underlying the functioning of the immune system need to be understood.

The different components of the immune system can be divided into two kinds of function: natural immunity (also known as primary immunity) and specific immunity (also known as acquired immunity or secondary immunity). Natural immunity is, from an evolutionary perspective, the older type of immunity. Natural immunity is designed to deal with any form of pathogen or foreign matter, whatever its type. The term antigen is used to refer collectively to substances to which the immune system reacts, so natural immunity is designed to deal with any form of antigen. By contrast, specific immunity involves the development of white blood cells and biochemicals that have a specific effect on particular antigens. Because the specific response is antigen specific, it also tends to be more effective. When the immune system detects a threat, there is an immediate response involving natural immunity and a delayed response involving specific immunity.

The immediate outcome of any form of internal assault on the body (e.g., an antigen or physical damage) is to stimulate the natural immune system, and this is done by the release of biochemicals whose function is to communicate the existence of a threat within the body. These activating biochemicals include the pro-inflammatory cytokines and Substance P, which enhances the pro-inflammatory cytokines as well as having an independent inflammatory effect. Substance P is a sensory peptide that is produced when tissue is damaged. Substance P is also produced when a person perceives an external (i.e., psychological) threat, so Substance P functions as a general indicator of a problem needing an inflammatory response (Rosenkranz, 2007). The inflammatory mechanism is complex and involves many pathways, and there is redundancy in that these pathways have similar effects: the overall result of these different inflammatory pathways is inflammation. Inflammation can occur throughout the body and involves a variety of changes to tissues that activate and help the action of immune cells. The inflammatory response is particular strong in barrier tissue. Barrier tissue means the barrier between the internal and external environment and includes the airways, the skin and the gut. Inflammation in barrier tissue creates a variety of other changes that make the barrier less susceptible to assault. For example, inflammation in the airways leads to production of mucus, which helps the expulsion of foreign matter. Inflammation in the gut leads to faster gut action, leading to expulsion of the irritating food.

After the initial, natural immune response, the immune system initiates a second response, but this time involving the specific immune system. Another set of chemicals, including other pro-inflammatory cytokines, then stimulate the specific immune system, which then develops the necessary cells and biochemicals to deal with the specific threat. The separation of natural and specific immunity is an example of the principle of efficiency. It is wasteful of energy to keep the immune system ready to deal with any antigen with a specific response. Instead, the body keeps the specific response in reserve and develops it for use at the time it is needed.

There are two kinds of health problem that arise from the way the immune system functions. One is when the immune system is not sufficiently active to deal with a pathogen. Interest in immune suppression characterises much of the early work by psychologists in the mind–immune system link. A second and more serious type of health problem arises from over-activity of the immune system when the white cells attack the body's own tissues. There are numerous diseases that have an inflammatory aetiology – that is, where the likelihood of developing the disease is increased by inflammation. They include diseases such as heart disease, cancer, inflammatory bowel disease, chronic obstructive pulmonary disease, asthma, rheumatoid arthritis, multiple sclerosis and many more diseases. Although drugs exist that suppress the inflammation, they tend to have side effects that are undesirable. Furthermore, the distal cause of these inflammatory diseases is not known, so treatment involves suppressing symptoms rather than curing the disease.

Recall from above that there is (a) an inflammatory response associated with the natural immune system and (b) an inflammatory response associated with the specific immune system. The consequence of this is that inflammatory diseases have two components. First, there is the inflammation that is specific to the part of the body involved and

Box 2.3 An overactive *and* underactive immune system

Note: a simplistic interpretation is that the immune system can be too inactive or too active, and the ideal is somewhere in between. It is important to emphasise that this interpretation is incorrect. The effect of long-term stress is to create over-activity in some parts of the immune system and under-activity in others. A dysregulated immune system has both over- and under-activity compared with the healthy immune system. The term *immunocompetence* is sometimes used to refer to an immune system that is neither over-active nor under-active but is functioning just right.

involves over-activity of the specific immune system. For example, the specific inflammation creates asthma when there is inflammation in the lung and inflammatory bowel disease when there is inflammation in the gut. Second, there is inflammation that affects the whole body; it is systemic and involves the natural immune system. The systemic inflammatory mediators tend to occur in all inflammatory diseases. All inflammatory disease tends to have raised levels, for example, of the pro-inflammatory cytokines associated with natural immunity such as tumour necrosis factor alpha (TNF-α), interleukin-1 (IL-1), interleukin-6 (IL-6) as well as Substance P. The systemic inflammatory mediators are *non-specific* in their contribution to disease.

The term *inflammatory response system* is used to describe the response of the natural immune system. Activation of the inflammatory response system is a consequence of an antigen, physical assault or an external threat that is input through a psychological route. The inflammatory response system is activated through both somatogenic (e.g., a virus) and psychogenic (e.g., psychological stress) routes. If the inflammatory response system is activated over a long period of time, then this increases the likelihood of a range of diseases, namely all those diseases that have an inflammatory component. The natural inflammatory response is a *non-specific* predisposing factor for disease. The specific inflammatory disease a person actually develops is affected by other factors, namely genetic predisposition and specific environmental factors. If a person lacks a predisposing gene for a specific disease, they are unlikely to develop the disease irrespective of the level of non-specific inflammation: if they do have the gene, then there is an increased chance of that disease developing. Not only does non-specific inflammation contribute to that chance of disease developing, but in addition, for some diseases, there are specific environmental predisposing factors. For example, excessive exposure to sunlight in people with light-coloured skin predisposes to skin cancer, but not to lung cancer. On the other hand, smoking predisposes to lung cancer. Environmental factors that irritate a specific part of the body have a specific effect on the development of cancer. When laypeople consider risk factors for diseases, they often consider only genetic and specific environmental factors. However, an equally important health message is to avoid non-specific inflammation over the long term.

Relationship between the mind/brain, behaviour and the immune system: psychoneuroimmunology

Almost a century ago (Ishigami, 1919) examined white blood cell activity in patients with tuberculosis and found that the activity of these cells as viewed under the microscope decreased if the blood sample was taken during periods of emotional excitement. Ishigami suggested that the 'stress of contemporary life' could impair the functioning of the immune system. Despite this early beginning, most research on the topic that is labelled *psychoneuroimmunology* has been conducted during the last 30 or 40 years.

The research falls into three categories. First, there is correlational research in which immune function is correlated with mental state, or more correctly, commonly those mental states referred to as mood. Some of this research involves correlations between immune parameters and mood in general populations and some involves comparisons between people with depression and matched controls – i.e., people without depression. A second kind of study involves manipulation of the internal environment in some way – through infection or drugs – and then observation on mood. A third kind of study involves manipulation of the external environment or observation of the effects of naturally occurring variation of external events, such as stress. The immunological consequences of this manipulation or variation are then observed.

The first category of research is very extensive and shows that measures of the immune system and measures of mood are correlated. This correlational research provides little information about the two kinds of causal direction shown in Figure 2.5 and 2.6 above. A correlation between mood and physiology may arise because the immune system changes to accommodate mental signals about the external environment, or it may arise because the mind is affected by the state of the immune system. Despite this limitation, the correlational research provides useful insights.

The early research (up to the mid 1990s) focused primarily on measures of immune activity, such as salivary IgA (which is comparatively easy to measure from a sample of saliva) and natural killer cell activity (which requires a sample of blood). The research shows suppressed activity on these and other parameters for people who are depressed or have poor mood (Irwin and Miller, 2007). Immune suppression comes about in part due to the effect of cortisol. Cortisol is a hormone and therefore part of the endocrine system. More specifically, the suppression of immune activity is the result of an interaction between the neurological, endocrine and immune systems.

Cortisol is produced through the following mechanism involving the hypothalamus, the pituitary (which is located at the base of the brain) and the adrenal glands (located over the kidneys), and hence is referred to as the hypothalamic–pituitary–adrenal axis, or HPA axis. In brief, stress leads to the production of corticotrophin-releasing hormone in the hypothalamus. Corticotrophin-releasing hormone acts on the pituitary, which produces corticotrophin. Corticotrophin produces cortisol from the adrenal glands. Cortisol has a number of effects on the body, not just the suppression of immune activity. Cortisol is an important hormone that communicates the fight or flight response throughout the body. Immune suppression is just one feature of the fight or flight response, a response that prepares the body for vigorous physical activity. Drugs that mimic cortisol (cortisone or corticosteroids) have the effect of suppressing immune activity. Note again the principle of efficiency: an external challenge can prepare the body for vigorous physical activity, but also suppresses the immune system.

Later research focused on other aspects of the immune system, in particular the pro-inflammatory cytokines. The general finding is that levels of these cytokines correlate with poor mood or depression (Irwin and Miller, 2007) and with stress (Kemeny and Schedlowski, 2007). Additionally, cytokines are known to be associated with fatigue (Straub and Männel, 1999). Thus, the correlational data show a complex pattern of immune changes associated with poor mood – some parts are up-regulated and some down-regulated. The down-regulation is associated with the parts of the immune system that actually deal with infection. For example, depression is associated with reduced lymphocyte proliferation, reduced virus-specific T-cell responses and reduced memory T-cell responses (Irwin and Miller, 2007). By contrast, the up-regulation is associated with those parts of the immune system that communicate the need for increased immune response, in particular the pro-inflammatory cytokines and other mediators that stimulate the acute phase of immune response.

The up-regulation and the down-regulation of the immune system involves two different but linked mechanisms, both of which are elicited by stress. Up-regulation is brought about by the inflammatory response system. Down-regulation is brought about by the HPA axis. Thus, the state of the immune system in response to stress depends on the competing effects of the inflammatory response system and the HPA axis, and in many cases these competing effects lead to some parts of the immune system being overactive, and others being suppressed.

Introduction to the immune theory of depression   The above section on correlational research shows that there has been a shift of interest from down-regulation to up-regulation of the immune system. This shift of research interest was due in part to recognition that the up-regulation of the immune system is clinically important. Long-term activation of the inflammatory response system is responsible for a variety of inflammatory diseases. In addition, activation of the inflammatory response system provides an explanation for the distal cause of depression. The hypothesis that the inflammatory response system plays in a role in depression has had a long history (see an early review in Maes, 1993 and a more recent one in Anisman *et al.*, 2005). According to the immune theory of depression, the changes observed in the brain associated with depression are themselves the result of immune dysfunction, namely ongoing activation of the inflammatory response system.

Although there is evidence of correlations between immune function and depression, this type of evidence does not establish causality. Additional support for the immune theory of depression comes from several additional types of evidence.

- Stress is a predictor of both depression and activation of the inflammatory response system (see next section).
- Antidepressant medications that increase serotonin levels also have the effect of reducing inflammation.
- Experimental increase in levels of pro-inflammatory cytokines tends to cause depression.

The last type of evidence, namely that the stimulation of pro-inflammatory cytokines leads to changes in mood, is important to establishing causality. Animal studies show that when animals are infected so as to produce an acute immune response, they engage in 'sickness behaviours', namely doing very little and not engaging in novel activities – i.e., behaviours associated with depression. There are a smaller number of studies that show a similar effect with humans. For example, Reichenberg *et al.* (2001) gave human subjects a mild immune stimulant (*Salmonella* endotoxin) or placebo by injection. Levels of depressed mood increased for those given the stimulant, and those given the stimulant also had poorer cognitive function – memory tasks were impaired. However, an important part of this study was that the authors showed that the degree of depression or cognitive impairment in those given the immune stimulant correlated with the degree to which they had increased their levels of pro-inflammatory cytokines. Thus, cytokines appear to have a direct causal role in poor mood and memory impairment. In a more recent study, Eisenberger *et al.* (2010) gave participants endotoxin or placebo, and measured the effects on pro-inflammatory cytokines, depression mood and social disconnection. Endotoxin, compared with placebo, produced increases in cytokines, depressed mood, fatigue and social disconnection, and these four variables increased on approximately the same timescale. Thus, there seems to be fairly clear evidence that cytokines (or, more accurately, that which stimulates cytokines) also have an effect on a range of mental states.

One implication of the immune theory of depression is that depression could be treated by pharmacological alteration of the immune system rather than pharmacological alteration of the brain. If pro-inflammatory cytokines are the distal cause of depression, then suppression of the effects of those cytokines should reduce depression. There have been a small number of clinical trials examining the effects of cytokine inhibitors on depression. The results (reviewed in Rosenkranz, 2007) have not been encouraging. Anti-cytokine or anti-Substance P therapy does seem set to replace conventional therapy for depression. There is just one footnote to the disappointing results with anti-cytokine therapy. Because lack of immune function is in itself a cause of health problems, an experimental therapy called cytokine therapy involves providing patients with those cytokines that stimulate immune function. Cytokine therapy is notorious in causing disturbances of mood, in particular depression. Not everyone becomes depressed following intake of cytokines, but a significant proportion do. Additionally, experimental treatment of healthy individuals with cytokines tends to lead to changes very similar to the sickness behaviours observed in animals. Thus, the results from the immune theory of depression are paradoxical.

Several types of evidence indicate a correlational link as well as a causal link between cytokines and depression. However, depression is not cured by anti-cytokine drugs!

There is one further paradoxical feature of the immune theory of depression. It is that there is no specificity between type of inflammatory mediator and type of mood. For example, it is not the case that high levels of IL-6 are associated with depression whereas high levels of TNF-α are associated with fatigue. This lack of specificity is inconsistent with the assumption of specificity that underpins modern Western medicine. These paradoxical findings need an explanation, which will presented later.

Box 2.4 Don't get too optimistic about brain therapy for depression!

A possible response to the failure of anti-cytokine therapy to cure depression may be that the real problem with depression is in the brain. The neurological theory of depression is that depression is caused by lack of serotonin. This topic will be examined in a later chapter. However, not only is the serotonin hypothesis widely disputed (Lacasse and Leo, 2005) but, in addition, serotonin-enhancing drugs are not very effective (Kirsch, 2009).

The failure of anti-cytokine drugs to provide an effective cure for depression does not obscure the fact that there is clear evidence that pro-inflammatory cytokines induce a range of symptoms that lead to illness behaviours (Dantzer and Kelley, 2007). When a person gets influenza, that person experiences a variety of symptoms that include temperature, fatigue, aching limbs and a general feeling of unwellness. These symptoms are not produced by the influenza virus. They are produced by the body's own response to the influenza virus, namely the inflammatory mediators. The effect of these 'sickness symptoms' is that they alter behaviour – i.e., they create 'sickness behaviour'. People with influenza typically respond to their feelings: they go to bed and rest. Owing to the principle of efficiency, resting when there is a threat to the internal environment of the body makes a lot of sense. By resting, the body is able to mobilise its resources for dealing with the internal threat, rather than use energy for other activities, such as dealing with external threats. If you have influenza it is not sensible to join a mammoth hunt. The response of the mind to pro-inflammatory cytokines is an adaptive response. The pro-inflammatory cytokines as well as other inflammatory mediators have a dual role – they change the organism's external environment via the mind–behaviour–external environment link, and they change the internal environment through their effects on the immune system.

How the external environment alters the internal environment   The correlational evidence between mood and immune function is also consistent with the causal pathway external world → mind → immune function. The external world is interpreted by the brain/mind. If this interpretation falls under the general category of stress, then the experience of stress creates changes in the immune system through a variety of pathways. In addition, stress alters the endocrine system via the HPA axis. Research over the last 40 or so years has revealed a simple principle. The acute response of the immune system to external stress seems to be the same as the response of the natural immune system to internal stress (Rosenkranz, 2007). That is, acute stress produces changes that include, among other effects, an increase in inflammatory mediators.

It is common to distinguish between *immunogenic* inflammation, meaning inflammation caused by immune challenge from *neurogenic* inflammation, where the latter is mediated via pathways descending from the brain. However, both sorts of cause of inflammation produce a similar effect, at least in the first instance. They *both* cause activation of the inflammatory response system (i.e., the inflammatory response

of natural immunity). It seems likely that immunogenic inflammation evolved first. However, inflammatory response to external challenge is also adaptive. It makes sense to prepare for infection when
you hunt mammoths. The inflammatory response to external stress
must have evolved as animals became more complex and began to alter
their external environments. Evolution is blind: rather than invent
an entirely new mechanism or structure, the existing inflammatory
response was exploited for the new challenge coming from the external
environment.

External stress produces Substance P, just in the same way that
Substance P is produced in response to antigens and physical damage.
Substance P therefore acts as a common pathway in stimulating the
inflammatory response system. Thus, the effect of the mind in producing an immune response is not some 'special' mechanism in which
mind influences the body. Instead, it is part of the same mechanism
whereby signals from various sources elicit an inflammatory response.

In general, research has shown that the effect of the acute response
to stress is an activation of the natural immune system and a slight
reduction in the activity of the specific immune system (note the principle of efficiency) (Segerstrom and Miller, 2004). This acute response
was labelled many years ago by Selye as the 'alarm stage'. If stress persists, then the body enters the 'stage of adaptation' during which other
immune changes take place, particularly those relating to the specific
immune system. Finally, if the stress is persistent, that is, if the person
experiences chronic stress, then there is suppression of both natural and
specific white cell activity, but with enhanced levels of inflammatory
mediators, such as the pro-inflammatory cytokines and Substance P.
This final stage, called by Selye, the 'stage of exhaustion', shows a
dysregulated immune system, where the pattern of dysregulation shows
the same pattern as that found in depression. Thus, the effect of stress
on the immune system differs depending on whether it is short-term
or long-term. Over the long term, stress produces the same pattern of
immune dysfunction that is implicated in giving rise to the sensation of
depression (Connor and Leonard, 1998).

Research into the short-term effects of stress shows that there is a
relatively rapid response of the immune system to stress brought about
by external challenge, i.e., within a few minutes (Wetherell *et al.* 2004).
The long-term research shows that numerous changes take place when
stress is experienced for a long time. For example, research shows that
the rate of wound healing is inhibited following stress such as the stress
of long-term care of a relative with Alzheimer's disease (Kiecolt-Glaser
et al., 1995, 2002). Stress can have long-term effects, long after the

stressor is no longer present. The conclusion from this research is that there is clear causal evidence that mental interpretation of events in the external world leads to changes in the immune system in the short term and in the long term (Irwin, 2008; Kern, 2007).

An important aspect of the stress response is that it stimulates the inflammatory response of natural immunity. As such, stress increases mediators that are associated with increased likelihood of developing a range of different inflammatory mediated diseases. Stress creates a *non-specific* tendency for inflammatory disease. There is a considerable body of research showing the relationship between psychological stress and immune-related diseases (Kemeny and Schedlowski, 2007).

However, stress does not only activate the inflammatory response system. Stress also activates the HPA axis (see above). HPA axis activation creates a variety of changes that prepare the body for vigorous physical activity, but it also produces cortisol, which acts as an immune suppressant. Thus, stress activates two systems that have different and sometimes opposing effects on the body. Why should there be two such systems?

The term stress is a general term for a variety of very different occurrences in the external environment. Some stresses, such as hunting mammoths, carry the risk of infection but also require vigorous physical activity. Other stresses, such as bereavement, do not carry the risk of infection. Modern stresses are different from those that commonly occurred when humans evolved – there is currently an unfortunate lack of mammoths – but the body responds to modern stresses in the same way that it responded to archaic stresses. The stress of competitive activity in an office situation is, from the body's perspective, similar to that of hunting mammoths. Thus, stressful office life activates the body to prepare for infection and vigorous activity, when neither is needed.

In the archaic environment, stresses would vary in the extent to which they signalled the risk of infection versus the need for vigorous activity. Thus, stresses would have varied in the extent to which resources needed to be allocated to managing the internal versus external environment. The *hypothesis of internal–external balance* proposes that the infornet evaluates any stress in terms of the resources needed to be allocated to immune challenge versus external challenge, and that the solution provided by this evaluation leads to the particular balance between the immune activation of the inflammatory response system and the immune suppression of the HPA axis. If the infornet anticipates increased external challenge, this leads to activation of the HPA axis. If the infornet anticipates increased internal challenge and the need for immune protection, this leads to activation of the inflammatory response system. As many stresses involve both external and internal challenge, a common solution is for pro-inflammatory cytokines to be raised but the activity of other immune parameters to be suppressed owing to the immunosuppressive effect of cortisol, which is produced by HPA activation.

In sum, the immune system and the mind are closely linked. Many authors suggest that there is a bidirectional causal link between the two. A better interpretation is that the mind is a signalling system that provides information about the state of the immune system and also provides the immune system with information about the external world. The reason for rejecting the bidirectional interpretation is that the evidence does not support a simple causal relationship between *particular* biochemicals in the immune system and psychological state. First, anti-cytokine and anti-Substance P therapy does not cure depression. Second, there are wide individual differences. A particular pro-inflammatory pattern may be associated with depression in one person but not in another. Third, the relationship between immune states and psychological states is by no means exact: there is no specificity. There must be some alternative theoretical model for explaining the link between the immune system and the mind.

Mood and emotion and internal–external balance

Psychologists distinguish mood from emotion. Mood refers to general psychological states that vary between positive and negative. Mood includes the states of depression, anxiety and fatigue. Emotion refers to more specific psychological states that are linked to particular experiences or external events. For example, fear, anger, disgust, love and elation are all emotions. Mood and emotion differ in two respects. Mood is more general and also does not relate to specific events. Emotion is less general and does relate to specific events. There is a relationship between mood and emotion. People who are depressed are more likely to have negative emotions such as fear and anger.

According to infonet theory, mood is a signal from the internal environment. Negative mood is a signal that provides information about the state of the infonet. By contrast, emotions, although influenced by mood states, reflect information about the external environment. Anger, love and fear are all emotions that provide information about external events. Thus, the causal sequences shown in Figures 2.5 and 2.6 can be redrawn as shown in Figure 2.7; or more simply as shown in Figure 2.8.

Different mood states have not been found to be related in a one-to-one fashion with immune or endocrine variables. The question of the relationship between emotions and physiological variables is less

Mood alters behaviour

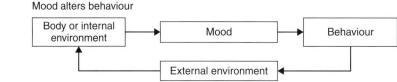

Emotions alter the internal environment

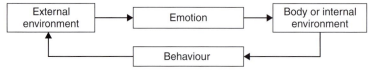

Figure 2.7 Mood alters behaviour and emotions alter the internal environment

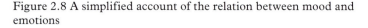

Figure 2.8 A simplified account of the relation between mood and emotions

clear, but recent publications suggest that a link is possible. A meta-analysis (Denson *et al.*, 2009) suggests that whereas global mood states are unrelated to physiological parameters, some emotional states do show a consistent pattern of response. For example, their results suggest that the HPA axis is consistently activated in response to threats to social status and threats to the social self. However, the conclusion from Denson *et al.* (2009) is disputed (Miller, 2009), though a later study also suggests specificity for emotions consistent with Denson *et al.*'s meta-analysis. In a study that investigated the short-term effects of anger and fear, Moons *et al.* (2010) found that whereas anger lead to increased cortisol, fear lead to reduced cortisol. These authors suggest the difference in response is adaptive: fear is associated with a greater likelihood of damage, and cortisol reduces pro-inflammatory action. Hence the reduction of cortisol allows an increase in the inflammatory response. Finally, bereavement has been shown to be related to reduced natural killer cell activity, whereas trauma is related to a slight increase in natural killer cell activity (Segerstrom and Miller, 2004). All these results suggest that the pattern of immune suppression is particularly associated with negative social emotions. The implication is that negative social emotions orient the internal–external balance towards external challenge, not internal challenge. Negative social emotions lead to activation of the HPA axis but not of the inflammatory response system. By contrast, stressful events that signify threat or fear lead to both HPA axis activation and inflammatory response system activation.

Infornet theory provides a perspective of the putative relationship between emotions and mood on the one hand and biological parameters on the other. The lack of specificity between mood and neuroendocrine markers arises because mood is an output from the infornet, and these markers contribute to the activation of this network system rather than having a unique causal relationship that would be expected from the assumption of disease specificity. Mood states are the result of a particular activation pattern of the infornet and therefore involve multiple biochemicals and receptors. By contrast, emotions provide information about the external environment, and as such provide information that is relevant to the internal–external balance. One would therefore predict that emotions lead to specific relations with immune parameters to the extent that they signal differences in the extent to which the external situation is interpreted as needing internal versus external resources. Fear indicates the risk of damage, and hence the need for immune preparation; anger does not. Trauma is associated with damage; bereavement and threats to social status are not. The specificity data cited above therefore fit the hypothesis of internal–external balance, but the hypothesis leads to additional predictions that require testing.

Immune conditioning

Classical conditioning was discovered at the end of the nineteenth century by Ivan Pavlov (1849–1936) (Pavlov, 1897, 1928). The phenomenon, which is also known as Pavlovian conditioning, can be illustrated with an example. Food (unconditioned stimulus) leads to salivation (unconditioned response). When a bell (conditioned stimulus) is paired repeatedly with food (unconditioned stimulus), then after a while the bell (conditioned stimulus) itself by elicits salivation (conditioned response). Classical conditioning demonstrates a phenomenon also known as associative learning, and this phenomenon was studied extensively by psychologists in the first part of the twentieth century. For example, if the conditioned stimulus is presented without the unconditioned stimulus (e.g., the bell but no food), then over a period of time the conditioned response reduces and disappears – a process described as extinction.

Immune conditioning was discovered (partly by accident) by Ader and Cohen in 1975 (Ader and Cohen, 1975; Ader *et al.*, 1995). Again the phenomenon can be illustrated with an example. If rats drink a fluid containing an immunosuppressant (unconditioned stimulus), then this leads to immune suppression (unconditioned response). When the immunosuppressant is paired repeatedly with a flavoured drink (i.e., the fluid in which the immunosuppressant is placed is flavoured), then the flavoured drink becomes a conditioned stimulus. After a while the flavoured drink will produce immunosuppression (conditioned response) in the absence of the immunosuppressant.

Although first demonstrated only in rats, immune conditioning has also been shown to exist in humans (Goebel *et al.*, 2002; Schedlowski and Pacheco-López, 2010). The implications of immune conditioning are substantial. If a person experiences a stressful event, and that event is associated with a conditioned stimulus, then over time the conditioned stimulus will create the same immune changes as the stressful event, namely a conditioned response. The discovery of immune conditioning is important, and implications of this phenomenon will be examined later in this book. For the moment it is worth noting that despite being discovered several decades ago, immune conditioning has not been exploited either in terms of explanations for disease or in terms of therapy. Studies have shown that it is possible to reduce unwanted inflammatory responses (e.g., allergic responses), but the studies have not always been consistent and they have not led to accepted new therapies (Schedlowski and Pacheco-López, 2010). Nevertheless, the phenomenon provides another example of the close relationship between the mind/brain and the immune system.

Independently of the work in immune conditioning, psychologists had become interested in the question of *why* conditioning occurred. It is now accepted that immune conditioning (and other learning phenomena) can be explained in terms of a neural network that operates according to some simple rules (Ellis and Humphries, 1999). The explanation of conditioning in terms of network theory will be described in Chapter 4. If classical conditioning is the result of a network structure, and immune conditioning has the same underlying mechanism as classical conditioning, then immune conditioning must also involve a network structure. The implication is that the brain and immune system form part of a single network structure.

Although researchers on immune conditioning were unaware of the development of classical conditioning in terms of network theory, they were interested in finding the way in which the immune system and neural system communicate with each other. Schedlowski and Pacheco-López (2010) review existing research on this topic and come to the conclusion that that the method of communication is not yet properly understood. They suggest that the immune system can communicate with the neurological tissue in two ways. It can communicate through a *systemic* pathway, where immune messengers (such as the pro-inflammatory cytokines) in the bloodstream affect the brain. For example, there are receptors for TNF-α in the brain. Second, the immune system can communicate with neurological tissue via a *neural* pathway in which immune messengers affect nerves in the periphery, and the nerves then conduct information up to the brain. The vagus nerve is a prime candidate for this kind of conduction. In the case of the neural tissue communicating with the immune system, this can also be achieved through two routes, *either* through the effect of efferent nerves (outgoing nerves) from the brain that have direct effects on the immune system (and the sympathetic nervous system is a prime candidate for this function), *or* through the HPA axis, where the activated HPA axis leads to higher levels of cortisol, which then reduce immune activity. If classical and immune conditioning are both examples of sequential processing, then one might expect one route or other to be involved in immune conditioning – though this has not been demonstrated. However, if immune conditioning is a network phenomenon, then the prediction is that multiple routes should be involved in the conditioned immune response. The reason researchers have had difficulty identifying a sequential route for immune conditioning may be that such a route does not exist.

The gut and mind

Introduction to the gut

Most people are familiar with the fact the function of the gut is to digest food. However, the gut has many other functions. One function is immunological: the gut is an important site of immune learning. The hygiene hypothesis suggests that inflammatory diseases (i.e., dysregulatory diseases of the immune system) arise in part because children are kept in too hygienic an environment and therefore do not come into contact with a sufficient variety of microorganisms (Yazdanbakhsh *et al.*, 2002). The hygiene hypothesis has been supported with a range of studies. Some studies showed that the gut microflora of children in Scandinavia – where the air was clean but asthma incidence high – was much less varied than the gut microflora of children in nearby Russia – where the air was polluted but asthma incidence low. Other research shows that children brought up on farms (and hence in more contact with 'dirty' animals) have a lower incidence of asthma than those brought up in rural areas but not on a farm. Furthermore, research shows that animals reared with sterile guts do not develop adequate immune systems. This large body of research leads to a general conclusion: the development of the immune system takes place primarily in the gut and involves the microbiota of the gut (Forsythe *et al.*, 2010). In addition, a person's health depends on the health of the gut microbiota, as these living organisms within the gut interact with the immune, neural and endocrine systems. Humans evolved symbiotically with microbiota – not in a sterile environment!

In addition to being part of the immune system, the gut is also part of the neurological system – being richly served by a network of neurons. The nervous system in the gut is referred to as the enteric nervous system and it has a coordinating function for gut activities (Wood, 2006). The enteric nervous system is sensitive to events that occur in the external environment, just as it is sensitive to events that occur within the gut itself. Technically, the contents of the gut are 'outside the body' and the gut wall is a barrier between the external and internal worlds – and hence a site particularly prone to inflammation. Particularly high levels of Substance P are found in the gut, and in fact this was the site where Substance P was first discovered (Rosenkranz, 2007). Inflammatory bowel disease (IBD) is defined by inflammation in the large or small gut, and is one of the more common inflammatory diseases in humans.

In order to achieve its function of digestion, the gut 'massages' the gut contents downwards toward the anus through an action called peristalsis. For effective digestion, the rate of peristalsis has to be neither too fast nor too slow – too fast produces diarrhoea and too slow produces constipation. Diarrhoea and constipation are symptoms of inflammatory bowel disease (IBD) and irritable bowel symptom (IBS), of which the latter involves the symptoms of IBD but no overtly measurable local inflammation (systemic inflammation is elevated in both IBD and IBS). In both cases these symptoms are symptoms of dysregulation – the control system controlling the rate of peristalsis is set at an abnormal level.

Relation of the mind/brain to the gut

Several studies show associations between mood states and poor gut function – for example, either IBS or IBD. In particular, depression and anxiety are often associated with gut disease. Correlational research typically fails to determine causal direction: is depression causing poor gut function, is poor gut function causing depression or are they both caused by a common factor? Longitudinal epidemiological research can shed some light on this problem, but the results do not lead to a simple conclusion. For example, in one study the association over time between

External world　→　Mind　→　Gut

(i.e., nasty things happen in the outside world, so I get upset, and so I have gastric problems)

Gut → Mind → Behaviour → External world

(i.e., I have gastric problems, so I get upset and don't do the things I want to do and so miss out on having fun)

Figure 2.9 Two causal pathways involving the mind and the gut

mood and IBD was assessed for two common types of IBD: ulcerative colitis and Crohn's disease (Kurina et al., 2001). Whereas depression preceded the onset of ulcerative colitis, it did not precede onset of Crohn's disease. Although pro-inflammatory cytokines are associated with both poor mood and inflammatory disease, it is unclear why the association in the study was found only for ulcerative colitis. Nevertheless, despite the above, there is clear evidence for both causal pathways as shown in Figure 2.9.

The effect of the mind on the gut　The stress response – or the fight or flight response – is mediated through two mechanisms. First, stress stimulates the HPA axis (see above) and therefore produces cortisol. Cortisol has a number of wide-ranging effects, but there is a time lag as it takes time for cortisol to be produced. Second, the effect of stress has a much more rapid effect that is mediated via the autonomic nervous system. The autonomic nervous system has two branches: sympathetic (which acts to prepare the body for fight or flight) and parasympathetic (which acts to create relaxation). Normally, when the sympathetic nervous system is active, the parasympathetic is not, and vice versa – the two parts of the autonomic nervous system function like either end of a see-saw. The effect of stimulating the sympathetic branch of the autonomic nervous system is to reduce the rate of gut peristalsis and in addition there is a reduction in blood flow to the gut. This response is adaptive and follows the principle of efficiency described above. If an organism needs to deal with an external threat, energy is removed away from the function of digestion to functions that are able to deal with that threat. So the effect of stress acts via the autonomic nervous system not only to reduce the flow of blood to the gut but also to increase the flow of blood to the large muscles and produce other changes (e.g., increased heart rate) that prepare the body for intense physical activity. In addition, the gut is sensitive to the inflammatory mediators associated with natural immunity. Consequently, stress caused by external threat leads to inflammatory response in the gut due to release of Substance P. Part of that inflammatory response in the gut involves increased peristalsis, as the way the gut deals with irritation in the gut contents is to increase peristalsis so as to eliminate the irritant as quickly as possible. Whether it is external threat or an internal threat, the immune system responds in the same way: activation of the inflammatory response system. Consequently, over the long term stress is associated with an inflamed and dysfunctional gut, and increased risk of gut disease. Of course, not everyone with stress experiences gut problems – there is no evidence of a consistent causal relationship.

The effect of the gut on the mind   The state of the gut affects a person's mood state. People report that they feel sluggish after a large meal. Like animals that tend to rest after eating, people experience sensations that induce rest – rather than engaging in stressful activity. There is a very good reason for resting, as after a meal the body's resources are directed at digestion, including increased blood flow to the gut. There is a popular advice not to swim immediately after swimming as doing so is more likely to lead to cramp – where cramp is caused by reduced blood flow to the legs and hence increased build-up of lactic acid. People with IBS describe how being constipated is not just a physical symptom but makes them feel unwell as a person. An unhealthy gut is detected by the mind/brain system and this registers in terms of negative mood (Forsythe *et al.*, 2010). Of course, not everyone with gut problems experiences depression – there is no evidence of a consistent causal relationship.

The gut is just one of several specific systems in the body, but it illustrates a general principle: The whole body is involved with the mind. The mind is a signal that indicates the state of the internal environment just as it is a signal providing information about the external environment.

In sum, the mind influences the gut via:

- the HPA axis and the production of cortisol;
- the autonomic nervous system; and
- the production of Substance P and the pro-inflammatory cytokines.

These different systems are part of the internal–external balance whereby the infornet provides a solution to external challenges that vary in their threat of immune challenge.

The behaviour inhibition system

The previous sections have examined the mind as a mediator between the internal and external environments. In this section we consider the mind as part of a system for managing the external environment, as shown in Figure 2.4.

As a general rule, the mind is a signal that helps initiate behaviour. A person who is presented with tasty food is more likely to eat it than if the food is hidden. Some 70 years ago, the psychologist Henry Murray proposed the existence of 'environmental press'. Environmental press refers to features of the environment that elicit motives – motives that are otherwise inactive until the press (i.e., the content of the environment) elicits motivational arousal. The mind is part of the behavioural activation system that elicits motivated behaviour, where the mind is influenced by both the external environment (the sight of the tasty bun) and the internal environment (low blood sugar). Although the function of the mind is often viewed in terms of its activating role, the mind can also inhibit behaviour.

Thorndike proposed his famous 'law of effect' (Thorndike, 1911) one hundred years ago. An organism is more likely to repeat a behaviour that has a satisfying effect. Thorndike developed his law by observing animal behaviour, but the general principle applies to humans though with additional refinements. Goal satisfaction, particularly the satisfaction of important or self-defining goals, leads to positive mood states (Carver and Scheier, 1982; Deci and Ryan, 1985; Sheldon and Elliot, 1999. Failure to satisfy goals is associated with depression (Hyland, 1987). Depression inhibits behaviour. Thus, by registering the *consequences* of behaviour, the mind is a signal that makes organisms more likely to disengage from unachievable goals and so redirect behaviour to realising other, hopefully more achievable, goals, whatever those goals happen to be. Disengagement of unattainable goals is an adaptive human response. Failure to disengage from unattainable goals is associated with a greater risk of depression (Carver and Scheier, 1998; Hyland, 1987). The story of 'sour grapes' is in fact an example of an adaptive psychological response. If you can't get the grapes then it is psychologically more comfortable not to have wanted them in the first place. To be happy, it is necessary for goals to be satisfied – for behaviour to have a 'good' effect. For behaviour to feel good, you need to stop doing things that feel bad – something that is rather obvious but not always acted upon.

Thorndike's law of effect has an exception. If a rat is placed in a T-maze (see Figure 2.10) and rewarded at whichever arm it first turns, the rat will continue to repeat the same behaviour.

So for example, if the rat turns right in the T-maze and receives food, then the rat will continue to turn right on the second and third occasions. Thorndike's law of effect is being followed: the rat is repeating behaviours that have positive consequences. However, as

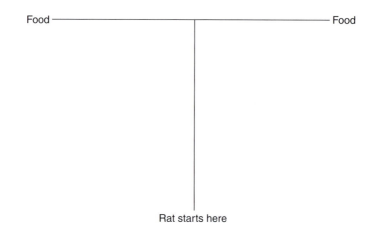

Figure 2.10 A T-maze where the rat is rewarded for turning either right or left

the trials continue, the rat will suddenly take the opposite arm of the T-maze – in the example it will turn left rather than right. Why? The reason suggested over fifty years ago was a mechanism called react-ive inhibition (Zeaman and House, 1951). Each time a behaviour is repeated, this generates inhibition for that same behaviour, inhib-ition that dissipates slowly over time. Although the rat is reinforced for turning right (in the example), inhibition gradually builds up for turning right. When that inhibition reaches a critical level, it over-comes the law of effect and the rat turns left. Reactive inhibition is a mechanism for inhibiting behaviour, and it confers an evolutionary advantage on organisms whose survival depends on understanding the external world. If the rat always turned right, it would not learn that there is tastier food in the left-hand arm of the maze. The consequence of reactive inhibition – curiosity – helps prepare people for whatever the external world throws at them. Humans experience reactive inhib-ition in a variety of ways, but primarily by the experience of boredom and fatigue. The author often has to mark students' essays and exam scripts; it is easy to imagine the cumulative effect of reading several very similar essays hour after hour.

The behaviour inhibition system is a system for inhibiting behaviour. Several factors can contribute to behaviour inhibition, including failure to attain a goal and reactive inhibition. In each case, the mind is presented with a signal that inhibits further activity. Depression inhibits any activity; boredom inhibits the particular ongoing activity.

The behaviour activation system

One of the design features of the body is that there are centres for inhibition behaviour and activating behaviour. For example, part of the hypothalamus is responsible for activating eating behaviour, and another part for inhibiting it. If there is a behaviour inhibition system, then it is plausible that there is a behavioural activation system.

It might be supposed that the amount of activity a child engages in during the day depends on environmental features; for example, those children who have the opportunity to do sport engage in more activity than those who don't have that opportunity. The research shows otherwise: that activity level appears to be constant. The *activitystat* hypothesis (Wilkin *et al.*, 2006) suggests that there is a biologically determined level of activity and that children modify their behaviour so that this level is achieved. Of course, in the short term activity may be increased for a variety of reasons. One reason for increased activity is an external threat. External threat leads to an increase in HPA axis activation (see above) and, depending on the nature of that threat, external threat also leads to anxiety and emotional states such as fear, guilt or shame.

Putting it all together: the infornet, the inflammatory response system, the HPA axis and the behaviour inhibition and activation systems

Let us return to the ideas introduced in Chapter 1: modern Western medicine is based on the principle of specificity. Specificity leads to predictions about the relationship between the immune system and the mind, as shown in Figure 2.11.

The problem is that, despite 30–40 years of research into psychoneurimmunology, the specificity hypothesis has not been confirmed for mood states. There is, however, recent research showing some specificity for emotions (Moons *et al.*, 2010), as described above. This difference between mood and emotion can be understood in terms of the way these two different mental states provide information about the external and internal world, namely that shown in Figure 2.8.

The lack of a specific relationship between immune parameters and mood is inconsistent with the specificity assumption of modern Western medicine. Neither simple patterns of immune function (e.g., only IL-6

Particular cytokines ⟶ Particular mood

Figure 2.11 Predictions from the specificity hypothesis

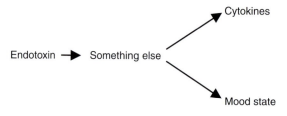

Figure 2.12 Causal sequence for studies showing the effect of endotoxin on mood

leads to depression) nor more complex patterns of cytokine combinations (e.g., both IL-6 and TNF-α together lead to depression) have been associated consistently with specific mood states. Additionally, anti-cytokine and anti-Substance P therapy have not been found to be effective therapies for depression.

The alternative must be that both the inflammatory response system and psychological states of depression and fatigue are themselves the consequence of something else. For example, in the studies where endotoxins lead to increased cytokines and negative mood states (Eisenberger *et al.*, 2010; Reichenberg *et al.*, 2001), the route is *not* endotoxin causes cytokines which cause mood state, but rather, the sequence shown in Figure 2.12.

Let us suppose that pro-inflammatory cytokines (and other inflammatory mediators) have two functions within the body. First, these cytokines act as part of a sequential processing system: they activate the immune system through their action on other parts of the immune system (i.e., the conventional understanding of immunology). They also form part of a sequence of events that involves the endocrine system. Second, they provide causal connections between the units of a parallel processing system, namely the infornet (details of how parallel processing systems function will be given in Chapter 4). The inflammatory mediators and immune parameters are just one of several different types of causal connection that occur between the units that make up the infornet. Other causal connections are made from the endocrine system and yet others from the neurological system, including neurons and neurotransmitters. So, the pro-inflammatory cytokines do not determine the state – and the outputs – of the infornet alone. Additionally, because networks often have considerable redundancy, changes in the pro-inflammatory cytokines alone will not necessarily alter the output from the infornet.

The infornet has physiological and psychological outputs. The physiological outputs include activation of the inflammatory response system. Thus, the distal cause (or origin) of the inflammatory

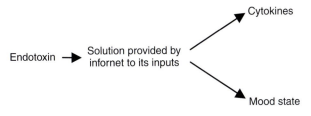

Figure 2.13 Causal sequence for studies showing the effect of endotoxin on mood with infornet included

response system is a signal from the infornet. Psychological outputs include moods. The causes of depression and fatigue are therefore not particular biochemicals but the output from a network that involves many different biochemicals. The association between mood and the immune system is not that they cause each other but rather that they are the consequence of a common cause, the infornet. The reason for the association (i.e., the common cause) will be explained in Chapter 3. Thus, the causal sequence from the endotoxin studies (Eisenberger *et al.*, 2010; Reichenberg *et al.*, 2001) is that shown in Figure 2.13.

Short-term stress has a different effect from long-term stress, so it makes sense to consider short-term effects on the infornet separately from long-term effects. Furthermore, the infornet responds not only to challenge but also to positive external events. We start by considering three examples of short-term effects on the infornet: (a) external threat (e.g., being faced with a tiger), (b) internal threat (e.g., a virus infection) and (c) a positive external event (e.g., response to infants while breastfeeding). These examples can be considered elaborations of Figures 2.5 and 2.6.

Let us suppose that a person experiences an external short-term threat, such as being faced with a tiger. The infornet interprets the threat as a state of alarm. Let us call this *infornet alarm*. Infornet alarm means that the infornet adapts the body to deal with the particular form of threat. That adaptation will depend on the extent to which the threat is interpreted as leading to external challenge (i.e., the need for additional activity) and internal challenge (i.e., the need for immune protection).

Let us suppose that infornet alarm activates the inflammatory response system because the tiger carries the risk of physical injury. The outputs from the inflammatory response system then initiate the cascade of immune responses that are part of the specific system and lead to systemic and specific inflammation. The interpretation that the tiger constitutes an internal challenge will tend to create behavioural inhibition. However, because it might be sensible to avoid the tiger, infonet alarm initiates other physiological changes that are associated with the fight or flight response, via the HPA axis and the autonomic nervous system, and that tend to create behavioural activation. So, for example, there is an increase in heart rate and blood flow to the large muscles and reduction of blood flow to the gut. Because the tiger is interpreted as constituting an external challenge, there will be an increase in the behaviour activation system, including the mental signal of anxiety. The more the tiger is seen as requiring an external challenge, the greater the HPA axis activation and behavioural activation. The more the tiger is seen to signal a risk of physical injury, the greater the activation of the inflammatory response system. The resulting behavioural activation/inhibition and immune activation/inhibition is a compromise made by the infonet as the best possible solution for preparing the body to deal with a tiger.

In the tiger example, the level of immune activation and level of HPA activation depends on the internal–external balance, that is, the extent to which the solution to the inputs provided by the infonet reflects the relative need for infection control versus physical activity. If the tiger induces the emotion of fear, then fear is a signal of potential physical damage, and so the internal–external balance will be oriented towards activation of the inflammatory response system along with the HPA axis. However, other forms of external stressor, for example, those inducing anger or guilt, will not signal physical damage and so there will be less activation of the inflammatory response system. In the example of the tiger, the behaviour inhibition and behaviour activation systems are both activated: the former owing to the risk of internal challenge, and the latter owing to the risk of external challenge. Note that the HPA axis and inflammatory response systems are interacting systems: HPA axis activation tends to suppress immune activity.

Consider now what happens when a person experiences a short-term challenge of a virus. Again the infonet interprets the challenge as requiring a state of alarm, infonet alarm, and activates the inflammatory response system. There is an upgrading of all parts of the natural immune system: an increase in pro-inflammatory cytokines and increase in immune cellular activity. In addition there are other physiological changes associated with infection, such as raised body temperature. Finally, the infonet alters the psychological state so as to produce a state of behavioural inhibition. Behavioural inhibition leads to symptoms of fatigue and depression that lead to a general decrease in behaviour. Notice that, in this case, the absence of external challenge means that there is no increase in the behaviour activation system: there is no increase in activity and no anxiety. There is no activation of the HPA axis – unless, of course, being ill leads to loss of income and hence psychological stress.

The above two examples can be put together diagrammatically, as shown in Figure 2.14. The two examples shown in Figure 2.14 illustrate that response to threat tends to be specific to that threat. There are different psychological responses and different physiological responses depending on the extent to which a stressor is interpreted, by the infornet, as constituting an external or internal challenge. More generally, different types of threat produce infornet alarm of a type that is best suited to deal with that particular threat. Activation of the inflammatory response system is not limited to infection, as it can be an adaptive response to external threat. If you are going on a mammoth hunt, there is a good chance you will be injured and it will be useful to have an activated natural immune system ready for such a challenge.

The infornet responds not only to challenge but also to positive events. The third example is that of breastfeeding. When a mother who is breastfeeding hears her baby crying, there is a physiological response

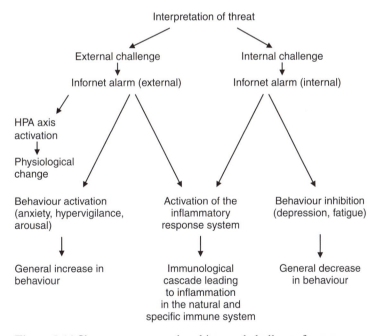

Figure 2.14 Short-term external and internal challenge from a potential threat

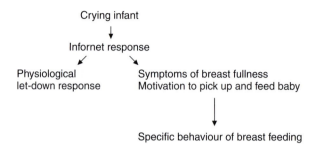

Figure 2.15 Short-term positive event

called 'the let-down response' whereby the breasts become ready for breastfeeding and milk starts to leak out. The let-down response is also accompanied by psychological symptoms, namely a sense of breast fullness, a sensation that increases motivation for breastfeeding. Thus, the informet responds both to challenging and other events with a response that is consistent with the situation. The informet controls the body's control systems so that the appropriate response is given. The example of breastfeeding is illustrated in Figure 2.15.

These examples show that the short-term response of the informet is specific to its inputs. The informet 'solves' the problem provided by its inputs and provides a solution, where the inputs are both physiological and psychological and the solution or output is both physiological and psychological. The theory of the internet suggests that mind affects the body because the mind is part of the body – i.e., the mind is a signal from the informet. Some of those signals are internally generated and some of them are externally generated. However, there is no 'disembodied mind' that has a causal effect on the body, because the mind and body are not separate: the mind is a signal of the body.

Informet alarm is an adaptive response to threat where the precise form of the response depends on the inputs received into the informet. Similarly, the let-down response of breastfeeding is an adaptive response to the crying infant. The *well-regulated* informet produces outputs that are appropriate for the current situation. The *dysregulated* informet, by contrast, produces outputs that are inappropriate to the current situation. The informet can be dysregulated in different ways, but an important form of dysregulation is *general dysregulation*. In the case of general informet dysregulation, irrespective of the current situation, the informet produces outputs that would otherwise be produced in response to external and internal challenge. That is, general informet dysregulation involves a response that could be described as non-specific alarm – as though there is both internal and external threat. General

Box 2.5 Perseveration of acute stress

If you nearly have an accident – a near miss in car, for example – then your body produces an acute physiological stress response involving the autonomic nervous system. However, that response persists (technically called perseveration) even though you realise you are now safe. This preservation response shows that the body is not responding directly to the cognitive input – i.e., the perception of danger – but rather to something else that has a slightly different timescale – one that perseverates. Other authors have explained this perseveration in terms of an unconscious part of the mind, and they refer to this hypothesis as the unconscious perseverative cognition hypothesis (Brosschot *et al.*, 2010). An idea developed throughout this book is that the infornet contains meaning that may not be available to consciousness. According to the present theory, the unconscious preservative cognitions are beliefs encoded in the infornet.

infornet dysregulation will be described in the next chapter. For the moment it should be noted that the outputs of general infornet dysregulation include those shown in Figure 2.14, namely:

- chronically heightened inflammatory response system, that is, a chronically high level of inflammatory mediators of the natural immune system, leading to a cascade of inflammatory effects in the specific system;
- HPA axis activation causing (a) autonomic changes associated with arousal and (b) suppression of natural and specific immune cellular activity leading to less effective management of infection in the specific system;
- behaviour inhibition (i.e. symptoms such as depression and fatigue) leading to a general reduction of behaviour; and
- behaviour activation (symptoms of anxiety and hypervigilance) and a general increase in behaviour.

The immune, endocrine and psychological characteristics of general infornet dysregulation are those of long-term stress. In terms of its physiological and psychological features, general infornet dysregulation is equivalent to Selye's state of exhaustion. The infornet is dysregulated because its response is inappropriate to the current situation, sometimes 'trying' to achieve incompatible activities at the same time. Thus, in a dysregulated infornet there may be simultaneous mental signals to increase behaviour (anxiety) and decrease behaviour (fatigue and depression) and also signals that activate parts of the immune system (inflammatory response system) and decrease others (the effect of cortisol produced via the HPA axis). The dysregulated infornet performs poorly on the principle of efficiency, described above, in that the body conserves its resources by carrying out specific functions at specific times.

The mind, the infornet and the specific system: a summary

The mind is a part of the body's communication system that provides information about the state of the internal environment – the infornet – and in so doing gives rise to mood states, including depression, anxiety and fatigue. In addition, the mind provides information about the external world. Information from the external world can be divided into two categories. First, there are symptoms, such as pain, that provide specific information about the body's interaction with the external world. Pain alerts you to the fact that you have injured yourself. Second, there are emotions, such as fear and anger, which provide more general information about the way the body is interacting with the environment. Fear provides information that there is some, unspecified threat that can create harm and therefore the need for immune protection. Emotions that indicate the need for immune protection increase the inflammatory response system compared with emotions that indicate otherwise. Any negative emotion caused by an external stressor can increase the HPA axis.

Figure 2.16 provides a summary of the several roles of the mind as part of the body's communication system. Note that Figure 2.16 is a simplification in that behaviour alters the external environment, and for simplicity these causal links are not shown.

In sum, the mind is a 'dial' that registers what is going on inside and outside the body. There are different dials, i.e., different mental states, depending on whether the dial is primarily registering what goes on inside or outside the body. Moods originate from the infornet, emotions from the external environment. In addition, symptoms arise from the specific system.

Mood states are not specific to any part of the body. The argument will be developed in the following chapters, i.e. that mood states such as depression and fatigue (as well as less tangible symptoms such as 'feeling unwell') are signals from the body that there is something causing a problem. To deal with the problem, it is necessary to get to the root cause – one needs to ascertain what the 'something' is before appropriate action can be taken. If your engine registers that it is overheating, you will not solve the problem by disconnecting the heat sensor indicator.

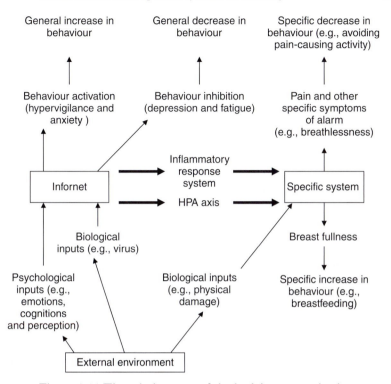

Figure 2.16 The mind as part of the body's communication system. Note that the infornet solves the problem: what is the best output given the current inputs?

If someone burns their finger in a flame, the sensible response is to learn to avoid putting the finger in the flame. That is, the sensible response to damaging your finger is to change behaviour to avoid the damage and so avoid the symptom. A less sensible response is to continue putting your finger in the flame and take some paracetamol so that it doesn't hurt so much. Depression, anxiety and fatigue are also signals from the body. A sensible response to such mood states is to avoid behaviours that cause them.

3 Personality, disease and the meaning of infornet dysregulation

Introduction

The idea that the personality or states of mind could cause disease has a long history. The Roman physician Galen suggested that imbalances in the four bodily humours create both mental states and physical diseases. The four bodily humours were those proposed by the ancient Greek Hippocrates, many years before, namely blood, black and yellow bile and phlegm. Galen used Hippocrates' proposal to suggest, for example, that melancholic women (i.e., depressed women) were more likely to develop cancer, as both depression and cancer were caused by an excess of black bile. In addition to medical texts based on the Hippocratic medical tradition, there are many examples in the literature of mind states influencing disease, in particular those relating to the idea of a 'broken heart' (Lynch 1977). For example, John Donne's (1572–1631) poem 'The broken heart' suggests that lost love could lead to disease, including the plague. There is a Japanese myth of an octopus farmer who, spurned by the octopus with whom he had fallen in love, died of a broken heart. The 'broken heart leading to disease and death' concept is worldwide.

The relationship between personality and disease is important because it provides insights into the idea of dysregulation. Infornet dysregulation has a number of psychological consequences, including consequences for personality. Thus, the personality–disease relationship is part of the way dysregulation manifests psychologically. This chapter on the meaning of infornet dysregulation therefore starts with an examination of research on the personality–disease relationship.

Academic research into the personality–disease relationship falls into two categories. First, there is research that takes as its starting point *existing* personality constructs and dimensions. This research examines to what extent constructs that were developed for some other purpose (typically to predict other behaviours) correlate with health or disease states. This programme of research is conducted primarily by

70

psychologists and in many cases health and disease are treated as part of a unidimensional construct (i.e., health versus disease). At least for some of this research, researchers are unconcerned with whether particular types of personality are linked to particular types of disease. Second, there is research that takes as its starting point the development of *new* personality constructs that are specifically linked to particular types of disease (e.g., heart disease versus cancer). This second type of research was started by medical researchers and continued by psychologists, and there is an assumption of specificity between disease and personality type – or state of mind. Over time these two research traditions have tended to merge.

This chapter starts with a review of both these research programmes, so as to examine *how* and *why* personality is linked to disease and health, with a particular focus on fatigue, depression and anxiety. The chapter goes on to explore how higher-order factors of the original five-factor theory of personality are relevant to infornet dysregulation, as well as the relevance of reinforcement sensitivity theory, and theories of coping style and cognitive style. In the final section the meaning of infornet dysregulation is examined in terms of the meaning that can be attributed to different forms of dysregulation.

Personality theory and disease

What is personality?

Personality provides a description of the way people differ. Hence, the personality–disease relationship provides a description of how different types of people are more prone to disease than others. There are, however, several different approaches to personality theory, so there are different ways of dividing up people into 'ways in which people differ'. In this section we will limit attention to trait theories of personality. Traits are consistent patterns of behaviour. More precisely, traits are behaviours that tend to be consistent across situations and across time, and hence provide a reliable and consistent way of describing differences between people. Personality traits were developed to predict these consistent differences in behaviour.

Trait theories of personality fall into two categories: five-factor theory and what is best described as 'other personality dimensions'. According to the five-factor theory, there are five orthogonal (i.e., uncorrelated) dimensions of personality, namely neuroticism versus stability, extraversion versus introversion, conscientiousness, agreeableness and openness to new experiences. According to this theory, all (or almost all) variation in trait behaviour can be understood in terms of these five dimensions – which are commonly referred to as the Big Five. What I have referred to as 'other personality dimensions' are those that do not fit naturally within the five-factor theory model, that is, where authors believe that there is something distinct about their dimension that cannot be accommodated within the Big Five. These other personality dimensions are usually developed for a specific theoretical purpose (i.e., to explain a particular type of behaviour) and they are very heterogeneous – varying from optimism to spirituality. Not surprisingly, the question of uniqueness of these other personality dimensions is disputed by those supporting the five-factor theory, but this controversy need not concern us. However, it is important to note that some of these other dimensions are closely related to emotions. Anger is an example of an emotion – and one that has been linked to increased cortisol levels (Moons *et al.*, 2010). Hostility is a personality dimension that is closely related to habitual levels of anger. Thus, some of the 'other personality dimensions' refer to consistent emotional responses to particular types of situation.

Of the Big Five, neuroticism explains more variance in behaviour than any of the remaining four dimensions, and neuroticism is also particularly important from the perspective of the personality–disease relationship. Consequently, it is important to understand exactly what is meant by this personality construct.

Sometimes people have negative mood states – where negative mood will include feelings of depression, disappointment, anxiety, worry, panic, lack of energy, etc. Transient mood states are referred to as *state affect*, and negative mood states as *negative state affect*. If a person consistently experiences negative state affect, then that person is said to have *trait negative affect*. Trait negative affect means that the person experiences negative mood states across situations and time. Trait negative affect and neuroticism are, in all practical details, the same construct. The mental representation of neuroticism consists of negative *mood* states – such as depression, anxiety as well as negative *emotional states*, such as hostile, guilty and scared. A list of negative emotional states associated with trait negative affect or neuroticism can be found in the *positive and negative affect scale* (Watson *et al.*, 1988). The empirical evidence for the construct of neuroticism comes from the finding that negative mood (depression, anxiety and fatigue) and negative emotions (e.g., hostile, guilty, scared) co-vary, and they co-vary independently of the remaining four of the Big Five. Thus, from the perspective of trait theory, neuroticism can be considered a combination of correlated negative mood states and emotions that tend to occur together. From the perspective of infornet theory, mood is a signal of the internal state of the body whereas emotions are signals about the external environment. The reason that negative emotions and negative mood correlate is that the interpretation of the external world is influenced by trait mood.

Extraversion–introversion is another personality dimension of the Big Five and one that explains the next greatest proportion of variance. Extraversion is, in all practical details, equivalent to trait positive affect. Positive affect includes emotions such as excited, proud, inspired and alert. Positive and negative moods tend to vary independently, but there is a weak negative correlation between the two (Crawford and Henry, 2004). In sum, the five-factor theory of personality suggests that there are two different types of affect: negative affect, which includes depression, anxiety and fatigue; and positive affect. Whereas excessive negative affect can be considered a health problem, it is not common to consider lack of positive affect a health problem. If a person complains of depression, then clinicians will recommend treatment. If a person complains about lack of joy – but without depression – then they are unlikely to be recommended treatment.

Trait dimensions and health

Trait scales were developed to predict behaviour, not to predict health. When researchers began investigating the relationship between these scales and health, it soon became apparent that most scales correlate with health outcomes to some extent, but some more than others.

Much of the early research on the health–personality relationship focused on the relationship between negative affect (or neuroticism) rather than positive affect (or extraversion) and health (Watson, 1988). The reason for this focus on negative rather than positive affect was because of research showing that negative affect was a better predictor than positive affect. For example, Knapp *et al.* (1992) found that the induction of negative emotions led to physiological changes (increase in systolic blood pressure and reduced immune cellular activity), whereas induction of pleasant emotions did not, and Emmons (1991) found that symptom reporting was correlated with positive but not negative affect.

There is a large body of consistent research showing that neuroticism and its components are associated with disease and poor health (Brown and Moskowitz, 1997). Some of this research shows that there are correlations between neuroticism on the one hand and measures of physical symptoms on the other. Other research shows that people with diagnosed disease tend to be higher in anxiety and depression. The relationship between neuroticism and health/disease is one of the most stable and consistent relationships in health psychology (Consedine and Moskowitz, 2007). If health is correlated with more than one personality dimension, neuroticism normally has the strongest correlation.

Although there is considerably more research on the relationship between negative affect and health, more recent research has also established that positive affect influences health, and it does so independently of negative affect (Pressman and Cohen, 2005; Steptoe *et al.*, 2009). Negative and positive affect are therefore both independent predictors of health.

Other trait scales are also related to health. Personality scales as diverse as hardiness, optimism, religiosity/spirituality and self-actualisation have been found to be associated with better health, either mental or physical, whereas neuroticism, hostility, loneliness and emotional repression (i.e., difficulty in expressing emotions or alexithymia) are negatively related to related health. Interpretation of these findings is made complex by the fact that many scales correlate (sometimes highly) with others, and in particular neuroticism (i.e., trait negative affect) and extraversion (i.e., trait positive affect). For example, optimism correlates negatively with neuroticism, though the authors of the scale measuring optimism claim that it is a different construct. It is impossible to review the whole of this large research field here, but it is worth noting that there are few personality scales that have not, in one study or other, been found to relate to one measure or other of health or disease.

A good way of characterising the correlations between personality scales and health is that mental and physical health are correlated. There is one possible exception: perfectionism as a personality trait is often associated with poorer health and is a good predictor of fatigue (Magnusson *et al.*, 1996). However, perfectionism is not obviously an unhealthy mental state, though perfectionism can be divided into a maladaptive and an adaptive form. Studies have found that only maladaptive perfectionism is associated with poor health (Bieling *et al.*, 2003) or CFS (Deary and Chalder, 2010), yet another has found that both adaptive and maladaptive forms are associated with poor health (Saboonchi and Lundh, 2003).

In sum, there is ample evidence of an association between personality traits and measures of health and disease. The more difficult question is why? What are the underlying mechanisms for this relationship?

Mechanisms

Any observed correlation between personality and disease can arise for one or more of five reasons – i.e., five different mechanisms. Each of these mechanisms is plausible and has empirical support. Each of these five mechanisms could lead to a correlation between either negative affect or positive affect and health, apart from the first of those reported (symptom reporting and diagnosis bias), which is probably responsible only for a negative affect with health correlation.

1. Symptom reporting and diagnosis bias   People who are high in the trait of neuroticism tend to perceive external events more negatively and tend to remember negative events more than those low in neuroticism. Symptom perception is a type of perception. People who are high on trait negative affect or neuroticism are more likely to report symptoms than those lower in neuroticism. People high in trait negative affect tend to recognise and recall their symptoms more than those low in negative affect (Watson and Pennebaker, 1989). Correlations between, for example, depression and physical disease reporting can be attributed to the effect of depression on symptom reporting. Neuroticism will influence the reporting of all self-report scales of physical illness, and there is a general rule that *any* self-report measure relating to health is affected by trait negative affect. These correlations vary in degree, but can be surprisingly high. For example, neuroticism correlates with measures of health-related quality of life, with reported correlations in the order of $r = 0.7$, that is, a degree of association consistent with convergent construct validity (Hyland, 1992b).

The question of whether reporting bias affects objective assessments of physical illness is more complex. People who are prone to anxiety are more likely to seek help for a problem than those who are not, leading to diagnosis bias. In addition, where a disease requires self-medication, people high in anxiety are more likely to solicit and hence be prescribed medication (Hyland *et al.*, 1993), leading to a correlation between anxiety and disease severity when the latter is measured by level of prescription. Thus, neuroticism (anxiety is a component of neuroticism) may also affect some objective measures of disease – i.e., those that require clinical judgement.

The symptom reporting and diagnosis bias mechanism is normally relevant only to concurrent correlations between personality and disease, that is, where both measures are taken at the same time. In principle, however, this bias could lead to correlations between personality measured at one time point and disease at a later time point if disease diagnosis is affected by neuroticism. If neuroticism leads to increased levels of diagnosis – because neurotic individuals are more likely to seek medical advice – then, assuming neuroticism remains constant, the link between neuroticism and disease at a later time point is a consequence of the concurrent relationship.

2. Disease affecting mental states   Physical or somatic diseases (i.e., non-brain diseases) often lead to physical symptoms. For example, a person with asthma may experience breathlessness. A person with inflammatory bowel disease may experience gastric pain. These physical symptoms have consequences for the way a person lives. For example, asthma can cause breathlessness and the anxiety about breathlessness may restrict the activity of someone with asthma. Someone with inflammatory bowel disease may be able to eat only particular foods, which therefore restricts social activity. In addition, people with chronic diseases have to manage those diseases and disease management imposes its own burdens.

In general terms, being ill can lead to a variety of changes in quality of life, including activity restriction, concerns about the future and worries about self-management. Being ill can have mental consequences. Thus, a relationship between depression and disease may arise because having the disease is a depressing experience. The relationship between anxiety and disease may arise because the disease elicits anxiety about the future. Additionally, for diseases where self-management plays an important role (e.g., asthma, diabetes and COPD), anxiety about self-management may be responsible for a correlation between anxiety and disease severity. Health-related quality of life scales are constructed on the assumption that disease has the capacity to cause deficits in quality of life, and these deficits include poor mood and activity restriction.

The concept of health-related quality of life is analogous to the retail price index. Scales measuring this concept assess a shopping bag of life's experiences that make up what is conventionally thought of as life's quality. The questionnaire items of such health-related quality of life scales assess the patient's self-report about how disease impacts on those experiences (Hyland, 1992a).

Box 3.1 Measuring disease versus measuring health

Note: although the term used is 'health-related quality of life', the scales would be more aptly described by the term 'disease-related quality of life'. Simply describing something as 'health' does not eliminate the fact that in health-related quality of life scales good quality of life is operationalised by the absence of disease – rather than something which, as suggested in the WHO definition of health, is more than just the absence of disease (see Chapter 1).

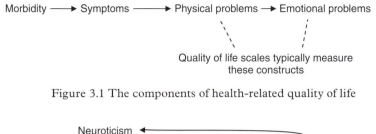

Figure 3.1 The components of health-related quality of life

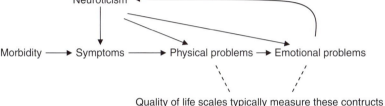

Figure 3.2 The effect of symptom reporting bias on quality of life

The experiences measured by health-related quality of life scales fall into two factorially distinct groups: those relating to the emotional and mental effects of the disease and those relating to physical limitations caused by the disease (Hyland, 1992b, Hyland *et al.*, 1994). These factorially distinct groups are found both in generic health-related quality of life scales (i.e., those that can be used for any disease) and those that are disease specific.

In sum, physical morbidity (i.e., disease) leads to symptoms which then lead to physical and emotional problems, as shown in Figure 3.1.

Putting the first two models together

The first two models, namely 'symptom reporting and diagnosis bias' and 'diseases affecting mental states' both involving perceptions, are put together in Figure 3.2.

Figure 3.2 shows how these two models act as a positive feedback system. In colloquial terms: having a physical symptoms makes you miserable; and being miserable makes those physical symptoms seem worse.

Research supports Figure 3.2: neuroticism is more highly correlated with emotional problems than physical problems, and disease severity is more highly correlated with physical problems than with emotional problems. However, the causal sequences shown in Figure 3.2 all involve the perception of symptoms – there is no suggestion in this model that morbidity (i.e., physiological processes that indicate pathophysiology)

Personality → Behaviour → External environment → Internal environment → Disease

Figure 3.3 The effect of personality on health-harming behaviours

is influenced by psychological factors. These first two models do not propose that psychological factors alter the physical course of a disease.

3. Unhealthy habits, external environment   If anxious people are more likely to smoke cigarettes, then anxiety will lead to behaviours that expose the body to an unhealthy external environment. If people who are depressed are less willing to go out and buy fruit and vegetables, they will have an unhealthy diet. There are several different ways that personality might induce people to modify their environment so that they have greater contact with those parts that are unhealthy or less contact with those parts that are healthy. In either case the external environment (e.g., smoking) affects the internal environment (e.g., irritation of lung tissue). The causal sequence is shown in Figure 3.3.

Anxiety and depression (i.e., the trait of neuroticism) is one of several personality dimensions that can alter behaviour in a way that leads to more or less self-harming behaviours. Another personality dimension that is related to self-harming behaviour is religiousness. Several studies show that religiousness is associated with better health. One possible explanation for this relationship is that religiousness contributes to better self-control so that people are less likely to smoke and drink to excess (McCullough and Willoughby, 2009). Thus, self-control appears to be an important mediator of the extent to which personality factors can lead to differential exposure to external harm.

Theories of coping provide a useful perspective on health-promoting and health-harming behaviours. When treated as a trait variable, it is possible to distinguish two main coping styles: problem-focused coping and emotion-focused coping. Problem-focused copers try to deal with the problem at hand. Emotion-focused copers try to deal with the emotion caused by the problem, but without necessarily dealing with the problem itself (Carver *et al.*, 1989). People who are emotion focused are less likely to respond to the practical, problem-solving advice that is part of health education. For example, the response 'I am not going to get heart disease so I don't need to exercise or eat properly' would be a typical emotion-focused response to a healthy heart education programme. As a general rule, emotion-focused coping protects people from the emotional trauma of sudden disease onset, but leads to poor long-term outcome because emotion-focused coping, compared with problem-focused coping, is less likely to lead to the behavioural change needed for healthy habits.

Box 3.2 Emotion-focused versus problem-focused coping

Imagine that a student is expecting a difficult examination. The problem-focused coper will work out a revision programme, revise hard including working in the evenings, and prepare for the examination. The emotion-focused coper will get drunk in the evenings and during the day complain how unfair it is to have examinations. Emotion-focused copers are less stressed by the examinations because they are distracted from the problem of the examination itself. The problem-focused coper gets more stressed but performs better.

Emotion-focused versus problem-focused coping can be treated as a trait dimension. This trait correlates (between a moderate and large extent) with neuroticism. Thus, the neurotic tends to be emotion focused and as a consequence has less adaptive behaviour in the long term. People high in neuroticism and those low in self-control are more prone, therefore, to non-adaptive behaviours that compromise health.

There is a final point to note about these external factors that contribute to disease. Many, though not all of them, are pathogenic because they contribute to inflammation. That is, habits are healthy to the extent to which they prevent people exposing themselves to inflammatory-prone environments. Excessive sunlight, smoking, poor diet, etc., all lead to increases in inflammatory mediators, because, as a general rule, anything that irritates the body's tissues has a pro-inflammatory effect.

4. Unhealthy habits, internal environment If a person has an aggressive personality, that person is likely to get into arguments and disputes, and this combative behaviour may lead to an increase in blood pressure, which then makes cardiovascular disease (e.g., heart disease and stroke) more likely. Anger is associated with greater HPA axis activation. Any personality trait that increases the likelihood that a person experiences more stressful situations – i.e., a stressful situation-inducing personality – is likely to experience health problems owing to changes to the internal environment, where these changes may involve cardiovascular changes, immune changes and changes to the gastric system. Thus, hostility, which is a consistent predictor of poor health, may have an effect because it increases the number of stressful situations experienced by a hostile person. The effect of stress on the immune and gastric systems was described in the previous chapter. The causal sequence is shown in Figure 3.4.

Personality → Behaviour → Internal environment → Disease

Figure 3.4 The effect of a stress-seeking personality on health and disease

People create their own environments, often through their emotional response to particular situations. There is a variety of reasons why a person may create an environment that is stressful, and they are not limited to hostility (i.e., it is not just 'nasty people' who create stress for themselves). For example, if a person is hardworking and committed to their job, and the job can be stressful, then that person will experience greater stress than a person who is less committed to the job. Commitment to a job, commitment to others and perfectionism can lead to greater experience of stress. The previous chapter outlined the immunological and other consequences of stress. In particular, stress leads to non-specific inflammatory processes that can contribute to disease. Thus, the two mechanisms, 'unhealthy habits, external environment' and 'unhealthy habits, internal environment' can both lead to increased inflammation, the former through a somatogenic physiological route (e.g., smoking) and the latter through a psychogenic route (e.g., psychological input from stressful situations).

Putting the third and fourth models together
The third and fourth models both suggest that psychological factors affect morbidity but do so via their influence on behaviour. These two models can be represented together, as shown in Figure 3.5.

Personality → Behaviour → Lifestyle causing somatogenic inflammation → Disease
Personality → Behaviour → Lifestyle causing psychogenic inflammation → Disease

Figure 3.5 Two ways behaviour affects health and disease

5. Common factors   A common statement in papers in psychoneuroimmunology is that there is a bidirectional causal relationship between the mind and the immune system. The common factors explanation is that there is no causal relationship. Instead, mental states, personality and immune parameters are all consequences of something else. Infornet theory is a version of the common factors explanation. According to this theory, dysregulation versus well-regulation in the infornet is responsible for variation in mental states (more specifically, mood states), personality and coping on the one hand, and variation in the inflammatory response system and HPA axis on the other.

The origin of depression, fatigue and anxiety, and specific diseases is therefore infornet dysregulation. The causes of infornet dysregulation fall into three categories:

- *Somatogenic causes* of dysregulation. Somatic causes will include biochemicals that irritate and therefore contribute to inflammation and so 'push' the network towards a dysregulatory state, as well as infection, nutritional stress and other adverse biological conditions.
- *Psychogenic causes* of dysregulation. Psychogenic causes include, but are not limited to, long-term stress. Later chapters will provide examples of other ways in which lifestyle can affect dysregulation and so contribute to activation of the inflammatory response system.
- *Genetic causes* interact either with the first two or have an independent effect whereby some people are more prone to infornet dysregulation.

Somatogenic and psychogenic causes of dysregulation occur throughout the lifespan, but they have a particularly high impact at particular times. The causes of infornet dysregulation will be considered in Chapters 5, 6 and 7, but it should noted at this point that somatic and psychogenic causes are particularly important in the fetus and young child.

Integration of the five mechanisms; the integrative model

The five mechanisms suggested above are all plausible. However, although commonly treated as separate mechanism, they are linked within a more general framework, which will be called *the integrative model*.

A useful way to understand the integrative model is to sketch out a scenario. Let us suppose that Peter has a personality that predisposes to the experience of stressful experiences. The precise type of personality is irrelevant at this stage but it might include, for example, hostility or neuroticism. It may be that Peter is prone to engage in hostile interactions with others and so increase objective levels of stress. Alternatively, Peter may be neurotic and experience stress in circumstances where others do not. According to the 'unhealthy habits, internal environment' mechanism, Peter gets angry more often than others, he experiences more stress and over the long term stress leads to network dysregulation via a neurogenic route and activation of the inflammatory response system.

According to the 'common factors' mechanism, personality and disease proneness are both consequences of a common factor, namely infornet dysregulation. This common factor then creates changes in personality and disease onset. Peter becomes more anxious and as a result takes up smoking, initiating the 'unhealthy habits, external environment' mechanism. Additionally, he starts to develop heart disease and this disease affects his quality of life via the 'disease effecting mental states' mechanism, changes in quality of life that include financial uncertainty, so that his environment becomes more stressful. Finally, because Peter is also becoming depressed via the 'common factors' mechanism, his interpretation of the world is more gloomy and he becomes more sensitised to his physical symptoms via the 'symptom reporting and diagnosis' mechanism, and his greater awareness of symptoms emphasises how ill he is, leading to further stress.

This scenario illustrates an important point: the five mechanism are actually different parts of a single system. This single system is shown in Figure 3.6. In this model, personality and environment each play a role. Note that in this model the environment should be interpreted as the subjective or psychological environment rather than the objective or physical environment – it was one of Kurt Levin's maxims that it is the psychological and not the physical environment that affects behaviour. The five mechanisms are shown within boxes. Other significant parts of the causal sequence are shown without boxes. One of the implications of this model is that it is possible to set up a vicious cycle whereby the consequences of inflammation and disease contribute to the continuation and enhancement of inflammation and disease. Dysregulated people live dysregulated lives, which maintains them in a dysregulated state.

There are two conclusions to be drawn from Figure 3.6. The first is that personality is not something that is fixed but something that can change. This point will be returned to later in the chapter. The second is that if a correlation is observed between personality and disease, the explanation for that correlation may be difficult to determine. There are many mechanisms.

The integrative model is an expanded version of the model presented at the end of Chapter 1, which showed that the infornet causes the specific system (large arrow indicating a larger effect) but also that the specific system causes the infornet (small arrow indicating a smaller effect). The effect of the specific system on the infornet is in part due to effect of physical illness on mental state: having a physical disease tends to make you miserable. Being miserable pushes the infornet towards a state of dysregulation. The dysregulated infornet then activates the

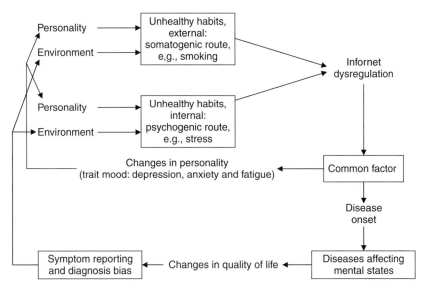

Figure 3.6 Integrative model showing relationship between different mechanisms linking personality with health and disease

inflammatory response system, which affects the specific system via the immune cascade. The implication of these models is that neither the infornet nor the specific system should be ignored.

Personality and disease: specific relationship investigations

The above sections provide a perspective on the link between mind and disease from the perspective of psychologists, with research starting in the 1970s. However, research into the mind–disease relationship started some 40 years earlier. During the 1930s a group of psychiatrists investigated the hypothesis that physical disease (i.e., non-brain disease) could be understood in terms of psychiatric theory that was used to explain mental disease (i.e., brain disease). These psychiatrists developed a new field of research and practice, which was called 'psychosomatic medicine'. The journal *Psychosomatic Medicine* was first published in 1939 and the research of that early period is summarised in a classic – but now largely unread – book: Franz Alexander's *Psychosomatic Medicine*, published in 1950 (Alexander, 1950).

Alexander identified seven groups of diseases that had a psychosomatic component – gastrointestinal, respiratory, cardiovascular, skin, endocrine, joints and skeletal muscles, and the 'sexual apparatus'.

Alexander and other researchers assumed that particular psychological states were associated with particular diseases, i.e., the assumption of disease specificity that underpins modern Western medicine. For example, asthma arose from an unconscious suppressed impulse to cry for the mother's help, whereas gastric symptoms arose from a conflict between a desire to remain in a childlike, dependent and infantile situation and an adult desire for independence and accomplishment. The explanations for these different diseases reflect the psychodynamic (i.e., Freudian) theoretical underpinning of the researchers. Each explanation provides an account of some kind of mental conflict that then leads to disease. Alexander considered the possibility that there was a non-specific relation between personality and mind and disease (what he referred to as 'the older view', p. 69, meaning the older Hippocratic view of non-specificity) but rejected it, suggesting that particular configurations of conflicts led to particular diseases. However, he recognised that there was a common element to all psychosomatic disease, namely a conflict between simultaneous sympathetic and parasympathetic activation. For example, in gastric disease, the infantile desire is parasympathetic and the desire for independence sympathetic, and both are activated at the same time. Alexander believed that it was the specific 'dynamic configuration' between these two different impulses that provided the end result of specific disease. The specificity hypothesis was, of course, consistent with the development of modern Western medicine, which may have had some influence in the way the field was presented (see Chapter 1).

The early psychosomatic research is largely forgotten, primarily because of its reliance on psychoanalytic theory. Nowadays, most psychologists and other scientists reject psychoanalytic theory as being either wrong, unfalsifiable or implausible. Nevertheless, the case studies of that period show that psychological treatment could benefit patients, even though the assumed reason for that benefit may have been incorrect. The idea of conflict between parasympathetic and sympathetic activity will be re-examined in Chapter 10.

During the 1950s interest in psychosomatic effects waned, in part owing to the rejection of the psychoanalytic approach but also, and possibly primarily, owing to the advances in pharmaceutical treatment. However, interest in psychological causes of disease did not disappear. In the late 1950s, the secretary of two cardiologists, Meyer Friedman and Ray Rosenman, noticed that the front edge of seats in their waiting room were wearing out – whereas seats normally wear out more evenly. This observation led the two cardiologists to discretely observe their clients. Their clients were often sitting in an impatient manner at the fronts of the seats. What they first labelled 'the hurry sickness' the cardiologists eventually labelled the Type A behaviour pattern (Friedman and Rosenman, 1974). Having medical rather than psychological training, they defined Type A as a type – rather than a trait. As they were cardiologists, not psychiatrists, there was no reference to psychoanalytic theory.

The Type A behaviour pattern was defined in terms of a combination of three characteristics: competitiveness, time urgency and hostility. The Type A concept owed nothing to the earlier psychoanalytic theory, and, significantly, did not involve the idea of conflict between parts of the mind. Just having a particular characteristic, the Type A behaviour pattern, predisposed to heart disease. However, the Type A theory did share one feature that was common with the earlier psychosomatic research: the assumption of specificity. Note that the Type A behaviour pattern was developed originally to explain a health outcome, namely heart disease – in contrast to trait theories, which were developed originally to explain behaviour.

Several different types of study were used to examine the Type A hypothesis, but some of the most convincing studies are those that are prospective. In the prospective longitudinal study, personality is measured at Time 1 and disease onset is measured at Time 2, where Time 2 is several years after Time 1. The advantage of the prospective study is that it rules out the effect disease might have on personality (i.e., the second model above). The first major longitudinal study to examine the Type A hypothesis was the Western Collaborative Group Study (Rosenman et al., 1976). Of the of 3,154 men in the study, those classified as Type A compared with those classified as Type B were 2–3 times more likely to develop heart disease during the following 8.5 years. This and other similar studies established the Type A behaviour pattern as a risk factor for heart disease, along with high levels of cholesterol and smoking.

Box 3.3 Types versus traits

Types are distinct patterns of behaviour. People are either Type A or Type B – nothing in between. Although some early psychologists used typologies in order to characterise personality, it is now commonly accepted that personality varies along continuous dimensions, rather than being, for example, a dichotomy. Traits are one way of describing a dimension of difference. People vary along a dimension of neuroticism – they are not either neurotic or stable.

Although several early studies supported the Type A hypothesis, others did not. A later study of 12,866 high-risk men (Dembroski *et al.*, 1989) found that global Type A behaviour did not predict heart disease, although people high in potential for hostility were about one and a half times more likely to develop heart disease than those low in potential for hostility. Furthermore, a follow-up of the Western Collaborative Group Study showed that of those people diagnosed with heart disease, those who had originally been classified as Type A were less likely to die during the follow-up period (Ragland and Brand, 1988). In sum, longitudinal studies of Type A and heart disease produced inconsistent results – some showing no relationship, some showing that Type A was a predictor, and a minority showing that Type B was a predictor of heart disease. Meta-analyses and reviews suggested that at least part of the variability of results could be attributed to methodological factors. For example, those studies using the original Friedman and Rosenman interview technique for identifying Type A are more likely to find significant findings than those using a questionnaire method of assessment, and studies using at-risk populations are less likely to find significant results than those using healthy populations. Despite these methodological effects, there also seems to be a trend towards null findings for Type A research over time, a trend that could not be attributed to known methodological factors (Miller *et al.*, 1991). Moreover, there is evidence that the relationship between Type A and heart disease varies as a function of the time point at which heart disease is measured, with higher risk occurring only in the earlier period after original assessment. These results suggest that Type A is not itself to blame but rather plays a role in exposing the person to other, heart-disease-inducing triggers (Gallacher *et al.*, 2003). Although research with the Type A behaviour pattern as a global construct has produced variable results, there is greater consistency in the relationship between hostility as a predictor of heart disease, with meta-analysis generally supporting the role of hostility as a risk factor for later heart disease (Chida and Steptoe, 2009; Miller *et al.*, 1996).

Following the initial success of the Type A hypothesis, researchers also began to search for personality predictors of cancer. The Type C, or cancer-prone, personality was proposed by Temoshok (1987) and consists of a combination of emotional repression and hopelessness/helplessness – the latter being related to depression. Rather confusingly, this combination of traits is also referred to as the Type D personality, but when applied to heart disease rather than cancer (Denollet, 1998). The research on the Type C personality parallels the Type A research. Early positive findings were later challenged by null findings. A large follow-up of an earlier study showing an association between emotional repression and breast cancer failed to find a relationship (Bleiker *et al.*, 2008). Spiegel and Giese-Davis (2003) conclude:

The literature on depression as a predictor of cancer incidence is mixed, although chronic and severe depression may be associated with elevated cancer risk. There is divided but stronger evidence that depression predicts cancer progression and mortality, although disentangling the deleterious effects of disease progression on mood complicates this research. (p. 269)

Inconsistent results can be due unknown factors. One possible 'unknown factor' is that personality is just part of the story and that other factors, such as culture and environment, are involved. For example, it may be that Type A behaviour has a different effect on health in the culture of the 1960s and 1970s compared with today. Another possibility is that other personality factors are involved. The earlier psychoanalytic approach to psychosomatics suggested that disease arose from mental conflict. It may be that whether, for example, depression predicts cancer, depends on other characteristics of the person. It would seem that the only honest conclusion from this research endeavour is that we do not entirely understand the processes involved, but that personality could be involved in some way in the development of disease.

The disease-prone personality

The Type A and Type C research was based on the assumption of specificity – that particular mind states are the cause of particular diseases. However, results began to emerge that showed that both types could be associated with other diseases. For example, not only was the Type C personality relabelled Type D in the context of heart disease, but the underlying construct of emotional repression, or alexithymia,

---

Box 3.4 A meeting with one of the founders of psychoneuroimmunology

George Solomon is often credited with inventing the term psychoneuroimmunology, though in fact the term he originally used was psychoimmunology. I met George in 1988, and found him to be a generous, charming and inspiring host. George told me that although it had not yet been established, he was absolutely convinced that there was a specific relationship between types of personality and disease – because that is how the body worked. The body works on the principle of specificity: that is, the logic of a mechanistic view of the body as a sequential processing system.

was shown to be related a number of diseases. The assumption of specificity was challenged in a meta-analysis conducted by Friedman and Booth-Kewley (1987). The authors included in their meta-analysis both prospective and concurrent studies that satisfied the following two criteria. First, the study should include measures that correspond to one of five descriptors of personality traits (anxiety, depression, extraversion and anger/hostility/aggression). Second, any of those five types of personality trait was correlated with any one of five diseases (coronary heart disease, asthma, ulcer, headache). For all five diseases there was a greater prospective risk and concurrent correlation for anxiety, depression and hostility. The relationship with extraversion was weaker and mixed, being positively associated with heart disease but negatively associated with arthritis, ulcer and (marginally) asthma. Thus, the authors did not find, for example, that hostility was associated only with heart disease and depression only with cancer. In fact, the pattern of personality data was very similar across diseases, with the authors pointing out that 'the degree of consistency is quite remarkable' (p. 549). Their conclusion was that there is no specific association between personality and disease type but, rather, there is a 'disease-prone personality,' that is, a type of profile of personality characteristics that predisposes to all diseases. Mindful of the different possible mechanisms linking personality and disease, the authors also point out that their data are also inconsistent with specific diseases causing particular personality problems (e.g., a specific version of mechanism 2 above).

The hypothesis of the 'disease-prone personality' has never been successfully challenged. Despite the early psychosomatic enterprise assuming specificity, the data seem to fit a non-specific interpretation, namely that certain types of personality are unhealthy across a range of disease types. Of course, this does not stop researchers examining specific disease–personality relationships, but the overall picture is that there is no specificity. Not only is there is little evidence for specificity, but also different types of negative dispositions tend themselves to be highly correlated: The authors of a review of the relationship between depression, anxiety and anger with heart disease (Sul and Bunde, 2005) conclude:

The overlap among the 3 negative dispositions also leaves open the possibility that a general disposition toward negative affectivity may be more important for disease risk than any specific negative affect. (p. 260)

Although research has shown that negative affectivity is associated with greater risk of mortality, one large study shows that it is the presence of positive affectivity rather than the absence of negative affectivity that is associated with reduced mortality (Xu and Roberts, 2010). Thus, although there seems to be a disease-prone personality, it would seem that it is consists of both the presence of negative affect and the absence of positive affect. The relative contribution of positive and negative to mortality or other health outcomes is uncertain on the basis of existing data. The relationship between different types of affect and health outcome is made more complex by the possibility that both types of affect can have a role in at least four of the five mechanisms described above. Although it seems likely that only negative affectivity is associated with symptom and disease reporting bias, the other four mechanisms (disease affecting mental states; unhealthy habits, external environment; unhealthy habits, internal environment; common factors) could, in principle, arise either because of high negative affect or low positive affect. Thus, to answer the 'relative contribution' question properly, research would need to address this question in terms of these four mechanisms.

In summary, research on the personality–disease link that was initiated by psychologists *assumed* there was no specificity, and showed links between a variety of personality traits and health and disease. Research on the personality–disease link that was initiated by psychiatrists *assumed* that there was specificity. However, subsequent research has failed to support the specificity argument. It does seem that psychological factors, at least at the general level of personality, contribute to disease without any specific relationship.

Fatigue, depression and anxiety in major illness

Infornet theory predicts that anxiety and depression should correlate, because they are both outputs from a dysregulated infornet. The correlation between anxiety and depression is well established statistically – they are both components of the trait of neuroticism. Additionally, patterns of comorbidity for depression and anxiety overlap and the overall pattern of symptomatology is inconsistent with anxiety and depression being separate diseases with a clear boundary. Instead, the 'fuzzy' boundary between these two symptoms is consistent with a network interpretation (Cramer *et al.*, 2010). The correlation between depression and anxiety and the fuzzy boundary between them is not easily explained from a conventional medical perspective. Anti-anxiety drugs have a different chemical structure to anti-depression drugs and work on different biochemical pathways (depression is assumed to be caused by lack of serotonin and anxiety by lack of GABA). Thus, the correlation between anxiety and depression cannot be explained easily in terms of the assumption of disease specificity on which pharmacological treatments of depression and anxiety are based. In point of fact, the idea that depression and anxiety have distinctly different biochemical causes involving different transmitter substances is inconsistent with several other types of evidence, to be reviewed in Chapter 8 (see also Hyland, 2010).

In the original Friedman and Booth-Kewley (1987) meta-analysis, depression and anxiety were found to correlate with both concurrent and future disease states. These two mental states are extremely common concurrent co-morbidities of physical illness. However, there is another mental state that is commonly found in major physical illness – as well as those without illness – and that is unexplained fatigue. The theory of the infornet suggests that people with major illness are more likely to have a dysregulated infornet. Hence, people with major illness should tend to experience anxiety, depression and fatigue. The following section examines some of the research on the prevalence of these three mental states, fatigue, depression and anxiety as co-morbidities to major illness.

It is difficult to measure the absolute or relative frequency and severity of depression, anxiety and fatigue in any major disease for several methodological reasons. Symptom severity of mental states varies, and the way this variation is measured varies between studies. Some studies use mean scores, some use incidence according to a criterion, and some use odds ratios. By way of illustration, in one study, the mean fatigue scores of people in 11 categories of physical illness were about one standard deviation greater than those people without disease (i.e., a 'large' effect size) (Watt et al., 2000). By contrast, another study used relative risk as a measure of association between depression and disease compared with healthy controls. The authors found no difference in relative risk for depression between seven categories of disease (note the consistency of this finding with the concept of the disease-prone personality) but that the overall odds ratio for depression and chronic illness was much higher than for the healthy population, the risk ratio being 2.2 for minor depression and 1.4 for major depression (Beekman et al., 1997). The comparisons between fatigue and depression are made yet more complex by the fact that each mental symptom varies in the general population. For example, in one population study of 1,741 individuals, 358 (20.6%) reported suffering from fatigue for 2 weeks or more in their lifetimes. Of those 358 individuals, 14% reported that their fatigue was the result of physical disease and 68% had no explanation (i.e., 14% of the total sample) (Addington et al., 2001). Some studies compare levels of more than one mental symptom within a particular disease. A weakness of such methodology is that clinically established cut-off points for symptoms between scales may not be equivalent. For example, in a study on COPD, 28% of patients anxiety and 19% depression compared with 6% and 3.5%, respectively, in a control group (Di Marco *et al.*, 2006). The authors measured anxiety and depression with standard questionnaires using established cut-off points, but the equivalence of particular levels of anxiety and depression at particular cut-off points is clearly a matter of debate.

Although precise comparison between mental symptoms is therefore difficult, the above and other data suggest that fatigue, depression and anxiety are extremely common features of major disease, and, also as indicated above, depression and anxiety are predictors of disease onset. Fatigue is also a predictor of disease onset, though this symptom has received less research. For example, people often experience 'vital exhaustion' (a feeling of extreme, unexplained exhaustion) just prior to a heart attack (Appels, 1997). The experience of fatigue prior to a heart attack is consistent with a common factor explanation – increased inflammation leads to the shedding of fatty plaques that create the blockage of the heart attack (Kop and Gottdiener, 2005).

In sum, the common occurrence of fatigue, depression and anxiety with major disease is consistent with the prediction from infornet theory that a dysregulated infornet contributes to physical disease as well as negative mood states. Physical diseases vary in that some are linked to inflammatory processes whereas others are not. Whalley and Hyland (2009) examined the relationship between fatigue and depression on the one hand and inflammatory and non-inflammatory physical symptoms on the other in a healthy population. Inflammatory symptoms were those that are associated with inflammatory disease – such as constipation and diarrhoea (associated with inflammatory bowel disease) and cough and wheeze (associated with asthma). Non-inflammatory symptoms were those associated with infectious diseases (e.g., colds and cold sores). After partialling out variance that could result from reporting bias, they found that fatigue but not depression correlated with the inflammatory physical symptoms. Neither fatigue nor depression correlated with the non-inflammatory physical symptoms. Thus, there is some evidence that symptoms of behaviour inhibition are associated particularly with inflammatory disease in contrast to non-inflammatory disease.

Other psychological variables that correlate with neuroticism
or its components (depression, anxiety and fatigue)

Fatigue, depression and anxiety are all characteristics of the trait of neuroticism. In addition to the emotions associated with negative affect, several other psychological variables correlate with neuroticism.

Coping style was described above: people high in neuroticism tend to be emotional copers rather than problem-focused copers. As emotion-focused coping is less adaptive in the long term, people high in neuroticism create circumstances that are more aversive than those low in neuroticism.

In addition, neuroticism is associated with cognitive style. People who are depressed and anxious perceive the world in a different way from those who are neither depressed nor anxious. Neuroticism is associated with an attributional style whereby the neurotic person attributes problems as (a) being caused by themselves and (b) likely to persist (referred to as a stable attribution). That is, the neurotic attributional style is one in which there are internal and long-term attributions for negative events. Where positive events occur, then they are attributed to chance and thought of as being of only temporary benefit – i.e., external and unstable attributions for positive events. The result is that the depressed person sees the world in a gloomy way, whereas the non-depressed person sees the world through rose-tinted glasses. In fact, the evidence seems to suggest that non-depressed people have falsely optimistic views about the world, whereas depressed people are 'sadder but wiser' (Alloy and Abramson, 1979).

In sum there is a cluster of characteristics that co-vary: depression, anxiety, fatigue, emotion-focused coping and negative cognitions, as well as emotions such as guilt, anger and fear. Mood, emotions, cognitions and behaviour are correlated. Negative thoughts, poor mood, negative emotions and socially maladaptive and health harming behaviours all tend to go together.

Recent developments in trait personality theory: the Big Two and the Big One

The five-factor model of personality (see above) is the dominant theory of personality. According to this theory, there are five 'big' factors of personality: neuroticism, extraversion, agreeableness, conscientiousness and openness to new experiences. These five factors are assumed to be orthogonal (i.e., uncorrelated) but they are made up of correlated traits. For example, neuroticism comprises anxiety and depression. Neuroticism is equivalent to trait negative affect – which comprises a number of negative mood states. Research shows that trait positive affect tends to be comparatively independent of negative affect, and that positive affect is associated with extraversion (Watson et al., 1988). Thus, the five-factor theory is consistent with affect theory: there are five independent personality factors; variation in trait negative affect is equivalent to variation in neuroticism and variation in positive treat affect is equivalent to extraversion. Trait mood or affect and personality are linked.

The five-factor model *assumes* that the five factors are independent, that is, that the five factors are uncorrelated. However, data from numerous studies show that the five subscales of any of the several measures of the Big Five always tend to correlate. Indeed anyone, whether student or researcher, who has used one of the Big Five scales will observe that there are correlations between the subscales. Similarly, scales of positive and negative affect (the Positive and Negative Affect scale is the one most widely used (Watson *et al.*, 1988) also tend to correlate. The correlations are not large, but they are clearly present. Those who support the Big Five theory suggest that such correlations are due to *measurement error*. They assert that the Big Five really are orthogonal, and they are at the top of the hierarchy of personality. However, the five subscales that are produced by personality questionnaires are not perfect measures of the underlying constructs, and measurement error leads to the observed correlations.

An alternative interpretation is that the correlation between the Big Five personality constructs is real and reflects a higher level of trait organisation. Factor analysis of the Big Five suggests that there is a Big Two. Given a world where data often correlate, albeit at a low level, it will come as no surprise to learn that there is also a Big One, i.e., a still higher level of organisation. The hierarchical relationship between personality factors is shown in Figure 3.7. The important point to note about Figure 3.7 is that *all* levels of interpretation are correct in the sense that they each provide a valid way of describing consistency in behaviour. However, the Big Two and the Big One lack the degree of specificity needed to make them useful theories of personality for predicting behaviour. It is unlikely that these higher-order theories of

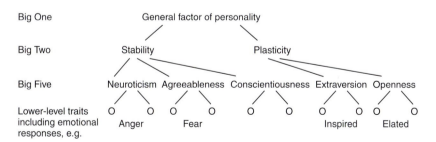

Figure 3.7 The hierarchical arrangement of personality and personality theories

personality will supplant the Big Five as the standard dimensions for predicting behaviour – which is how, in the main, they are used.

Although the Big Two and Big One are not useful as predictors of behaviour because they are at too general a level, a central argument of this book is that these dimensions are theoretically interesting. In particular, the Big Two provides a way of understanding different types of dysregulation in the infornet.

The Big Two was suggested by Digman (1997), who used data from several studies to indicate that there was a higher-order level of factors, which he called Alpha (Emotional stability, Agreeableness, Conscientiousness) and Beta (Extraversion and Openness). This research was replicated by both DeYoung et al. (2002) and DeYoung (2006), who re-labelled Alpha as Stability and Beta Plasticity. The reason for these changed terms was based on network theory. To function effectively, networks must be stable to prevent oscillatory changes, but also sufficiently plastic to respond to change (Grossberg, 1987). A well-regulated network must be both stable *and* plastic – and stability and plasticity must be balanced in the sense that both features must be present. De Young (2006) suggested that the Big Two exist because they reflect the properties of a network – namely stability and plasticity. According to this perspective, a dysregulated network can be characterised as being low in stability or low in plasticity, or both.

It is useful at this stage to consider what is meant by a network that is low in stability or one that is low in plasticity. A network that is low in stability is one that tends to over react to situations of threat, leading to an increased tendency to negative affect. A moment's reflection will show that trait negative affect is not only associated with neuroticism, but also with disagreeableness and lack of conscientiousness. Although from the perspective of the five-factor theory it is common to equate negative affect with neuroticism, in terms of the Big Two theory it makes sense to equate negative affect with lack of stability. By contrast, a network that is low in plasticity is one that cannot adapt to novel situations. Within the five-factor theory, positive affect is equated with extraversion. However, those who are open to new experiences will also tend to experience positive affect. Thus, from the perspective of the Big Two theory, positive affect is associated with plasticity and lack of negative affect with stability. Stability and plasticity therefore represent dimensions that have wider theoretical application: they relate to the two-factor theory of affect.

The Big One (or a 'general factor of personality') was first demonstrated by Musek (2007) and replicated by Rushton and Irwing (2008). The Big One is a combination of the stability and plasticity factors of the Big Two. The Big One explains just under half the variance in personality scales – there is a general statistical rule that the more factors are extracted in a factor analysis, the greater proportion of variance explained. Thus, The Big One is even less useful for making precise predictions about behaviour than the Big Two. What is a plausible explanation for the existence of a Big One? A network is dysregulated if it fails to exhibit stability and plasticity, and so the general factor of personality can be characterised as a factor of well-regulation–dysregulation. The implication is that those high in the general factor (plastic and stable) are more regulated than those low in the factor.

Note that the Big One, Big Two and Big Five are at different levels, and are related to each other in that they are arranged hierarchically. One way of thinking about this relationship is that the Big One 'colours' rather than determines the factors that fall below it in the hierarchy. Thus, someone who is high in the general factor of personality will tend to be agreeable, but there will also be many other factors that contribute to agreeableness. The lower down the hierarchy, the less the general factor is going to predict variation in the lower construct.

Personality and underlying biological approaches: a biological explanation for the Big Two

Research into the Big Five, the Big Two and the Big One is conducted primarily through the use of factor analysis, that is, a statistical procedure for determining latent variables (i.e., inferred common causes). This procedure makes no assumptions about the physiological basis of those latent variables. However, some authors have provided a biological rationale for the existence of these latent variables (e.g., Eysenck, 1967).

Reinforcement sensitivity theory, first suggested by Jeffrey Gray (Corr, 2008; Gray, 1987) is now the commonly accepted explanation for the biological basis of personality – though the exact form of the theory varies. According to reinforcement theory, neuroticism and extraversion arise from two separate systems, punishment sensitivity and reward sensitivity. The neurotic is more sensitive to punishment, and this leads to greater experience of fear and anxiety and so avoidance behaviour. The extravert is more sensitive to reward and so experiences more hope and elation, leading to more approach behaviour. Empirical support for reinforcement sensitivity theory comes from a number of sources, including evidence that different areas in the brain relate to punishment sensitivity versus reward sensitivity. Punishment of all kinds is associated with a system spanning the periaqueductal grey, medial hypothalamus, amygdala and anterior cingulate cortex. Conflict between goals (e.g., approach avoidance conflict) is associated with the septo-hippocampal system and amygdala. By contrast, reward and hence reward sensitivity are linked to the basal ganglia, with an emphasis on dopaminergic activation.

According to reinforcement theory, neurotic people respond particularly badly to environments that are characterised by negative events. Such environments include stressful environments, so the neurotic is adversely affected compared with the non-neurotic by stress. By contrast, the extravert gains particular advantage from environments that are rich in novel, pleasant events. The differences in neuroticism and extraversion therefore emerge only in particular environments.

Reinforcement sensitivity theory suggests that personality can be understood in terms of variation in sensitivity to punishing and rewarding stimuli, and that this variation has a neurological basis. How does this theory fit with the Big Five, the Big Two and the Big One? Reinforcement theory is commonly linked to two of the Big Five factors, namely neuroticism (punishment sensitivity) and extraversion (reward sensitivity). However, reinforcement theory was developed before the evidence demonstrating the existence of the Big Two and Big One. A moment's reflection will show that punishment sensitivity links well with the stability factor of the Big Two and reward sensitivity with the plasticity factor.

A person who is high in plasticity will not only have the characteristics of an extravert but will also be open to new experiences. New experiences have the potential for reward and so are attractive to the person high in reward sensitivity. This person who is high in plasticity will therefore tend to seek out and experience positive affect as a way of life.

By contrast, consider a person who is low in stability. Such a person will tend to perceive other people as a source of threat and will therefore tend to be less agreeable. This person will not only perceive the world as a threat but will create situations where the world is threatening. The person low in stability focuses on present emotional concerns (emotion-focused coping) rather than conscientiously completing tasks (problem-focused coping), so conscientiousness will be low. The person low in stability is high in punishment sensitivity, and tends to experience negative affect.

In conclusion, Big Two theory, affect theory and reinforcement sensitivity theory are all consistent with the idea that there are two separate systems involved in the production of mental states. Negative affect and positive affect involve different underlying mechanisms.

A well-regulated network system must not be overly sensitive to punishment or the system will become locked in a pattern of avoidance. However, a well-regulated system must not be entirely insensitive to punishment because, were this to be case, the system would not learn to avoid negative situations. In addition, a well-regulated system must be reasonably sensitive to reward, otherwise the system will not be able to exploit positive aspects of its environment. However, a well-regulated system cannot be dominated entirely by reward, otherwise the system will become locked into a limited number of reward situations (as, for example, found in addiction). Thus, the well-regulated system has moderately low but not zero levels of punishment sensitivity, and moderately high levels of reinforcement sensitivity. The regulated system is balanced between extremes – in other words, the regulated system is high in the general factor of personality. In sum, reinforcement sensitivity theory and affect theory fit neatly with the more recent ideas of the Big Two and Big One.

The meaning of infornet dysregulation

The above sections have provided an account of research into the relationship between personality and disease and the structure of personality. Using this information, it is now possible to provide a description of infornet dysregulation.

The infornet is a psychoneuroimmunoendocrine information system that is distributed through the neurological, immune and endocrine systems. There are two ways of representing this idea. One way of representing the infornet is in terms of the biological structure of those interaction systems. For reasons that will be explained in the next chapter, biological description of the state of the infornet is likely to be extremely difficult and will not be attempted. The second form of representation is in terms of the information represented within the infornet, and it is this form of representation that will be presented here. The infornet can be described in terms of its *meaning*.

The infornet contains information: it is a meaning system. The infornet controls the body's control loops through instructions that alter the settings of those control systems. Those instructions are based on the way the infornet interprets the situation – i.e., the internal and external environment. The infornet's interpretation of the situation can be called *infornet beliefs*. Infornet beliefs represent the meaning the infornet has about the situation in which the body is placed. The information contained in the infornet can therefore be represented as a set of infornet beliefs. These infornet beliefs are not represented in consciousness but they can be treated as analogy to the beliefs that are familiar to lay people and to psychologists, by whom they are sometimes referred to as cognitions.

First, let us consider how ordinary beliefs or cognitions work. Many beliefs are connected in such a way that there are several beliefs that are mutually supporting. Beliefs exist in *interconnected clusters*. For example, the belief in God does not exist in isolation but is connected to other beliefs concerning the purpose of life, the nature of the universe and so on. All these related religious beliefs tend to be consistent with each other and they will be different from those of persons who do not believe in God. For individuals who do not believe in God, the related non-religious beliefs are mutually supporting of the 'no-God belief'. The consequence of this belief-interconnectedness is that it is always difficult to change any one belief because it is supported by many other beliefs.

However, not all beliefs are interconnected. The belief in God is unrelated to beliefs about the proper way to build a brick wall. There will be a set of building beliefs, but this will be entirely separate from that of God beliefs. In sum, there are clusters of beliefs and some of the clusters are connected, but some are unconnected to each other. The beliefs of the infornet can be considered as sets of beliefs some of which are interconnected, and some of which are not.

The infornet can be characterised as having a set of beliefs that have a particular sort of organisation and structure. The structure of infornet beliefs is central to infornet theory. To reiterate, the use of the term infornet belief should be treated as an analogy – these are not real beliefs in the sense of having conscious content. The infornet beliefs are just ways of representing meaning in the system.

Infornet beliefs can be described as dysregulated when the infornet produces outputs (i.e., alters control loops and creates mental states) that are inappropriate to the current inputs. An example will illustrate what is meant. Let us suppose that the situation is one where there is neither an internal challenge nor an external challenge. The person is neither engaging in a mammoth hunt nor suffering any infection, is well fed and should be perfectly content. The appropriate infornet response is one where there is no activation of the inflammatory response system, no activation of the HPA axis and no negative mental states. However, if the infornet produces activation of the inflammatory response system and negative affect, then the output is inappropriate to the input. One of the characteristics of a dysregulated infornet (see Chapter 2) is that there is chronic activation of the inflammatory response system along with negative affect.

The crucial questions are 'what are the infornet beliefs, how do they cluster together and how do they differ when they are well regulated versus dysregulated?' The nature and structure of infornet beliefs can be inferred from two sorts of evidence: (a) the nature and structure of personality, which includes the relationship between different mental traits; and (b) covariation in physiological parameters and co-morbidities associated with specific disease. The theory proposes that patterns of correlations between somatic and psychological symptoms reflect different ways the infornet becomes dysregulated, and hence reflect the underlying infornet beliefs. We begin by considering three sets of beliefs: beliefs associated with stability, plasticity and the inflammatory response system.

The Big Two personality theory suggests that there are two dimensions of dysregulation: stability–unstability and plasticity–nonplasticity. The infornet beliefs that would lead to variation in stability can be characterised as:

STABILITY–UNSTABILITY INFORNET BELIEFS:
Life is a punishment versus life is not a punishment.

On the basis of reinforcement sensitivity theory this belief can be expanded as follows:

It's a nasty old world out there. Things tend to go wrong. I expect to be punished. There are threats round the corner. I am doing things wrong. I am not getting where I want to be. Whatever it is that I am doing is leading to this bad situation.

The opposite set of beliefs is:

It's a wonderful world. Things go right. There is no punishment. There are no threats, things are going as well as I want them to go.

If these beliefs are inappropriately negative, then such beliefs would be consistent with punishment sensitivity and be associated with negative affect (depression and fatigue) and emotion-focused coping.

The infornet beliefs that would lead to variation in plasticity can be characterised as:

PLASTICITY–NONPLASTICITY INFORNET BELIEFS:
There are rewarding opportunities in the external situation versus no rewarding opportunities.

On the basis of reinforcement sensitivity theory, this belief can be expanded as follows:

The world is OK so long as nothing changes. Let's not rock the boat and do anything new or different. Let's avoid doing too much of anything. Keep quiet and everything is OK. I don't expect to be rewarded from what I do.

The opposite set of beliefs is:

There are plenty of opportunities out there. Let's go out and seek new worlds and boldly go where no one has gone before. Let's explore and try out new ways of making the world a better place. Rewards are out there – I just need to go and get them. Life is fun.

If such a cluster of beliefs were inappropriately negative, then such beliefs would be associated with lack of reward sensitivity, low extraversion and low openness to new experiences.

The stability-related and plasticity-related beliefs are themselves related. They are part of a more general belief that

The external situation is bad.

The above describes infornet beliefs associated with personality theory. We now consider infornet beliefs associated with immune response. The infornet belief associated with the inflammatory response system can be characterised as:

INFLAMMATORY RESPONSE SYSTEM INFORNET BELIEFS:
The internal situation is bad versus the internal situation is not bad.

Such beliefs can be expanded to:

It's a nasty old world out there. Things tend to go wrong. I need to protect the body from foreign bodies. Let's get the immune system set up to deal with what is going to happen.

versus

It's a nice world. I don't need to protect the immune system from foreign bodies.

If the inflammatory response system beliefs are inappropriately set to expect the internal situation to be bad, then there will be a chronic activation of the inflammatory response system.

The infornet beliefs that the internal and external situations are bad and are themselves part of a more general belief, that:

The general situation is bad versus the general situation is good.

The belief that the general situation is bad will tend to produce beliefs that the internal and external situations are both bad.

Chapter 2 showed how the inflammatory response system is linked to behaviour inhibition, whereas the HPA axis is linked to behaviour activation. The beliefs associated with the HPA axis are similar to the beliefs that are associated with stability–unstability beliefs.

HPA AXIS INFORNET BELIEFS:
More physical activity is needed versus less physical activity is needed.

One way of representing the influence between infornet beliefs is in terms of a meaning space. Figure 3.8 represents a hypothetical infornet meaning space showing the overlap between different types of infornet beliefs. Although the stability–unstability and plasticity–nonplasticity beliefs are logically distinct, self-evidently they have some degree of connection through the superordinate belief that *the external situation is bad* and so the stability–unstability and plasticity–nonplasticity beliefs are shown as overlapping in Figure 3.8. In addition, these infornet beliefs that determine behavioural responses also have some relationship with infornet beliefs that determine physiological response, because they are all related to the super-superordinate belief that *the general situation is bad*. Therefore the stability–unstability and plasticity–nonplasticity beliefs are shown as overlapping with the with the inflammatory response system beliefs and the HPA axis beliefs.

In Figure 3.8, each group of beliefs is best characterised as a node in a network, such that the beliefs associated with one node influence other beliefs to which the node is connected. These beliefs form clusters identified by the node, but there is no firm boundary round the clusters of beliefs. Thus, the overlap between the stability and plasticity beliefs is the result of causal connections between the two clusters, albeit weaker causal connections than those within each cluster. The overlapping circles shown in Figure 3.8 should be considered as having fuzzy boundaries. The exact form of Figure 3.8 is uncertain, and may vary between

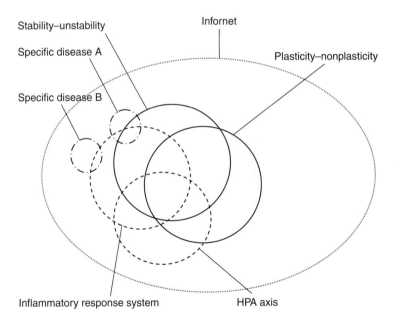

Figure 3.8 The infornet meaning space
Notes: circles show regions of infornet beliefs of varying kinds. Specific disease B shows beliefs where there is overlap with the inflammatory response system but little psychological distress (e.g., asthma). Specific disease A shows beliefs where there is overlap with the inflammatory response system as well as the psychological states associated with stability–unstability

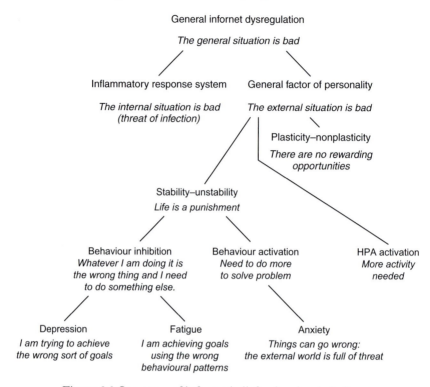

Figure 3.9 Structure of infornet beliefs, showing *in italic type* infornet beliefs at the different levels and in standard type the system to which the beliefs apply

people. One particular question that is of interest is the comparative extent to which stability–unstability and plasticity–nonplasticity beliefs overlap with those of the inflammatory response system and HPA axis. The hypothesis of internal–external balance proposes that the infornet forms a belief based on the likelihood that a stressful event leads to physical damage and hence the need for immune activation – mammoth hunting carries the risk of personal injury as well as requiring vigorous physical activity. The internal–external balance belief can be characterised as *to what extent is it necessary to prepare the body for infection versus vigorous activity?*.

Figure 3.8 is an oversimplification in order to illustrate the overlap between beliefs. Although anxiety, depression and fatigue tend to correlate, they do not correlate perfectly. Thus, within the space shown as stability–unstability in Figure 3.8 there are smaller groups of clusters of infornet beliefs that give rise to the different psychological states.

An alternative way of representing the relationship between infornet beliefs is therefore with a hierarchical structure shown in Figure 3.9.

Figure 3.9 shows how lower-level infornet beliefs are linked to superordinate level beliefs. The infornet belief that *the general situation is bad* is at the highest level and is associated with negative infornet beliefs at all levels. The infornet belief that *the external situation is bad* is associated with HPA axis activation as well as infornet beliefs that determine mood states such as fatigue, depression and anxiety.

The theory shown in Figure 3.9 explains *why* anxiety and depression are correlated, and *why* the inflammatory response system correlates with negative mental states, such as depression, anxiety and fatigue. The reason is that all are signals from the infornet, and when the infornet becomes dysregulated, then the beliefs driving these different signals are themselves connected. Thus, the theory being presented is not that the inflammatory response system is equivalent to behaviour inhibition and activation, rather that both physiological and psychological systems are driven by some common infornet beliefs. It is the beliefs represented in the infornet that determine health and disease.

The meaning of general infornet dysregulation, and different types of dysregulation

General infornet dysregulation can be defined as follows:

General infornet dysregulation occurs when there is persisting infornet belief that *the general situation is bad*, a belief that persists irrespective of inputs to the infornet, where the outputs from this belief have both psychological and physiological consequences

The idea of general infornet dysregulation was introduced in the previous chapter. General infornet dysregulation was associated with activation of the inflammatory response system (and therefore immune activation), activation of the HPA axis (and therefore immune suppression), behaviour inhibition (depression and fatigue) and behaviour activation (anxiety). The reason for this association is that the infornet belief that *the general situation is bad* will tend to be associated with a variety of other beliefs about the internal and external environment, all of which promote the various co-varying outputs which, in the earlier chapter, were proposed as hallmarks of general infornet dysregulation.

Although general infornet dysregulation is characterised by the belief that *the general situation is bad*, it follows that this general belief can be associated with a variety of more specific beliefs associated with this general belief. Consequently, general infornet dysregulation is defined in terms of a general infornet belief that has psychological consequences (e.g., depression *versus* fatigue *versus* anxiety) as well as physiological consequences, such as activation of the inflammatory response system and somatic symptoms associated with that inflammation *versus* activation of the HPA axis with a different set of physiological changes associated with increased demand for physical activity versus immune challenge. The consequence is that the precise form of general infornet dysregulation will vary.

As infornet beliefs are connected, and because infornet belief strength varies continuously, it is to be expected that variation between different forms of infornet dysregulation will be continuous rather than forming discrete disease categories. The idea of continuous variation of symptoms has been suggested with regard to anxiety and depression (Cramer *et al.*, 2010), but this principle of continuous variation should apply much widely. Cramer *et al.* (2010) show that patterns of co-morbidity between anxiety and depression are inconsistent with these diseases, having different and distinct causes. In sum, general infornet dysregulation is consistent with continuous variation between its different forms, rather having discrete different types of dysregulation.

The idea of general infornet dysregulation presents a different way of thinking about health and disease from that found in modern Western medicine. Modern Western medicine is based on the assumption of specificity and the consequent assumption that there are firm boundaries between diseases. For example, there is a clear boundary between heart disease and a broken leg. Although a minority of people will suffer from both heart disease and a broken leg, there is never any doubt as to whether the disease is heart disease or a broken leg. In the case of general infornet dysregulation, however, there are no clear boundaries between different forms of dysregulation. The reason is that the meaning of the dysregulation in the infornet can be conceptualised as interconnected beliefs. Each of these beliefs can vary so that, between people, there can be gradual variation in beliefs, with the consequence that there is a gradual variation in the form of dysregulation. Thus, the difference between a person diagnosed with anxiety and one diagnosed with depression is not that they have fundamentally different diseases, but that their infornets have different beliefs, albeit only slightly different beliefs because infornet beliefs leading to depression and anxiety are connected via the higher level belief that *the general situation is bad*. Infornet theory and the idea of general dysregulation leads to the prediction of continua of different types of symptoms, but with no clear boundary between different types of people.

The consequences of general infornet dysregulation are not limited to inflammation and dysphoric mental states and the physiological consequences of HPA axis activation. Coping and cognitive styles are also affected by infornet beliefs. The dysregulated person will not only experience the world as a threatening place but may also behave in ways that are counterproductive and create threat and negative emotions. Such counterproductive behaviour can be contrasted with that of a person whose infornet has a well-regulated set of beliefs and sees the world as benign. Figure 3.8 provided an integrative model for the relationship between personality and disease, and the implications of this model can now be understood in relation to the beliefs associated with dysregulated infornet. The infornet is dysregulated because its beliefs do not contribute to effective functioning of the body. That set of beliefs contributes further to that dysregulation. The world is indeed a threatening place to an animal that attacks everything in sight.

The meaning of specific infornet dysregulation: allergy and asthma

General infornet dysregulation can be defined as dysregulation where the information encoded in the infornet – i.e., the infornet's beliefs – has both physiological and psychological consequences. It follows that some of the infornet's beliefs may have a dysregulatory effect *only* on psychological outputs or *only* on psychological outputs. Such dysregulation can be described as specific. So, general dysregulation can be contrasted with specific dysregulation in terms of the generality of its effects and in terms of the generality of infornet beliefs. Because beliefs in a network tend to be interconnected, however loosely, general versus specific dysregulation is best thought of as being on a continuum – some dysregulation involves multiple outputs, others only a few outputs. Allergy provides an example where the dysregulation is comparatively specific.

Allergy is the response of the immune system to an antigen – i.e., a substance that produces an immune response. The immune response involves a cascade of immune changes that includes the production of immunoglobulin E (IgE). Allergy can be defined in terms of the production of IgE.

Allergic diseases are those in which there is excessive inflammation. Asthma is a common allergic disease affecting about 5% of the population. In the case of asthma, the airways become inflamed in response to substances that are normally treated by the body as harmless. These substances or allergens vary between different people who have asthma – for some it might be cat dander (the powder that comes from cat skin), for others it might be house dust mites (actually, it is the faeces of the dust mite that matters), yet for others it may be tree pollen – the list of potential allergens is long. When exposed to the allergen, the person with asthma responds with an allergic response as though the allergen were a threat, that is, with inflammation that is specific to the airways.

When the body is exposed to a parasite, it produces IgE. IgE is part of the cascade of immune changes that the body uses to protect against parasitic infection. Levels of IgE are raised in the airways of people with asthma. So, in the case of asthma, the immune system is responding as though it perceives the harmless allergen to be a parasite – it is a state of alarm created by a misperceived event. The airways inflammation characteristic of asthma would be adaptive if there were lung parasites.

Asthma involves a form of dysregulation where the infornet has incorrectly encoded that the lungs are exposed to the threat of a parasite.

The cascade of immune changes that take place with the asthmatic allergic response is well understood and leads to inflammation of the airways and bronchoconstriction (i.e., narrowing of the airways). The distal cause of this sequence (i.e., what starts it off in the first place) is the expression of one or more asthma-causing genes. Gene expression means that the gene is 'switched on' and is therefore producing the particular biochemical the gene is designed to produce. There are several asthma genes and different genes appear responsible for different types of asthma (Baines *et al.*, 2010). Many people carry asthma genes but do not have asthma: their asthma genes are 'switched off'. The question that is not well understood is 'what switches on the asthma gene?'. Infornet theory suggests that particular infornet beliefs are responsible for switching on genes, including asthma genes. The relationship between infornet and specific system described in Chapter 1 can therefore be expanded to that shown in Figure 3.10. Details of how this might occur for asthma and supporting data will be presented in Chapter 7.

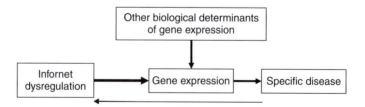

Figure 3.10 The infornet, gene expression and the specific system

All inflammatory diseases, including allergic diseases such as asthma, have a specific inflammatory component and a systemic inflammatory component. The specific inflammatory component in the case of asthma is the inflammation in the lungs – linked to IgE. The systemic inflammatory component involves higher than normal levels of pro-inflammatory cytokines, that is the pro-inflammatory cytokines associated with the natural immune system and the inflammatory response system (see Chapter 2). Thus, in the case of asthma, there are two sets of infornet beliefs, one that there is a parasite in the lung and the other is that there is a more general risk of immune challenge. These two sets of beliefs may be interconnected – if the world is a dangerous place, then it is more likely that there are lung parasites around.

General infornet dysregulation occurs when there is a belief that *the general situation is bad* and where this general belief has both physiological and psychological outcomes. An obvious question is whether the infornet beliefs that drive the physiology of asthma are linked to those that have psychological consequences. Available data would suggest that the overlap (i.e., the degree of general infornet dysregulation) is probably very small. It is certainly the case that anxiety is slightly higher in the asthma population than in people who do not have asthma, and anxiety is a signal of psychological dysregulation. However, these raised levels of anxiety may be due to a variety of factors, such as the effect of illness on psychological state (see earlier sections in this chapter). The likely conclusion is that asthma tends to be a rather specific disease. Although there may be some psychological dysregulation caused by infornet beliefs that are common to the inflammatory response system and stability–unstability, these would appear to play a relatively minor role (see Figure 3.8).

The disease of asthma can be contrasted with another inflammatory respiratory disease, namely chronic obstructive pulmonary disease (COPD). Compared with asthma, depression and anxiety are much more common in COPD, where 80% of patients have clinical levels of either anxiety, depression or both (Kunik *et al.*, 2005). It may be that these higher levels of psychological distress are the consequence of the greater severity of COPD. Alternatively, it may be that in the case of COPD general infornet dysregulation is more common, so the underlying infornet beliefs create a greater level of psychological distress in addition to the physiological outcomes. Specific diseases vary in the extent to which the inflammatory response system is involved. One predicts on the basis of infornet theory that diseases where there are higher levels of systemic inflammatory mediators should be characterised by higher levels of psychological distress.

The meaning spaces for two specific diseases are shown in Figure 3.8, one where there is an overlap between the specific disease and stability–unstability and one where there is not. It could be that the former characterises COPD and the latter asthma. However, the presentation of both COPD and asthma is variable. Within both patient groups some will have the specific disease without appreciable general infornet dysregulation whereas others will have considerable general infornet dysregulation and the specific disease is associated with negative mood states. For some COPD patients, the glass is half empty. For others, the glass is half full.

When the specific disease of asthma is coupled with infornet dysregulation, then one would predict that self-management of the disease should be compromised. The reason is that people with infornet dysregulation will tend to lead dysregulated lives, and the latter is likely to compromise self-management, and in particular, failure to adhere to medication that is important to manage the specific disease. About 80% of fatal or near-fatal asthma attacks are due to poor management. Confidential enquiries into fatal asthma shows a strong relationship between fatal asthma attacks and the psychological characteristics of depression and denial (Bucknall *et al.*, 1999; Sturdy *et al.*, 2002). Depression is a signal of infornet dysregulation. Denial is a feature of emotionally focused coping, which is described above as an indicator of general infornet dysregulation. In sum, dysregulated people who live dysregulated lives are more likely to suffer the consequences of specific disease because they manage their diseases less well.

A classification of diseases

According to infornet theory, inflammatory diseases of the specific system, such as asthma, have as their distal cause dysregulation in the infornet. Thus diseases, can be divided into three main categories, depending on the presence or absence of dysregulation and specific disease:

- *Diseases where there is infornet dysregulation but **no** specific disease.* For example, medically unexplained symptoms, functional diseases such as irritable bowel syndrome, repetitive strain injury, chronic fatigue syndrome and mental states such as depression and anxiety. Such diseases will be characterised by (a) psychological symptoms (e.g., fatigue or depression) that will have fuzzy boundaries between them; (b) physiological abnormalities (e.g., raised levels of pro-inflammatory cytokines); and (c) physical symptoms, (e.g., pain, gastric symptoms), none of which are specific to the psychological symptomatology.

- *Diseases where there is infornet dysregulation **and** specific disease.* For example, all inflammatory diseases and those where there is an inflammatory aetiology, such as asthma, chronic obstructive pulmonary disease, heart disease, arthritis, multiple sclerosis, cancer, etc. Such diseases will be characterised by (a) disease-specific physiological abnormality and, depending on the degree of specificity versus generality, (b) non-specific physiological abnormality (e.g., raised levels of natural immune system pro-inflammatory cytokines), (c) physical symptoms (e.g., gastric symptoms) and (d) non-specific psychological symptoms.
- *Diseases where there is specific disease but **no** infornet dysregulation.* For example, physical damage (such as a broken limb) and some infectious diseases, in particular those where the disease has a specific time point of infection, (such as malaria and food poisoning). Such diseases will have disease-specific physiological abnormality and specific psychological symptoms that are associated with that abnormality.

Diseases where there is infornet dysregulation *only* and diseases where there is specific disease (with or without dysregulation) can be distinguished in two ways. First, specific diseases should have a pathophysiology that is specific (i.e., unique) to that particular disease. Second, specific diseases should exhibit a pattern of symptomatology that is consistent with the conventional principles of nosology, namely symptoms should cluster into distinct nodes that represent the different diseases. By contrast, dysregulatory diseases should have no specific pathology, although non-specific immune and HPA axis abnormality is predicted. In addition, for dysregulatory diseases, symptoms should show continuous variation between different types of disease. That is, there should be fuzzy boundaries between disease types, as illustrated by the fuzzy boundary between anxiety and depression (Cramer *et al.*, 2010). Empirical research into co-morbidity can therefore provide useful insights into dysregulation of the infornet.

General infornet dysregulation: summary

Infornet theory suggests that that there is a general factor of dysregulation–well-regulation, which is summarised in Figure 3.11. Figure 3.11 shows the kinds of variables that are likely to correlate. However, because general infornet dysregulation takes a variety of different forms, the particular pattern of psychological symptoms and physiological responses will vary.

Theoretical framework	State	
Description of the infornet	General well-regulation	General dysregulation
Big One	High general factor of personality	Low general factor of personality
Big Two	High plasticity and stability	Low plasticity and stability
Coping style	Problem-focused coping	Emotion-focused coping
Cognitions	Internal and stable attributions for positive events and external and nonstable attributions for negative events	External and non-stable attributions for positive events and internal and stable attributions for negative events
Reinforcement sensitivity	Fairly low sensitivity to punishment, fairly high sensitivity to reward	High sensitivity to punishment, low sensitivity to reward
Mood states	No behaviour inhibition: no fatigue or depression. No behaviour activation: no anxiety	Behaviour inhibition: fatigue and depression. Behaviour activation: anxiety
Emotions and affect	Low negative affect High positive affect	High negative affect Low positive affet
Environment created	(a) No long-term stress (b) Less health-harming behaviours and exposure to external damage	(a) Long-term stress (b) More health-harming behaviour and exposure to external damage
Characteristic of immune system	(a) Low levels of inflammatory mediators, e.g., tnf-α (b) Active cellular immune activity, e.g., Natural Killer Cell	(a) High levels of inflammatory mediators, e.g., tnf-α (b) Suppressed cellular immune activity, e.g., Natural Killer Cell

Figure 3.11 Dysregulation versus well-regulation of the infornet

Some potential tests

One way in which different forms of general infornet dysregulation vary is in terms of the balance between the competing demands of responding to external challenge (e.g., physical activity) and internal challenge (e.g., infection). The hypothesis of internal–external balance is that the infornet uses its inputs to determine to what extent an external threat (e.g., a mammoth hunt) is likely to require external versus internal challenge. If the threat is perceived as requiring only external challenge, then this will be associated with HPA axis activation, the production of cortisol and hence reduction in the activity of some components of the immune system. In terms of psychological symptoms, external challenge is associated with symptoms of behaviour activation, and in particular, anxiety. However, if the threat is perceived as carrying a risk of internal challenge, then this will be associated with activation of the inflammatory response system. In terms of psychological symptoms, internal challenge is associated with symptoms of behaviour inhibition, namely depression and fatigue.

Using the above argument, the hypothesis of internal–external balance leads to the prediction that depression is more associated with immune activation and anxiety with immune suppression. In addition, limited research, cited above and in Chapter 2, supports the idea that specific emotions might be associated with internal versus external balance. The idea of specificity could be tested further using a theory-driven perspective. For example, the Positive and Negative Affect Scale (PANAS) (Watson et al., 1988) contains ten negative affect items. Of these, Scared, Afraid, Jittery and Nervous would indicate a potential threat that involved both internal and external challenge. However, Guilty, Upset, Distressed, Ashamed and Hostile would indicate only external challenge. Thus, the theoretical prediction is that the latter set of emotions from the PANAS should be associated with more HPA axis activation and less inflammatory response, in contrast to the former set of emotions. More generally, the hypothesis of internal versus external balance leads to the suggestion that trait emotions, when organised according to infornet beliefs of external versus internal challenge, should lead to specific associations between neuroendocrine, immune and psychological states.

There is a limited number of very useful studies examining experimental injection of endotoxin on psychological states in humans (Eisenberger et al., 2010; Reichenberg et al., 2001) (see Chapter 2). Such research could be expanded to look at a wider range of psychological variables – one would predict that the endotoxin should have a greater effect on behaviour inhibition than behaviour activation.

Finally, the hypothesis of internal–external balance may have applications to clinical cases. Post-traumatic stress disorder (PTSD) is associated with HPA axis disturbance (Yehud, 2003) and takes two forms, one in which the primary feelings are those of shame and the other in which the primary feelings are those of fear (Adshead, 2000; Herman, 1992). Infornet theory would predict that shame-type PTSD should be associated with more HPA axis disturbance and less inflammatory response system activation. However, fear-type PTSD should be associated with more inflammatory response system activation and less HPA disturbance.

4   Networks and their properties

Introduction

The previous chapters have used the terms network and infornet without any formal attempt to describe the difference between network or parallel processing systems on the one hand versus sequential processing or non-network systems on the other. The aim of this chapter is to describe the emergent properties of networks, particularly as they relate to the infornet, and to provide some detail about how those emergent properties arise as a function of network structure. The chapter expands on ideas introduced in earlier chapters. It shows how networks solve problems, and therefore how the infornet solves the problem of how best to adjust the reference criteria of homeostatic loops. The chapter provides an introduction to the emergent properties of control systems and describes the network learning rules that are the basis for infornet dysregulation.

A very brief history of networks

In the 1940s, a small number of authors (e.g., Hebb, 1949; McCulloch and Pitts, 1943) presented a theory that could be used to explain the learning phenomena that psychologists were then investigating. They pointed out that the brain was a network of neurons and that it was possible to explain learning phenomena in animals if the brain, as a network structure, followed a simple rule. This simple rule explained *why* classical conditioning took place and *why* habits were formed. The rule was subsequently called the association rule or Hebbian rule. It sometimes happens that important theoretical suggestions are ahead of their time and so have little immediate impact. Such was the case with these early theoretical suggestions. It was not until the mid 1980s that the developments in mathematics, computers and the relationship between computers and intelligence (McClelland and Rumelhart, 1985) led to the science of connectionism or parallel processing systems.

A full understanding of connectionism and network theory requires an analytical (and mathematical) understanding of networks and is beyond the scope of this book. There are many textbooks and review papers on this topic (e.g., Bechtel and Abrahamsen, 1991; Ellis and Humphries, 1999; Smolensky, 1988). However, networks can also be described synthetically in terms of their overall behaviour – the emergent behaviour – of the network as a whole. The aim of this chapter to focus on this emergent level. There is no mathematics! The chapter starts with an intuitive portrayal of the difference between network and non-network structures.

Clocks versus flocks: an intuitive first understanding

A clock is an example of a non-network mechanism or sequential system. In Chapter 1 I suggested that clockwork was one factor in the emergence of modern medicine. The body is assumed to be a mechanical system (e.g., the heart pumps the blood) and has the same sequential form of causality as a clock. By contrast, a flock of birds is an example of a very simple network. If even the smallest cog of the clock is damaged, the clock will stop. However, if a bird in the flock is shot as it flies past, the flock flies on without interruption. Clocks and flocks work in different ways. Network causal structures are not uncommon in the natural world. Although a simple structure such as a flock of birds could not be considered a living structure, it is the network structure that is considered responsible for the special features of life, including the ability to grow and self-heal (Bedau, 1998; Larson-Freeman (1997).

How does a flock of birds actually work? Imagine, first, a flock of birds that is feeding on the ground and will shortly take off so that the birds can return to their roosting site for the night. Before they leave, there are little disturbances when a few birds take to the air briefly and then return to the ground again. Then suddenly the flock takes off as a rapid ripple flows over the flock and in a second they are all in the air. Next, the flock in the air weaves backwards and forwards a few times, before setting off towards the roosting site. The flock flies in a beautiful pattern of birds that sweeps across the sky. How does all this 'magic' happen? The important point to realise is that it is not magic – magic is a description given to the unexplained.

The behaviour of each bird is controlled by its own motivations as well as, to a far greater degree, by the behaviour of its neighbours. Each bird is, in effect, locked into doing what its neighbours are doing. As the end of feeding approaches, the motivation to return to roost increases, but however great that motivation is in any one bird, that bird cannot escape from its neighbours. Sometimes a cluster of birds has sufficient motivation to roost so as to create a local and temporary ripple when a few birds take a few strokes into the air, but the effect of their feeding neighbours is still too strong. Then, only when the motivation to roost is sufficiently great in the *whole* flock will the flock, acting as one, take to the air. Once in the air, very small changes in motivational trends in the flock will cause deviations in flight pattern, but eventually the flock moves on. The behaviour of a flock of birds looks like magic only if one uses the wrong mental model of how it works – the wrong model is that there is some co-ordinator or leader that makes the birds fly in a particular way. There is, however, no co-ordinator – or prime cog as there would be in a clock. The flock of birds exhibits the behaviour it does simply because that is the way a network structure works. It illustrates an important principle of complex systems: complexity arises from simple rules when the structure is a network.

Does structure make a difference?

The familiar PC at home or work and the supercomputer in military or research institutes are basically the same type of machine. They are sequential processing machines, also known as von Neumann machines. They carry out calculations one at a time (or with dual processors, just a few at a time). Their parentage can be traced back in time through mechanical calculators (older people may remember how you used to crank a handle to multiply or divide), back to medieval clockwork. Computers can carry out a range of computational tasks, and, in that sense, they are capable of 'thinking'. However, computers do not think in the same way as humans. Some tasks that are difficult for humans are easy for computers – reliable detection of spelling error is difficult for humans who tend to miss the odd mistake, but the standard spell-checker on a computer is excellent, which is why we use them. Other tasks that are easy for humans (e.g., recognising handwriting) are difficult for computers. Comparison of human cognitive abilities and computer computational abilities suggests that humans and computers are using different strategies to think.

The science of artificial intelligence grew out of a need to construct computers to think like humans. How can computers be designed to think like humans? One way would be to construct a computer with the same kind of network structure as the brain – but this is currently very difficult for practical reasons. An alternative strategy is to program a computer so that it simulates a network system, that is, it makes the mathematical calculations that would be made if it were a network. It is this second strategy that has been adopted and that forms the main route to current understanding of networks and artificial intelligence.

Current understanding of networks is based largely on the use of sequential computers that are programmed to act like network (parallel processing) computers. In fact, this kind of simulation is not just for research as it is used in commercial applications. Computers with a handwriting recognition facility simulate a network system to achieve this human facility of recognising handwriting.

Computers are sequential systems. Human brains appear to be network systems – at least, they are partially network systems. Computers and human brains have different structures; they are organised in different ways. If a sequential system can simulate a network system, does structure actually matter? The reality is that, in principle, the output from any parallel processing system (i.e., network system) can be simulated by a sequential system (i.e., conventional computer), assuming that the sequential system is powerful enough. Equally, a parallel processing computer, were it to be made, could, in principle, simulate any output from a sequential system. Each type of computer can, in principle, *compute* what the other can compute. However, structure does matter for several reasons. One reason has to do with the efficiency of computation.

Sequential systems can simulate parallel systems only by very elaborate computations, and to do this they need considerable computing power. It is no coincidence that network theory and increased computing power developed at the same time. Modern computers are so much more powerful than their forbears. Twenty-five years ago, a university computer took up the space of a whole room, and processing speed was so slow that programmes now running in seconds on a modern PC had to be run overnight. In those days using a computer – '*the* computer' – was a challenge. Modern computers are able to simulate networks because they are so powerful that it doesn't really matter that they are working very inefficiently. In principle, structure does not matter to computation given unlimited resources, but in practice it does matter as resources are always limited in the real world of biological structures. Biological systems cannot afford to work inefficiently (see Chapter 2). It is wasteful to use a sequential system if you are trying to achieve the functionality of a parallel system, and nature is not wasteful. It will come as no surprise, therefore, to learn that the body has the structure within it that allows parallel processing – as well as sequential processing. The structure is most apparent in the brain because neurons have a physical representation, but biochemical communication, as found in the immune and endocrine systems, can also function as a network (Tyrone, 2009; Varela and Coutinho, 1991).

The following section describes the computational functions that networks are particularly good at. Towards the end of the chapter I will return to the issue of parallel versus sequential systems and show that there are emergent properties that can occur only in network systems – life is more than just computation.

How networks work

The following sections provide an account of the parts of a network, and how the parts work together.

Units, causality and stability

A network consists of a number of *units* that are causally connected to other units. The word *unit* is a technical term and the unit can consist of cells or other structures that have causal connections, either through biochemicals (e.g., ligands and receptors) or through electrical (e.g., neural) pathways. The units are sometimes referred to as nodes, because they are the points of connection in the network. In terms of the mathematics of network theory, it is irrelevant what the units consist of: what matters is that units vary in their *state*. The state of a unit is treated as a mathematical quantity. The state of a unit varies either in a binary fashion (e.g., the unit is on or off) or continuously (i.e., can take many values). Note – we return to this point in a later chapter – it is assumed that the unit varies along only one dimension, for example, level of excitation in a cell.

The units are connected by causal connections in the sense that any one unit influences others. Because the historical routes of network theory derive from psychology and neurology, it is easy to think of these connections as the synapses between neural cells in the brain, but in fact any form of causal connection will do. Ligands (i.e., biochemical communicators) and their receptor sites provide another form of connection within the body. Such biochemical communicators include hormones, as well as the pro-inflammatory cytokines and Substance P referred to in previous chapters. According to infornet theory, the neurological and biochemical forms of causal connection are all part of the same system, in just the same way that mobile phones and land-line phones are all part of the same telecommunication system. The mobile phone corresponds to biochemical communication in that information is widespread and the receptor (or receiving phone) responds to the information. The landline phone corresponds to neurological communication in that information is sent down particular localised routes. Psychoneuroimmunoendocrinology is the term sometime used to include all these different forms of connection. So the biopsycho-social information network that is the infornet is represented in terms of its physical structure in terms of psychoneuroimmunoendocrinol-ogy. For the rest of this chapter, there will be no further discussion about the precise physiological form of the connections. However, all these causal connections (i.e., neurological and biochemical) can be either excitatory (e.g., agonist) or inhibitory (e.g., antagonist). Equally, the excitatory and inhibitory connections can be binary (e.g., on/off) or they can be continuous.

Figure 4.1 shows a schematic representation of a very simple network. The network (A) consists of units (shown as circles) that are joined by excitatory causal connections (shown as solid lines) or inhibitory causal connections (shown as dotted lines). The units are either 'on' (shown by filled circles) or 'off' (shown by open circles). Now let us invent a rule: The state of any unit depends on the summa-tion of the excitatory and inhibitory effects of the 'on' units to which it is connected. Note that in this rule the 'off' units have no effect on their neighbours – they can be ignored. Returning to Figure 4.1, the sequence of events of the network can be followed. Let us suppose that the top left unit is turned on (B) – as shown by the filled circle. The effect of the top left unit will be to activate three other units and switch them on (C). Those additional units then have two kinds of effect. One is to switch on an additional unit (D), but also one 'on' unit will be switched off. Note how the middle left-hand unit receives one excitatory and two inhibitory connections: $1 - 2 = -1$, so the unit is not being activated. The result is that the middle left-hand unit is switched off. Finally, note that once the network has achieved the state shown in D, then it ceases to change.

Network theorists describe networks as *relaxing* into a stable state. However, the term relaxing has specific meanings in health so I shall use the term *resolving*. The network resolves into a particular state depending on its initial state, where that initial state may be the result of outside influences.

A clockwork mechanism is easily grasped by the mind. A clock is a sequential mechanism and it is easy for attention to focus sequentially on different parts. You start with the first cog, move on to the second and so on. Networks are more difficult to understand because all the parts are happening at once and the mind simply cannot comprehend much simultaneous causality. Of course, if the network is very simple,

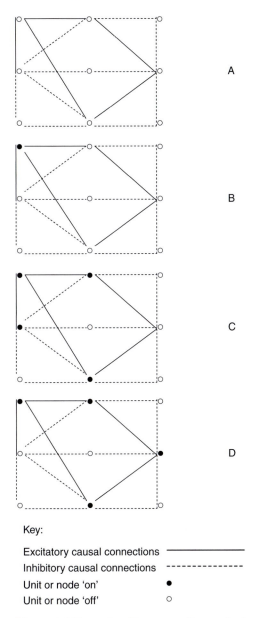

Key:

Excitatory causal connections   ——————
Inhibitory causal connections   --------------
Unit or node 'on'   ●
Unit or node 'off'   ○

Figure 4.1 Example of how causality works in a network

then it is possible to follow how the network changes. A network as simple as that shown in Figure 4.1 is comprehensible, but it is far too simple to have any useful network properties. However, the example does show what is meant by the network resolving. The way the network resolves can be said to 'solve' the problem of its inputs.

When a network is exposed to new inputs, those new inputs can alter the solution into which the network resolves. When the infornet is exposed to either somatogenic or psychogenic stress, then that stress acts as new inputs into the network. Stress therefore has the ability to change the solution of the infornet in terms of the states of its nodes, and hence leads to outcomes that are based on the interpretation of that stress. Chapters 2 and 3 provided an account of the hypothesis of internal–external balance. Thus, the state that the infornet resolves into, and hence the pattern of HPA activation and inflammatory response system activation, depends on the inputs to the infornet, and how those inputs are interpreted as requiring an internal (i.e., immune) versus external (i.e., increased motor activity) response.

Resolution is a relatively fast response, so the effect of stress on the network is relatively fast. The speed of resolution will depend on a variety of factors, but the order of change will be in the order of minutes and hours – i.e., the time taken to create the physiological changes associated with the HPA axis and immune system, as well as changes in mental state. Of course, once the stress is removed, then the infornet resolves back into its earlier state, and the inflammatory response, HPA activation and behaviour activation are abated. The dysregulated system (see later) misinterprets all situations as stressful, as well as other forms of misinterpretation that lead to maladaptive solutions to external and internal events.

Perception, pattern recognition and hidden layers

The ability to recognise handwriting is something that is taken for granted, but in reality it is an extraordinary skill. Figure 4.2 shows two letters, *e* and *a*, written in different ways. A human finds it easy to distinguish between these two letters. How could you design a sequential machine, such as a PC, to recognise handwritten letters? One way is to use a technique similar to that of a spell-checker. Stored in the computer's memory are a number of 'templates' of different types of *e*s and *a*s. These templates would have to be at different orientations – and there would have to be a lot of them. Of course, if an *e* or *a* were written very badly, in a way that did not correspond to a template, it would not be recognised. None of the *e*s and *a*s in Figure 4.2 correspond to any known

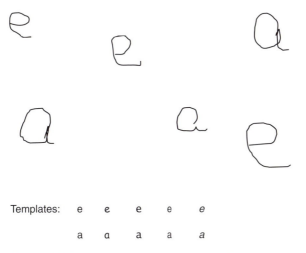

Templates: e   e   e   e   e

          a   ɑ   a   a   a

Figure 4.2 Pattern recognition from templates versus networks

template of the letters – some templates are shown at the bottom of the figure. Thus, the template strategy does not work, simply because an *e* and an *a* can be written in so many different ways. Humans, by contrast, are able to recognise an *e* or an *a* that has never been seen before. That is the extraordinary factor in pattern recognition. Humans can recognise things they have not seen before. The human does not use a template to recognise letters. The template method is a very limited method and is not used in practical applications. Pattern recognition needs to use a method other than template matching in order to be effective.

Figure 4.3 shows a network that has three different types of unit: output units, input units and hidden units. The hidden units are arranged in layers, and Figure 4.3 shows two layers. In fact, there can be one or more layers of hidden units – single-layer, hidden-unit systems have limited functions. Figure 4.3 shows a basic pattern recognition device in which an array of inputs (the input layer) is interpreted by the hidden layers, leading to the recognised pattern (the output layer). For example, suppose that there are 26 output units corresponding to each of the letters of the alphabet, and many more input units that correspond to points on a page of paper. Then, depending on the hidden units and the causal relationships between them, the device should be able to recognise handwritten letters. How does it do it? It all depends on the activation rules that connect the input units to the hidden units, the hidden units to each other, and the hidden units to the output units. In the previous example of Figure 4.1, the activation rules were

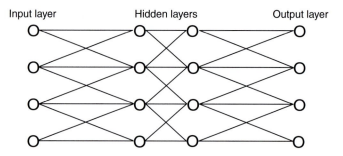

Figure 4.3 A simple network for recognising patterns

binary, and the units were either on or off. For the pattern recognition device shown in Figure 4.3, however, the activation rules are not binary. Instead, the activation of any one unit by another varies along a continuum, so it is possible to refer to the 'weight' with which one unit affects another. The pattern recognition device recognises handwriting when the 'weights' between the different units are just right. Just how one gets these weights 'just right' is something that will be covered in a later section on learning. For the moment, it should be noted that the success of this machine in recognising patterns depends crucially on the weights by which the units affect each other. Additionally, as stated above, the number of layers makes a substantial difference, and there is a general rule that pattern recognition improves with the increase in number of hidden layers. There is one final point: the network mechanism of pattern recognition is the same mechanism that allows the infonet to resolve into a solution given a stressful situation. Pattern recognition is a form of problem solving, and stress requires a solution to the question 'how can the various control systems be altered to best accommodate the situation that is currently presented?'.

Some general features of networks

Structure matters in the sense that network structures are 'better' at doing some things than sequential processing structures, and vice versa. This section reviews some of the emergent properties of networks to show how networks function differently from sequential structures.

Pattern recognition

Pattern recognition is one of the most useful features of networks, and it is a feature that is already being exploited. Computers that are able to recognise handwriting do so by simulating a network computer, that is, by simulating the structure shown in Figure 4.3. What exactly is a pattern? Towards the beginning of the twentieth century a group of psychologists, later called Gestalt psychologists, demonstrated that perceptions are holistic. When people view a picture they impose meaning onto the elements of which the picture is based – the elements consist of the colours, lines, dots, shapes, etc. When people interpret what a picture is, e.g., a picture of a face, they see more than just the elements themselves. In perception the whole is greater than the sum of its parts, and this Gestalt principle has been confirmed time and time again. There is, however, one important player in recognising a picture: the observer. When an observer looks at a picture, it is the observer who takes the elements and constructs something that is not present in the elements alone.

Patterns need an observer. The observer constructs the pattern from the elements on the basis of knowledge. So patterns are *elements informed by knowledge*. In the case of the pattern recognition device shown in Figure 4.3, knowledge is in the activation rules between the units of the system. Notice how the pattern is an emergent property of the elements that make up the pattern. However, this property only emerges on the basis of knowledge contained in the activation rules.

One property of parallel processing systems is that they can respond to complex interrelationships between stimuli in the environment, instead of simply responding to the stimuli themselves.

The above shows that infornet alarm occurs in response to *patterns* in the environment. That pattern can be mediated psychologically (psychogenic stress) or biologically (somatic stress), or the pattern may be some combination of the psychogenic and somatic stress. Stress comes about through the recognition of a pattern and leads to a particular solution. A corollary of this realisation is that patterns leading to infornet alarm may be complex. Depending on the way the pattern is interpreted as reflecting external versus internal challenge, there will be corresponding activation in the HPA axis and the inflammatory response system.

Tolerance of local error

If a cog in a clockwork mechanism is damaged, then, however small the cog, the clock will stop. If a software or hardware fault develops on a computer, the computer will stop working and show an error. By contrast, if a bird in a flock of birds suddenly falls down dead, the flock flies on as if nothing has happened. One of the interesting features of network systems is that they are relatively insensitive to local error.

Let us return to the pattern recognition device shown in Figure 4.3, and let us suppose that the all the hidden units and weights are set up so that the system is able to recognise handwritten letters. What happens when one of those units is damaged, or when one of the weights is changed? The answer is surprisingly little. The device is likely to function just as well as ever. Network systems have redundancy built into them, so that small local error makes little difference. However, as more and more units are damaged or removed, the pattern recognition device starts making errors. For example, it may start confusing *es* with *cs*. The decline in function is not catastrophic, as would be the case with a clock, but gradual. Network systems exhibit gradual malfunction with increasing local error. This is a crucial point to the arguments developed later – that dysregulation happens slowly, and healing (i.e., recovery of regulation) also occurs very slowly.

Tolerance of local error is a feature that has some clear advantages for biological systems. In the group of cells that make up a multicellular individual it is inevitable that some cells will die or malfunction. Some local error is inevitable, and systems that can cope with local error have advantages in terms of survival.

When errors occur in a parallel processing system, this leads to gradual degradation of function in contrast to catastrophic degradation of function. Similarly, when the system is corrected, this leads to gradual improvement in function.

Distributed memory and distributed cause

When information is stored on PC (i.e., a sequential processing device), information is stored at a particular point in space. It is localised. For example, when this sentence is stored on the hard drive of my computer, it will be encoded in binary code at a particular location on the hard drive.

Consider now the pattern recognition device shown in Figure 4.3. When the system recognises a letter, it does so using the whole of the network. Recall that pattern recognition involves the elements plus knowledge. The knowledge that is needed to recognise the pattern is in the activation rules of the network and so is distributed throughout the network. Recognition of each letter uses the whole of the network, or at least that part dealing with recognition. One of the findings of neuroscience is that different parts of the brain are active with different types of mental activity, so there is evidence that parts of the network that is the brain have specialised functions.

Pattern recognition requires the activation rules of the system as a whole – collectively, these activation rules are referred to as the activation pattern. The memory that confers the ability to recognise patterns is distributed over the whole system. In network systems, memory is distributed rather than localised. In fact, it is because memory is distributed rather than localised that network systems are tolerant of local error. Memory is an important part of infonet theory, because the body is capable of *experience-based learning*. That is, the body can remember what has happened to it in the past.

In a standard PC, instructions are given in the form of computer programs. Computer programs comprise a list of sequential instructions. In a network computer, there is no computer program: there are no sequential instructions. The instructions and the information in a network are encoded in the form of the activation rules of the units, that is the activation pattern of the whole system. Indeed, it is because information is stored in this way that network computers are difficult to make in practice. Imagine that instead of loading a program onto your computer you had to physically change the weights of the connections between the different units – perhaps millions of connections. Writing a program is much easier, which is why we still use sequential computers to simulate network systems.

In parallel processing systems, information is distributed in the form of strength of connections (activation rules) between the units of the systems.

This point is crucial to the holistic approach needed to understand how the infonet functions. The infonet involves connections throughout the whole body, not just in the brain or just in the immune system.

Intuition, soft decisions and multi tasking

Here is a problem for you to solve:

It is big, red, transports people, and it can be found in London. What is it?

You should have the answer straight away: a bus. How did you manage to work it out? Let us start with how you *didn't* work it out. You didn't list all the red objects you know, then all the objects that transport people, and then all the objects in London, and see where there is an overlap in those three lists. Doing it that way, i.e., doing it sequentially, would take far too long. The way you did it can be illustrated in Figure 4.4. You activated three units in a network, the units red, transports people and London. The activation in those three units then spread out through the network, activating and inhibiting other 'hidden layers', and the

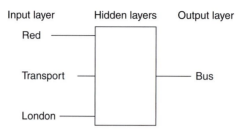

Figure 4.4 Pattern recognition example

unit that then became most active was the unit of a bus. The problem was solved using each of the clues in parallel, not in sequence.

Let us now suppose I were to set you a second problem, a problem for which there is no clear and obvious solution. The problem this time is:

It lives in the Arctic, it is a mammal and it is large. What is it?

Again, the clues activate the network, but there is no one unit that becomes active overall. There are several possibilities – such as polar bear and whale. You haven't been able to find a solution, but you have been able to find *possible* solutions. What you have done is demonstrate the beginnings of intuition. Networks are able to recognise the pattern in things. They are able to come up with novel solutions. In other words, the information in a network is not constrained by what it has been taught. Networks can discover.

Consider now a third problem. This time there are lots of clues but it is impossible to find any single object that corresponds to all those clues. The instruction is to try find something that provides a reasonably good fit to as many clues as possible.

It lives in the water, it has legs, it has no hair, and it is a mammal. What is it?

Possible examples include whale, and seal – though neither satisfies all clues, but at least it is possible to come up with solutions that approximate.

Networks can solve this problem of inadequate task specification using the technique of spreading activation, as before. However, networks are much better at this type of task than sequential systems: networks are good at 'soft decisions' where multiple constraints need to be satisfied, some of which are incompatible with each other. In common-sense terms, networks are good at making the best of a bad job.

The ability of networks to solve multiple problems simultaneously is an important biological characteristic. In brief, the body needs to ensure that all of its feedback systems are running correctly. There are many different feedback systems running simultaneously in the body, so this is clearly a multi-task problem. As noted in previous chapters, a stressful activity such as a mammoth hunt signals the need for vigorous physical activity, but also the possibility of injury and immune challenge. Thus, there is a competition between setting up the body so that it deals with internal versus external challenge. A soft compromise is made – perhaps activation of inflammatory mediators but down-regulation of some cellular immunity. This compromise is achieved through a network structure, the infornet, rather than a series of coincidentally connected feedback loops.

Parallel processing systems have features that are reminiscent of humans rather than machines: they are able to make intuitive decisions.

Resolution, history and local minima

One of the properties of networks is that they tend to 'resolve' into a stable state. The stable state that a network resolves into can be altered by external factors. Psychogenic and somatogenic stress may alter the resolved state of the infornet – that is, it comes to a different solution under stressful situations. However, some networks are able to resolve into more than one stable state, in the sense that they can come to different solutions for the same stressful situation. If you return to Figure 4.1 and change the starting point so that some of the 'on' units are 'off' and vice versa, then it is possible to end up with a different final solution. The history of events affecting the network is important: networks are sensitive to history. Infornet alarm is not simply a function of the current stressful inputs to the network, but is also affected by recent events. For example, someone may find a stressor less stressful if they have recently had their self-esteem enhanced by other another person (possibly a therapist). The fact that it is possible to end up at a different position shows that networks are sensitive to history: where you end up depends on where you begin. Infornet alarm is not a simple mechanical response to the external environment but a complex interpretation that includes recent events.

In network terminology, the different solutions of the network can be referred to as 'energy minima', and it can be the case that one solution is best (i.e., network minimum is lowest). The best solution is referred to as the overall minimum, and others as local minima. Figure 4.5 is a way of representing an overall minimum and one local minimum of a network system. Whether one ends up in the local minimum or the overall minimum depends on history. Depending on where you start, it is possible to end up in a state of the network that is stable but not optimally stable.

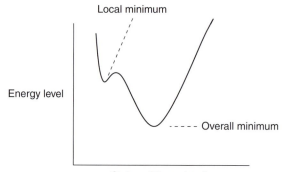

Figure 4.5 A local minimum and an overall minimum

Note in Figure 4.5 that in order to move from the local minimum to the overall minimum it is necessary to move 'uphill', that is, to move to a state away from the overall minimum in the first instance. The implication of local minima is that once a network has resolved into a particular state, shift to another state may be abrupt rather than continuous.

Parallel processing systems can be disturbed from the optimal states, and generally tend to return spontaneously to their optimal state. Sometimes, the system is prevented from returning to its optimal state.

Networks as learning devices

Information in a network is encoded in the form of activation rules. Learning entails *changes* in those activation rules. Along with pattern recognition, learning is perhaps the most important feature that distinguishes network from non-network systems. Network systems are able to learn by interacting with their environments.

Learning in networks can be understood as the application of *learning rules* that lead to changes in the activation rules of the network. These changes occur slowly. Network learning is a slow process: network resolution is fast.

Learning and learning rules are crucial to dysregulation in the infornet, and it is for this reason that it will be necessary to examine network learning rules in some depth. The preceding sections have focused on infornet alarm: the following ones focus on infornet dysregulation. Infornet dysregulation comes about through the application of learning rules.

Learning rules

Three different types of rule will be covered in this section: (a) associative learning, (b) supervised learning and (c) unsupervised or
competitive learning.

Associative learning

Over a century ago, psychologists discovered that animals learned to
associate simultaneously occurring events. Pavlovian conditioning (also
called classical conditioning) is a good example of this phenomenon.
Pavlov found that if a bell is rung whenever a dog is fed food, then
eventually the dog will salivate when the bell is rung in the absence
of food. This type of learning is called associative learning. Immune
conditioning was described in Chapter 2.

In 1949, Hebb explained the phenomenon of Pavlovian conditioning
in terms of the behaviour of networks, with the result that the *Hebbian
learning rule* is the name sometimes given to learning rules underlying
associative learning. The Hebbian or associative learning rule can be
stated as:

If two units are activated at the same time, then increase the weights
connecting those two units.

The associative learning rule is illustrated in Figure 4.6. If units A
and B are activated at the same time (owing to some external influence
on the network) then the network responds by increasing the weights of
all connections between those two units. Increasing the weights means
that the activation rule between any two units is changed so that activity
flows more readily between the units A and B. Hence, activation of A
will lead to the activation of B and vice versa. The associative learning
rule is sometimes expressed mathematically: the appropriate weight is
the product of the activity of the two connected units. However, for
present purposes it is enough to understand that networks, if they are

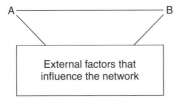

Figure 4.6 The associative learning rule: when A and B are activated
simultaneously the connections between them strengthen

designed with the associative learning rule, are good at judging the degree of association between units that are contiguously activated. They are good at adjusting the activation rules so that when one unit becomes active, the other becomes active to the extent that the activity of those units has been associated on past occasions.

Not only can the associative learning rule explain why classical conditioning occurs, it also can explain the formation of habits. Animal research had established that if animals learned a behaviour for a particular reward, then even after that reward was removed, the behaviour tended to persist (elsewhere known as Thorndike's law of effect). Habits form owing to the repetition of behaviour. In fact, the importance of habits – and promoting good habits – had been recognised by many of the earlier psychologists (James, 1899). Habits can be explained by the same learning rule. If a situation repeatedly induces a particular behavioural response, then the network connections associating the situation and behaviour will be strengthened.

The phenomenon of immune conditioning (see Chapter 2) is closely related to classical conditioning. If classical conditioning can be explained by associative learning, then so can immune conditioning. If immune conditioning occurs because of associative learning, then the immune system and neurological system must be part of the same network.

One feature of associative learning is that, for it to work effectively, the rate of change in activation rules must be reasonably slow – because otherwise the system responds too rapidly to events that may not in the long run be shown to be associated. Network learning using the associative rule must therefore be a gradual process. As Pavlov observed in his early experiments, associative learning is slow. Immune conditioning (see Chapter 2) is a similarly slow process. Immune conditioning is an example of the associative learning rule applied to the infornet – rather than limited to that part of the infornet called the brain.

Parallel processing systems can exhibit classical conditioning or associative learning. Conditioning is not a unique feature of the brain, as it has also been demonstrated in the immune system and is probably a property of the whole body.

Supervised learning

Let us return to the pattern recognition device shown in Figure 4.3. Recall, that this device will be able to detect patterns *so long as the activation rules are 'just right'*. Supervised learning is a way of ensuring those activation rules get 'just right'.

Supervised learning occurs only in networks that have certain characteristics. In order to learn, the units of the network and the activation between them both need to be capable of varying continuously, rather than in a binary fashion. In the case of a physiological network, this means that that the activation of a cell or other structure must be able to vary in strength – and this is a feature of many physiological cells and structures.

Supervised learning involves two phases: a learning phase when the system is adjusting its activation rules, and a test phase when one tests to what extent the system has got it right. In the learning phase, the system is presented with a pattern in the input nodes that feed through the network to create an arbitrary output at the output nodes. This arbitrary output is the *actual* output, and the aim of learning is to convert this initial actual output into the *desired* output. To do this, the weights in the system are changed. The change is done systematically, starting with weights for causal connections between the penultimate units (i.e., the last hidden layer) and the output units. The following procedure is adopted.

First, calculate the difference between the actual and desired output and multiply this by some function of the inputs to that output unit. This calculation creates an error term. Then, using that error term, adjust the weights of the connections from penultimate layer in the network to the output unit. Repeat this procedure between the penultimate units and the layer behind them, and then repeat back through all the other network layers back to the input layer.

The method is often called the back-propagation method, as the correction is 'back-propagated' through the network. In practical terms it means that if the actual output unit has a level of activity lower than the desired output, then the weight of the excitatory connections to the output unit is 'tweaked up' a little (and the inhibitory weight tweaked down). The extent of this 'tweaking' is actually quite crucial for the ability to learn and can be expressed mathematically. Assuming, however, that the correct changes are made, then the network will learn gradually through repeated presentations of different patterns. The detail of how these changes are made is not essential here. The important message is that if the pattern recognition device shown in Figure 4.3 is presented with many different patterns and a particular learning rule (the back-propagation rule) is adopted, then, gradually, the activation rules connecting the units will change so that the device correctly recognises the set of patterns. Note, that the 'tweaking' is quite small, as otherwise the system will over-respond to any particular pattern, and therefore not learn the total set of patterns. Supervised learning is necessarily a slow process, as is associative learning.

A————————————————➤ B

Figure 4.7 The pattern that is specified by the genome. The genome specifies the pattern: if there is an A, then the A should be followed by a B.

Researchers in network theory have often suggested that supervised learning is not very biological in the sense that there does not appear to be anything biological that can supervise. However, the genome is ideally suited to this task, and supervised learning is a perfectly reasonable biological phenomenon. Hox genes are a class of genes that have the function of specifying patterns in the body – for example, the position of the limbs. Current knowledge of genetics suggests that genes can specify complex patterns. If it is possible to specify a pattern (as can be achieved through the genome), then a system can learn to recognise – or behave in accordance with – that pattern.

Parallel processing systems can learn to perform better if they are told whether or not they are performing correctly. To put it technically, when given feedback, parallel processing systems can 'self-organise' so as to function more effectively.

The genome as the supervisor

Because the role of the genome as a supervisor in network learning is essential to the theory being proposed here, a possible mechanism will be described in some detail in this section.

First, suppose that the genome is a pattern detector, in the sense that it is able to detect patterns of events that occur in the body. An example of such pattern is 'B follows A' as shown in Figure 4.7.

Figure 4.7 illustrates the pattern: if there is an A, then A should be followed by B. There are many examples of how the body changes one state to another so as to be consistent with the pattern specified by the genome. Two examples are shown below; in each case the 'correction' of the wrong pattern to the right pattern can be achieved by a mixture of internal adjustment (i.e., physiological change) and external adjustment (i.e., behaviour).

Example 1
  A = body temperature below 36.4°C
  B = body temperature at 36.4°C

Example 2
  A = inadequate nutrition
  B = adequate nutrition

Notice that in both these examples, B is the desired or ideal state as defined by the genome and A is some state that deviates from ideal state.

Let us suppose that the output from the network is A. Using the information from the genome, the network 'learns' to produce state B using the back-propagation method of supervised learning. That is, the activation rules in the network change until the network starts to produce pattern B. In example 1, the network finds out through trial and error that in order to increase body temperature, there are several changes that can be made including increases in metabolic rate, decreases in heat loss, and because the network also controls behaviour, changes are made in behaviour (e.g., lighting a fire, putting on more clothes). In the case of example 2, the body finds out through trial and error that in order to improve nutrition, it is necessary to give a mental signal of 'hunger', a signal that then motivates the body to engage in behaviours that increase nutrition. In sum, the network – i.e., the infornet – learns to create the pattern specified by the genome through a process of discovery, using whatever method the network discovers. The network finds a *means* to an *end* and different networks may find different means to the same end.

Note that for this means–ends relationships to be formed, the network must be capable of recognising patterns over time. Sensitivity to the dynamic properties of patterns is sometimes referred to as the binding problem. Suffice it to say that networks are capable of detecting patterns of events not only cross-sectionally, but also longitudinally over time (Shastri and Ajjanagadde, 1993).

Infornet theory proposes that the genome is the supervisor of the infornet. The consequence of this proposal is that the genome does not specify the activation pattern of the infornet (i.e., the information contained in the infornet). The genome specifies what the pattern should be (i.e., what 'should happen'), and the network does the rest. The particular way the network back-propagates in order to achieve what 'should happen' (i.e., the pattern specified by the genome) will depend on a variety of environmental and other factors. So the genome tells the infornet what to do – but not how to do it. One of the implications of this hypothesis is that genes can be used efficiently – you do not need to specify every little detail because the network will be able to work out some of the detail for itself. A second implication is that even if two people have the same genome (i.e., identical twins), they may have different 'styles' of self-regulation, particularly if they develop in different environments. A final implication is that control loops – the basis on which bodies function – are not predetermined by the genome in the sense of a pre-formed kit. Instead, control loops are constructed by a network using the instructions from the genome about how the control loop should function.

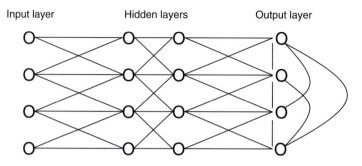

Figure 4.8 Network structure needed for competitive learning (learning that discovers)

Competitive learning

I have been unable to find a role for competitive learning within infornet theory. As a role may be found in future, it is included here for completeness. Some readers may want to skip to the next section. The network structure for competitive or unsupervised learning is slightly different and shown in Figure 4.8. Each input unit is connected to an output unit, but also the output units are connected to each other. The distinguishing feature of the competitive network is that the output layer works in a 'winner-take-all' manner. That is, the unit that receives the greatest activation from the input units ends up in an active state, whereas all other output units end up in a non-active state. The learning rule is: increase the weights between the active output unit only and the input units.

This simple arrangement and rule confers a rather interesting property on the network. The network is able to 'discover' patterns. That is, it can find regularities in the input units and then classify those regularities in terms of different output units. Whereas the supervised network has to be 'told' what the pattern is that it is trying to recognise, the unsupervised network can discover patterns for itself.

Parallel processing systems can discover new rules.

Self-regulation

Self-regulation and self-organisation are different concepts. This section examines how networks function as part of a *self-regulatory* system, and will be followed by a section that examines how networks *self-organise*.

Networks can be organised in different ways. In the recurrent network (Figure 4.9) outputs are connected to inputs, so the whole systems feeds

Input layer   Hidden layers   Output layer

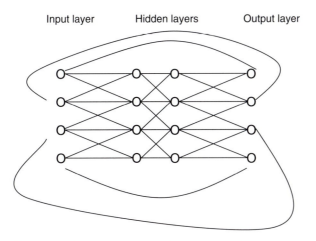

Figure 4.9 A recurrent network: a network that also acts as a control loop. The output layer sends information to the input layer

back on itself. Recurrent networks have several interesting features, one of which is that they can become time sensitive – because the rate of flow through the network and back again is time dependent. Recurrent networks, or indeed any networks where there is some feedback within the network, can function as self-regulatory systems.

One of the features of a recurrent network is that it feeds back on itself. The idea of feedback is not new – it predates network theory by several hundred years. Feedback or self-regulation can be a property of certain types of networks (i.e., recurrent networks), but it is also a property of simple control systems. Additionally, networks and control systems can themselves be linked together into a single system. As simple 'stand-alone' control systems themselves have important emergent properties, they will be described initially as independent functioning units.

A negative feedback loop is the basic unit of a control system. Examples of control systems of one kind or another occur throughout history. An early mechanical example is the 'governor' used by James Watt in his steam engine (Figure 4.10).

James Watt needed to overcome a mechanical problem. The boiler of the steam engine drives a piston, and the piston makes a wheel go round. The rate at which the piston goes in and out and the speed with which the wheel goes round depends on the pressure of steam. If the pressure if very low, the engine will stop. If the pressure if too high, the engine will go faster and faster until it breaks. Watt first solved this problem by having an assistant open or shut a tap to keep the engine running at

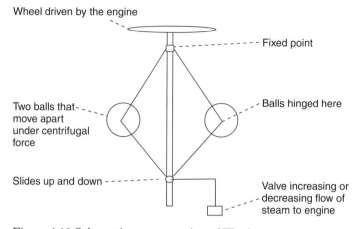

Figure 4.10 Schematic representation of Watt's steam governor

a constant speed. The assistant turned the tap on to make it go faster, or off to make it go slower. However, an assistant costs money, so Watt invented something he called a 'governor' to do what had previously been done by hand The significance of this historical example is that the governor *did what humans did*. In engineering contexts, control systems are designed so that machines can replace the functions of humans. The philosophical implication of this was not lost on later control theorists who applied control theory to humans (Powers, 1978). Humans' goal-oriented behaviour is controlled by control systems. Control theory provides a useful way of understanding goal-oriented behaviour (Carver and Scheier, 1998; Hyland, 1988). Humans function because of control systems that control both the internal and external environment.

A diagram of a basic control system is shown in Figure 4.11. Such systems work by comparing a reference criterion (sometimes called the goal or set point) with a perceptual input (sometimes called the perception or environmental input), and then generating an output (sometimes called behaviour) that affects the environment in such a way as to reduce that error. This negative feedback system is very common in all walks of life, a familiar example being a thermostatically controlled central heating system. Because of their familiarity, control systems are often thought of as relatively simple and it is assumed that they always work. Neither is true. Negative feedback systems are complex and work effectively only under certain circumstances. Imagine you are taking a shower, and you are unfamiliar with how showers work. You switch on the water, and water comes out freezing cold.

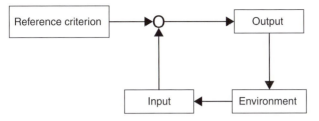

Figure 4.11 A control loop (feedback loop)

The reference criteria and input are compared at the comparator (O) and the difference generates an output. The output affects the environment, which alters the input.

So you turn the knob that adjusts the temperature up as hot as it will go. Soon the water starts getting tepid, then warm then scalding hot. Because the water is scalding you rapidly turn the knob right down to cold, and you end up in an oscillating cycle of being too hot and too cold. Of course, you won't do this because you have an intuitive understanding of showers and know that you should make small adjustments. However, the shower example illustrates that stability in control does not follow inevitably from the structure of the control system. The stability of a negative feedback system arises from the connections between the elements of the system, and it is an emergent property – it is a property of the system as a whole.

Stability in control systems is a function of two parameters. The *gain* of the system is the strength of the output for any given level of error; that is, it is extent to which error generates behavioural change. In the shower example, gain is represented by the extent to which the temperature knob is adjusted – sensible people make small adjustments to the shower knob, i.e., a small gain. The second parameter is *lag*, which is the time information takes to travel round the loop. In the shower example, lag is a function of the distance between the temperature knob and the shower head. Control systems that have high lag and high gain tend to oscillate (if you give the shower example some thought you will see why this is the case). However, if the gain is not sufficiently high, then external circumstances are not sufficiently controlled. When control engineers develop control systems (for example, for robots or for flight systems of jumbo jets) they do so by making careful calculations about the gain and lag.

Let us suppose that there is a thermostatically controlled heating system, but the temperature is found consistently to be too low. There are two possibilities that should be considered. One is that the reference criterion is wrong (i.e., the thermostat is set too low), and the other is that the gain is insufficient (i.e., the size of the boiler is too small).

Evidently, complex control systems can exist independently of networks, and when they are used in modern machinery that is precisely how they are used. However, a control system can also be embedded within a network. After all, a network is simply an arrangement of units, and that arrangement can incorporate a control system. A control system is embedded in a network system when the various parameters of the control system, such as the reference criterion or gain, are controlled by (i.e., are outputs from) the network. When a control system is embedded in a network system, self-regulation can have all the advantages that go with network systems. For example, if self-regulation is achieved through a network, then the reference criterion of the control system can be the output from the network. The result of this arrangement is that the reference criterion of the control system can be a pattern rather than a simple unidimensional parameter.

Homeostasis and homeodynamics

Some control systems are homeostatic. The word *homeostasis* is derived from the Greek, *homoeo* = 'same' and' and *stasis* = 'stand'. Some of the body's biochemical values remain reasonably constant – for example, blood glucose levels vary only slightly despite input of glucose via food and depletion of glucose via exercise. For homeostatic control systems,

Box 4.1 Why is self-regulation important to disease?

Many diseases can be understood as a malfunction in a control system. For example, in the case of inflammatory diseases, the inflammatory response is set at a level that creates damage within the body's own tissues. Endocrinological disorders, such as low levels of thyroxine and diabetes, can be understood as a failure of the body's ability to maintain correct levels of biochemicals. In the case of irritable bowel syndrome (IBS), gut motility varies between too active (diarrhoea) and too inactive (constipation). People with bipolar disorder show oscillations in mood. Many chronic diseases involve intrinsic oscillation in underlying morbidity.

Diseases where there is a failure of a control system fall into two categories. First, there are those diseases (particularly endocrine diseases) where there is a control loop failure because the output or input fails to function properly. Second, there are those diseases where the reference criterion is set incorrectly. This latter category includes those diseases where there is an inflammatory component: the inflammatory response is set too high.

the reference criterion remains fixed. The reference criterion (or set point) of the glucose control system maintains the level of glucose constant at about 90 mg per 100 ml of blood. If the level is too low, the hormone glucagon is secreted, which has the effect of increasing blood glucose. If the level is too high, then the hormone insulin is secreted, which has the effect of decreasing blood glucose. Blood calcium levels are also comparatively fixed, varying between 9 and 11 mg per 100 ml of blood. Again, this effect is achieved through two competing hormones: calcitonin and parathyroid hormone.

However, other control systems within the body are not homeostatic in that the reference criterion varies. This variation is controlled and occurs as a result of external events, including diurnal variation. For example, cortisol level is controlled but varies in a predictable manner according to external events – it is increased by stress. Similarly, heart rate is controlled but varies in a predictable manner – it increases with increased physical activity. Such control loops with changing reference criteria are called homeodynamic (from homeo = same and dynamic = force or movement). Homeodynamic systems are different from homeostatic systems because, although a parameter is controlled, the controlled parameter varies in a controlled way – or at least a way that is more controlled than mere oscillation. Many of the body's control loops are homeodynamic rather than homeostatic. Both the inflammatory response system and the HPA axis provide examples of homeodynamic variation, as both systems are sensitive to external events.

Where a control system is homeodynamic, health is characterised by variability in that control system. Heart rate is homeodynamic parameter: heart rate increases with exercise and HPA activation. However, the heartbeats are not completely regular – there are small

Box 4.2 Example of a homeodynamic system

Suppose you live a room whose temperature is thermostatically controlled. Suppose that you want to want to increase the temperature gradually throughout the day, and then decrease the temperature gradually at night. One way of doing this is to sit next to the thermostat and change it gradually. An alternative is to create a machine to change the thermostat for you.

Body temperature also increases during the day and decreases at night. Not only is this variation controlled, but also, when you have a fever, the fever adds a constant increase in temperature to the diurnal variation. The system is controlled but can also be changed in response to external events.

changes in the interval between individual heartbeats. Heart rate variability decreases in states of poor health, particularly those associated with autonomic disturbance, and increases when health is good (van Ravenswaaij-Arts *et al.*, 1993). The reason is that heart rate variability results from the dynamic interaction between the many physiological determinants of heart rate, primarily from neural inputs from the sympathetic and parasympathetic nervous systems (i.e., it is intimately connected to the HPA axis and stress). The healthy heart is sensitive to this dynamic interaction – the unhealthy heart is insensitive to those inputs and is functioning as though it were a stand-alone device (Bilchick and Berger, 2006). Thus, heart rate variability is an indication of health because it shows that heart rate is *not* controlled by a stand-alone control loop. Instead, the control loop that controls the heart rate is homeodynamic and the reference of that homeodynamic loop is sensitive to other inputs. The body works poorly if it functions as though it is made up of different modules, each with its own unique function. It works best if the different homeodynamic control systems are sensitive to inputs controlling their reference criteria and gain.

The theory of the infornet: its representation in network theory

There are two ways of achieving homeodynamic control. One way is for the reference criteria of the homeodynamic control system to be the output from a higher-level control system. For example, if one wanted to increase room temperature at night, a room thermostat could be altered by a higher-level control system that detects external light intensity. Control systems can be stacked up, metaphorically, one on top of the other, so that higher-level systems control the reference criteria of lower-level systems, as shown in Figure 4.12.

An alternative way of achieving a homeodynamic system is to use a network such that output from the network alters the reference criterion of the control loop. With regard to the way the body functions, the data are more consistent with the latter explanation. When an external event leads to changes in the reference criteria of control systems,

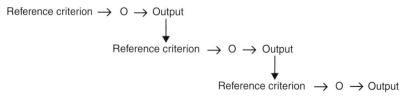

Figure 4.12 Hierarchically arranged control systems

several homeodynamic control systems are altered at the same time. For example, a stressful event will alter all the control systems found in the mutually interacting inflammatory response system and HPA axis. This alteration is coordinated – all the different control systems change in an intelligent and mutually supporting manner. Furthermore, the coordination of change in the body's homeodynamic systems requires 'soft decision making', and this is a particular feature of networks. Finally, networks, unlike stand-alone control systems, are capable of self-organising. Self-organisation is described in a later section of this chapter but is a characteristic of the way the body's homeodynamic systems are themselves controlled.

Infornet theory proposes that there is an intelligent network system that is distributed throughout the body and that provides inputs to the homeodynamic control systems that are essential for the organism to function. The theory is represented in Figure 4.13.

Notice that the infornet coordinates control systems that control the internal *and* external environments. It is this seamless and elegant coordination that leads to the conclusion that the homeodynamic control systems are being controlled by an intelligent system, that is, a system that is capable of encoding meaning.

Chapter 2 introduced the idea of the principle of efficiency, the principle that the body conserves its resources by carrying out specific functions at specific times. A network system such as that proposed in the infornet is ideally suited to redirecting resources to maximise the current task. So, for example, when you hunt mammoths, then the

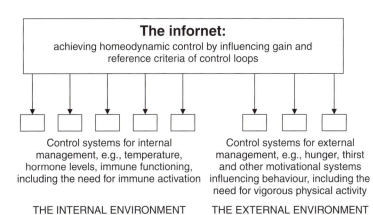

Figure 4.13 Relationship between homeodynamic control systems and the level of organisation at which the infornet functions

homeodynamic systems change so as maximise the body's resources for hunting mammoths; and when you eat the mammoth, the homeo dynamic systems change to maximise the body's resources for digesting food. Network systems are ideally suited to making the compromises necessary to keep many homeodynamic control systems functioning at the same time.

Life is a pattern of change: living systems are always changing. If life is a *pattern* of change, then it is possible that there is an emergent knowledge existing at the level of the body, rather than at the level of a body subsystem (e.g., brain, immune system, endocrine system). Infornet theory proposes that this emergent knowledge is not at the level of a single control system level, nor at the communication system level (e.g., brain, immune system, endocrine system) but at the level of the infornet. The infornet is the repository of information in the body, where information is stored in the form of activation rules between the nodes of the network. Change in that knowledge means change in the activation rules of the infornet.

Self-organisation

Networks have the capacity to learn. Three learning rules were described above: associative learning, supervised learning and competitive learning, of which the first two are relevant to infornet theory in its current form. If a self-regulatory system learns, then it is said to self-organise. A network that has the capacity to self-organise also has the capacity to improve the quality of its self-regulation. That is, the network can learn so as to achieve better self-regulation. Equally, networks that have the capacity to self-organise can undergo a deterioration in the quality of self-regulation. They can learn so that self-regulation is less effective – i.e., there is dysregulation.

The network learning rule of supervised learning can be used to explain how the body improves the quality of self-regulation in response to information provided to the infornet. Let us suppose, as proposed above, that the supervisor of the infornet is the genome. The genome specifies the patterns that the body should achieve – the infornet self-organises until that pattern is achieved. The process of supervised learning has two phases. First there is a 'test phase' during which the genome detects whether the pattern has been achieved or not. If the pattern has not been achieved, then there is a learning phase. In the learning phase the infornet changes the activation rules, i.e., the strength of connection between the units, until the desired pattern is achieved. So, for example, let us suppose that the desired pattern is a particular fluctuation of cortisol throughout the day. That is, what is specified by the genome is that cortisol levels should rise rapidly in the morning and decrease during the night. Supervised learning of the network with the genome as supervisor then creates a self-regulating system so that the pattern of cortisol that is produced is the one that corresponds to that contained in the genetic information. The body learns to do what is specified by the genome.

In sum, infornet theory suggests that the body learns to be an efficient self-regulator, rather than being created as an efficient self-regulator. The control loops of the body are not fixed – they are not genetically predetermined. Instead, the body self-organises until the control loops are doing the job they are supposed to be doing, as defined and detected by the genome.

If self-organising systems have the capacity to learn and become more effective, and if the infornet is a self-organising system, then the logical consequence would be that the infornet should always be effective – it should never become dysregulated. We should all have perfect health. However, according to the theory developed here, networks do become dysregulated, and this dysregulation should be considered a form of learning. Network dysregulation results from network learning rules that normally produce more effective self-regulation but which, under particular circumstances, lead to poor self-regulation.

Infornet dysregulation occurs when the learning process of self-organisation produces less effective regulation – it is a form of self-organisation that 'has gone wrong'.

In sum, infornet dysregulation is the consequence of network learning rules that normally produce more effective self-regulation but for one reason or other lead to less effective self-regulation.

Box 4.3 Life and self-organisation

Chapter 1 covered some of the problems of using a mechanical analogy for explaining living matter. One of these problems is that life involves decreased entropy: it becomes more complex, whereas the second law of thermodynamics is that systems should become less complex over time. Mechanical systems, such as jumbo jets, computers or robots, are unable to heal themselves, grow or reproduce. Self-organisation is an emergent property that can, in principle, account for those properties of organisms that go beyond mere self-regulation. Self-organisation shows how systems can increase their complexity and extract negative entropy from their surroundings. Self-organisation is a property of life. Living systems are *always* self-organising.

Representation of the meaning of the infornet

The previous chapter described the infornet as a meaning system. How is this meaning represented in network systems such as the infornet? A good way of understanding infornet meaning is in terms of a computer program. A computer program contains a list of instructions, just as the infornet contains the infornet beliefs that determine how the parameters of homeodynamic control systems are altered. Both programs are ways of representing meaning.

In the case of a computer program, the program is represented physically by a unique location in three-dimensional space on a hard drive. Of course, if one wanted to find out about a computer program, it would make no sense to use micro-analysis (see Chapter 2), i.e., the method of reductionist science, and measure the magnetic locations on the hard drive. Putting the hard drive under a microscope is not the right way to find out what program a computer contains, though it is theoretically possible to investigate the program in terms of a binary sequence of magnetised material. From a practical perspective, if one wished to investigate the program of a computer, the sensible way of doing this is to run the computer and see how it operates.

In the case of a network system, the program is represented by the activation rules of the network. Unlike the program of a computer, these activation rules do not have a unique location in the network. Instead, the activation rules are spread out throughout the network. The consequence is that it is even more difficult to determine the program of a network through micro-analysis than with a sequential processing computer. Thus, it is difficult for micro-analysis to reveal the meaning of the infornet. Meaning such as *the general situation is bad* or *there is threat from a parasite* cannot be easily extracted from the activation rules of a network. The meaning of the infornet is therefore best understood in terms of the functioning of the system, that is, by observing health and disease in relation to external conditions. Even though it is a biological entity, the meaning of the infornet is best understood through its emergent properties, namely how it affects health and disease.

Several authors have noted that connectionism tends towards an *instrumentalist* philosophy of science wherein the theory is evaluated in terms of its ability predict accurately, in contrast to a *realist* philosophy of science wherein the theory is evaluated in terms of how well it describes objective reality (for a discussion see Garcon and Rodriguez, 2009). That is, connectionism, and certainly the type of theory being presented here, does not provide an account of underlying structure. This is a perfectly valid criticism – but it may be that instrumentalism is the best way to understand complex systems. That is, it may be necessary to consider the infornet as a kind of black box, and make inferences and predictions from its inputs and outputs, rather than trying to look inside the black box itself. The relative merits of instrumentalist versus realist philosophies of science are beyond the scope of this book.

Summary of network properties and the infornet and a prediction

A network consists of units that are massively connected to each other by activating or inhibiting causal connections. Networks have fundamentally different properties compared with sequential processing machines such as clocks and jumbo jets. In networks, local error causes gradual rather than catastrophic malfunction (tolerance of local error) because information is distributed rather than localised. Networks resolve into stable states (solutions), referred to as local minima and an overall minimum, and are good at pattern recognition.

Infornet theory proposes that the body functions in part as a network system. The infornet is that part of the body's system that controls the homeodynamic control systems, where these systems control the internal environment and, via behaviour, the external environment. Infornet alarm occurs when the infornet resolves into a new state brought about by the external challenges of somatogenic and psychogenic stress. However, the infornet does not respond only to stress. Chapter 2 provided an account of the let-down response that occurs prior to breastfeeding. The infornet resolves into whatever state is appropriate for dealing with its current inputs.

Networks can learn, where learning takes the form of change in the rules governing the connections between the nodes of the network. Infornet self-organisation occurs when it learns, and the process of infornet learning is slower than the process of infornet resolution. Infornet learning and self-organisation normally lead to more effective self-regulation by altering the parameters of lower-level control systems, parameters such as the reference criterion and the gain. Infornet dysregulation occurs when the learning rules that normally improve self-regulation go wrong and the network learns to become less effective rather than more effective at self-regulation. When the infornet is less effective at self-regulation, the lower-level control systems no longer function effectively because their parameters are set in ways that affect the sequential processing system, thereby leading to specific disease.

A prediction from infornet theory

Control systems are of two kinds, homeostatic and homeodynamic (see above). Many diseases involve an error in the way the control system works. Error in a control system can occur for several reasons. One possible reason is that the reference criterion is set at the wrong level, and this is the case for inflammatory diseases. In the case of inflammatory diseases, the immune reaction varies, but always at too high a level. Another possible reason for error is that there is a break in the control loop, either because of the failure to produce an output or of the failure to detect and input into the comparator. Such errors occur in diabetes. In the case of Type 1 diabetes there is a failure to produce insulin, and in the case of Type 2 diabetes a failure for insulin to have its desired effects of reducing blood glucose. Homeodynamic control systems could, in principle, have error of either kind. By contrast, infornet theory suggests that homeostatic control systems will typically exhibit only the error resulting from a break in the control loop, rather than because the reference criterion is set at the wrong level. The reason for this prediction is as follows. The reference criterion of a homeostatic control loop is relatively fixed, and so events in the infornet, including dysregulation, should have little impact. However, the reference criterion for a homeodynamic loop is constantly being changed by the infornet. Hence infornet dysregulation may lead to errors in that reference criterion. The prediction, therefore, is that pathophysiology involving homeostatic control loops should consist of diseases in which there is a break in the control loop. Thus, the type of error found in Type 1 and Type 2 diabetes is the type of error one would expect with a homeostatic control system. By contrast, the reference criteria and gain of homeodynamic control loops are influenced by the infornet, and such loops should therefore be subject to infornet dysregulation where the reference criterion or gain is at level. Such errors are characteristic of inflammatory diseases. Thus, the conclusion is that diseases involving homeostatic control loops should exhibit a different type of error from those involving homeodynamic control loops.

5 The causes of dysregulation: associative learning, food intolerance and the effects of stress throughout the lifespan

Introduction

This chapter brings together two ideas that were developed in previous chapters. The first of these is that of *dysregulation*. When the infornet is dysregulated it produces an inappropriate output to the inputs from the current situation. The second idea is that of *learning in networks*. There are two types of learning rule that are relevant to the infornet: associative learning and supervised learning. This chapter focuses on the origin of health and disease from the perspective of associative learning. The impact of supervised learning is discussed in the next chapter.

Here is a brief summary of some of the points made in earlier chapters. It is a requirement of living organisms that they constantly self-organise to achieve better self-regulation (see Chapter 1). Self-organisation is achieved through the application of network learning rules (Chapter 4). Under certain circumstances these self-organisational rules lead to poorer self-regulation, i.e., infornet dysregulation (Chapters 2 and 3). Infornet dysregulation can be defined as follows:

Infornet dysregulation occurs due to experiences that affect the learning rules of the infornet. These patterns of living lead to self-organisation change which, under normal circumstances is adaptive, but which due to the particular experience is maladaptive

Associative learning

Associative learning is based on a simple network learning rule. The rule is to strengthen the connection between units of a network that are simultaneously activated (Chapter 4). The consequence of this rule is that events that are contiguous in time tend to become associated. Associative learning is responsible for classical conditioning and immune conditioning (Chapter 2). This chapter shows how two phenomena can arise from associative learning. The first is biologically unexplainable

147

food intolerance. Food intolerance is a problem that is often reported by people who have dysregulatory diseases. The second consists of two linked phenomena: the effect of biological and psychological stress on health, and the delayed effect of fetal and early childhood stress on adult health many years later.

Food intolerance: description of the phenomenon

To the general public, the words food intolerance and food allergy are often used interchangeably. There are, however, several reasons for 'adverse reactions to food' and the words refer to different mechanisms. The mechanism of allergy involves an increase in immunoglobulin E (IgE) (see Chapter 3). The meaning of food intolerance is problematic because not only do doctors disagree about the meaning of this term (Nelson and Ogden, 2008), but also the written literature provides different definitions or interpretations of intolerance (compare, for example Brostoff and Challacombe, 2002 with Zopf et al., 2009). For present purposes, it is necessary only to note that there is a biological interpretation of some non-allergic adverse food reactions whereas there is no biological explanation for others. Lactose intolerance is an example of a non-allergic adverse food reaction that has a biological explanation – i.e., absence of or reduced activity of the enzyme lactase. The prevalence of true food intolerance is 1–2% of the population, that is, where food intolerance can be explained by a biological abnormality (Young et al., 1994). However, about 20–33% of the population, depending on the survey, report that they have food intolerance (Knibb et al., 1999). Thus, the greater proportion of people who report that they have food intolerance have no known biological basis for their symptoms. It is these 'psychological' types of food intolerance that are the focus of concern here, and that are controversial. To the extent that these non-biologically-based food intolerances are troublesome to the patient, they can also be described as medically unexplained symptoms (MUS).

Where conventional medicine provides no clear answer to a health problem, it is not unusual for complementary medicine to provide an alternative. There are several tests for food intolerance offered by complementary practitioners, and these include kinesiology and the VEGA test. In the case of kinesiology, the client is touched with various foods or holds them in one hand while holding out the other arm horizontally. The tester puts pressure downwards on this other arm, and when the client touches food for which he or she is intolerant, the arm becomes weak and can be pressed down. The VEGA test involves measuring electric current at acupuncture points while the person is exposed to various foods, often presented in sealed tubes. Neither test has been shown to be reliable using double-blind techniques (Lewith *et al.*, 2001). However, practitioners and clients provide anecdotal reports of these techniques correctly identifying intolerance, and once the particular food is avoided, then health improves. The issue of food intolerance and improved health by food avoidance cannot be dismissed out of hand.

Those conventional medical practitioners who accept the reality of a non-biologically detectable form of food intolerance recommend that the only reliable method of detection is an exclusion diet (Brostoff and Challacombe, 2002; Brostoff and Gamlin, 1998). When following an exclusion diet, the person starts with a very simple diet that is unlikely to include foods for which they are intolerant and then adds in additional foods one at a time. When a person follows an exclusion diet, the introduction of a food to which they are intolerant produces a noticeable and pronounced increase in symptoms. Foods for which people are commonly intolerant include dairy products, eggs and wheat; however, a person can be intolerant to many more foods.

Food intolerance has several features, which are listed below and which provide evidence that it involves some of the learning process.

- People are almost never intolerant of foods that are seldom eaten. Intolerance develops for commonly eaten foods, and sometimes for foods that are particularly liked by the person concerned and therefore frequently eaten.
- Reactions to food intolerance following ingestion of the food can be slow. The onset of symptoms is often not immediate, unlike the response to an allergen. Appearance of symptoms can take half an hour and sometimes up to 48 hours after the food has been eaten.
- Symptoms include all possible gastric symptoms, but also mouth ulcers, itchy skin, muscle and joint pain, headache, fatigue depression and a general feeling of being 'run down'. Symptoms are highly varied.
- The severity of symptoms increases with the amount of food eaten. The severity of symptoms can also be affected by the current psychological state.
- When food intolerance is detected (e.g., through an exclusion diet) and the particular food avoided, then it is possible to develop intolerance to some other food. If the person then avoids that second food, intolerance may then develop to yet another food – leading to an

increasingly restricted diet. Although development of new intolerances is not inevitable, it is a clinically recognised phenomenon.

- The onset of food intolerance can be gradual and involve a slow deterioration of health, or it can be rapid after a particular event, such as a flu or some physical or psychological trauma.
- If the food to which a person is intolerant is avoided, sometimes intolerance to that food disappears. The timescale of the disappearance of food intolerance varies widely, but it can require abstinence for over a year.
- Food intolerance is sometimes reported by people with chronic specific diseases, as well as functional diseases such as irritable bowel syndrome and chronic fatigue syndrome. Avoidance of the particular food can reduce symptoms.
- People with food intolerance score higher on measures of neuroticism (Knibb et al., 1999) and anxiety and depression (Lillestøl et al., 2010).

Many people with adverse reactions food report that their response reflects a combination of psychological state plus the food that is eaten. This common report leads to the following conclusion:

If adverse food reactions result from an interaction between biological input (i.e., food) and psychological input (i.e., feeling upset) then there must be some common mechanism that links the biological with the psychological.

Box 5.1 Idiosyncratic food problems in gastric disease

As part of a qualitative study into the quality of life of people suffering from gastro-oesophageal reflux disease (GORD, popularly known as heartburn), the author asked about 40 diagnosed sufferers whether particular foods increased symptoms. Apart from foods that commonly upset (fatty and sweet foods), patients would also report idiosyncratic responses to particular foods. One patient could eat soft lettuce, but not the hard cos type of lettuce. One could eat brown bread but not white, another white bread but not brown. Some were upset by red wine but not white. Some could not tolerate tea, or not tolerate chocolate. One could tolerate both tea and chocolate but not both combined. Most people said that they could tolerate a small amount of the 'naughty' foods but not a lot. Most people said that the amount of 'naughty' foods they could tolerate diminished when they were emotionally upset.

Explanation for non-biologically mediated adverse food effects

Several of the clinical features of food intolerance problems suggest that the atypical response to food is due to some process of learning: the gradual acquisition and extinction of the response point to a learning phenomenon. The relationship between neuroticism is significant in that people high in neuroticism (i.e., high in punishment sensitivity) condition faster (i.e., faster associative learning) than those low in neuroticism.

The explanation being proposed here is that food intolerance arises when a food becomes a conditioned stimulus for infornet alarm. The explanation is based on a premise: that the stomach and gut are capable of recognising food, but without that recognition leading to the mental signal commonly described as taste. The mouth and tongue are specialised in the recognition of food and such recognition leads to the mental signal of taste. Taste tells the body what the food consists of. Additionally, according to the present hypothesis, the stomach and gut also have a limited capacity to recognise food but without that recognition necessarily leading to any mental signal. The premise is not unreasonable, as the process of digestion involves the recognition of the stomach and gut contents.

Let us suppose that a person eats sandwiches at work, and that work is stressful. Let us also suppose that the person does not eat bread at other times of the day. According to the principles of associative learning, the one consistent feature of the sandwiches, namely bread, would become associated with the stress of the work. Bread (or more generally wheat or gluten) is therefore associated with the stress of work. Stress at work produces infornet alarm associated with work, so bread is associated with that particular type of infornet alarm. Thus, food intolerance is defined as a particular form of dysregulation of the infornet such that when the body is presented with a particular food, the infornet resolves into the state that is associated with the particular stress, namely a state of alarm associated with the stressor.

One criticism of this theory is that conditioning in humans is not easily achieved. Furthermore, the normal requirement for conditioned responses is that that the conditioned stimulus (the bell in the Pavlovian conditioning experiment or in this case the food) occurs fractionally before and certainly no more than a few seconds before the unconditioned response (the food in the Pavlovian conditioning experiment or in this case the stress). The associations described in the paragraph above are not sufficiently time specific to develop conditioned associations.

The response to this criticism is that there is evidence that conditioning is *adaptively specialised* in that particular patterns of conditioning are associated with particular responses. Controversially, it has been suggested that there are no universal laws of conditioning. The best known example of adaptively specialised conditioning is *taste aversion learning* (Domjan and Wilson, 1972). In the case of taste aversion learning, the animal eats a food, which then makes the animal sick at some later time. The animal will subsequently avoid the food. There are two distinctive features of taste aversion learning. First, it is a very rapid form of learning, and can occur after only one experience of sickness. Second, this learning takes place even though the interval between eating the food and getting sick is several hours. The evolutionary advantage of taste aversion learning is clear. Poisonous and infected foods often create sickness not immediately but after a period of time. Thus, it is biologically useful to be aware of the connection between the eating of food and its consequence at some later time. If the animal can learn to avoid food that creates sickness, it is less likely to eat that food in the future.

Box 5.2 Food aversion learning: a practical example

Black bears were a nuisance at a military camp in North America. They had become habituated to humans and they ate packs of ready-to-eat meals. The camp authorities gave the bears ready-to-eat meals that were laced with thiabendazole, which caused the bears to become ill between 60 and 90 minutes after eating. None of the bears so treated subsequently completely ate a ready-to-eat meal, and interest in the meals declined (Ternent and Garshelis, 1999).

Whether food aversion learning should be considered a special type of conditioning or something completely different is controversial, but this controversy is irrelevant here. Infonet theory shows how associative learning can take place, and as networks can be sensitive to time factors (see Chapter 4), so the delay between conditioned stimulus and unconditioned response is entirely consistent with the rules of network learning.

Food intolerance as a derivative of taste aversion learning

The theory proposed here is that the mechanism underlying food intolerance is related to the mechanism for food aversion learning. That is, the body evolved one mechanism, the mechanism of food aversion learning, and food intolerance is a case where that mechanism is elicited in a different format. In the case of food aversion learning, the animal becomes sick after eating the food, and therefore avoids the food. In the case of food intolerance (according to the theory) the person is stressed by lifestyle factors after eating the food. That is, the person eats the food and then, for one reason or another, experiences stress. Why, then, should a person who experiences stress after eating not simply learn to avoid the food? There are two crucial differences between taste aversion learning and the proposed mechanism for food intolerance. In the case of food aversion, the experience after the food is one of sickness and nausea. This is a specific symptom, that is, a symptom associated with a specific body system, the stomach. Sickness is one of the signals the body uses to alter behaviour: the symptom of sickness inhibits eating. By contrast, in the case of food intolerance, the experience after eating the food is not sickness or nausea. Instead, it is the experience associated with infornet alarm where the alarm is not associated with a particular part of the body but rather an external stressor. Thus, the person with food intolerance has a form of infornet dysregulation in which the body responds to food as though it were an external threat. There is no avoidance of food – just the experience that the situation is now one of threat.

Because they are interconnected (see Chapter 3), the association between the food and the external stress will also elicit other infornet beliefs, for example, those that lead to activation of the inflammatory response system. Thus, the external stressor becomes associated with not only a response specific to that stressor but also other responses that involve external and internal challenge. The particular pattern of symptomatology experienced by the food intolerance sufferer therefore reflects (a) the particular external stressor and (b) the pattern of interconnection between infornet beliefs. Thus, for any such individual, the co-morbidities in terms of symptom clusters provides information about the meaning space in which those infornet beliefs are located.

The association between intolerance and neuroticism provides evidence of a learning phenomenon. Although this association may be the consequence of reporting bias, it is also the case that people who are high in neuroticism are more sensitive to punishment and condition more quickly to negative stimuli. Thus, if intolerance is a learned phenomenon, then conditioning theory would predict an association between neuroticism and intolerance.

Many other clinical features of food intolerance are consistent with this learning interpretation. The strength of response to a conditioned association depends on the strength of the unconditioned stimulus, so the amount of the intolerant food consumed should correlate with symptom strength. Reports that food avoidance can lead to the development of new intolerances is consistent with the substitution of a new conditioned response – and suggests that it is not what the person eats that is important but how the person eats the food. Most importantly, this mechanism provides a rationale for clinical findings that are otherwise difficult to explain. A person who is intolerant of a food does not always respond badly to that food. Response seems to be affected by a combination of dietary factors (eating too much of the food or combinations of 'bad' foods) and psychological factors (being upset). So, whether or not the infornet resolves into a state of alarm on presentation of the food depends not just on the food but on the other inputs to the infornet. The infornet is a system for integrating psychological and biological inputs. Food intolerance is it not a simple mechanical response to the 'bad food', but rather the solution the infornet provides to a particular combination of inputs from internal and external sources. It remains to be seen whether it is possible to extinguish food intolerance through some form of desensitisation technique. Such a technique might involve presenting people with food (in very small doses) to which they are intolerant in relaxing situations and then ensuring that they relax for at least an hour afterwards.

Detecting food intolerance

As stated above, one of the reasons why some conventional doctors dispute the existence of food intolerance is that there is no commonly accepted diagnostic test. According to the present hypothesis, food intolerance is a characteristic of the infornet, and is therefore reflected in small differences in activation patterns rather than gross pathology. It therefore cannot be detected by tests of gross pathology, only by the way the system functions.

Why might complementary tests such as kinesiology and the VEGA test work in clinical practice? There are two possibilities. One is that they don't actually work – that people are intolerant of particular common foods, and that by chance the tester sometimes gets it right. Given that some foods are commonly linked to intolerance, it is not surprising if a therapist sometimes gets it right. In addition, the suggestion that a person is intolerant of a particular food will lead to the expectation that, when avoided, there will be therapeutic benefit. Thus, the benefits of food avoidance may be mediated via a placebo effect.

The other possibility is that people are aware, at some subliminal level, of foods for which they are intolerant. Signals from the stomach and gut about food content do not emerge in a fully conscious form. However, there is some kind of awareness that certain foods have negative effects, so that when a person touches food – or thinks they are eating food – for which they are intolerant, then the person reacts in a way consistent with suggestion, namely a weakening of the arm. Thus, tests of intolerance might not work when practitioner and patient are blind to the procedure, but they might work when the patient is aware of the food being tested. This psychological interpretation of intolerance testing has not been tested, but it presents a possibility that is interesting both for practical and theoretical reasons. It is theoretically possible that the sight of food – or touching food – leads to the fight or flight response or to activation of the inflammatory response system. Thus, if research does establish that eating food to which a person is intolerant leads to particular physiological responses, then it would be of interest to see whether the sight of or intentional contact with the food has a similar effect.

The effect of stress in adults, in the fetus and in childhood

Chronic stress can be defined as repeated episodes of acute stress. Chronic stress, whether mediated via the inflammatory response system or the HPA axis, leads to disease (see Chapters 2 and 3). An activated inflammatory response system predisposes towards specific diseases by enhancing the specific inflammatory response (e.g., Kemeny and Schedlowski, 2007). A suppressed immune response also predisposes to disease: it increases the risk of infection and the reduced activity of natural killer cells predisposes to cancer, as these cells detect and remove pre-cancerous cells. Long-term psychological stress, which is associated with both immune changes, is associated with the development and enhanced progression of a large number of diseases, such as heart disease and cancer.

Chronic stress produces long-term changes in the body, including a slower rate of wound healing (Marucha and Engeland, 2007). In a classic study, Kiecolt-Glaser et al. (1995) showed that wound healing was delayed in carers of Alzheimer's patients whose loved ones had died several years before. This research established that long-term stress has enduring effects, long after the stressor has disappeared. The body exhibits learning on the basis of past experience.

In addition to psychological stress, biological stress in the form of infection can also predispose to disease. Viruses are implicated in the development of many chronic diseases, including the autoimmune destruction of insulin-producing cells in Type 1 diabetes, bronchiolitis in young children and the development of asthma, glandular fever and chronic fatigue syndrome, and viruses are also implicated in the development of certain cancers (e.g., cervical cancer).

The above research focuses on the effect of psychological and biological stress on the development of disease shortly afterwards – i.e., within a few months or years. However, there is another strand of research showing that stress in the fetus or in the early years of life can lead to disease onset decades later. The Barker hypothesis, named after David J. P. Barker (Barker, 1992), proposes that fetal stress 'programmes' the fetus to develop disease in later life. Fetal stress can have a variety of causes, including poor nutrition during pregnancy leading to low-birth-weight babies, as well pre-eclampsia (pregnancy-induced high blood pressure), smoking, alcohol and viral infection of the mother.

Low birth weight is associated with mental health problems (Schlotz and Phillips, 2009), as well as a range of chronic diseases including heart disease, stroke, hypertension and Type 2 diabetes (Barker, 2007; Barker et al., 2009). Low birth weight is associated with attention-deficit/hyperactivity disorder (ADHD) (Mick et al., 2002), and very low birth weight is associated with a range of cognitive and social disadvantages. The incidence of schizophrenia increases if, during the pregnancy, the mother was exposed to psychological stress (particularly in the first trimester), including bereavement, war, famine and natural disasters such as floods and earthquakes (Malaspina et al., 2008). In addition to psychological stress, prenatal exposure to bacterial infection leads to increased incidence of schizophrenia (Sorensen et al., 2009), and infection during the first years of life increases the risk of rheumatoid arthritis (Carlens et al., 2009) developing from age 16 onwards.

Not only is fetal stress associated with increased disease prevalence many years later, but stress in the young child can also have delayed effects on health. Childhood abuse or trauma are associated with many health problems in later life. They are associated with medically unexplained symptoms (Roelofs and Spinhoven, 2007), pseudo-seizures, (i.e., people with epileptic fits but without the normal brain activity of epilepsy) (Fleisher et al., 2002), chronic fatigue syndrome (Heim et al., 2006, 2009; McCauley et al., 1997), arthritis (Fuller-Thomson et al., 2009) and cancer (Fuller-Thomson and Brennenstuhl, 2009). In addition, women who have been abused as children are more likely to abuse drugs and alcohol and have higher scores on measures of depression and anxiety (McCauley et al., 1997).

Insight into the possible reason for these effects is provided by data showing that low birth weight is associated with greater adult hostility and greater adult weight (Räikkönen *et al.*, 2008). Hostility is an emotion that is part of the stability–unstability cluster of mental states. Coupled with data from animal research (Shanks and Lightman, 2001), the conclusion is that the stressed early or prenatal environment leads to long-term changes that include raised levels of system inflammatory mediators, mental health problems and major disease.

The above brief review shows that acute and chronic stressful biological and psychological events have long-term effects that predispose towards disease. That is, the stressor changes something in the body that then predisposes to disease at a later date.

Long-term effects of stress explained by associative learning

This section addresses two linked questions:

1. Why do the physiological changes produced by repeated acute stress persist after the stressor has disappeared?
2. Why is it that the effects of stress in the fetus and early life persist for so long? What exactly is being 'programmed' (to use the term from the Barker hypothesis) by these early events?

The associative learning rule is: strengthen the excitatory connection between the units of a network that are simultaneously activated. This rule explains several psychological phenomena, including classical conditioning (i.e., the basis for immune conditioning) but also *habits*. Habits are formed when a behaviour is repeated many times. Each time the behaviour is repeated, the connection between the network units governing that behaviour are strengthened – because of the associative learning rule. Thus, habits become fixed simply by repetition. Of course, the reason for the behaviour occurring in the first place is often due to the response to some external demand. A man turns left at the end of the drive because of the coffee shop where he buys his coffee. However, after the coffee shop has closed down, the habit of turning left persists and he follows the same route to work. The early educational psychologists stressed the importance of developing good habits – because habits are difficult to change later (James, 1899).

Let us suppose, as suggested in Chapter 2, that psychological or biological challenge leads to infornet alarm – i.e., resolution of the infornet where the outputs are appropriate for the presenting challenge. The infornet alarm can be characterised as an infornet belief appropriate for that situation – for example, an infornet belief that an external threat will lead to external and internal challenge. If the threat is repeated on several occasions, then, owing to the associative learning rule, the connections between the units of the network will become strengthened. The infornet beliefs and the solution that is provided by the infornet tend to become fixed. Thus, the persistence of the infornet alarm (i.e., activation of the inflammatory response system and activation of the HPA axis) can be considered as analogous to the formation of a habit. The infornet develops the habit of treating the situation with the belief that *the general situation is bad*. Thus, the repeated occurrence of stress – in exceptional circumstances, one very crucial stressor – will lead to a long-term change in the infornet. General infornet alarm, i.e., the infornet belief that *the general situation is bad*, can therefore arise as a kind of habit from the repeated exposure to psychological and biological challenge.

Chronic stress (i.e., repeated acute stress) can lead to the infornet developing the belief that *the general situation is bad*. However, it is generally accepted that the young organism is more plastic and more responsive to learning than the older organism. Consider, for example, that is easier to learn a new language when young compared with when adult. There are critical periods of learning, when learning is much more rapid and becomes more established. These critical periods occur when organisms are young. Evidence suggesting that the infornet exhibits age-sensitive learning is found in the observation that personality is more variable when young (Caspi *et al.*, 2005). According to infornet theory, personality, in the form of the Big Two dimensions, is an indicator of the level of general infornet dysregulation. The fact that personality becomes more fixed as life proceeds shows that the stability–unstability beliefs and the plasticity–nonplasticity beliefs become more fixed as life proceeds. In brief, when circumstances are bad, the young organism is particularly prone to developing the beliefs that lock the infornet into a state where *the general situation is bad*.

Although the fetus is located within the mother, it is exposed to biochemicals that provide information about the external world. Both biologically and psychologically mediated maternal stress increases cytokine production (Coussons-Read *et al.*, 2007). So, if the mother is stressed, the fetus is exposed to biochemicals that provide information about the external world, namely that *the general situation is bad*. The finding that low birth weight is associated with greater adult hostility (Räikkönen *et al.*, 2008) is consistent with the idea that fetal stress influences personality. Hostility is a component of the stability–unstability cluster of infornet beliefs, comprising the personality dimensions of neuroticism, conscientiousness and agreeableness. The finding that low birth weight is associated with a greater incidence of ADHD

(Mick *et al.*, 2002) suggests that behaviour activation is increased by an adverse fetal environment, though without an increase in anxiety. The association between low birth weight and adult weight gain (Räikkönen *et al.*, 2008) is consistent with the hypothesis that the infornet forms a belief that food is scarce when inputs provide information that it is scarce. Consequently, the infornet sets up the phenotype so as to maximise the use of food – for example, by storing food in the body in the form of fat.

The infornet beliefs formed when the organism is young will tend to persist, because the infornet is particularly plastic at this stage of development. Habits formed when young tend to persist, and infornet beliefs that *the general situation is bad* tend to persist. However, there is a second reason why infornet beliefs associated with general dysregulation tend to persist. Chapter 2 outlined the way in which dysregulated people create dysregulated lives which then create further dysregulation. This spiral of poor health can now be extended to the maternal environment and the raising of children. Dysregulated people live dysregulated lives and because of this produce children who are themselves dysregulated. Well-regulated people live well-regulated lives and produce well-regulated children. The social implications of this mechanism are obvious.

The infornet responds to the early environment, including the prenatal environment, so that the infornet's beliefs are informed by that early environment. That is, the infornet forms a set of persisting beliefs that are consistent with the early environment.

Thus, when the mother is experiencing a challenging environment, the child develops in a way which is consistent with that environment being challenging. Of course, the challenges that mothers experience in the twenty-first century are very different from the challenges they experienced 100,000 years ago. Consequently, the response of the developing child to the modern mother's environment is no longer adaptive – the modern environment differs from the environment in which humans evolved.

As an illustration, children born with low birth weight tend to be heavier when older. Food sensitivity is adaptive in an environment where there is little food. If the adults experience a scarcity of food, then it is adaptive for their children to be particularly motivated to search for food. However, food sensitivity in an environment where food is easily available is not adaptive. Obesity is caused by eating too much. Obese people have higher levels of hunger motivation, and are more sensitive to food cues in their environment (Schachter, 1971). In addition, stressed environments require greater activity. The greater activity found in children with ADHD might be adaptive in an environment where physical activity is needed, but not in an environment where children spend much of their time in front of a television.

Although early programming of infornet beliefs is important, infornet learning never ceases. Hence, changes to infornet beliefs can occur throughout the lifespan. A good deal of research shows that enrichment of the environment can mitigate the negative effects of low birth weight, in particular tactile stimulation and massage (Vickers *et al.*, 2004; Weiss *et al.*, 2004). By contrast, stress at later stages of life also changes infornet beliefs towards *the general situation is bad*. For example, long-term care of a loved one with Alzheimer's disease leads to changes that are then characteristic of long-term stress, namely general infornet dysregulation.

The association rule can also explain changes in reinforcement sensitivity and hence changes in personality over time. The rule of increasing connections between simultaneously activated units leads to the following prediction: repeated punishment will lead to increases in punishment sensitivity, and repeated rewards will lead to increases in reward sensitivity. More generally, negative events, irrespective of whether they are psychological or physiological, will push the infornet towards a state characterised in Chapter 3 as general infornet dysregulation – a state where the infornet responds to both the external and internal environments as though threats are imminent.

Predictions from infornet theory

The effects of an adverse fetal environment have been studied with regard to mental health and disease. However, infornet theory suggests that early experiences should also affect personality. Low birth weight should be associated with unstability (Big Two theory) and the relevant three dimensions from the five-factor theory (neuroticism, agreeableness, conscientiousness). However, it is unclear what the relationship will be between birth weight and plasticity (Big Two theory) and the relevant two dimensions of the five-factor theory (extraversion and openness). The relationship between birth weight and personality provides a novel way of investigating infornet structure, but also answers a simple empirical question: to what extent is personality laid down as part of the prenatal experience?

According to the hypothesis of internal–external balance, acute stress varies in the extent to which it signals external versus internal challenge, where the former biases the response towards HPA activation and the latter towards activation of the inflammatory response system. As chronic stress is commonly an aggregation over time of a particular type of acute stress, this leads to the expectation that the particular pattern of immune change associated with a particular type of long-term stress should be the same as the response to the equivalent short-term stress. Emotions vary in the extent to which they relate to internal–external balance (i.e., fear indicating the risk of internal challenge, but not anger; Moons *et al.*, 2010). One would predict, therefore, that if trait-like emotions are classified in terms of the extent to which they signal external versus internal stress, then this classification should map onto the relative activation of the inflammatory response system and HPA axis (see prediction at the end of Chapter 3).

Summary

Pavlov discovered a form of learning now called classical conditioning about 100 years ago (Pavlov, 1897). Some 60 years ago, Hebb suggested that classical conditioning as well as habit formation could be explained by a neural network that obeyed a simple rule, later known as the association or Hebbian rule (Hebb, 1949). Immune conditioning was discovered by Ader and Cohen about 30 years ago (Ader and Cohen, 1975). The existence of immune conditioning suggests that networks are not only neural but also extend throughout the body (Hyland, 2002).

First, this chapter has shown how non-biologically mediated reports of food intolerance can be explained in terms of associative learning that involves the gut and brain. Food intolerance that appears to have no biological cause can be explained as a form of conditioning between stressful events and particular foods. Second, this chapter shows how the persistence of the inflammatory response and the persistence of HPA axis activation following fetal stress, stress in childhood and chronic stress in adult life can be explained in terms of the association or Hebbian rule. The persistence of the inflammatory response occurs for the same reason that ordinary behavioural habits persist – the infornet is modified by the repetition of patterns of activation. The long-term effects of stress occur because the infornet develops the habit of reacting to repeated stressful situations.

6 The causes of dysregulation: supervised learning, repetitive strain injury, attention-deficit/hyperactivity disorder, chronic fatigue syndrome and depression

Introduction

Supervised learning is a type of network learning and therefore a type of network learning rule that can lead either to dysregulation or to well-regulation of the infonet. Supervised learning works according to the back-propagation rule, where the connections between nodes in the network are strengthened or weakened (starting from the output and working backwards) according to feedback provided by the supervisor. In the biological network system that is the infonet, the genome is the supervisor. Supervised learning therefore provides a mechanism that links the genome (the repository of long-term information acquired from the parents) with the infonet (the repository of information acquired during the organism's life).

In network systems, complexity arises out of simplicity. According to infonet theory, there is one simple rule that normally leads to more effective self-regulation but under certain circumstances leads to dysregulation. This rule is called the compensation rule. This chapter shows how this single rule leads, under different circumstances, to the prediction of repetitive strain injury, attention-deficit/hyperactivity disorder, chronic fatigue syndrome, depression and asthma

The compensation rule

Let us start from the assumption, described in Chapter 4, that the genome specifies patterns and the body learns to achieve those patterns. As before, we suppose that the ideal pattern is that A leads to B. But now let us suppose that the pattern of A leads to B is interrupted or attenuated by the effect of C (Figure 6.1).

Figure 6.1 shows that two units in the infonet (or two patterns in the infonet) cause each other, but the causation is inhibited by the input from another unit (or pattern). The result is that the effect of A on B is weakened. Now suppose that the inhibitory effect of C is a regular occurrence. If the A → B pattern is specified by the genome (i.e., a

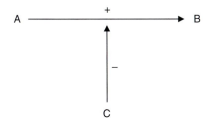

Figure 6.1 The compensation rule. The infornet compensates for
any deviation to the pattern specified by the genome. The specified
pattern is A leads to B – and compensation occurs when this
expected pattern is interrupted by C

supervisor), the infornet should learn to compensate for this interruption.
This compensation could take one of two forms. Either there will be an
increase in the activity of A (i.e., activation of units A are increased) or
there will be an increased sensitivity of B to the input B receives from
A. Either way, the infornet will learn to compensate for the inhibiting
effects of C by learning to compensate for this inhibition.

The compensation rule states that the infornet finds ways of compensating for
anything that makes it deviate from the pattern specified by the supervising
genome.

The following example will illustrate the compensation rule in a
familiar mechanical system, that of domestic central heating. Imagine
a heated room where the temperature is thermostatically controlled,
and where there is a central heating boiler that heats a radiator placed
in a room. The room has a thermostatic switch so the temperature is
kept at a constant temperature (the more observant reader will realise
that the temperature will oscillate slightly, but that detail is irrelevant
here). Now let us suppose that someone leaves the window of the room
open. The temperature of the room drops, the thermostat switches the
boiler on and the boiler heats the radiator. However, although the boiler
is on full, the room remains cold because the window has been left
open. The supervisor – the person in the room – gets cold. The supervisor (who hasn't noticed the open window) notices that the feedback
system is no longer working and therefore decides to make a change.
Two changes are possible. One is to turn the thermostat up (i.e., change
the reference criterion). The other is to get a new boiler with a greater
thermal output and add another radiator (i.e., increase the gain). If the
window is sufficiently large, neither strategy will work. This example
illustrates a general point – self-organisational change does not always
work if the external conditions are wrong.

If the above example is applied to the infornet, the compensation rule shows that the infornet finds ways of compensating for anything that makes it deviate from the genetically determined pattern.

The application of the compensation rule to the body means that if a pattern is not achieved, the body will do *something* to try and achieve it. That something may not always be an effective solution. The *something* also means that different infornets may find different ways of dealing with the problem – the *something* is not fixed.

The following sections show how diseases can arise from the compensation rule. In each case there is a brief description of the disease followed by an explanation using infornet theory.

Repetitive strain injury: a disease of specific dysregulation

Repetitive strain injury is a disease that involves a specific form of infornet dysregulation but without a specific pathology – i.e., without specific disease. Repetitive strain injury can therefore be classified as one of the dysregulatory diseases.

Repetitive strain injury: description of the disease

If a person over uses or strains a joint in the body, the result is pain. Typically the pain is associated with inflammation and swelling. Inflammation is the body's normal response to tissue damage, and inflammation leads to swelling of soft tissue. The pain that is associated with inflammation and the overt signs of pathophysiology are well understood. In addition to analgesics, these are treated by anti-inflammatory medication and other techniques to reduce the inflammation (aspirin is an analgesic with anti-inflammatory properties). A sensible person responds to the sensation of pain and therefore does not over use or strain the joint.

However, pain sometimes occurs without any biological marker of pathology. Repetitive strain injury is one example of non-specific pain syndrome where the pain persists in the absence of any signs of inflammation or damage.

The existence of repetitive strain injury has been controversial – a court decision in the UK in 1993 decided that it did not exist as a separate medical condition. A survey published in 1995 found that 50% of doctors did not think that repetitive strain injury was a genuine disease (Diwaker and Stothard, 1993). Assuming that this condition exists, at least in some form, repetitive strain injury occurs in response to repetitive action, particularly with keyboard users. The rate of onset appears to be very gradual – taking place slowly over months. Stress appears to be a factor in that stress produces enhanced muscle activity: additional neuroticism is also related to the risk of repetitive strain injury (Rietveld *et al.*, 2007). There are a variety of unproven remedies for repetitive strain injury, but the most effective is rest. In this case, rest means no longer engaging in the specific movement that causes the pain. Following rest, the pain normally subsides. However, the pain can recur once the repetitive action is resumed. Sometimes the only way of avoiding the pain is a change of job.

Repetitive strain injury: explanation

Let us suppose that a person engages in a repetitive action, for example key strokes on a computer keyboard. If that action is very repetitive, the action will create a sense of discomfort – and may even create inflammation and pain. Pain is a signal from the body. It is a signal with a purpose. The pattern defined by the genome is that pain should lead to cessation of the activity causing the pain. The 'right pattern' is to respond to pain by stopping the particular action.

However, a person can ignore the discomfort or pain of repetitive action because they are focused on what they are doing. People using a computer are so focused on what they are writing that their fingers and shoulders are not salient parts of their environment. What happens if the sensation of pain is ignored? The application of the compensation rule means either that the signal of pain or discomfort is enhanced, or that the sensitivity to the signal is enhanced. Either way, ignoring the signal leads to the perception of pain being increased. If the person routinely ignores the signals of pain – for example, continuing with the action after inflammation has started, then self-organizational change is likely. The infornet sets itself to a new point that prevents the action from happening; see Figure 6.2.

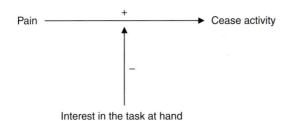

Figure 6.2 The compensation rule and the development of repetitive strain injury

Box 6.1 Headache and analgesics

One additional prediction from the above explanation of repetitive strain injury is that analgesics for signals of pain might increase the pain signal. In fact, analgesic overuse is a well-known cause of chronic headaches (Grosset and Grosset, 2004).

Learned associations become extinguished over time, and if the person ceases the activity, then the enhanced pain gradually reduces. However, repetition of the action can lead to a recurrence of an enhanced pain response.

The infornet interpretation of repetitive pain injury is that it is the result of an ignored pain signal. The clinical features of repetitive pain injury – that the only effective treatment is rest – are consistent with this interpretation. Additionally, the recurrence of repetitive strain injury is consistent with its hypothesised cause, namely ignored signals of discomfort, being repeated in a similar situation.

Repetitive strain injury provides signals of pain that prevent the person from engaging in *specific* actions. Recall, from Chapter 2, that pain was presented as a signal from a specific part of the body. Repetitive strain injury is a specific form of infornet dysregulation – specific in the sense that it occurs in relation only to infornet beliefs about the joint that is associated with pain. That is, the infornet beliefs associated with repetitive strain injury tend to occupy a small local space in the infornet's meaning space. Of course, it is inevitable that infornet beliefs tend to influence each other, so beliefs relating to lack of unstability will tend be connected, albeit weakly, to those of specific pain. People high in punishment sensitivity are particularly sensitive to negative events. The theory therefore predicts that neuroticism should correlate with the incidence of repetitive strain injury – which is in fact the case. However, repetitive strain injury should be considered a specific infornet dysregulation rather than one that is linked with the more widespread features of general dysregulation.

Attention-deficit/hyperactivity disorder (ADHD): a disease involving the behaviour activation system

Attention-deficit/hyperactivity disorder (ADHD): description of the disease

Although the characteristics of attention-deficit/hyperactivity disorder (ADHD) have been recorded for over a century, the present terminology has been adopted only since about 1980. Earlier labels of the disease include minimal brain damage syndrome, hyperkinetic reaction of childhood and attention-deficit disorder, with the labels reflecting changing beliefs about underlying aetiology (Rowland *et al.*, 2002). The disease occurs frequently though not exclusively in children (reviews suggest a prevalence of between 2% and 18%), and the characteristics of the disease and its diagnosis include poor attention span and impulsive and hyperactive behaviour (Rowland *et al.*, 2002). The DSM-IV criteria include, under the former category, 'is often easily distracted by extraneous stimuli' and, under the latter category, 'often fidgets with hands or feet or squirms in seat' and 'is often "on the go" or often acts as if "driven by a motor"'. Subtypes of ADHD can be identified in terms of whether they are primarily that of poor attention, hyperactivity or both. In addition, ADHD can be characterised as either with or without anxiety. Abnormality of HPA axis function is observed in some children with ADHD, but this abnormality is not diagnostic of the disease, even though it appears that different types of ADHD tend to have different patterns of abnormality (van West *et al.*, 2009). HPA abnormalities are common in several diseases, including chronic fatigue syndrome (see next section).

Treatment for ADHD is almost exclusively based on medication, of which Ritalin (methylphenidate) is the best known. The largest study to date is the NIMH Multimodal Treatment Study of ADHD (MTA), which compared three management strategies for children with ADHD: medication, behavioural management and a combination of medication and behavioural management. All three management strategies were compared with routine community care. After 14 months of treatment, the results showed that most effective treatments were medication alone and medication with behavioural management, which were significantly better than behavioural management or routine community care. For most outcomes, medication alone was equivalent to that when combined with behavioural management. The conclusion from this very large study was that medication was effective but that behavioural management was ineffective except for a subcategory of children where anxiety was a pronounced co-morbidity (i.e., an anxiety subtype of ADHD), where there was a slight benefit on some outcome measures (Jensen *et al.*, 1999a, 1999b). These results established the use of medication as the only effective treatment for ADHD. It therefore came as a surprise that a 3-year follow-up of the MTA study failed to find significant differences between the treatment modalities, though with the repeat of the slight advantage of behavioural management for children with high levels of anxiety (Jensen *et al.*, 2007). This follow-up therefore poses a challenge for any understanding of ADHD, its aetiology and management. Not only was medication shown to be ineffective over the long term but, in addition, the 3-year follow-up showed that medication led to long-term retardation of growth (Swanson *et al.*, 2007).

ADHD explained

The behaviour activation system, when activated, leads to an increase in behaviour and, to the extent that there is an infornet belief of external danger, to an increase in anxiety. Let us suppose that there is a genetically determined dispositional level of behavioural activation. Such a supposition is consistent with the data relating to the activitystat hypothesis (Wilkin *et al.*, 2006). The activitystat hypothesis is that children's activity levels are biologically determined rather than being determined by opportunities in the environment. Thus, let us suppose that the level of the activitystat is specified by the genome. Such a hypothesis is consistent with data showing, for example, that for children who have exercise as part of their school day their level of required activity is met at school so that they engage in less activity at home. By contrast, for those who do not have exercise as part of their school day, the level of required activity is not met and so they engage in more activity at home (Wilkin *et al.*, 2006).

Now let us suppose that the normal feedback system that leads to the correct activity fails. The child could fail to achieve the desired level of activity for several reasons. A rather unusual one is that the child is physically restrained from engaging in activity. Another is that the child is placed in an addictive situation that leads to the child inhibiting their own activity level; for example, the child watches television. The relationship between these events is shown in Figure 6.3.

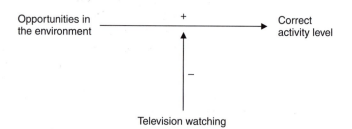

Figure 6.3 The compensation rule and attention-deficit/hyperactivity disorder

According to the compensation rule, there should be potentiation of the value of the correct activity level. That is, because the child is no longer achieving the level of activity proposed by the infornet, the infornet will increase the reference criterion of the activitystat so that the desired level is achieved. The description of children with ADHD as 'often acts as if "driven by a motor"' sums up the overactivity resulting from the potentiated activitystat.

Several features of ADHD are consistent with the infornet interpretation of an enhanced behaviour activation system. First, ADHD sometimes occurs with and sometimes without anxiety. Increased behavioural activity and anxiety are both outputs from the behaviour activation system. Second, watching television is associated with poorer attention. Several cross-sectional studies have shown the length of reported television watching to be associated with attention deficits, but these studies can be criticised on the basis that the direction of causality is uncertain (it may be that children with poor attention span watch more television). However, there has a been a series of longitudinal studies that have confirmed that television watching at an earlier age leads to attentional problems at a later age (Christakis *et al.*, 2004; Landhuis *et al.*, 2007; Miller *et al.* 2007), though there is limited research failing to support this relationship (Stevens and Mulsow, 2006). In addition, television watching is associated with greater hostility (Manganello and Taylor, 2009) and psychological stress (Hamer *et al.*, 2009), suggesting that this activity might also increase general infornet dysregulation.

Finally, the research showing the comparative ineffectiveness of psychological therapy – except where there is anxiety and then only to a small degree – is consistent with ADHD being a disease that is specific to the behaviour activation system. The finding that drug therapy is effective in the short term but not in the long term is consistent with a system where the activitystat is being changed by a higher-level system according to circumstances, rather than one where the activitystat is broken. The specific intervention of the drug is overridden by the self-organising infornet – just as a person can learn to compensate for a car that tends to steer to one side.

Infornet theory suggests the following remedy for ADHD: more opportunities for physical activity, less television watching and greater tolerance of children who are likely to fidget and let their attention wander if their natural tendency to engage in intrinsically motivated activity is inhibited by the demands of parents and teachers. These suggestions are not new (DeGrandpre, 1999). Indeed, research reviewed later in this chapter shows that persistence with non-rewarding goals is associated with depression, so the inattention of ADHD children may be an adaptive response to a maladaptive situation.

General infornet dysregulation: diseases involving the behavioural inhibition system

The behavioural inhibition system, when activated, leads to two highly correlated types of mental output: fatigue and depression. This section focuses on fatigue; the related mechanism leading to depression will be discussed towards the end of this section. Chronic fatigue is a disease whose underlying mechanisms are closely linked to that of repetitive strain injury – except that all behaviour is being inhibited rather than a specific behaviour.

Chronic fatigue syndrome: description of the disease

Just as the nomenclature of ADHD has changed over time, so have the labels used for the disease now known as 'chronic fatigue syndrome'. Names have included neurasthenia, yuppie flu, myalgic encephalo-myelitis or ME, chronic fatigue syndrome or CFS, chronic fatigue immune dysregulation syndrome or CFIDS, and post-infectious fatigue syndrome (PIFS). The word 'burnout' is sometimes used for fatigue associated with excessive activity (including sport- and work-related activity). In the UK the term ME/CFS is now often used as a compromise between patient groups and clinicians. Patient groups point out that the disease is more than fatigue so can be hos-tile to the term CFS. For simplicity, the term CFS will be used here. Although doctors now accept the reality of CFS, there was a time when the existence of the disease was disputed (Wessely *et al.*, 1998). Repetitive strain injury and CFS are both diseases whose existence has been disputed.

For most diseases there are internationally agreed diagnostic criteria. Not so for CFS, for which there are UK (or Oxford) criteria (Sharpe *et al.*, 1991), US criteria (Fakuda *et al.*, 1994) and Canadian criteria (Carruthers *et al.*, 2003) as well as paediatric-specific criteria (Jason *et al.*, 2006; Sharpe *et al.*, 1991). Other countries typically use one of these criteria; for example, the Australians use the Canadian criteria. All three criteria are based on patient symptoms as no physiological diagnostic test has been discovered. Despite years of searching for a biological basis of CFS, this Holy Grail of CFS researchers has not been found: there is as yet no consistent biological marker of CFS. Additionally, fatigue is a common problem of specific disease (see Chapter 2), and levels of

Table 6.1 *Some symptoms that can occur in patients with CFS*

Fatigue
Post-exertion malaise and/or fatigue
Sleep disturbance, waking up feeling unrefreshed, vivid dreams
Pain in muscles or joints, sometimes moving round the body, headaches
Muscle weakness
Impairment of memory and concentration (a feeling of a mental fog), muscle weakness, hypersensitivity to noise
Nausea, light headedness, dizziness, urinary frequency
Irritable bowel syndrome, development of new food intolerances
Difficulty keeping the right temperature (often feeling very cold), sweating, loss of appetite, loss of tolerance to stress
Tender lymph nodes, recurrent sore throats or flu-like symptoms
Just simply feeling 'ill'
Depression

fatigue in CFS patients and patients with fatigue and specific disease are comparable (Jones *et al.*, 2009).

The British, American and Canadian diagnostic criteria all agree on one thing: to be classified as having CFS the patient must have experienced unexplained fatigue for 6 months or more. Where the criteria differ is in terms of other symptoms that need to be satisfied in order to acquire the diagnosis of CFS. These other symptoms include immune manifestations (such as sore throat, flu-like symptoms and sore lymph nodes), autonomic symptoms (such as light-headedness and nausea) and psychological symptoms (such as impaired concentration). A list of common symptoms is shown in Table 6.1. Because the symptoms vary between patients, the US and Canadian criteria require that a certain number out of a list of possible symptoms need to be present. The UK criteria simply state that other symptoms may be present. The precise details of the differences in criteria are not relevant here, other than noting that different criteria produce different estimates of prevalence – varying between 0.03% and 1% (Bates *et al.*, 1993). Self-report of persistent severe fatigue has been found to be 4% among adolescents (Viner *et al.*, 2008).

Why are there no universally agreed criteria for CFS? The reason is in part that the mechanisms underlying CFS are controversial and the different criteria are influenced by belief in these different mechanisms. The three most commonly cited mechanisms are:

1. *Cognitive dysfunction.* CFS is caused by over-attention to symptoms and false cognitions about illness that lead to illness behaviours (i.e., inactivity) and hence a general deterioration of physical fitness. CFS

patients interpret symptoms in a negative, catastrophising way that, coupled with a hard-driving, perfectionist personality, leads to CFS being an incorrect learned response to bodily signals (Fry and Martin, 1996; Lawrie et al., 1997; Wessely et al., 1998). The person becomes ill because they think they are ill. Supporters of the cognitive explanation cite that pre-existing depression is a predictor of CFS, and is often co-morbid with CFS. Moreover, muscle weakness is perceived rather than being due to any real physiological weakness.

2. *Immune dysfunction.* CFS is caused by immune disturbance caused by infection (Landay et al., 1991; Lloyd et al., 1994; Tirelli et al., 1994; VollmerConna et al., 1998). The immune system is unable to deal effectively with infection and there are raised levels of pro-inflammatory cytokines. The presence of painful lymph nodes and flu-like symptoms indicates that the problem is immunological. In addition, CFS is characterised by chronically raised markers of natural immunity (Raison et al., 2009), though this characteristic is not unique to CFS.

3. *Neurological dysfunction.* CFS is caused by neurological abnormalities that involve blunted response of the hypothalamic–pituitary–adrenal (HPA) axis to external events and abnormalities of the autonomic nervous system (Demitrack and Crofford, 1998; Demitrack *et al.*, 1991; Pagani and Lucini, 1999; Scott *et al.* 1998). CFS sufferers can experience a range of neurological disturbances, including poor temperature regulation and dizziness. HPA axis abnormalities are not unique to CFS.

Each of these mechanisms explains some of the symptoms and data relating to CFS. There are immune irregularities in many patients, as well as evidence of neurological disturbances and psychological symptoms. However, none of these irregularities is consistent across all patients, and none of the biological abnormalities, where they occur, is sufficiently great to explain the extreme fatigue experienced by CFS patients. Additionally, several predictors of CFS have been identified (see Table 6.2), many of which can be linked with one of the three mechanisms above. However, none of the three mechanisms is consistent with all the predictors. In sum, none of these three kinds of explanation or mechanisms explains all of the symptoms and data.

Because the different explanations of CFS are often treated as competitors with each other, it is easy to overlook an important finding about the biological basis of CFS, which is that:

CFS is characterised by small abnormalities in the neurological, immune and endocrine systems, but these abnormalities are inconsistent across patients.

Table 6.2 *Several predictors of CFS onset have been found, though not necessarily consistently across studies*

Virus or infection
Atopy or allergy proneness
Reported stress
Ethnicity
Female
Perfectionism
High or low levels of exercise
Persistence in exercise despite fatigue
Anxiety
Depression
High night-life activity for adolescent girls
Higher social class
Poor sleep quality
Childhood trauma

References for predictors of CFS: Bakker *et al.* (2009); Deary and Chalder, 2010; Dinos *et al.*(2009); Harvey *et al.*, (2008); Heim *et al.* (2009); Luyten *et al.* (2006); Magnusson *et al.* (1996); Rimes *et al.* (2007); Tashman *et al.* (2010); ter Wolbeek *et al.* (2008); Viner and Hotopf (2004); Viner *et al.* (2008).

The combination of raised pro-inflammatory cytokines and HPA axis dysregulation plus negative affect is by no means unique to CFS (Raison *et al.*, 2009). This particular combination was reviewed in Chapters 2 and 3 as indicators of chronic stress. Thus, CFS has the characteristics of a stress-related disease. The challenge in explaining CFS, therefore, is not to explain this characteristic pattern of chronic stress (i.e., the changes in HPA axis, immune system and mood) but rather why this common response to chronic stress is associated with disabling fatigue. According to infornet theory, fatigue is a signal of behavioural inhibition. Hence the explanation of CFS must explain (a) why this severe behavioural inhibition occurs and (b) why the behavioural inhibition takes the form of fatigue rather than depression.

One of the reasons CFS poses such a problem in terms of conceptual understanding – and hence diagnosis and treatment – is that there is no consistent presentation of the disease. Although clinicians recognise a commonality in the way the disease presents, the exact way it presents is highly variable. Sometimes there is a rapid onset, sometimes the onset is slow. Sometimes the onset is associated with an infection, sometimes it is not. Some have lowered levels of cortisol or a blunted cortisol response, others do not. Sometimes it is associated with depression, sometimes not. Some patients experience repeated viral infections, others do not. Some experience irritable bowel syndrome and food intolerance, others do not. Some experience dizziness, some nausea, and so on. The list of symptoms is highly variable between patients. CFS is a highly variable disease, leading some to question whether it is indeed a single disease or rather a label given to a family of diseases. Finally, and most crucially, outcome varies between patients. Research papers tend to give a rather pessimistic view of outcome as patients in these research cohorts tend to be tertiary referrals – i.e., the most challenging cases – for example, where the disease persists for 10 years or more. However, many people with CFS get better by themselves without any form of therapy. One study of a cohort of patients receiving CBT found that 23% were fully recovered after treatment, but those with co-morbidities were less likely to recover (Knoop et al., 2007). The timescale for recovery is generally slow, often taking something in the region of 6 years. The reason for good or poor outcome is not well understood, but the belief that CFS is caused by a virus infection in contrast to psychological factors appears to be associated with poor outcome – possibly because such a belief does not lead to lifestyle modification (Huibers et al., 2004). Despite a belief by some patient groups that a virus is the cause of CFS, and that it is therefore treatable as a 'physical disease' with a 'physical treatment', this belief is not matched by data (van Kuppeveld et al., 2010) – despite a concerted research effort to find a specific CFS-causing virus.

A commonly asked question about CFS is whether it is a psychological or physical disease. As shown in Chapter 2, the distinction between psychological and physical disease is based on a false assumption, so this question needs to be reformulated. There is an important binary divide between, on the one hand, the cognitive explanation and on the other the immune or neurological explanations. Many patients vigorously reject the cognitive explanation – i.e., they insist it is not 'just' a psychological disease and that they are not simply misperceiving their symptoms. Several factors appear to contradict such claims from patients. No consistent biological marker of CFS has been found – which leads some to conclude (on the basis of the incorrect assumption of dualism) that it must be mental. No biochemical has been found to help or treat CFS. From time to time promising biochemicals have been found (including vitamin and mineral supplements), but after careful investigation none has been shown to be better than placebo. Perhaps most importantly, there is evidence that the physical fatigue experienced is not due to weakness of the muscle itself but is neurological in origin. The muscles of CFS patients are not actually weak – they just appear to the patient to be weak. Finally, psychological factors (e.g., poor mental state prior to the disease) predict disease onset, and failure to recognise psychological factors in the cause of CFS leads to poor recovery (Huibers *et al.*, 2004).

The cognitive explanation is that CFS arises from over-attention to symptoms that lead to illness beliefs, which then lead to a marked reduction in activity. The reduction in activity then leads to general deterioration of health. The cure for CFS, according to this explanation, is to change cognitions so that there is less attention to symptoms leading to a gradual increase in exercise tolerance. In support of the cognitive explanation, two treatments have been shown to be effect: cognitive behaviour therapy, or CBT (which changes the patient's cognitions) (Deale *et al.*, 1997) and graded exercise therapy (which increases exercise tolerance) (Fulcher and White, 1997). The NICE (National Institute for Clinical Excellence) guidelines recommend both CBT and graded exercise therapy.

There are several problems with the cognitive explanation, and not just that it has difficulty explaining the frequent but inconsistent biological abnormalities. First, although CBT and graded exercise therapy have both been shown to be helpful in clinical trials, the effect sizes compared with alternative therapies or natural disease progression are small (Deale *et al.*, 1997; Fulcher and White, 1997; Prins *et al.*, 2001; Sharpe, 1997). Second, the fact that a therapy is effective does *not* mean that the therapy is working according to the mechanism believed by the therapists who devise the therapy. (Chapter 8 will expand on the difference between what therapists think is happening and what appears to be happening.) CFS is also improved to an equal degree by counselling – which purports to work according to a different mechanism from CBT (Ridsdale *et al.*, 2001). It is worth bearing in mind, when considering the value of various therapies, that there are few therapies that have not, at one time or other, been reported by patients to be helpful. Patients often try one or more types of complementary medicine: some people find some of them helpful but there is no one complementary therapy that has consistently good results. Finally, informal patient report does not support CBT and exercise therapy as universally beneficial forms of therapy, and they certainly do not cure all patients (Knoop *et al.*, 2007). On the contrary, many patients find these therapies unhelpful. Patients and their support groups find that the most effective therapy is *pacing* (Shepherd, 2001). Pacing involves not overdoing things, as over-exertion leads to deterioration the following day (called post-exertion malaise). According to the recommendations of pacing, the patient should try to keep doing things, but only do 50% of what they feel they are able to do.

Box 6.2 Post-exertion malaise: implications for theory

If a well person goes for a run or engages in vigorous activity with which they are unfamiliar, they normally feel tired afterwards. They feel tired immediately afterwards. The following day they may feel a bit stiff but the fatigue has worn off. In the case of CFS, however, the pattern is different. The person who engages in 'too much' activity does not feel tired immediately afterwards. Indeed, that person often feels that he or she is 'doing very well'. However, the following day, they feel completely and utterly exhausted. The time scales of fatigue in healthy people and those with CFS are different. Furthermore, CFS patients have to deal with a different concept – that of 'too much'.

The question of 'too much' activity is problematic as it appears to be less than that which many patients accept. Because CFS patients tend to overdo things (anecdotally, CFS patients are people who tend to be very active prior to illness), there is a tendency for them to oscillate between doing too much, feeling exhausted with post-exertion malaise, gradually getting better again, then doing too much again.

Post-exertion malaise has a time delay that is not found in normal fatigue. Any acceptable explanation for CFS must be able to explain this time delay. However, it would seem at the very least that fatigue in CFS is not simply 'depletion' of an energy store or battery. If CFS were simply lack of energy, then the fatigue should be immediate. The fact that it takes a day for the post-exertion malaise to set in suggests that a much slower process is involved. Self-organisational change is a slow process: infornet alarm occurs rapidly, whereas infornet dysregulation occurs more slowly. The phenomenon of post-exertion delay suggests a different analogy than the depletion of energy. Instead, the analogy is one of 'putting the brakes on'.

The aim of pacing is to avoid post-exertion malaise. Post-exertion malaise is a feature of CFS that has important theoretical implications (Box 6.2).

The infornet explanation of CFS and depression: introduction

Any complete explanation of CFS must do five things. First, it must provide some rationale for the different mechanisms and different diagnostic criteria that exist. It is reasonable to assume that although researchers and clinicians can have different and sometimes strongly held views, they are all intelligent people and their theories must have some substance, even if any one theory fails to tell the whole story. Second, the explanation must fit with the patient's experience, and, crucially, it must explain pacing. Pacing has received comparatively little formal evaluation, and has been investigated only recently in clinical trials. The lack of evidence regarding pacing may be because it is a patient-derived idea, and it is only in the last few years that patient input has played an important role in the research process. Third, the explanation must be able to provide a rationale for the variability of the way CFS manifests. Any explanation must explain why such variability is found in this challenging disease. Fourth, the explanation must be consistent with the predictors of CFS onset, in particular the evidence both from patient report and epidemiology that an overactive lifestyle predicts onset. Finally, the explanation must explain why stress, which is a predictor of both depression and fatigue, sometimes leads to depression and sometimes leads to fatigue.

Although many researchers support any one of the three major explanations of CFS cited above, a small minority have favoured an interactive perspective. For example, Jason *et al.* (1999) suggest that psychoneuroimmunology might provide a useful insight. A network theory was presented about 10 years ago (Hyland, 2001b, 2002). However, this explanation proposed just one route into CFS and does not provide an explanation for the benefit of pacing, or the variability of the disease. The theory presented here is a development of that earlier network theory, the main difference being the proposal that infornet dysregulation comes about in several different ways; that is, *there are several routes into CFS*. The following sections show three ways in which lifestyle can lead to behavioural inhibition, followed by a section that explores the different mechanisms of CFS and depression. The theory should be evaluated in terms of the five criteria listed above.

Three ways in which the compensation rule leads to
long-term activation of the behavioural inhibition system

The behavioural inhibition system is the body's own way of stopping it from engaging in behaviour. It is an active process of putting on the brakes rather than running out of energy. There are three possible mechanisms that lead to long-term activation of the behavioural inhibition system and hence to the symptoms of CFS:

1. combination of infection and stress;
2. ignoring reactive inhibition: the effect of repetitive exploratory activity; and
3. goal-based explanations of negative affect: self-actualisation, learned helplessness, goal conflict and interruption of goal pursuit.

Combination of infection and stress

Research into the antecedents of CFS shows that there are two patterns of onset: rapid onset and gradual onset. Rapid onset is often found after an infection, typically but not invariably a virus infection. The common experience in these cases is that the infection creates a sense of fatigue – which is to be expected as the virus will stimulate the inflammatory response system. However, the fatigue then persists after the virus infection is resolved. Thus, one route into CFS appears to involve an infectious agent. Additionally, atopy or allergy proneness is also a predictor of CFS onset, though some studies fail to find an association (Viner and Hotopf, 2004)

The body is designed to hunt mammoths and fight infection but not do both at the same time. Imagine that you are a member of a palaeolithic group some 50,000 years ago; you are suffering from a cold and so resting in the camp. Suddenly, a sabre-toothed tiger attacks. It is maladaptive to say to the tiger 'Sorry I have a cold, I can't fight you today'. It is not surprising that the body has evolved ways of over-riding those sensations of fatigue when external circumstances demand, namely when there is external challenge. Sabre-toothed tigers exist only in museums and few people hunt mammoths these days, but there are a variety of modern equivalents of external threat that carry the risk of internal challenge (i.e., infection) and external challenge (i.e., the need for enhanced physical activity).

Let us suppose that that the threat is an examination and a person is revising for that examination. If the person develops flu while revising for exams, the body's normal response to the flu virus is to create fatigue, plus other symptoms such as achy limbs. It is, however, possible to override the sensations of fatigue. The fear of exams can lead students to revise even though they feel tired. In more general terms, environmental challenges tend to inhibit feelings of fatigue by creating a state of arousal. Activation of the arousal system in the brain is known to be brought about by novel, non-rewarding (frustrating) or punishing stimuli (Gray, 1987). Thus, the threat of failure in an examination is often enough to ensure that a person continues working when unwell, even though they might otherwise rest.

Let us suppose that the person's ability to suppress the feelings of fatigue, either through cognitive control or through the use of a variety of stimulants (e.g., caffeine) is a consistent behavioural pattern. That is, the fatigue-producing effect of infection is constantly inhibited. This pattern of behaviour is represented in Figure 6.4.

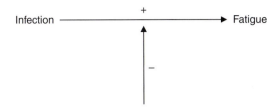

Figure 6.4 The compensation rule and the development of fatigue through ignored signals arising from infection

An application of the compensation rule leads to the prediction that there will be an increase of the fatigue symptom for any given level of infection. Eventually, the fatigue signal will be set at such a level that fatigue is experienced even in the absence of infection. Consequently, even though the infornet is set to produce low levels of pro-inflammatory cytokines, there will still be the sensation of fatigue. The infornet finds a way of stopping the person ignoring the signals of fatigue. The way this is done is to make the fatigue signals more salient. The infornet has corrected what it perceived as inappropriate behaviour.

Several predisposing variables of CFS are consistent with the above explanation. Infection and atopy are predisposing factors because they create the immune response (i.e., increase in pro-inflammatory cytokines and Substance P) that normally creates fatigue but which in this circumstance is ignored. Indeed, onset of CFS is often associated with a combination of stress and infection, for example, the student preparing for an examination, a busy mother trying to balance life and home activities. Harvey *et al.* (2008) suggest that:

Continuing to be active despite increasing fatigue may be a crucial step in the development of CFS. (p. 488)

Why should someone ignore their signals of fatigue? Perfectionism is a personality characteristic that predicts the onset of CFS (Luyten *et al.*, 2006). The perfectionist is more likely to work when ill, and so the perfectionist is more likely to override feelings of fatigue when ill.

There is some evidence that so-called maladaptive perfectionism is more harmful to health in general than adaptive perfectionism (Bieling *et al.*, 2004), though there are exceptions to this finding (Saboonchi and Lundh, 2003). Comparison of different types of perfectionism has not yet been carried out for CFS. There are several ways of defining adaptive versus maladaptive perfectionism, but all definitions of maladaptive perfectionism tend to align themselves with the dimension of neuroticism versus stability. Neuroticism is a predictor of poor health for a variety of reasons (see Chapter 3). As stress mediates the effect of perfectionism on fatigue (Tashman *et al.*, 2010), any difference between these two forms of perfectionism may simply be that maladaptive perfectionism is associated with greater stress, and therefore leads to worse health outcomes.

Some CFS patients experience repeated bouts of infection. If CFS arises through this route of internal plus external challenge, then there is the following implication for therapy. It is that patients should reduce activities that involve external challenge during the bouts of infection, and increase activity when the infection is absent. Thus, rather than maintain a constant level of activity, patients should listen to their bodies and try to regain activity, but vary the amount of activity in a way that reflects immunological changes that are taking place as part of the oscillatory pattern of the disease.

Ignoring reactive inhibition: the effect of repetitive exploratory activity

The second route into CFS does not necessarily involve infection. After all, infection is not a necessary condition for developing CFS.

Reactive inhibition refers to the inhibition of behaviour by the act of carrying out that behaviour (see Chapter 2). If rats are consistently reinforced for turning right in a maze, they will nevertheless sometimes turn left. The level of reactive inhibition depends on the time interval between the preceding behaviour and the number of times that behaviour has been carried out, and it is independent of reinforcement. From an evolutionary point of view, it makes sense for exploratory behaviours to be more prone to reactive inhibition rather than non-exploratory behaviours, as the function of evolutionary advantage of reactive inhibition is that it increases exploratory activity. The concept of reactive inhibition is linked to Eysenck's theory of the biological basis of personality – extraverts develop reactive inhibition more quickly and dissipate it more slowly, and people may become more sensitive to the effects of reactive inhibition as they age (Eysenck, 1967).

Repeated actions activate the behavioural inhibition system. There are two possible reasons why a person might ignore this effect of reactive inhibition. First, the person overrides the inhibition through cognitive control. For example, suppose someone is engaged in a repetitive task that over time becomes boring but is paid to do the boring task and so persists in doing it. Application of the compensation rule means that

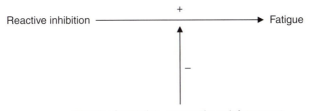

Figure 6.5 The compensation rule and the development of fatigue through ignored reactive inhibition

the signal associated with behavioural inhibition – i.e., fatigue – should increase. It should increase because the infornet is compensating for the failure to follow one of its rules, namely to stop working when it gives the signal of boredom.

A second reason to persist in a repetitive task is that the person finds the task intrinsically interesting, and that intrinsic interest and motivation overrides any sense of boredom. Note that research has shown that the development of reactive inhibition is independent of reinforcement. Finding a task enjoyable does not stop the development of reactive inhibition. If reactive inhibition is ignored, the prediction from the compensation rule is that the signal of fatigue should be increased (see Figure 6.5). People high in perfectionism are more likely to persist in a task, owing to either cognitive control or intrinsic interest. Thus, the perfectionist living style predicts fatigue, both for this mechanism of ignored reactive inhibition and for the mechanism of combined external and internal challenge.

If a person's lifestyle is characterised by suppression of reactive inhibition, there will be a gradual increase in behavioural inhibition and signals of fatigue. Those signals of fatigue are inhibited, either by cognitive control or by interest, that is, by a mechanism that can override the sensation of fatigue. In some cases of CFS there is a gradual increase in fatigue, and fatigue onset is gradual. Such cases can be explained by the gradual accumulation of undissipated reactive inhibition. Other cases of CFS involve a sudden increase in fatigue, often brought about by infection. In such cases of sudden fatigue an event such as infection – or even having time to rest – will lead to a catastrophic failure of the override mechanism. Because the suppression of fatigue is no longer present, there is an acute increase in fatigue symptoms. Thus, if ignored reactive inhibition is the cause of fatigue then the infection is not itself a contributor to the dysregulation, but merely creates a change in lifestyle that allows the underlying dysregulation to become apparent.

Infornet beliefs tend to be interconnected, so the fatigue associated with the activity to which there is over-persistence generalises to other activities. All activities become inhibited owing to ignored reactive inhibition to just the one activity. CFS is a form of general behavioural inhibition, in comparison with repetitive strain injury where only one type of behaviour is inhibited. According to this mechanism, CFS is a kind of distributed repetitive strain injury where all behaviour is being inhibited.

Several features of CFS support this mechanism of ignored reactive inhibition. Perfectionists are more likely to ignore symptoms of fatigue, and the finding that perfectionism is a predictor of CFS (Luyten *et al.*, 2006) is therefore consistent with both this and the above mechanism of ignored infection. Additionally, for both gradual and rapid onset of CFS, there are reports of awareness of disturbance before the onset of the disease. CFS patients will report increased symptoms before the rapid onset of CFS. Thus, although the disease may appear to strike suddenly, people are aware of something beginning to go wrong beforehand (Ray *et al.*, 1998). In addition, some patients assert that CFS strikes them down just when things were going really well – for example, a new job or new activity that was really exciting and fulfilling. The fact that a job is exciting and fulfilling does not prevent the build-up of reactive inhibition. Indeed, one would predict that it is precisely those people who find their work interesting and exciting who are most likely to develop CFS – because they put all their energy into their work and 'forget to turn left in the maze'. 'Overdoing things' is a common description of events prior to developing CFS (Ray *et al.*, 1998). Finally, once CFS has developed, the disease is often characterised by the patient doing very little, feeling better and then doing too much, leading to a cycle of over- and underactivity. Such behaviour can be expressed as that shown in Figure 6.6.

Most importantly, the reactive inhibition explanation for the development of CFS provides a theoretical rationale for the effectiveness of pacing. If a person does too much exercise – or too much of any activity – then this will contribute to further reactive inhibition and so lead to a deterioration of the patient (i.e., post-exercise malaise). Too little activity, however, leads to a general deterioration of health – as suggested by the cognitive explanation. Thus, the patient has to engage in limited activity while reactive inhibition dissipates – which it does by itself, given the right circumstances, slowly, over time. Because of the increased sensitivity to reactive inhibition, the patient has a small window of 'the right level' of activity. Too little activity and health deteriorates due to inaction. Too much activity and reactive inhibition is elicited.

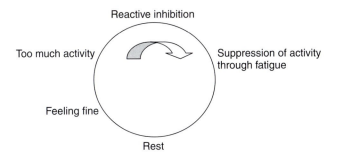

Figure 6.6 The cycle of over-doing things, having to rest and then over-doing things again

There is an important theoretical implication from the observation of pacing and post-exertion malaise. Recovery from CFS is very gradual and is best measured in terms of months or half-yearly intervals. However, post-exertion malaise appears after about 24 hours. Thus, it would seem that the rate of self-organisational change within the infornet varies. There would seem to be a general, long-term form of dysregulation, but also a shorter, more easily changed form of dysregulation. A way of thinking about this is that general dysregulation occurs at different levels with a more fundamental and less fundamental kind, each varying in terms of rate of change. The more fundamental form of dysregulation may make the infornet more sensitive to reactive inhibition – i.e., a person is reactive inhibition sensitised. Hence, the severe CFS patient can tolerate only very short periods of activity without creating reactive inhibition again. As excess activity leads to enhanced reactive inhibition, and excess activity occurs only too easily (particularly with perfectionists), there is a constant recurrence of reactive inhibition and dysregulation at the less fundamental level, so that the more fundamental level of general dysregulation persists.

Various predictions follow from the hypothesis that CFS is the result of ignored reactive inhibition. The first is that it is not so much the repetition of a single type of behaviour that is important but rather the failure to engage in other behaviours. If a person is always turning right in a maze, this will not be a problem so long as they occasionally turn left. But if the lifestyle always requires right turning without any left turning, then there is going to be a problem. The implication of the above is that variety of activity is important to the development of behavioural inhibition and hence to health. There is an old adage, variety is the spice of life.

The therapeutic implication of the reactive inhibition route into CFS is that it takes time for reactive inhibition to dissipate. Recovery is slow, as indeed clinical experience shows. However, dissipation of reactive inhibition will not take place if the person persists in their original activity, and recovery will be helped if a person engages in novel activities. The person needs to 'turn left in the maze'. Because CFS is such a debilitating illness, there is a tendency for lifestyle to become restricted and monotonous, and this restriction will not assist recovery. Reactive disinhibition therapy is based on the idea of doing small amounts of enjoyable activity – but always paying attention to the principle of pacing. The patient should do small amounts of activity so as not to initiate further reactive inhibition. This small amount of activity should differ from those that led to disease – for example, someone who, prior to the disease, spent much time revising an academic subject, should do something completely different such as music or art. Reactive disinhibition therapy is an untested idea – but it is consistent with reports from patients that pacing is the most effective therapeutic intervention, and that some significant life event can sometimes trigger the start of recovery.

> *Goal-based explanations of negative affect:*
> *self-actualisation, learned helplessness, goal conflict and*
> *interruption of goal pursuit*

Many theories and a wealth of empirical data show that goal satisfaction tends to happiness whereas failure to satisfy goals leads to unhappiness (Carver and Scheier, 1990, 1998; Deci and Ryan, 1985, 2000; Maslow, 1954; Sheldon and Elliot, 1999). The link between failure to satisfy goals and poor mood is one of the most well-established findings in psychology, and, in one form or another, is a common explanation for depression (Hyland, 1987). According to infornet theory, depression is a signal of behavioural inhibition. Why then, is it adaptive to become depressed when goals are not satisfied? The answer comes from observation about the way people respond to failed goals. One possible response is to disengage from the failed goal and do something else. If you cannot catch a mammoth, you might be able to catch a cow. A second possible response is to persist in the previously failed goal – to keep trying to catch the mammoth even though you have failed to do so. Evidently, it makes sense to disengage from unattainable goals after a period of failure. Research shows that failure to disengage from unattainable goals is characteristic of people who develop depression (Carver and Scheier, 1998), because people who fail to disengage tend to experience more failure. In terms of the present theory, signals of behavioural inhibition (such as depression and fatigue) have an evolutionary advantage in that they signal a person to stop trying to achieve the unattainable and engage in a different pattern of living.

Few people get upset if the supermarket does not stock their favourite cereal; but most get upset if they are sacked from their job. As a general rule, the satisfaction of or failure to satisfy *self-defining* goals has the most impact on a person's state of mind. Maslow's (1954) theory of self-actualisation suggests that people differ in the goals that provide them with self-actualisation, that is, they differ in their self-defining goals. Maslow suggests that this difference between people is to some extent biologically determined, and that there is a unique form of self-actualisation for each person. Each person has a unique 'true self' that they seek when they self-actualise.

Although a person's goals are to some extent unique, goal-based theories of personality suggest that goals (i.e., human motivation) can be represented on two dimensions. There is considerable agreement over one of these dimensions, the dimension of self-transcendence and spirituality versus the self-enhancement and/or hedonism (Grouzet *et al.*, 2005; Schwartz and Boehnke, 2004).

Let us suppose that a person's goals are such that the person is high on self-transcendence and spirituality. Moreover, let us suppose that this person is unable to satisfy this goal in everyday life for a variety of reasons, which might include a mixture of work, child care, cultural influences and so on. Thus, our hypothetical person is unable to self-actualise. Failure to self-actualise is associated with poorer mental health (Maslow, 1954), so the person in our example will experience poor mental health, namely depression and anxiety.

Maslow's theory of self-actualisation is concerned with goals that are unique to each individual. However, there are also goals that all people seek. People are motivated to control their environment, and failure to do so leads to learned helplessness – a state associated with sad affect, motivational deficit and cognitive decline. The need for control and learned helplessness theory can now be seen as part of a more general theory, that of self-determination theory. According to self-determination theory there are three basic goals, competence, autonomy and relatedness, which when satisfied lead to better health and well-being (Deci and Ryan, 1985; Ryan and Deci, 2000). The need for control is encompassed by the needs for competence and autonomy. The need for relatedness is a different need that expresses a basic human need for people to need to relate to others. Failure to satisfy these common basic human needs leads to poorer mental health, including the depressive symptoms that are associated with learned helplessness.

If failure to satisfy a goal leads to negative affect, then a special case arises when a person has multiple goals and can only satisfy one of them. More generally, if a person experiences goal conflict there will be a tendency for goals to remain unsatisfied. A more common occurrence will be where goal activity is interrupted on a regular basis, as each interruption is a signal that the goal has not been satisfied. The Zeigarnik effect refers to the tendency of people to remember incomplete unsatisfied tasks more than those that have been completed. The Zeigarnik effect illustrates that failure to achieve a task is not simply ignored by the infornet, but leads to a trace indicating that the goal is unfulfilled. A possible extrapolation from the Zeigarnik effect is that constant interruptions shift the infornet towards behavioural inhibition and dysregulation, because the infornet recognises that the lifestyle is not satisfying goals.

In sum, if people are unable to satisfy their goals, whether they are unique self-actualising goals or goals that all people share, or if the satisfaction of these goals is constantly interrupted, then this lifestyle pattern is inconsistent with that specified by the genome. The infornet therefore self-organises so as to alter that lifestyle pattern, doing so by increasing the level of behavioural inhibition.

The therapeutic implication of the goal-based route into CFS is that the patient needs to make a change to lifestyle so that these goal failures no longer occur. For example, some people get better only when they retire from their work and do something completely different. Of course, some people make the change from an unsatisfying life to a more satisfying one without the need to experience CFS!

Box 6.3 A hypothetical case of how lifestyle can contribute to CFS through several routes

Joe is a perfectionist. His self-actualisation requires satisfaction of a need for spirituality. However, he works as a market trader in a bank, and he is not a member of any religion as he believes religions to be irrational. He is sympathetic to New Age ideas but doesn't have time for this kind of thing. Joe is good market trader and his work is exciting, keeping him trading for long hours doing a repetitive but interesting job. However, there are many interruptions as Joe has to deal with queries from junior staff. Joe cannot afford to get ill, because he will miss out on market trades, so he comes into work even when suffering from flu. According to the theory being advanced, Joe is a prime case for developing CFS.

*Explanations why some people develop fatigue and
others depression*

The above three mechanisms (combination of infection and activity, ignored reactive inhibition and failure to satisfy goals) all lead to the prediction of behavioural inhibition. Behavioural inhibition has as its outputs the mental states of depression and fatigue. Why, then, despite the correlation between fatigue and depression, do some people develop a disease that comes to be called depression (i.e., primarily depression symptoms) whereas others develop a disease called CFS (i.e., primarily fatigue symptoms)? There are two differences between CFS and depression that must be accounted for. The first is that there are different psychological states, namely fatigue and depression. The second is that CFS is characterised by a much greater pattern of co-morbidity. Although people with depression are more likely to have minor health complaints, the occurrence and severity of co-morbidity, and specifically somatic medically unexplained symptoms is much higher in the case of CFS.

A central idea of infornet theory is that mental states such as depression and fatigue are outputs from the infornet and therefore reflect infornet beliefs about the state of the organism. Depression and fatigue are subjectively different. It seems plausible that two different signals evolved because they represent different infornet beliefs and that they have different functions.

Chapter 3 suggested that the infornet beliefs were organised hierarchically. The infornet belief associated with behavioural inhibition was characterised as *whatever I am doing is the wrong thing and I need to do something else*. Thus, both fatigue and depression indicate that the infornet is trying to generate a different kind of behaviour from that currently being acted out, but according to the theory, each of these mental states must be associated with a different, more specific belief.

A possible hypothesis is as follows:

- In the case of depression, the goals are incorrect and the individual needs to pursue other goals. Thus, the infornet belief associated with depression is *I am trying to achieve the wrong sort of goals*.
- In the case of fatigue, the goals that are being sought are consistent with the genome, but the pattern of seeking those goals is incorrect. The infornet belief associated with fatigue is *I am achieving goals using the wrong behavioural patterns*.

The evidence for the above hypothesis comes in part from a consideration of the predisposing variables mechanisms described above.

The first two mechanisms (combination of stress and infection, and ignoring reactive inhibition) are mechanisms where the pattern of seeking the goal is incorrect, and it is these two mechanisms whose predisposing variables have been particularly linked with CFS. By contrast, there is little theory or evidence linking depression with prior infection. However, depression has been linked to failure to satisfy goals, and the goal-based explanations for depression have been, traditionally, linked to depression rather than fatigue. Thus, depression would seem to be a more fundamental signal that the pattern of living is incorrect, in terms of the goals sought by a person, but fatigue is a signal that whether or not those goals are correct, the way in which those goals are being sought is inconsistent with the genome.

The co-morbidity of depression and fatigue – which is a feature of some patients diagnosed with CFS and some diagnosed with depression – occurs because the infornet beliefs leading to depression and fatigue are themselves related, as they are both part of the higher-level belief: *whatever I am doing is the wrong thing and I need to do something else*. Thus, depression and fatigue are both result of applying the compensation rule to patterns of living, but different patterns tend to produce one symptom or the other.

In sum, according to the hypothesis presented here, depression is caused by lifestyles in which *what* you are doing is fundamentally wrong in the sense that the person's important goals are not being satisfied. Fatigue is caused by lifestyles in which the *way* that you are seeking goals is wrong: it is not the goal-seeking behaviour that is at fault but rather the timing or amount of that behaviour. According to this rationale, depression is a signal from the infornet that shows that the lifestyle pattern is fundamentally wrong in terms of the goals that are being sought. Fatigue is a signal from the infornet that although the goals are OK, it is time to stop engaging in that particular behaviour.

Readers familiar with the treatment of depression will point out that whereas there is no agreed pathophysiology for CFS, there is an agreed pathophysiology for depression, namely low levels of serotonin in the brain. Moreover, antidepressant medication – which increases levels of serotonin – is a widely used treatment in clinical practice. Data showing that this interpretation of depression is likely to be invalid will be presented in the next chapter. Suffice it to say that, despite being the basis for a multi-billion-pound industry, the serotoninergic hypothesis is widely disputed (Lacasse and Leo, 2005). Furthermore, *at least* 80% of the effectiveness of antidepressant medication is placebo-mediated (Kirsch, 2009). Although there is a widespread belief that depression, unlike CFS, fits the pattern of disease specificity, this belief may be more optimistic than true.

The above provides an explanation for why the primary symptom for some patients is depression whereas for others it is fatigue. However, CFS and depression differ not only in terms of the psychological states experienced. Both patients can exhibit immune and HPA axis abnormalities, but the CFS patients tend to have far more co-morbidity, where this co-morbidity includes immune symptoms (e.g., painful lymph nodes, repeated infections) and autonomic symptoms (e.g., dizziness, nausea).

The hypothesis of internal–external balance proposes that the infornet estimates the extent to which an external challenge requires vigorous physical activity versus defence against infection. The former tends to increase activity in the HPA axis; the latter tends to increase activity of the inflammatory response system. The particular pattern of immune and neuroendocrine changes that occurs reflects the infornet's judgement of the internal–external balance. In Chapter 5, I showed how the associative learning rule explains how repeated acute stress leads to the psychological and physiological pattern associated with chronic stress, where the internal–external balance of the acute stress is reflected in the long-term changes. One apparent difference between chronic depression and CFS is that the latter would appear to be a consequence of stress that reflects more strongly the internal in the internal–external balance, whereas depression reflects primarily a response only to external challenge. Thus, although stress is a predictor of both depression and fatigue, infornet theory predicts that different kinds of stress predict either form of symptom – or as is often the case, the particular strength of two symptoms, depression and fatigue, which co-occur.

In what way do external events trigger an infornet belief that there is likely to be an internal challenge *as well as* an external challenge? The example given in earlier chapters of hunting mammoths does not apply today – and not only because of a lack of suitable mammoths. Research by Moons *et al.* (2010) suggests that fear produces a greater immunological response than anger, whereas anger produces greater HPA axis activation. The most likely modern psychological equivalent of mammoth hunting is an activity in which there is a problem that needs to be solved and where, if it goes unsolved, the problem has negative consequences. Thus, threats where there is the repeated possibility of failure (i.e., generating fear) would seem to be those that are particularly prone to creating immunological disturbance. Of course, stress can be created in many ways. Constant interruption of work activities is stressful. Having targets that cannot be achieved is stressful. Being angry is stressful. Being told you have failed is stressful. Repetitive, boring activity is stressful. Having to work when you are feeling ill is stressful. Failing to do the kind of work you would like to do is stressful. Infornet theory suggests that although stress leads to both depression and fatigue, different types of stress tend to lead to one type of symptom or the other, and that depression is linked with failure to achieve important or self-defining goals. Of course, any form of stress will tend to create general infornet dysregulation – i.e., the infornet belief that *the general situation is bad* and so any form of stress will predispose towards both depression and fatigue.

In summary, this section has examined why some people experience depression and others fatigue. According to infornet theory,

- CFS is a disease that is associated with (a) an overload of challenging tasks that have potential for failure, and where failure has important consequences and (b) particular patterns of living that that involve combination of stress and infection and ignored reactive inhibition; and
- depression is a disease in which the person is living a life that is inconsistent with the pattern specified by the genome, and in particular is not achieving those goals or becoming the person that is specified in the genome.

Stress is an aversive state that can lead to both depression and fatigue, but there should be a relationship between the type of stress and type of symptom. Using the hypothesis of internal–external balance, external and internal challenges are more likely to lead to fatigue and external challenges to depression. The question of whether stress leads to fatigue or depression therefore depends on the way the infornet judges external stressors in terms of internal–external balance.

As a final comparison, it is worth reflecting on the patient's perspective. Many CFS patients reject the idea that their illness is 'only psychological'. Nevertheless, research shows that patients who accept that their disease has a psychological component recover faster (Huibers, *et al.*, 2004). Both positions have validity. Compared with depression, CFS has more somatic symptoms and therefore does not 'feel' like a mental illness. However, at the same time, because the disease is one of infornet dysregulation, vitamin supplementation and other forms of biological intervention may be less effective than lifestyle management.

*Biological contributors to general behavioural inhibition
and infornet dysregulation*

The infornet and specific systems have a bidirectional causal relation-ship. Although biological inputs may be more important for specific diseases, it is also possible that biological factors may also contribute to general infornet dysregulation. Possible biological factors are mentioned briefly in this section: our understanding is limited.

Several biological inputs affect the immune system. Diets containing fish oils or those high in omega-3 fatty acids have an anti-inflammatory effect on the immune system, and it is possible that they also contrib-ute to reduced infornet dysregulation. By contrast, omega-6 fatty acids (which tend to be high in the Western diet) are pro-inflammatory. In addition, vegetables contain antioxidants, and these may protect against disease. Exercise inhibits the production of one of the pro-inflammatory cytokines, TNF-α (Starkie *et al.*, 2003), and brown fat (which tends to be deposited round the waist) is pro-inflammatory and associated with allergic disease (de Winter-de Groot, 2004), as well as with depression (Rivenes *et al.*, 2009). Thus, a biologically healthy lifestyle would be expected to reduce the inflammatory response, and vice versa.

There are considerable data on diet and disease. The risk of heart disease is reduced by green leafy vegetables (Hung *et al.*, 2004). Green leafy vegetables and other 'healthy' foods are associated with lowered levels of biochemical markers of systemic inflammation (Esmaillzadeh *et al.*, 2007). An association between leafy vegetables and lowered risk for some (but not all) cancers is found in case–control studies (Steinmetz and Potter, 1991). However, a very large prospective study of diet and cancer onset showed only a weak relationship (only a 3% increase) between low vegetable consumption and risk of cancer onset, and that only in women (Boffetta *et al.*, 2010). However, interpretation of epi-demiological data should be treated with caution as diet is not randomly allocated. People choose their diets, and it may be that unhealthy people (i.e., people with a dysregulated infornet) eat more 'unhealthy' food.

If food has an effect on the infornet, then diet should alter psychological state. However, low intake of omega-3 fatty acids has not been found in depressed patients (Hakkarainen *et al.*, 2004), nor has use of omega-supplements been found effective in treating depres-sion (Appleton *et al.*, 2006). By contrast, exercise has been found to be effective for depression (Stathopoulou *et al.*, 2006) – although it remains unclear whether the mechanism is mediated through a biological or psychological route (Crum and Langer, 2007).

If healthy food (e.g., leafy vegetables and omega-3) is associated with reduced incidence of cancer and heart disease, but is unrelated to psychological state, then the conclusion would be that food acts as a precursor of diseases, but independently of the infornet. This possibility is consistent with the finding that biological treatments, including diet, have not been shown to be efficacious for CFS – though they may be effective for psychological reasons. With current data it would seem premature to come to any conclusion about the effects of biological inputs, such as food, on infornet dysregulation.

Summary and predictions

This chapter has presented four diseases that can be explained by infornet theory.

Repetitive strain injury (RSI) is disease in which the compensation rule leads to a specific dysregulation where pain signals are enhanced, but only in relation to a specific part of the body.

Attention-deficit/hyperactivity disorder (ADHD) is a disease in which the compensation rule leads to an increase in behaviour activation, which is manifested as a raised activitystat, with or without anxiety.

Chronic fatigue syndrome (CFS) is a disease in which the compensation rule leads to an increase in behavioural inhibition. The inhibition involves the way in which goal-oriented behaviour is achieved and leads to the primary symptom of fatigue.

Depression is a disease in which the compensation rule leads to an increase in behavioural inhibition. The inhibition involves the type of goals, and this leads to the primary symptom of depression.

All four diseases are dysregulatory diseases in that there is no consistent and unique pathophysiology associated with them. However, there is a unique and specific biological basis to each of these different diseases – but this unique biological basis is to be found in the activation rules of the infornet, not in gross pathology. All diseases are biological – there are no free-floating minds to get ill – but the biological basis of these dysregulatory diseases differs from the more familiar diseases that have a specific pathophysiology. Consistent with the idea of lop-sided specificity described in Chapter 2, depression and fatigue have different types of activation pattern (i.e., encoded information) within the infornet, but there may not be a unique activation pattern for either depression or fatigue.

All four diseases are caused by lifestyle. That they are caused by lifestyle leads to the following prediction. Any successful management strategy for these dysregulatory diseases will be based on lifestyle management. At best only short-term gains are achieved through medication. In the case of RSI the management strategy is avoidance of the action that causes pain. In the case of ADHD, a lifestyle requiring greater activity – as well as tolerance for inattention motivated by lack of interest – should lead the infornet to gradually self-heal. There are several possible lifestyle modifications associated with CFS, including pacing (and the theoretical development of pacing, namely reactive disinhibition therapy), and avoidance of activity and stress when experiencing infection. Management of depression is best achieved through lifestyle activities that increase the attainment of important, self-defining goals. An important point to emphasise is that for all dysregulatory diseases the system is not locked into the disease, as might occur with specific diseases (see the next chapter). Given the assumption that the body is naturally self-healing, which it must be in order to function (see Chapter 1), then all dysregulatory diseases should in principle be improved by the correct lifestyle. Getting that correct lifestyle is far from easy, however, but seeking and taking part in therapy is one form of lifestyle change that will be discussed in later chapters.

7   The causes of dysregulation: asthma and precursors to specific disease

Repetitive strain injury, attention-deficit/hyperactivity disorder and CFS are all dysregulatory diseases in that they do not have a specific pathology. They are not diseases of the specific system. The aim of this section is to show how infornet dysregulation can be a precursor to a specific disease. Asthma is used as an illustration of a specific disease, in part because the specific pathology of asthma is well understood.

Asthma: description of the disease

Asthma is a disease of variable airways obstruction that is caused by an allergic response. Although asthma sufferers can differ in the type of allergic response, the cause of the allergic response can be interpreted as an upgrading of a response that is designed to manage parasite infection (see Chapter 3). The person with asthma has an overactive inflammatory response in the airways, and this overactive response leads to inflammation of the bronchioles (the airways of the lung) causing swelling, the release of mucus and increased irritability, and hence constriction of the bronchiole muscles. The overall result is reduced airflow through the bronchioles, leading to shortness of breath, wheeze, cough and other symptoms associated with asthma. The inflammation of asthma is controlled by anti-inflammatory drugs, but asthma is not cured, in part because there is no understanding of the origin of that inflammatory response. Asthma can develop in childhood or in later life. Several factors are known to be associated with asthma onset.

- Asthma belongs to a group of diseases called *atopic* disease, which includes eczema and rhinitis. There are predisposing atopy genes (that predispose towards all three diseases) as well as asthma-specific genes. However, genes explain relatively little of the variance of asthma prevalence. The majority of people with atopy and asthma genes do not develop the disease. Nor is the presence of these genes a necessary condition for the development of the disease.

- Dirty air, including cigarette smoke, pollution from cars, pollution from factories and dander produced by pets. There is well-established evidenced that exposing children to air pollutants is associated with asthma, in particular that caused by traffic pollution (Duhme *et al.*, 1996). Some air pollutants are particularly prone to cause asthma, particularly those in industrial environments.
- If a child is brought up in a highly hygienic environment this can lead to a lack of variety of gut microbes, which is then associated with atopy (Bjorksten, 1999). There are now several different types of evidence supporting the *hygiene hypothesis*, including the findings that rural children brought up on farms tend to have less asthma than rural children not brought up on farms, and that the childhood practice of washing hands before meals leads to less gastric upset but more asthma.
- Infection is a common cause of asthma onset in young children, and in particular viral infection of the lungs (bronchiolitis) is known to precede asthma in some cases (Sugars *et al.*, 2000).
- Obesity leads to a greater prevalence of asthma onset in children (Gilliland *et al.*, 2003) and persistence of asthma in children (Guerra *et al.*, 2004), and is also a predictor of adult asthma onset (Camargo *et al.*, 1999).
- Intake of leafy vegetables is associated with a lower risk of developing asthma (Romieu *et al.*, 2006).
- First-born children are more likely to develop asthma, probably because later siblings are exposed to more infection (Cullinan *et al.*, 2003).
- Stress is associated with asthma onset. The stress experienced by caregivers at 2–3 months after birth predicts asthma during the first 14 months of the child's life (Wright *et al.*, 2002). Women who experience domestic violence are more likely to develop asthma (Subramanian *et al.*, 2007). The positive relationship between moving house and asthma onset (Hughes and Baumer, 1995) is probably due to stress: moving house is just one of several possible stresses associated with the home (Sandel and Wright, 2006).

On the basis of current understanding of asthma, explanations of asthma onset can be divided into three types of mechanism:

1. the *non-specific inflammatory response*, that is increase in systemic inflammation that tends to increase the specific inflammatory response (i.e., the kind of inflammatory response associated with general infornet dysregulation);

2. the *atopic inflammatory response*, that is, the mechanism predisposing towards allergy of several kinds (i.e., asthma, eczema and rhinitis); and

3. the *asthma-specific inflammatory response*, that is, the mechanism predisposing towards asthma.

If the infornet were to act as a precursor to the development of asthma, then it should act as a precursor to each of the above three mechanisms. Thus, the infornet explanation of asthma needs to be able to explain the non-specific inflammatory response, the atopic inflammatory response and the asthma-specific inflammatory response.

Explanation of precursors of asthma

According to infornet theory outlined in Chapter 3, the dysregulated infornet resolves into an inappropriate response to external circumstances owing to incorrect infornet beliefs. Chapter 3 provided the following description of the infornet beliefs associated with asthma:

Asthma involves a form of dysregulation where the infornet has incorrectly encoded information that the lungs are exposed to the threat of a parasite.

There are three factors that increase the likelihood of this infornet belief forming:

The non-specific inflammatory response

General infornet dysregulation is characterised by the infornet belief that *the general situation is bad*. Because infornet beliefs are connected, the general infornet belief that there is the threat of immune challenge (i.e., the belief associated with the inflammatory response system) tends to connect with the *specific* infornet belief that a parasite is present. Thus, anything that increases the general infornet belief that *the general situation is bad* will predispose towards the infornet belief that *the internal situation is bad*, which will in turn predispose towards the specific belief *the situation in the lung is bad*.

Several of the predictors of asthma onset give rise to the general infornet belief that *the general situation is bad* and hence *the internal situation is bad*.

- *Stress predicts asthma onset.* Stressed carers provide a psychological environment that communicates external threat to their children. External threat leads to beliefs of internal and external challenge, which, if repeated over a period of time, become fixed. Thus, the stressed carer provides the child with an environment that predisposes towards activation of the inflammatory response system via a psychogenic route.

- *Obesity predicts persistence of asthma.* Obesity is associated with inflammatory brown fat. Obese children therefore have an activated inflammatory response system via a somatogenic route.
- *Dirty air predicts asthma onset.* Irritants in the air create an inflammatory response in the lungs. Anything that irritates contributes to systemic inflammation.
- *Leafy vegetables predict reduced asthma onset.* Leafy vegetables have an anti-inflammatory effect.

The atopic inflammatory response

The specific immune system is a learning system. The specific immune system learns by recognising patterns – i.e., the patterns of antigens. Imagine that you are trying to teach someone the alphabet, using different patterns of letters. Your pupil knows that there are 26 letters in the alphabet and even knows the names of these letters, but doesn't know what shapes go with which names. During the course of training you forget to show your pupil the letter *e*. Your pupil knows that the letter *e* exists even though you have never shown an example. The consequence is that your pupil will attribute *e* to shapes that are not actually *e*. The hygiene hypothesis can be understood in terms of this kind of failure in learning. In addition, the sibling effect, in which first-born children are more likely to develop asthma, can be explained as part of the hygiene hypothesis. Much of the learning of the immune system takes place in the gut – the gut is the immune system's classroom. The failure to present the parasites that the gut expects to find leads to a tendency to misunderstand other biological signals as being that of a parasite threat. Atopy is a failure to learn due to inadequate training. Atopy therefore predisposes towards the formation of incorrect infornet beliefs about the external situation, that is, it predisposes towards the infornet belief that *there is a parasite in the lung*.

The asthma specific response

Many of the predictors of asthma onset are *either* immune challenges (e.g., viral infection, house dust mite, animal dander) *or* immune suppressants (e.g., cigarette smoke, car fumes and stress). Children brought up with these immune challenges and suppressants are more likely to develop asthma.

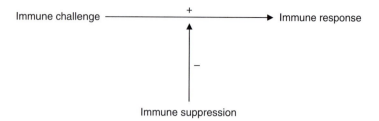

Figure 7.1 The compensation rule and the potentiation of immune response

When an immune challenge is presented with an immune suppressant, the immune response to that challenge is less than that defined in the pattern specified by the genome. The compensation rule predicts that, under such circumstances, the informet should self-organise so as to increase the immune response. Hence, the increased immune response can be understood through the application of the compensation rule to the combination of immune challenge and immune suppression (Hyland, 1999, 2001a); see Figure 7.1.

Once asthma has developed, the immune challenges and immune suppressants cited above also act as triggers that exacerbate asthma, but there is considerable individual variation as to which factors act as a trigger for which person. Combinations of biological immune challenges and suppressants are particularly powerful as triggers of asthma exacerbations (D'Amato, 2000; Svartengren *et al.*, 2000). The idea that asthma arises out of a combination of factors is supported by data showing that children of parents who experience stress are more likely to develop asthma when exposed to the harmful effects of traffic-related air pollution (Shankardass *et al.*, 2009). The implication of this research is that stress produces physiological changes that then interact with other causal factors.

From precursor to specific disease

The above explanation for the origin of asthma shows how lifestyle and environmental inputs to the informet can lead to informet changes that predispose towards the particular type of informet belief associated with asthma, namely that *the lung is exposed to a parasite*. However, though the dysregulated informet may act as a precursor to specific disease, the question remains, 'How does the precursor produce the specific disease?'. Data to help answer this question are lacking, but there are two theoretical possibilities: gene expression and influence of mechanisms in the specific system.

Gene expression

The genetic explanation for disease is that people carry genes that, when expressed, cause the disease to occur. In healthy individuals, these disease-causing genes are switched off. The genes are switched on by environmental factors and they are also switched on by age – diseases are more likely as people age. So, in the case of cancer, there are oncogenes that are switched off in healthy individuals but that cause cancer when switched on. In the case of asthma, the switching on of asthma genes leads to asthma.

According to infornet theory, the dysregulated infornet is a precursor of disease. If specific disease is due to gene expression, then the dysregulated infornet increases the probability of the expression of disease-causing diseases. Let us assume that asthma is caused by asthma genes; then each of the three mechanisms above increases the probability of genes related to asthma becoming expressed. The probability of asthma genes becoming expressed is increased when a combination of immune challenge and immune suppression leads to increases in the immune response. The probability of activation of atopy genes is increased by the poor immune learning that results from a hygienic environment. Finally, activation of the non-specific inflammatory response increases the probability of all inflammatory-related genes being expressed.

According to the gene expression explanation, the infornet is part of a communication system that involves gene expression. Not only does the genome act as a supervisor and thereby changes the infornet, but the infornet also alters gene expression, thereby altering the way the phenotype is expressed. The genome is part of the body's network system, namely the infornet.

Asthma is an example of a disease that spontaneously remits in some cases but not in others. Children who develop asthma some-times 'grow out of it', by which it is meant the asthma remits spontan-eously. Twenty-two per cent of children with asthma show complete remission and a further 30% show clinical improvement (Vonk *et al.*, 2004). Adult asthma seldom remits, but there are nevertheless examples where remission does occur. This difference between the reversibility of childhood and adult asthma suggests that children have some char-acteristics that allow the asthma genes to be switched off. It may be that the increased plasticity of infornet beliefs in children allows, under appropriate circumstances, for the infornet to 'forget' the belief that *there is a parasite in the lung.*

If the dysregulated infornet leads to an increased probability of expression of disease-causing genes, it also follows that other factors may influence the probability of gene expression independently of the infornet. The data on the relationship between food and disease onset cited above raise the possibility that the inflammatory/non-inflammatory effects of food may predispose to disease independently of the infornet. In general, it seems very plausible that infornet dysregulation is only one component that influences the expression of disease-causing genes. For example, age may be a factor that influences oncogenes irrespective of infornet dysregulation – men over 85 years typically have prostate cancer even though the cancer is often slow growing.

Mechanisms in the specific system

Once asthma develops it tends to persist, at least in adults. One possible explanation for the persistence of asthma is that inflammatory processes tend to be self-perpetuating in the specific system. Thus, once inflammation is caused in the lung, that inflammation tends to create more inflammation. It is possible, therefore, that part of the persistence of asthma is caused by persisting factors in the specific system. There is, though, a counter-argument. Steroid treatment is effective for people with asthma and can abolish the inflammatory response in the lung. However, even though the inflammatory response can be suppressed with medication, once the medication is removed then the inflammatory response returns. Thus, there must be something driving asthma that is separate from the self-perpetuating effect of inflammation.

Cancer is a disease in which there is uncontrollable growth of tissue. In the healthy individual, cells are constantly dividing, and in so doing some cells form precancerous growths. The precancerous growths are recognised and destroyed by the immune system, in particular, the Natural Killer Cells. In the healthy individual this process of disease formation and disease prevention is a constant process, such that disease formation is kept at bay. The development of disease can therefore be understood in terms not only of factors that increase precancerous tissue (e.g., chemical irritation) but also the body's own system for dealing with disease. A dysregulated infornet leads to a dysregulated immune system. In particular, stress leads to HPA activation and down-regulation (via the effect of cortisol) of cellular immune activity, such as Natural Killer Cell activity. Thus, the infornet may affect specific disease by altering (disabling or enhancing) the specific mechanisms that are in place to prevent disease formation. This alteration may occur either due to specific or general infornet dysregulation – any form of dysregulation may reduce the specific system's ability to protect against disease.

The prognosis for cancer varies widely with different sorts of cancer, and coupled with the evidence from asthma it would appear that there are multiple routes by which the infornet acts as a precursor to specific diseases. For some cancers, early detection and (specific) treatment leads to a positive outcome. In these cases, a good outcome is achieved by correcting the specific pathophysiology. By contrast, suppression of inflammation in the lung in asthma does not cure asthma. Nor does specific treatment always have such a positive outcome for some cancers. It would seem to be the case that some diseases become more self-perpetuating owing to the specific system and hence more resistant to treatment the longer the duration before specific treatment. However, for other diseases the tendency to self-perpetuate occurs irrespective of the duration between disease onset and treatment, and therefore irrespective of events in the specific system.

Similarities across chronic diseases

Chapter 3 provided a tripartite classification of diseases, namely:

- diseases in which there is infornet dysregulation but *no* specific disease;
- diseases in which there is infornet dysregulation *and* specific disease; and
- diseases in which there is specific disease but *no* infornet dysregulation.

Diseases in which there is infornet dysregulation (i.e., either with or without specific disease) have features in common. The consequence is that although specific diseases have specific pathophysiologies, they often have features in common. Specific diseases share similarities that betray their origin in the infornet.

Idiopathic variability

For many diseases, the level of symptoms or the underlying pathophysiology varies over time. Idiopathic variability means that the variability appears to come from within the person rather than in response to an external event, and there is no explanation for why this variation occurs. For two diseases this idiopathic variability is very pronounced. Irritable bowel syndrome (IBS) is a functional bowel disease where there is no observable gut pathology but the bowel can oscillate between constipation (i.e., insufficient gut motility) and diarrhoea (i.e., too much gut motility). Between 50% and 90% of IBS patients (depending on survey and method) experience generalised anxiety and major depression (Lydiard, 2001). Bipolar disorder is a disease in which the person varies between extreme dejection – i.e., low levels of stability (e.g., depression, fatigue) and high levels of plasticity (i.e., elation) when the patient feels anything is possible. Although IBS and bipolar disorder are characterised by their variability, all chronic diseases provide examples of idiopathic variability, though of a less dramatic nature. The idiopathic variability typically takes the form of a correlated increase in somatic and psychological symptoms. That is, the increase in somatic symptoms goes hand-in-hand with the increase in psychological symptoms.

What is the cause of idiopathic variability? A control system oscillates when the gain is set too high in relation to the lag (see Chapter 4). Thus, one possible explanation for idiopathic variability is that the infornet has set the gain of the control loop at too high a level.

There are two ways in which an intelligent monitoring system, such as the infornet, can change control loop parameters in order to achieve better control. One is by altering the reference criterion. The other is by altering the gain. In the previous chapter and in this one I have suggested that the compensation rule explains the setting of a reference criterion at too high a level. For example, inflammatory states found in asthma or fatigue signals found in CFS can be explained in terms of elevated levels of the reference criteria – for inflammation and fatigue, respectively. However, an alternative response of the infornet to a control system that is failing to achieve control is to increase the gain. That is, an alternative response to the detection of poor control is to increase the amplitude of the controlling response. Idiopathic variability can therefore be interpreted as another kind of response to the interpretation of poor control. As both changes in reference criteria and increased gains are possible responses to poor control, it is not surprising that diseases where there is an abnormal reference criterion also exhibit idiopathic variability. Thus, IBS can be characterised as a disease in which the infornet is trying too hard to obtain the correct level of gut motility. Bipolar disorder can be characterised as a disease in which the infornet is trying too hard to obtain the correct level of mood. In either case, the theory suggests that the reason the infornet has increased the gain in these control loops is that the infornet has detected that control in the relevant control loop is poor.

Trigger factors

In addition to idiopathic variability, chronic diseases are made worse by trigger factors. These triggers tend to have some disease specificity – for example, dirty air is primarily a problem for those with respiratory disease rather than gastric disease. Nevertheless, there are many examples of triggers that are common across all diseases.

The triggers can take the form of either a biological or a psychological input. Biological inputs include infection and food. People with asthma typically experience a worsening of symptoms with infection, and there is a smaller proportion who experience some exacerbation with food. Not surprisingly, particular foods can act as a trigger for people with gastric diseases, such as irritable bowel syndrome, inflammatory bowel disease and gastroesophageal reflux, and food triggers lead to an increase in both gastric symptoms and psychological symptoms such as fatigue. When foods act as a trigger this can be described by laypeople as food allergy or food intolerance. Food intolerance is a common feature of chronic diseases, though the particular foods perceived to cause exacerbation are highly idiosyncratic.

Triggers can also involve a psychological input. Many patients with chronic diseases report that somatic and psychological symptoms are exacerbated by stress. For example, stress commonly creates exacerbation of asthma. Two routes are involved. One leads to increased bronchodilation (Wright et al., 1998), while the other involves an increase in the inflammatory response in the lung (Chen et al., 2010). In both cases the trigger is providing a signal that creates infornet alarm: in the case of asthma, a response to the infornet belief that there is a challenge to the lung.

The study by Chen et al., (2010) is particularly interesting in that children of lower socioeconomic status had a greater inflammatory response to a stressful task than those of higher socioeconomic status. Socioeconomic status correlates with general psychological stress; so children of low socioeconomic status tend to experience more chronic stress. The interpretation of Chen et al.'s data is that a chronically stressed system is more likely to respond with inflammation to acute stress than a system that is not chronically stressed. Triggers therefore seem to have a characteristic of creating more alarm in a system that is already prone to interpreting the situation as requiring some form of alarm response. The more there is a general tendency to alarm, the more the specific trigger acts to create the specific alarm. Chen et al.'s data supports the idea that infornet alarm is a solution made by a system with multiple inputs and which is affected by previous experiences. General and specific responses of the infornet are linked.

One of the peculiar features of triggers is that they are so variable within diseases. For all chronic diseases, some patients will report that getting stressed makes things worse in terms of the presenting symptom. However, the impact of stress on symptoms does not occur with all patients. This variability occurs for both psychological and biological inputs. One possibility is that trigger factors act as triggers because the trigger was involved in the original aetiology of the dysregulation. The possibility of a link between factors involved in disease onset and disease exacerbation needs further investigation. The possibility of a link is consistent with the associative learning rule (Chapters 4 and 5) whereby acute stressors, when experienced regularly, produce long-term changes that are consistent with the acute stress.

If disease onset is linked to disease exacerbation, then a possible explanation is that the infornet 'remembers' the route into dysregulation, and factors involved in the original development of that dysregulation are sensitised in terms of their later effect on the dysregulated infornet. Thus, triggers act by increasing infornet alarm of an already dysregulated system, and do so because the cause of that dysregulation is linked to the particular trigger.

Fuzzy boundaries between dysregulatory disease

Cramer *et al.* (2010) provide evidence that there is no firm boundary between anxiety and depression. In fact, the principle of fuzzy boundaries should apply to all dysregulatory diseases.

The astute reader will have noticed that food intolerance and irritable bowel syndrome (IBS) were among the list of symptoms listed as characteristic of chronic fatigue syndrome (CFS) (see Chapter 6). The question whether CFS is different from IBS has been a matter of some debate. Although both IBS and CFS are diagnosed on the basis of symptoms (neither has a unique pathophysiology), there is no unique pattern of symptoms that identifies either disease. IBS is diagnosed by internationally agreed criteria, called the Rome criteria. To be diagnosed with IBS the patient must have 3 months or more of pain *plus* at least two of a list of four other symptoms. For CFS, according to the CDC criteria (i.e., the US criteria, see Chapter 6) the patient must have fatigue for 6 months or more *plus* at least four from a list of eight symptoms.

Questions such as, 'are IBS and CFS the same disease?' and 'are there different kinds of CFS?' are based on the assumption that all diseases exist as discrete entities. Modern diagnostic theory (nosology) is based on the assumption that diseases exist as discrete entities with firm boundaries. According to the present theory, questions such as, 'are there different kinds of CFS?' are based on an incorrect assumption. Diseases of dysregulation have a different nosology from that of specific diseases, and the way of classifying dysregulatory diseases is different.

If the infornet is a single integrated system, then dysregulation in one part of the infornet will tend to spread. More specifically, infornet beliefs tend to be interconnected (see Chapter 3). Consequently, dysregulation in one part of the meaning space that the infornet tends to spread to other parts in a way that is continuous rather than discontinuous. There are therefore no firm boundaries between dysregulatory diseases, and classification is a matter of grouping people according to their main symptoms. As people with specific disease have some form of infornet dysregulation, they also have symptoms that are shared across diseases (such as fatigue, see Chapter 3). Indeed, immune disturbance and HPA activation, along with fatigue, depression and anxiety, are common in most specific diseases, but in each case there is variation within the disease, presumably because of variation in the form of infornet dysregulation.

Common predictors

For each disease, researchers have been able to show that particular variables predict disease onset. Some of the predictors of asthma onset were listed above. However, it cannot be an accident that the predictors of disease onset are common across a range of diseases. This book has focused primarily on stress. Stress is a predictor of all diseases because it leads to activity of the inflammatory response system, or at least, according to the theory being advanced here, to the extent that the stressor acts as a signal for possible internal challenge. Stressors act as a signal for possible internal challenge not in terms of some rational, cognitive judgement about the likelihood of internal challenge but rather in the way stressors signalled challenge during human evolutionary history. As a consequence, the kind of stressful activities commonly encountered in work situations are those that elicit activity of the inflammatory response system. Activation of the inflammatory response system then acts to increase the likelihood of any disease that has an inflammatory aetiology.

Obesity is another variable that predicts disease onset across a range of diseases, including cancers, heart disease, diabetes and asthma. Obesity is also associated with psychological problems: it correlates with depression (Stunkard et al., 2003) and is a characteristic of children with attention-deficit/hyperactivity disorder (ADHD) (Cortese et al., 2008). Obesity is associated with brown fat, i.e., the kind of fat commonly deposited in the abdomen. White fat is deposited on the hips and bottom but this does not have an inflammatory effect. Obesity and, in particular, waist to hip ratio, is a predictor of numerous diseases, for the same reason that stress is a predictor of numerous diseases. Diseases in which there is an inflammatory aetiology are made more likely by the presence of large amounts of brown (abdominal) fat.

Poor diet leads to greater risk of many diseases. For example, lack of green vegetables is associated with risk of onset for asthma (Romieu et al., 2006), heart disease (Hung et al., 2004) and, to a greater or less extent, cancer (Boffetta et al., 2010; Steinmetz and Potter, 1991).

Moderate levels of exercise are associated with better mental health and a reduction in a wide range of diseases. Exercise leads to reduced levels of pro-inflammatory cytokines (Starkie et al., 2003).

Finally, fetal stress and early childhood trauma are associated with increases in most somatic and psychological diseases (see Chapter 5), presumably because the early stress leads to long-term changes in infornet beliefs.

There are three conclusions from these commonalities among predictors:

1. Although specific diseases have specific pathologies, there are predisposing mechanisms that are common to many diseases. This suggests that some predisposing mechanisms are common across diseases – and there may be common factors for the treatment of specific diseases.
2. There are numerous factors that predispose towards disease. Anything that is pro-inflammatory tends to increase risk, and anything that is anti-inflammatory reduces disease risk.
3. The level of systemic inflammation is influenced by both psychological and biological inputs. Psychological and biological inputs are both relevant to the prevention and development of somatic and mental disease.

Summary

This chapter has shown how specific infornet dysregulation can predispose towards specific diseases, but also that general infornet dysregulation can have a predisposing effect for specific diseases. Specific and general infornet dysregulation can predispose towards specific disease, either by enhancing the expression of disease-causing genes or by reducing the disease-preventing capacity of the specific system. The way the infornet acts as a precursor to specific disease is poorly understood.

8 Three different types of psychologically mediated therapy: placebos and the art of medicine, psychotherapy and complementary and alternative medicine

There are two parts to any therapy: the part that the therapist believes is important to therapeutic outcome and 'the other part'. The aim of this chapter is to review the concepts and evidence that suggest that, at least in some circumstances, the other part is important. This chapter begins with a history of the placebo concept, and then applies this concept to three topics: drug therapy for depression, psychotherapy and complementary medicine. The final section examines the extent to which psychological interventions have psychological and physiological benefits.

The placebo in medicine and the art of medicine

Placebo researchers can have an ambivalent attitude towards the term *placebo*. On the one hand, the term describes a topic of research. On the other, the term is used in a variety of different ways, and so is potentially ambiguous. Placebo is used to mean different things because the word is always used for a particular purpose. That purpose (a) has changed over time and (b) is different between groups of researchers. So an understanding of the term placebo requires an understanding of (a) when the term is being used and (b) why and by whom. Ambiguities over the term 'non-specific' occur for the same reasons.

The term placebo has a long and varied use in medicine. That use is best understood in the context of the history of medicine as a social organisation. All professional organisations set up institutions that protect their members' interests and ensure that the benefits of membership are limited only to those members. Medicine is no different in this regard from any other professional body. The organisation now known as the Royal College of Physicians was granted a charter by Henry VIII in 1518. The aims of the college (as stated in an early translation of the original Latin) include:

To curb the audacity of those wicked men who shall profess medicine more for the sake of their avarice than from the assurance of any good conscience, whereby many inconveniences may ensue to the rude and credulous populace.

'Rude and credulous' means 'uneducated and gullible'. The Royal College of Physicians, like other medical organisations afterwards, was concerned with protecting the general public from false medicine (Davenport et al., 2001).

The term *placebo* is a Latin word meaning 'I shall please'. Its use today can be traced back to a Latin translation of the 116th Psalm verse 9, which was said, during the Middle Ages, by (normally, hired) mourners over the body of the dead to signify the dead person's salvation. (In fact, the Latin text is *Placebo domino in regione vivorum. Placebo* is a mistranslation from the original Hebrew: modern bibles give the text correctly as 'I will walk before the Lord in the land of the living' rather than 'I shall please the Lord ...'.) Because of the use of hired mourners, the word *placebo* gained the connotation of pleasing others. In the late fourteenth century the name Placebo was used by Chaucer in one of his stories for a character who always tries to please (the hired mourners were there to please). The first definition of placebo appears in the second edition of Motherby's 1785 *New Medical Dictionary*, where it is defined as 'a commonplace method or medicine'. This definition suggests that the placebo was used as a technique in medicine. A later definition in Hooper's medical dictionary gives the definition of the placebo as 'An epithet given to any medicine adopted more to please than benefit the patient'. This and other evidence shows that it was acceptable to give an inert substance as part of treatment for a patient during the seventeenth, eighteenth and nineteenth centuries. What was referred to as 'the pious fraud' was considered ethically acceptable by the majority of physicians. Even up to the 1940s the view of the placebo or inert substance was that 'it cannot harm and may comfort the patient (Pepper, 1945). At the present time, many doctors use placebos – one survey gives a figure of 45% (Sherman and Hickner, 2008). There are ethical issues in the prescription of placebos, primarily arising over deception and trust between doctor and patient, that are beyond the scope of this book. It is sufficient to note that, despite the advances of modern Western medicine, placebos are used in clinical practice.

The first report of what would now be interpreted as a placebo-controlled trial was provided by John Hayworth in 1801 (de Craen et al., 1999). At the time many diseases were treated by applying metallic rods, known as Perkin's tractors, to the body of the patient. The metal was supposed to exert an electromagnetic influence. Hayworth was able to show that the same effect would be achieved if the rods were made of wood. This demonstration was important because it was able to show a difference between the psychological impact of the treatment and the physiological impact – and hence the difference between true and false medicine.

Despite attempts by medical organisations such as the Royal College of Physicians to protect their profession, there were numerous individuals during the nineteenth and early twentieth century who purported to provide cures for all kinds of ailments and who were not registered doctors. The purveyors of inert substances (such as 'snake oil') made a living out of people, namely the 'rude and credulous populace' that the original charter of the Royal College of Physicians was trying to protect. Thus it was important to distinguish quacks who sold inert substances whose only effect was psychological from 'proper doctors' who sold 'genuine medicine' that had a physiological effect – in addition to any psychological effect.

The placebo-controlled trial provided a criterion for distinguishing true from false medicine. The first time the word placebo was used in a randomised control trial was in 1938 (Diehl *et al.*, 1938), and within a few decades the randomised, placebo-controlled trial had become the gold standard for distinguishing genuine medicines from fake medicines. Today, it is this test that is used by all regulatory bodies, along with tests of safety, for a drug to be licensed. For a drug to be licensed it must do no harm (or at least the risk of harm versus benefit must be firmly on the side of benefit) and the drug must be shown to be more effective than placebo in at least two large, randomised controlled trials. Randomised controlled trials are those in which patients are randomised to receive either the real drug or the control, i.e., the placebo.

The placebo test can be extrapolated to surgery. Placebo surgery involves a sham operation in which the patient is operated on but only so far as making and repairing an incision. The placebo surgery is compared with the real surgery. Note that in surgery, placebo refers to an inactive procedure rather than an inactive substance. Tests of placebo surgery are carried out only if there is genuine doubt of the effectiveness of therapy, and some types of surgery that were originally thought helpful were later abandoned because they failed the placebo test. Whereas new medicines are *always* evaluated by the placebo test, new surgical procedures do not require placebo evaluation for their acceptance.

The consequence of defining the placebo as any physiologically inert substance or procedure has a consequence that, when it is used as an adjective, the term 'placebo mechanism' means *any* psychologically mediated effect. So the quacks who sell snake oil achieve therapeutic benefit do so owing to psychological mechanisms. Note that *any*

A: Good communication → More medication used → Better health outcome.

B: Good communication → Psychological effect on the infornet → Better health outcome.

Figure 8.1 The effect of good communication on patient behaviour

psychological mechanism can be involved, and it is unimportant, as far as the gold test of the placebo is concerned, to distinguish between different mechanisms. Medical texts on the placebo often refer to both the therapeutic bond and expectancy as important mechanisms in the placebo effect. However, the exact mechanism does not matter so long as the medicine under test can be shown to be more effective than the inactive (i.e., psychologically active) placebo.

Because of its association with 'not proper treatment' in clinical trials, and therefore with quackery, the term *placebo* carries negative connotations. Nevertheless, physicians and surgeons recognise the importance of the therapeutic bond in clinical practice. Terms such as 'the art of medicine' and 'doctor–patient communication' provide a positive wording for a topic that elsewhere is referred to as placebo. The science of medicine is the pills and procedures that have physiological effects. The art of medicine is the unscientific business of talking to patients. Despite its lower status, the art of medicine is recognised both in clinical practice and in modern medical training where students are often taught communication skills.

There are two ways in which doctors can influence patients through good communication: improved adherence with medication and improved well-being. These two different ways involve different mechanisms. If good communication produces better adherence to medication, then better outcome is achieved through a biological or somatic route (see Figure 8.1A).

However, if good communication improves well-being directly, then the outcome is achieved through a psychological route, which might be represented as shown in Figure 8.1B.

There is evidence consistent with good communication having a beneficial effect on the infornet. Thomas (1987) carried out a study on 200 patients who had medically unexplained symptoms (MUS). Some were treated, some were not. For some, the consultation was carried out in a positive manner; for others in a negative manner. Outcome was measured 2 weeks later. There was no effect of treatment, but those patients who had the positive consultation had a better outcome than those who had the negative consultation. If medically unexplained symptoms are explained in terms of general infornet dysregulation, the implication is that positive communication by a doctor can help undo the effects of infornet dysregulation.

It is common to distinguish patient-centred communication from doctor-centred communication. In the former, the doctor pays attention and listens to what the patient says. Patient-centred communication is associated with better adherence, particularly with that communication style associated with the *concordance model* of patient management. In the concordance model, the clinician listens to what the patient has to say, and together they agree a plan of self-management that is acceptable to the patient (Irwin and Richardson, 2006). The concordance model involves compromise. By contrast, in the *compliance model*, the clinician tells the patient what the optimum strategy is for self-management but without taking into account the patient's views.

The patient-centred concordance model of patient management has much in common with the psychotherapeutic approach suggested by Rogers (Chapter 1), where the therapist listens and responds to what the client says. It is therefore not surprising that patient-centred communication generally leads to greater satisfaction. As a general rule, and certainly as far as disease management is concerned, good patient satisfaction with the doctor is associated with better adherence with medication (Gross *et al.*, 2003), so at least part of the reason good doctor–patient relationships lead to better outcome is due to a biologically mediated route of better medication. The extent to which this good communication has an effect on symptoms and disease via a psychogenic route is difficult to determine, but there is a belief among some medical doctors that 'good' clinicians have an effect on disease through some psychogenic route, for example, by providing more positive expectations of outcome or a better therapeutic bond.

The word *placebo* has a particular meaning in medicine. The term *non-specific* also has a particular meaning in medicine. Recall that modern medicine is based on the hypothesis that there are specific pathophysiologies that cause specific diseases. Consequently, treatments should always be specific to those pathophysiologies and diseases and there should be no non-specific treatments. The quacks who sold snake oil in the nineteenth and early twentieth century often suggested that their medicines would cure all kinds off illness – from baldness to cancer. The idea of cure-alls is considered highly suspect by conventional doctors. Non-specific therapies are rejected on the basis that they refer to a mechanism that, according to conventional medicine, should not exist. Placebo treatments, on the other hand, are rejected on the basis that the effect is mediated only through psychological mechanisms.

Although medical practitioners may reject the idea of non-specific therapies *as part of medicine*, there is no such rejection if the therapy is treated as something different from a medical treatment. There is increasing evidence that exercise has a range of benefits, which include not only better physical health but also better mental health (Stathopoulou *et al.*, 1996). Exercise would therefore appear to have non-specific benefits. The way round this conundrum is to consider exercise not as a medical treatment but rather a lifestyle intervention. Of course, the word therapy also has a good cachet, so exercise therapy, art therapy, music therapy all exist as concepts, but they are not what proper doctors do. Proper doctors give genuine pills and carry out genuine operations, thereby allowing a boundary to be drawn between medicine on one hand and lifestyle and care on the other. Nevertheless, many doctors and GPs are highly sympathetic to lifestyle and other forms of patient management, for the simple reason that many patient consultations with a GP do not involve a diagnosable illness. If patients do not have a diagnosable illness (surveys suggest between 15% and 30% of patients visiting a GP; Kirmayer *et al.*, 2004), then the GP has to find some other way of managing the patient.

Drug therapy and the problem of depression

Medical, psychology and nursing students are all taught one simple fact. Depression is caused by lack of serotonin in the brain: people who are depressed have lower levels of serotonin than those who are not depressed. Serotonin is the 'happy' transmitter substance. If you don't have enough of it, you become sad. Antidepressant drugs increase levels of serotonin and so treat depression. Serotonin levels can be increased in different ways through drug treatment, so there are several classes of antidepressants drugs, each of which increases serotonin. The most recent are the serotonin selective reuptake inhibitors (SSRIS), of which a well-known brand name is Prozac. These drugs do what they say on the tin: they increase serotonin levels in the parts of the brain where they are needed. Herbalists are taught that St John's wort has a similar effect of increasing serotonin levels in the brain, and so the herbalist approach to treatment is based on the same underlying theory: the serotonin hypothesis.

Despite the serotonin hypothesis supporting a multi-billion-pound industry, and despite its widespread acceptance in education, many researchers are far more sceptical. In a paper entitled 'Serotonin and depression: a disconnect between the advertisements and the scientific literature', Lacasse and Leo (2005) provide a review of the widespread doubt expressed about this hypothesis by a range of eminent researchers.

Leaving aside these doubts, there is a simple test of the serotonin hypothesis: can the predictions of the hypothesis be observed in the experimental data?

If depression is caused by lack of serotonin, and cured by replacing that serotonin, then depression should be easily treatable by these powerful antidepressants, and consequently depression should be as rare today as tuberculosis. If the serotonin hypothesis is correct, depression should be treatable in almost all patients. The fact that patients are hospitalised owing to intractable depression, and that depression is a major cause of disability and cost in the West (Murray *et al*, 1996) leads one to question the effectiveness of antidepressant medication and hence the validity of the serotonin hypothesis. In the UK, depression is the third most common cause for consultation with a GP (Gilbody *et al.*, 2003).

Antidepressant medications are evaluated through *randomised controlled trials* or RCTs. In the RCT, patients are randomly allocated to receive a pill that is either the real drug or a placebo – a drug that looks the same but contains no active ingredient. Neither the researchers nor the patients know whether the pill is the real drug (the verum) or the placebo. The purpose of the RCT is to compare the improvement in those patients receiving the real drug with those receiving the placebo. Most published clinical trials of antidepressants show that the active drug is better than placebo. Not all clinical trials are published.

A meta-analysis is a way of summarising the data from a large number of RCTs, combining the data from these studies using statistical procedures. Irving Kirsch and colleagues have published three meta-analyses

Box 8.1 Efficacy versus effectiveness

Although the two words efficacy and effectiveness sound similar, they have different meanings in medical research. Efficacy refers to the degree to which the drug has an effect that is different from that of placebo. Efficacy is the 'pure drug' effect, that is, the biological effect. Effectiveness is the 'overall' effect, that is, the biological effect combined with the psychological effect. The effectiveness of a drug includes a combination of the physiological effect of the drug, the extent to which patients actually take the drug and psychologically mediated or placebo effects, which include the effect of the therapist and other psychosocial factors that affect outcome. RCTs are designed to demonstrate whether a drug is efficacious. In the RCT, verum is compared with placebo. Pragmatic trials are designed to determine to what extent the treatment is effective. In a pragmatic trial, verum is compared with a natural history control – i.e., patients who are not treated.

of antidepressants RCTs (Kirsch, 2009). These analyses compared the additional benefit of all classes of antidepressant with placebo. The first analysis was restricted only to published studies (Kirsch and Sapirstein, 1998), and the last two analyses to the antidepressant trials for both published and unpublished studies (Kirsch et al., 2002, 2008). His conclusion was that the placebo accounted for at least 80% of the effect of the benefit of antidepressants, and that this figure was the same irrespective of the type of antidepressant. That is, of the total gain from antidepressants, 80% was caused by placebo and the remaining 20% by the active drug. The first meta-analysis, which was based only on published studies, showed that placebos were slightly less (about 5%) effective. This difference can be explained in terms of publication bias: non-significant studies are less likely to be published.

The last two meta-analyses (Kirsch et al., 2002, 2008) took as their sample *all* those studies that had been submitted to the American Federal Drug Administration, the FDA. In order for the FDA to give permission for a drug to be sold, the manufacturers have to demonstrate that the drug is better than placebo in at least two clinical trials. As part of their application for drug registration, drug companies are asked to provide the FDA with information about all trials they have sponsored, *irrespective of whether the trial is published*. It should be noted that for drug registration by the FDA, two clinical trials need to be significant – there is no limit on the number of trials that are not significant. Under freedom of information legislation, Kirsch obtained data on all antidepressant trials submitted to the FDA. The resulting meta-analysis showed that although, overall, these drugs were *statistically* better than placebo, the level of benefit was not *clinically* better than placebo for mild and moderate depression, according to the National Institute for Clinical Excellence (NICE) guidelines. That is, the degree of benefit from antidepressants for mild and moderate depression was so low that, according to the NICE guidelines, they were insufficient to be considered useful for therapy.

The implications from these meta-analyses are simple:

Antidepressants are effective but not very efficacious.

Kirsch's meta-analyses have been criticised. For example, looking only at studies registered with the FDA means that other studies are ignored. However, the FDA-registered studies are important because it is those studies that lead to drug registration in the USA – and hence have a major impact in the rest of the world. Additionally, it is possible to argue that the NICE guidelines set too high a threshold, and that smaller effect sizes should be considered still clinically useful. Nevertheless, whatever the arguments, the data from these meta-analyses send a very clear message. In clinical practice, antidepressant drugs work primarily through a placebo effect. The active effect of the drug is very small, and may be so small to have little clinical effect.

Although Kirsch's research exposed the lack of efficacy of antidepressants, knowledge of this fact is not new. Pharmaceutical researchers know that 'their dirty little secret' is the immense difficulty in obtaining statistically significant findings in clinical trials of antidepressants. Large studies are needed, and those in the industry know that it is necessary to plan for several studies as there is a good chance that some will fail to reach significance.

So, if the cure for depression is not the raising of serotonin levels, what is the alternative? The alternative is to look for events that are causally distal to the low levels of serotonin, and which might therefore be the root cause of depression. The major biological alternative to the serotonin hypothesis is the immune theory of depression. The inflammatory response system hypothesis was described in Chapter 2. In brief, the immune theory of depression suggests that depression is the consequence of raised levels of inflammatory mediators, in particular the pro-inflammatory cytokines and Substance P, i.e., the mediators of the innate immune response to psychogenic and immunogenic stress.

To summarise from Chapter 2, the evidence in favour of the immune theory of depression is:

- levels of pro-inflammatory cytokines of the natural immune system correlate with depression and fatigue;
- drugs that alter levels of serotonin also reduce inflammation;
- experimental addition of cytokines in animals and clinical use of cytokines in humans is associated with illness behaviours and depression; and
- stress activates the inflammatory response system and is a precursor of depression.

Box 8.2 Antidepressants in clinical practice

Many GPs prescribe antidepressants for depression. Many – though not all – patients report benefit. If patients report benefit, perhaps it does not matter whether the effect is due to psychological or biological effects of taking the pill. The only problem is that antidepressants have side effects. Some of these side effects – such as risk of suicide in children prescribed antidepressants – are very dangerous. If one is going to take a placebo, then there are others that are a good deal less dangerous.

The evidence against the immune theory of depression is:

- lack of specificity between particular cytokines and mental states of depression and fatigue;
- large individual differences; and
- lack of evidence that anti-inflammatory drugs (i.e., anti-cytokine or anti-Substance P) have an appreciable effect on depression.

The lack of efficacy of anti-inflammatory drugs as treatment for depression has some interesting parallels with the research on serotonin-enhancing medications. In two large multi-site trials where anti-Substance P medication was compared with placebo and selective serotonin reuptake inhibitors (SSRIs), neither the anti-inflammatory nor the SSRIs outperformed placebo (Kramer, 2002; Rupniak and Kramer, 1999). If anti-inflammatory medication was as good at treating depression as it is at treating inflammation, then it would now be in routine use as an antidepressant.

Even with the evidence from clinical trials that medication has only weak effects on depression, there is a methodological reason why any interpretation that depression is treatable by medication should be treated with caution. Active medications often have side effects. Placebos do not. In a clinical trial, patients are randomly allocated to an active medication and placebo, and they and the researchers are blind to which they are given. However, patients on the active medication are often able to guess that they are on active medication – because they notice the side effects. This is called 'breaking blind'. Research indicates that patients in the placebo arm of a study guess their treatment correctly about 50% of the time (i.e., are guessing at random). However, both patients and doctors in the verum arm guess correctly about 80% of the time (Holroyd *et al.*, 2006; Rabkin *et al.*, 1986). If patients believe that they are on the active medication, this increases the placebo effect compared with those who are unsure. Thus, clinical trials tend to overestimate the effect of drug therapy for depression. The effect of breaking blind is difficult to quantify, but the implication is that the meta-analyses conducted by Kirsch and colleagues are overgenerous with regard to the efficacy of antidepressants.

Within the total field of medicine, the lack of efficacy of antidepressants is unusual. Most drugs (antibiotics, steroids, insulin, etc.) are highly efficacious. However, there are several conditions where drug treatment is known to be of limited efficacy. For example, there is no drug to relieve fatigue. Drugs for IBS (they take the form of reducing diarrhoea) are efficacious in some patients but not in others. Nevertheless, in such cases taking a pill for an illness may be effective

Box 8.3 An example of the effect of placebos in clinical trials

The author once helped a pharmaceutical company evaluate a new medication for IBS in a large (500+ subjects) clinical trial. The drug had proved successful in Phase 2 clinical trials, i.e., dose-ranging studies in which different doses of the drug are compared in small groups of patients but where there is no placebo. The drug was ready for testing in the Phase 3 trial, i.e., where verum is compared with placebo and the efficacy of the drug is established. After considerable effort collecting data in several countries, it was found that there was no significant difference between verum and placebo. However, about 85% of patients in the placebo arm of the trial improved and 86% in the active drug or verum arm. If a condition responds so well to placebo, it is difficult to obtain a significant result.

for reasons other than those suggested on the tin; they may be effective because of psychologically mediated effects.

The weak efficacy of serotonin-enhancing and (at best, very weak efficacy) of anti-inflammatory drugs is consistent with the hypothesis that the distal cause of depression is something else. The hypothesis outlined in the previous chapter was that this something else is general infornet dysregulation. Let us suppose that serotonin and inflammatory cytokines are all part of the communication system within the infornet (see Chapter 4). Consequently, when the level or effect of these biochemicals is changed through pharmaceutical interventions, there will be a change in the activation pattern of the infornet. However, because the infornet has considerable redundancy, these biochemical changes will have only a small and not necessarily consistent effect on the way the infornet performs – in the same way that killing a bird in a flock of birds makes little difference to the behaviour of the flock. If depression is the consequence of the way the infornet responds to its inputs, then the problem is only effectively solved by changing those inputs.

In conclusion, this section has shown that the 'other part' of drug therapy for depression is important in clinical practice. If the other part of anti-depression drug therapy, namely the psychological or non-biological component is important, then it is necessary to understand what that other part is operating on. At several points in this book I have suggested that the distal cause of depression is infornet dysregulation. It is possible that this dysregulation can involve changes in levels of serotonin and pro-inflammatory cytokines. However, although pharmaceutically induced change of these biochemicals alters the functioning of the infornet to some degree, these changes have little impact on the underlying trend towards dysregulation. Going to the doctor and taking the pills is far more effective than the pills themselves. Going to the doctor is part of a lifestyle modification and is only through lifestyle modification that effective change is made to general infornet dysregulation.

Placebos in psychotherapy research

The discipline of psychology, by comparison with medicine, is very much the junior partner. Psychologists have been active in treating patients for mental illness only in the last 50 years, and at the beginning of that period there was conflict between the role of psychiatrists and that of psychologists, when the former supported a psychoanalytic and the latter a behavioural interpretation of mental illness. The history of clinical psychology is one in which psychologists have had to make considerable efforts to make themselves heard and to carve out a place for their profession.

In order to justify their techniques as 'genuine', psychologists have to play by the rules that were set up by physicians to protect the 'rude and credulous populace'. From a medical perspective, all psychological therapeutic mechanisms are biologically inactive and could easily be classified as placebos. Psychologists would not get far if they approached those who control the medical purse strings with the marketing pitch, 'we do the best placebos'. Clinical psychologists therefore reinvented the placebo concept so that it could be applied to psychology in a way that would provide justification for psychotherapy within the rules of medical evidence.

Psychotherapists had to show that their therapy was better than placebo, but for this to happen the placebo concept needed to be redefined. Two parts of the psychotherapeutic encounter were distinguished: the specific or active component and the non-specific or inactive component. The specific component is that part of the therapy that is specific only to the therapy under consideration. That is, it is the unique therapeutic contribution of the psychotherapy. The non-specific component is all those aspects of therapy that are common to all therapeutic encounters, namely the therapeutic alliance (comprising therapeutic bond, expectancy and behavioural commitment). The non-specific component is also referred to as the 'inactive' component, because this component is not the active part of the therapy under consideration. However, as many placebo researchers point out, to describe the non-specific component as inactive is illogical, as it has active effects (Kirsch, 2005).

The great psychotherapy debate

The Great Psychotherapy Debate is the title of a book written by Bruce Wampold (2001) that sets out, in detail, an argument that has existed in the field of psychotherapy for over 80 years. In Chapter 1, I explained how theories of psychotherapy fall into two groups. The major group consists of those where there is an assumption of some kind of specific pathology that the therapist then corrects. Cognitive behaviour therapy (CBT) is the dominant form of psychotherapy today. In the case of CBT the principal pathology concerns the patient's cognitions – people with mental health problems have 'wrong' cognitions that are corrected with the help of the therapist. By contrast, humanistic and counselling psychotherapies start from the position that the person is naturally self-healing. According to the latter approach, the therapist does not correct anything but merely sets up the right conditions that enhance self-healing. According to the humanistic perspective, the right conditions include the therapeutic alliance. So, in the case of CBT, the therapeutic alliance is the non-active part of therapy. In the case of humanistic psychology the therapeutic alliance is the active part. The difference between these two positions has been explored experimentally. Two different kinds of research study enable conclusions to be drawn: (a) research into the relative merit of different types of psychotherapy, which, for reasons that will be explained shortly, has the heading of *the dodo bird effect* research; and (b) studies whose aim is to determine what exactly are the active ingredients of psychotherapy. As these latter studies examine the different components of psychotherapy, they are called *component studies*.

The dodo bird effect

Many studies have compared the effectiveness of different types of psychotherapy. Fortunately, several meta-analyses have been carried out on these studies, and the conclusions are consistent across the different meta-analyses. The meta-analyses show that the effectiveness of different types of psychotherapy is either equal or approximately equal (Luborsky *et al.*, 1975, 2002; Smith and Glass, 1977; Wampold *et al.*, 1997). The equality of different types of psychotherapy is called the dodo bird effect – after the use of the use of this word in one of the early papers (Rosenzweig, 1936). (The quote comes from the book *Alice in Wonderland*: 'At last the Dodo bird said "*Everyone* has won and all must have prizes."' The word 'all' is not italicised in the original book but is in Rosenzweig's paper, and is shown as such in the reference list of this book.) Despite the conclusions from these meta-analyses, there are those who disagree that psychotherapies are equivalent in effectiveness, and consider that their preferred therapy is best. As CBT is the dominant therapy today, the arguments for therapeutic superiority often come from those who support this type of therapy. Conclusions from meta-analyses can be criticised because any meta-analysis depends on the inclusion criteria of studies selected. Selection of studies can lead to meta-analyses supporting the use of CBT. Separating out these different views is made more difficult by research showing that researchers who support a particular type of therapy tend to produce results supporting that therapy, irrespective of what that therapy is. This research bias towards supporting one's own therapy is called an *allegiance effect* (Wampold, 2001). Allegiance effects occur for a variety of reasons beyond the remit of this book, but they should not be interpreted as fraud.

A balanced conclusion from these different points of view is that even if 'CBT is the best therapy available', any sensible scientific analysis of the data would suggest that the superiority of this (or any) therapy is very small. Interestingly, the NICE guidelines for treating depression (NICE, 2004) include CBT but do not rule out other therapies, on the basis that there is insufficient evidence to support one therapy over others. Although they are often quoted as supporting CBT therapy – which is true – this support is not exclusive. However, given the strong feelings generated in this area, and the political implications involved, there will always be those who believe that their own therapy is best. Beliefs are not necessarily shifted by scientific data.

Where psychotherapists are aware of the equivalence of outcome between psychotherapies it is sometimes referred to as 'our dirty little secret'. Researchers who carry out comparison studies know that it is 'risky' to compare their preferred therapy with another talking therapy. Nevertheless, when compared with waiting list controls, psychotherapy *is* very effective. By and large, about 75% of people show some improvement with psychotherapy, and psychotherapy is at least as effective if not more effective for depression than is pharmacotherapy (Wampold, 2001).

Component studies

Mechanisms underlying psychotherapy are investigated through the use of the component or dismantling study. In such studies, patients are randomly allocated to groups, some of whom receive the full therapy and others particular components of the therapy. The aim of such studies is to determine which components are active, i.e., have a therapeutic effect. As components are linked theoretically to mechanisms, discovery of the active components of psychotherapy provides information about underlying mechanisms. Component studies are therefore used to provide empirical support of particular therapies, as inclusion or exclusion of the active ingredient of the therapy should make a difference. Meta-analyses on component studies are less contentious than those relating to the dodo bird (Ahn and Wampold, 2001). There is really no evidence to support the assumption that particular components are better than any other. Numerous component studies show equivalence between the full therapy and partial components of the therapy.

Explanations for the dodo bird effect and null results from component studies

There are two explanations for the dodo bird effect and the null results from component studies. The explanation favoured by Wampold and some others is that the active ingredients of psychotherapy are those features that are common to all therapies (i.e., the therapeutic alliance) and that the components that distinguish one therapy from another (i.e., the therapy specific components) are inactive.

This *common factors* explanation is as follows. All psychotherapies have common features, which include the relationship with the therapist, the expectancy by the patient that the therapy will be effective, and behavioural engagement by the patient in the therapeutic process. It is these common factors that are responsible for therapeutic benefit as they elicit therapeutic mechanisms. Because all therapies have these common factors, the therapies are equally effective. Because all components of a therapy have these common factors, there is no difference between groups of patients receiving different components. The therapy-specific components do not elicit therapeutic mechanisms – they produce no benefit.

The term 'common factors' implies that the factors that contribute to therapeutic benefit are identifiable and distinct. As this implication may not be true, an alternative and preferred term is the *contextual model of psychotherapy*. The use of the word 'contextual' does not imply that there are distinct factors, as the patient may be responding to the context as a whole. As perception tends to be holistic (i.e., gestalt), it seems reasonable that the term *contextual model* provides a better description of the way patients respond to the therapeutic counter than *common factors model*.

There is a second, alternative explanation for the dodo bird effect and the null results from component studies: it is that both common factors and the therapy-specific components (i.e., the component distinguishing one therapy from another) are both active in that they produce therapeutic benefit. Why then do the dodo bird and component studies produce equivalence? The answer is that the logic of the equivalence and components studies is based on a false assumption. The assumption is that the mechanism of benefit experienced by the patient is determined by the type of therapy offered by the therapist. However, there is an alternative assumption. Suppose that the therapist merely provides a therapeutic environment, and that the patient selects from that environment those features that are most therapeutic for himself or herself. Each patient needs something from the therapeutic environment. Each patient takes something different from the same therapeutic environment. Although the therapist provides a particular sort of therapeutic environment, that environment suits some patients more than others. However, with any particular style of therapy there are always winners and losers in terms of patient–therapy-style fit, so some patients do better and others do worse. Thus, different therapies and different components do not produce equivalent results for individual patients, but overall, there are no differences between them.

This second explanation has some limited evidence in support. The effectiveness of flower essences was evaluated in a large study of 251 participants in which participants were provided with different descriptions of the way in which flower essences work (Hyland and Whalley 2008). For some participants, flower essences were described as a spiritual therapy; for others as a suggestive therapy. (Note: this was a placebo study as flower essences have been shown to be no different from placebo; Walach et al., 2001.) Spirituality predicted outcome for those with the spiritual contextualisation of flower essences, but not for those with the suggestive contextualisation (the correlations were significantly different). However, the overall improvement between the two groups was almost identical. The results showed no significance between the groups in terms of mean improvement, but the groups exhibited significantly different correlations between predictors and outcome – showing that different sorts of people responded best to the different types of therapy. These data show that equivalence in mean outcome between two therapies does not mean that the two therapies are working according to the same mechanism.

A summary of these two versions of the contextual model – the conventional and the alternative being proposed here – is set out in Table 8.1.

Table 8.1 *Two interpretations of the cause of outcome in psychotherapy*

Conventional contextual model	Alternative contextual model
The mechanisms of therapeutic benefit depend on the actions of the therapists.	The mechanisms of therapeutic benefit are selected by clients/patients from those available in the therapeutic context.
The mechanisms are those common to all therapies, and specific components have no role.	Any mechanism can contribute to benefit, and the labelling of common factors versus specific components is irrelevant to the patient/client.
Good therapists are those who provide the therapeutic alliance.	Good therapists are those who provide a range of opportunities for patients/clients to select from and achieve benefit.

If the alternative contextual model is correct, then the distinction between specific and common factors becomes unimportant: what is important is the therapeutic environment provided by the therapist and whether clients/patients can find opportunities within that environment to benefit from mechanisms of therapeutic change.

As a final point in this section, it should be noted that the placebo concept in psychotherapy is defined in a way that makes it functionally equivalent to the common factors or contextual model of psychotherapy. This equivalence provides an explanation for the considerable hostility directed by some clinical psychologists towards those advocating the common factors or contextual model of psychotherapy. At a professional and political level, psychotherapists need to establish the credibility of their craft. Failure to do so leads to lack of income and low self-esteem. Having created a criterion that fits within the medical model, and then shown that their therapy meets that criterion, it is very unwelcome to practising psychotherapists when research psychologists say that they have failed on that criterion. Not surprisingly, those involved in the politics of psychotherapy disagree that their therapy is different from placebo using the placebo test they have created. As is always the case with scientific debate, there are arguments in favour of both positions. Nevertheless, meta-analyses of equivalence studies (dodo bird effect) and component studies suggest one of two possibilities: *either* that the common factors or context play the major role in therapeutic outcome *or*, as I have suggested here, that patients elicit mechanisms of benefit from the context provided by the therapist, without regard to the therapist's intentions. Either way, these meta-analyses create problems for psychologists who are trying to justify their profession within a medical context.

Eclecticism and clinical practice

Modern research into the comparative effectiveness of psychotherapies (i.e., dodo bird effect) and component studies both use *manualised* psychotherapy. Manualised psychotherapy means that psychotherapy is strictly delivered according to a written manual – the psychotherapist does only what the manual specifies. The reason for editors and referees now insisting on manualised psychotherapy in research studies is that it is well known that in clinical practice psychotherapists use a variety of different techniques, and most do not practice according to their particular training. Therapists in clinical practice do not follow manuals! There is a common belief that after two years out of training, all psychotherapists, whatever their previous training experience, become *eclectic* psychotherapists. Eclectic means that they use whatever technique from whatever theoretical position they think might be useful for treating the patient (Garfield, 1995). There is some evidence that manualised psychotherapy might be *less* effective than allowing psychotherapists to be as eclectic as they wish. This last factor suggests that individualisation of therapy to the patient may be a factor in outcome – i.e., eclecticism as a strategy may be developed because it is found to work.

Eclecticism is not just limited to post-training practice. Informal examination of, for example, CBT training courses shows that students are provided with a range of information and techniques, not just those that might strictly be deemed CBT. To add to the confusion, the meaning of CBT varies. Although the original term was proposed by Aaron Beck (1967), CBT is now interpreted in a much broader way than originally conceived. For example, 'mindfulness-based CBT therapy' has been proposed as a form of CBT therapy (Teasdale *et al.*, 2000). Mindfulness is a meditative technique originally associated with Buddhism, but here coming with the politically accepted framework of CBT. One would imagine that the label 'Buddhist meditative technique' would not impress journal referees or those who provide the funds for therapy. 'Mindfulness-based CBT' sounds much better. Thus, labels of different types of therapy are probably less helpful than the specific techniques used in that therapy. Labels are politics; techniques are what happens in practice; mechanisms determine what actually happens in terms of the patient's benefit.

Therapist effects

There is something that probably applies to all types of therapy but which has only been investigated to any degree in psychotherapy: the effect of the therapist on outcome, or *therapist effects*. Research (Luborsky *et al.*, 1997; Okiishi *et al.*, 2003) shows that psychotherapists have consistent differences in their success rates, and these differences are substantial. Some psychotherapists achieve improvement in about 80–85% of their patients; others have levels of improvement that are very modest indeed (in exceptional circumstances, no change in the mean symptoms of patients). Therapist effects are difficult to explain. They are unrelated to the type and length of training – which is not too surprising if psychotherapists tend to end up as eclectic psychotherapists irrespective of training. They are also unrelated to the age or sex of the therapist. Therapist effects *are* related to the therapeutic alliance (Martin *et al.*, 2002). The therapeutic alliance includes the bond that the patient feels with the therapist as well as expectations of therapeutic benefit. Patients who feel a good bond with the therapist tend to get better quicker, and some therapists generate this bond more easily. Patients will be able to provide an estimate of therapeutic alliance after their first meeting, and this estimate then correlates with eventual outcome. However, therapeutic alliance explains a comparatively small amount of the variance of outcome (about 4%) (Martin *et al.*, 2002). Furthermore, it remains unknown what exactly the therapist does in order to create either therapeutic alliance or better outcome. 'Good' therapists seem to behave in a variety of different ways. Wampold's (2001) recommendation for anyone seeking psychotherapy is to select a psychotherapist on the basis of their past record of success. There is nothing else that provides a valid prediction of the likelihood of successful outcome.

There is a curious additional finding associated with therapist effects. Some patients receive both psychotherapy from a psychotherapist (whose average success rate will vary) and drug therapy (which is given by another person, a medical doctor). Research shows that if a patient goes to a 'good' psychotherapist (good in the sense of consistently providing better outcome), then the patient will also gain more benefit from the drug therapy (McKay *et al.*, 2006). Psychiatric medication works better if the patient is seeing a 'good' psychotherapist compared with a 'less good' psychotherapist. This additional finding has theoretical significance. An interaction of this kind suggests that the action of the psychotherapist and the effect of the drug are not working on disconnected parts of a system, but on a single system. The traditional perspective of Western medicine is that the drug is affecting the brain whereas the psychotherapist is affecting the mind – i.e., different 'bits'. That drug therapy and psychotherapy interact suggest that an alternative model is needed.

Box 8.4 How much does the 'other part' of therapy matter in psychotherapy?

The table shown below gives estimates of how much different components of psychotherapy contribute to outcome.

Source of effect	Proportion of variance in outcome explained (%)	Effect size
Effectiveness of psychotherapy comparing treatment with natural history	13	0.80
Relative effectiveness of different psychotherapies, comparing one with another	0–1	0.00–0.20
Relative effect of different components of therapy	0	0.00
Relative effectiveness of 'minimal' treatments compared with natural history	4	0.40
Correlation between therapeutic alliance and outcome	5	0.45
Correlation between allegiance of researchers to therapy and outcome	Up to 10	Up to 0.65
Therapist effects: contribution of different therapists to outcome	6–9	0.50–0.60

Source: adapted from Bruce E Wampold, *The Great Psychotherapy Debate*, Mahwal, NJ: Lawrence Erlbaum, 2001, with permission from publisher and author.

Overall, comparatively little variance is explained. It would seem that the client/patient is contributing to outcome. The idea that the client makes a difference has an important theoretical implication. Perhaps the client is not an inactive substance waiting to be cured. It may be that the client is on a road to recovery or is not and the therapy merely hastens or provides a catalyst for recovery. It may be that what matters is what the client gets out of the therapy rather than what the therapist gives.

Complementary and alternative medicine (CAM)

The term complementary medicine and alternative medicine is commonly defined as those treatments that are *not* part of the state-provided medical service. This negative definition is problematic in two ways. First, what is or is not provided by the state varies between countries and over time. Homeopathy is provided by the state in Germany, traditional Chinese medicine in China, and in the UK cancer patients are frequently offered a range of complementary treatments to help the patient feel more comfortable. The second problem is that a large and very disparate group of therapies are lumped together.

There are several ways of classifying different complementary therapies, and therefore of providing some way of distinguishing between them. For example, in the USA, the National Institutes for Health's National Center for Complementary and Alternative Medicine (NCCAM) divides complementary and alternative medicines (CAMs) into the following categories:

- whole medical systems, which include homeopathy, traditional Chinese medicine and Ayurvedic medicine;
- biologically based practice, which includes herbs and vitamins (note that vitamin supplements are therefore classified as a CAM);
- manipulative and body-based practices, which include osteopathy, chiropracty and massage;
- energy medicine, which includes spiritual healing, Reiki as well as techniques involving magnetic fields; and
- mind–body therapy, which includes cognitive behaviour therapy (CBT), prayer, meditation and support groups.

Such classification systems are easily criticised. For example, many CBT therapists might feel affronted at (a) being classified as a practitioner of alternative medicine and (b) being included with prayer and support groups. More importantly, there is considerable variation of belief and practice within each different type of CAM. For example, homeopathy was invented by Samuel Hahnemann (1755–1843), who wrote of his therapy as being a spiritual therapy – and by implication with links to spiritual healing (Hahnemann, 1999). While some homeopaths accept a spiritual basis for homeopathy, others see it as a purely mechanical technique based on ultra-dilution of substances (ultra-dilution means diluted to such an extent that no molecules remain). Additionally, acupuncture can be applied using the theory of Chinese medicine (i.e., the body becoming out of balance) or, in a Westernised form, by treating specific symptoms. In the case of the former, the clinician diagnoses and treats in terms of general signs such as tongue colour and the feel of the pulse. In the case of the latter, the clinician diagnoses and treats on the basis of the presenting symptoms. It is interesting to note that within both acupuncture and homeopathy there is a debate about the extent to which treatment should be based on the characteristics of the person versus the characteristics of the presenting symptom. In sum, classifications of CAMs tend to be undermined by the variability of practice within each CAM.

A more useful form of classification, and one that is found in a UK government report (House of Lords, 2000) is to divide CAMs into those that purport to diagnose and treat the person, and those that do not diagnose but simply aim to improve the health of the patient. Homeopathy, acupuncture, chiropracty, osteopathy and herbal medicine fall into the first category. Massage, healing and meditation fall into the latter category. This classification based on the intent of the therapist is useful because it divides therapies on the basis of the specificity of their effects. CAMS that 'purport to diagnose and treat the person' purport to do so on the basis that there is some form of specificity. That specificity may take the form of treating particular symptoms (i.e., the approach taken in modern Western medicine), or it may take the form of treating particular types of unbalance (i.e., the approach taken in traditional medicines), but there is always some kind of specificity. There is always some form of diagnosis that precedes treatment. As such these therapies accept the idea of specificity that is at the heart of all medical systems.

By contrast, there are those CAMS that aim to improve the health of the patient but have no specificity in the type of treatment delivered. The massage therapists will provide (approximately) the same massage, irrespective of whether a patient is depressed, anxious or terminally ill. There is no diagnosis prior to treatment. Similarly, there is no attempt to link particular types of meditation with particular diseases or people. Advocates of meditation recommend a particular technique or techniques.

The *non-specific CAM treatments*, namely those that improve health and so can treat any disease, have an interesting parallel with those psychotherapies associated with the humanistic tradition. In both cases, the treatment involves a therapeutic bond with a therapist and expectancy of benefit. The authors of a review into the effectiveness of massage therapy concluded that massage was as effective at treating

Box 8.5 Specificity for meditation?

The assertion that meditative techniques are not specific to diseases is not entirely true. There is a form of Kundalini meditation in which different body movements are said to be best for treating particular mental problems (Shannahoff-Khalsa, 2004). So, for example, depression would be treated with one type of movement and anxiety with another. There is no evidence to support such specificity.

depression as psychotherapy, but that it works through the same common factors route (Moyer *et al.*, 2004).

Does complementary and alternative medicine work? The problem of placebos in CAM medicine research

One of the most important differences between the specific and non-specific CAMs is that the question of evidence is treated differently in each case. When discussing any form of CAM, a common question is, 'does it really work?' The meaning of this question differs between the specific CAMs (those that purport to diagnose and treat) and the non-specific CAMs (those that do not).

If the aim of therapy is to diagnose and treat, then the question 'does it work?' is reinterpreted as 'does it work better than placebo?', thereby providing a direct comparison with conventional drug therapy. However, if the aim is to improve health, then the question 'does it work?' should be interpreted as 'does it work better than no treatment?' (in practice, 'no treatment' approximates to waiting list control), thereby putting it on a par with at least some of the research in psychotherapy. There is sometimes considerable hostility towards complementary medicine. If the CAM advertises itself as a physiologically active treatment when it is in fact just a placebo, then the complementary practitioner is exploiting the 'rude and credulous populace' (to use the words in the charter of the Royal College of Physicians) and should be stopped. However, if the complementary practitioner (such as massage) is not proposing a physiologically active treatment but is just providing care and lifestyle intervention for the patient, then this falls outside the realm of medicine. If the CAM is 'just' providing care and lifestyle management, then this, after all, is an activity already practised by nurses and so can be welcomed as ancillary support for medical treatment. CAM is most accepted within conventional medical systems when it is ancillary to conventional medical care. If CAM just makes people happy, then it is not a competitor for conventional medicine. Holidays often make people happy, but doctors do not prescribe holidays for their patients.

Given the large number of CAMs (there are about 50 distinct types), it is very difficult to summarise the research in a short space. However, as summarisation is necessary, an overview is provided by saying that the two questions 'does it work in relation to placebo?' versus 'does it work in relation to no treatment?' lead to different conclusions.

Any complementary therapy, irrespective of which group it belongs to, produces better results, on average, than no treatment. That different types of complementary medicine 'work' in this sense is uncontroversial. *All therapy works.* What is controversial are two linked ideas: (a) whether working in this sense is sufficient and (b) whether the complementary therapy works in relation to placebo. Broadly speaking, researchers and practitioners fall into three categories. There are those, particularly complementary therapists, who think that (a) it is sufficient that complementary works better than no treatment and (b) in any case it is better than placebo. Others, including some conventional medical researchers, think that (a) to be useful CAM needs to show that it is better than placebo rather than better only than no treatment, and (b) complementary medicine is in fact no better than placebo. There is a small group of people (including some psychologists) who fall into a third category: they believe that (a) it is sufficient for CAM to work better than no treatment and (b) it does not matter that it is no more effective than placebo.

Let us leave these three theoretical positions to focus on the data. There are numerous studies of both the effectiveness (comparison with natural history) and the efficacy (comparison with placebo) of different complementary medicines. Effectiveness studies consistently show that acupuncture reduces insomnia when pre-treatment is compared with post-treatment (Sok *et al.*, 2003). Massage leads to improvement in anxiety and depression with effect sizes similar to those in hypertension (Moyer *et al.*, 2004). Meditation has been shown to have clinically significant effects for hypertension (Anderson *et al.*, 2008), with effect sizes of 0.5 for mental and 0.4 for physical health outcomes (Grossman *et al.*, 2004). Thus, the effect size for meditation is the same order of magnitude as for psychotherapy (see Box 8.4), where the effect size is estimated to be about 0.8.

The efficacy studies are the ones we focus on here, as the effectiveness studies merely establish the obvious. Meta-analyses of efficacy studies from the pro-complementary medicine and anti-complementary medicine camps tend to produce different conclusions. These differences arise from the selection of studies to be used in the meta-analyses (Linde and Willich, 2003). There is an additional complication that, for many complementary medicines it is impossible to obtain adequate placebo controls, so the issue of placebo control itself is thrown in doubt.

For example, sham acupuncture is used as a placebo control in acupuncture studies. Sham acupuncture can take one of two forms. The first is to use sham needles, that is, a needle that looks real but that disappears into its handle rather like a stage dagger. The second is to use real needles but to insert the needle in a slightly incorrect position. In each case, the sham and real acupuncture have to be delivered by an acupuncturist. The acupuncturist *has* to be aware which patients are receiving the real and which the sham acupuncture. Unlike drug trials where therapist and patient are both blind to the condition to which the patient is allocated, therapists are not blind in acupuncture studies. Of course, in drug trials, the patient may break blind for reasons given above. Additionally, sham needles do not feel like real needles (though naive subjects may not recognise which is which), so the sham is not psychologically equivalent to the real thing. Whatever method is used to achieve placebo control in an acupuncture study, that method is open to criticism. Inserting a needle in the skin produces endorphins (i.e., endogenously produced morphine-like chemicals that reduce pain) and therefore inserting a needle at any point will have biological effects. By contrast the sham needle touches the skin, and the technique of acupressure is based on the assumption that skin contact is sufficient to have a therapeutic effect.

One might imagine that it is easier to create an adequate control in homeopathy, in that it is possible to create 'inert' homeopathic remedies. However, even here there are problems. Homoeopathists prescribe their remedies on the basis of a wide-ranging consultation that lasts up to an hour. Because the correct remedy (from over 2,000) may not have been selected on the first occasion, the homoeopathist sees the patient again some time (e.g., two weeks) later and, on the basis of the patient's report of symptom change, either changes the remedy or leaves things as they are. Homoeopathists report that if they do not know whether the patient is receiving sham homeopathy, then they cannot deliver homoeopathy in the way they should, so the treatment will be less effective (Weiner, 2002) Whether one believes this to be a valid argument will depend on therapeutic allegiance – homeopaths tend to be more sympathetic to the argument than others. The overall consequence of these methodological difficulties is that either side (the pro and anti camps) can usually find adequate data to support their own position.

Given the strong feelings in this area and given the methodological problems involved, is it is possible to come to any conclusion? There has been over the years a steady accumulation of data, and there are associated meta-analyses, so a tentative conclusion is possible, even though many authors of meta-analyses note the lack of good-quality trials. Some, but no means all, of these meta-analyses of randomised controlled trials are listed in Table 8.2. Some meta-analyses suggest that the CAM is more effective than placebo, but many do not. A sensible interpretation is that if there are differences between a CAM and placebo (i.e., efficacy studies) then the differences are at most small and limited to particular clinical indications.

Table 8.2 *Some meta-analyses of different types of CAM*

Homeopathy: Linde *et al.* (1997)	'The results of our meta-analysis are not compatible with the hypothesis that the clinical effects of homeopathy are completely due to placebo. However, we found insufficient evidence from these studies that homeopathy is clearly efficacious for any single clinical condition.'
Homeopathy: Ernst (2002)	'There was no homeopathic remedy that was demonstrated to yield clinical effects that are convincingly different from placebo.'
Homeopathy: Shang *et al.* (2005)	'Biases are present in placebo-controlled trials of both homoeopathy and conventional medicine. When account was taken for these biases in the analysis, there was weak evidence for a specific effect of homoeopathic remedies, but strong evidence for specific effects of conventional interventions. This finding is compatible with the notion that the clinical effects of homoeopathy are placebo effects.'
Homeopathy: Lüdtke and Rutten (2008)	Re-analysis of that by Shang *et al.* 'Homeopathy had a significant effect beyond placebo.'
Chiropracty: Ernst and Canter (2006)	A review of reviews: 'The conclusions of these reviews were largely negative, except for back pain where spinal manipulation was considered superior to sham manipulation but not better than conventional treatments … Collectively these data do not demonstrate that spinal manipulation is an effective intervention for any condition.'
Chiropracty: Proctor *et al.* (2006)	Treatment of dysmenorrhoea: 'There is no evidence to suggest that spinal manipulation is effective in the treatment of dysmenorrhoea. In the one trial reporting on adverse effects there was no greater risk of such events with spinal compared with sham manipulation.'
Acupuncture: Martin *et al.* (2002)	Did not find evidence of an effect of acupuncture in reducing asthma. The authors note that the meta-analysis was limited by shortcomings of the individual trials.
Acupuncture: Manheimer *et al.* (2005)	'For the primary outcome of short-term relief of chronic pain, the meta-analyses showed that acupuncture is significantly more effective than sham treatment.'
Acupuncture: Smith *et al.* (2010)	Meta-analysis of treatment for depression: 'There was insufficient evidence of a consistent beneficial effect from acupuncture compared with a wait list control or sham acupuncture control.'
Acupuncture Langhorst *et al.* (2010)	Meta-analysis for fibromyalgia: 'Strong evidence for the reduction of pain (SMD -0.25; 95% CI -0.49, -0.02; $P = 0.04$) was found at post-treatment. There was no evidence for the reduction of fatigue and sleep disturbances, or the improvement of physical function at post-treatment. There was no evidence for the reduction of pain and improvement of physical function at the latest follow-up.'

Distant healing: Astin *et al.* (2000)	57% of trials found a positive effect. Methodological problems were noted.
Distant healing: Crawford *et al.* (2004)	Compared clinical and laboratory studies: 'Of the clinical studies, 31 (70.5%) reported positive outcomes as did 28 (62%) of the laboratory studies; 4 (9%) of the clinical studies reported negative outcomes as did 15 (33%) of the laboratory studies'. Methodological problems were noted.
Distant healing: Masters *et al.* (2006)	No evidence that distant healing (prayer) is effective.

Box 8.6 The example of homeopathy

A very large homeopathic study of asthma found no significant difference in respiratory function (the primary outcome measure) at the end of the study between placebo and verum (in fact, those in the verum group did slightly worse than the placebo group) (Lewith *et al.*, 2002). Where multiple outcome measures are taken, medical researchers are required to specify their primary outcome prior to the study, and so their finding is classified as finding no evidence for homeopathy. However, there was a significant ($p = 0.02$) oscillation for several secondary outcome measures in the verum arm that was not predicted before the study but could be explained retrospectively (Hyland and Lewith, 2002). This significant result can either be dismissed as being a random occurrence (multiple testing has a substantial effect on significance levels; hence the need to distinguish primary from secondary outcomes) or taken as evidence that 'something' is going on. Dear reader, take your choice: this book is about the non-specific not the specific effects of CAM.

It is worth noting that one of the studies shown in Table 8.2 examines the efficacy of acupuncture for depression (Smith *et al.*, 2010). Their negative conclusions should be seen in the light of the weak efficacy for conventional antidepressants shown in the various meta-analyses carried out by Kirsch (2009) but the effectiveness of psychotherapy and placebos in reducing depression. The results of meta-analyses depend on the studies included. In the case of Kirsch's later meta-analyses, published and unpublished trials were included. Only published trials were considered in Smith's, so publication bias would tend towards the likelihood of finding an effect However, antidepressants have side effects and as, patients and doctors break blind, the efficacy of the active treatment is exaggerated: this would not be case for acupuncture where blinding appears effective, even though the adequacy of the control can be questioned (sham acupuncture is similar to acupressure, see above).

The debate about the efficacy of CAM obscures an important observation: many CAMs do not purport to treat diseases in any traditional sense and for these CAMS there is no effective placebo comparison. For example, massage therapy neither diagnoses nor provides any clear rationale for therapy effectiveness. Neither patients nor therapists can be blind to the fact that massage is taking place. There is no placebo control. Meta-analysis of massage therapy studies shows that massage is effective compared with no treatment (Moyer *et al.*, 2004). The effect sizes from combining several studies were 0.75 for anxiety, 0.62 for depression and 0.31 for delayed pain conditions. Note the similarity in effect size for psychological outcomes compared with that given by Wampold (2001) for psychotherapy and by Kirsch (2009) for placebos. Massage also showed reductions in cortisol, blood pressure and heart rate, indicating that massage also has physiological effects (effect sizes between 0.4 and 0.1). Moyer and colleagues (2004) conclude that because the benefit of massage occurs over a period of time (i.e., weeks), the benefit of massage is not mediated through a biological route (e.g., the effect of touch on the endocrine system) but through a psychological route – i.e., the effect of the psychological experience of massage on biological systems.

Use of complementary medicine and alternative medicine

It has been suggested that there is little point in carrying out randomised controlled studies of CAM as, whatever the results, those who believe in it continue to do so, and those who do not believe in it continue to be sceptical (Weiner, 2002). This factor is in itself interesting: why is complementary medicine popular and why is incidence of its use so high? In the UK, 10% of the population have seen a complementary practitioner in the last year, and 30% have used some form of CAM, accounting for almost half a billion pounds of expenditure per year. In the USA, 40% of the population use some form of CAM during the year, of which non-mineral, non-vitamin natural products (17%) and deep-breathing exercises (12%) are the most common (Barnes *et al.*, 2008; Thomas *et al.*, 2001).

There are several factors associated with the use of CAM (Furnham, 2003). These include:

- longer and better interpersonal contact with a clinician;
- failure of conventional medicine to resolve the problem; and
- convergence between the client's beliefs and the holistic health beliefs expressed in complementary medicine.

Note: Use of CAM and holistic health beliefs are correlated (Hyland *et al.*, 2003) and both correlate with absorption and spirituality (Petry and Finkel, 2004; Wheeler and Hyland, 2008).

However, research into the use of CAM in medical settings obscures the fact that people use CAM for different reasons, and not necessarily to treat illness. CAM is sometimes used by people who have a diagnosed illness (e.g., cancer) where there is a hope that the complementary medicine will have either psychological or physiological benefits (Catt *et al.*, 2006). However, CAM is also a 'lifestyle choice' by people who have no diagnosed illness (Feldman and Laura, 2004; Sointu, 2006). The idea that complementary medicine – and other therapies – acts as a form of lifestyle choice blurs the line between medicine and lifestyle. Recall that going on holiday can make people happy, but holidays are not considered part of medicine.

In Chapter 1 a distinction was made between systems that improve health and those that treat disease. If the aim of therapy is to treat disease, then there is a clear divide between medical treatment and lifestyle choice. Medicine involves doing something to the body that treats the disease – it is treatment selected by the doctor to correct the specific pathophysiology. However, if the aim of therapy is to improve health, then there is no boundary between therapy and lifestyle. If the aim is to improve health, then that which improves health is both simultaneously part of therapy and part of lifestyle.

Specific and non-specific revisited

The terms *specific* and *non-specific* are used in different senses in psychotherapy and in medicine. In medicine the word *specific* refers to a specific pathology, namely the specific physiological abnormality that is responsible for the (specific) disease. In psychotherapy the terms *specific* and *non-specific* refer to the components of therapy, namely that which is treating the pathology. It is easy to suppose that a specific component is inevitably linked to a specific pathology, but this is not necessary the case: the two concepts are logically distinct.

The concept of a specific component is socially determined – just in the same way that the meaning of CAM is socially determined. For example, the specific component of CBT is different from the specific component of psychodynamic therapy. More importantly, the meaning of specific component versus non-specific component is not constant. Although both CBT and psychodynamic therapy treat the therapeutic alliance as non-specific, it is the therapeutic bond that is specific in Rogerian counselling. Of course, it is possible to argue that Rogerian counselling is CBT minus the specific component, but Rogerian therapists would argue to the contrary. From a Rogerian perspective, the therapeutic bond plays a unique and specific role and has an emphasis not present in CBT therapy. Additionally, positive psychology techniques (Seligman *et al.*, 2005; Sin and Lyubomirsky, 2009) are different from the therapeutic bond, but are specific in the sense that they involve specific techniques (details are provided in the next chapter).

Rather than conceptualise components of therapy as being specific or non-specific, it is more useful to distinguish the intent of therapy: whether it is intended to have an effect *only* on a specific pathology, or whether it has a non-specific effect on multiple pathologies. CBT therapy is based on an assumption of specificity – that there is a specific component of therapy that affects only a particular pathology. This assumption derives from a more fundamental belief that the pathology involves specific errors in a system. There is therefore a specific treatment for the specific error. By contrast, Rogerian therapy and other more recent therapies called positive psychology (see Chapter 9) are based on the assumption that a specific component of therapy has a non-specific effect. This second assumption derives from the more fundamental belief that the body is a self-healing system (see Chapter 1).

What does the evidence tell us? There are strongly held views in each direction, but the evidence cited above points to a general conclusion that the specific components of psychotherapy have non-specific effects. For example, a form of positive psychology intervention called gratitude therapy has been shown in several studies to reduce symptoms of depression (Sin and Lyubomirsky, 2009). Gratitude therapy involves cultivating the sense of being grateful for something, and there is a logic why such an experience might lead to reduced depression. However, there is no logical reason why gratitude therapy should reduce body dysmorphia (extreme dissatisfaction with body appearance). Nevertheless, self-help gratitude therapy has been shown not only to be effective but also to be as effective as self-help CBT for dysmorphia (Geraghty *et al.*, 2010a, 2010b). In addition, McDonagh *et al.* (2005) compared CBT with present-centred therapy for the treatment of post-traumatic stress disorder (PTSD), selecting the latter treatment on the basis that it should not be beneficial for PTSD. However, the data showed that present-centred therapy was as successful as CBT. In addition to studies examining the effects of psychotherapy, research shows that the effect of psychologically mediated therapy is not limited to psychological effects. The study by Thomas (1987) cited above showed that a friendly doctor compared with an unfriendly doctor leads to a greater reduction in medically unexplained symptoms. Medically unexplained symptoms include somatic symptoms. The above shows the generality of some 'specific' sorts of psychological intervention.

The question remains, 'does CBT also have non-specific effects?'. The answer to this question comes from the component studies referred to above. If CBT has *only* specific effects, then the specific component of therapy must be active. However, as the meta-analysis by Ahn and Wampold (2001) shows, there is no evidence that the specific component is active. There is only one possible conclusion to all this evidence: irrespective of whether it is psychotherapy or complementary medicine or the placebo effect in a clinical trial, all these treatments appear to have non-specific effects. Psychologically mediated treatment, whether designated as specific or non-specific, has non-specific benefits. Mechanisms of therapeutic benefit will be considered in the next chapter.

How effective is non-specific therapy?

The above review shows that there are therapeutic effects that are non-specific in that there is no one-to-one relationship between the therapy and the benefits for a particular pathology. Consequently, any such therapy will have or purport to have a wide range of benefits. Placebos are a non-specific type of therapy; so is the contextual model of psychotherapy; so is positive psychology. The effectiveness of antidepressants and CAM is also primarily mediated through a non-specific route. The difference between placebos and the contextual model of psychotherapy is conceptually messy because the term placebo is used in many ways, as is the concept of a non-specific component of therapy. The conclusion to be drawn from the review above is that psychologically mediated therapies have non-specific effects.

Modern medicine is predicated on the assumption of specificity. Diseases have specific causes and therapies therefore have specific effects: one disease, one pill, one cure. There is therefore an obvious question: how effective are therapies that have non-specific effects compared with those that have specific effects? This question can be answered by examining data from two sources: from the placebo research and from psychological treatments for mental and physical illness.

The power of the placebo

How effective is the placebo? No simple answer is possible because the term placebo can be used for a variety of different situations in which effectiveness is very different. It is useful to distinguish:

- *Short-term laboratory studies of placebo effects versus long-term therapeutic studies.* In short-term laboratory studies, participants are led to believe that they receive a beneficial substance when it is in fact inert. Such studies are often *analogue* studies in the sense that they provide an analogy to real therapy. An example of an analogue study is one in which a pain stimulus is presented to students who do not have health problems and are not motivated to get better. The implication is that the results of the laboratory study generalise to clinical situations of pain control. Long-term therapeutic studies typically involve patients with genuine illness, and who are motivated to get better. Almost all long-term studies are based on randomised controlled trials in which researchers examine the improvement in the placebo arm of a study, rarely compared with a natural history control. Randomised controlled trials require patients to be fully informed that they will get either the real treatment or placebo. As patients do not know whether they are getting the real treatment, the placebo effect may be diminished.
- *Studies in which the outcome is a psychological variable versus studies in which the outcome is a physiological variable.* Pain and depression are examples of psychological variables; lung function and blood pressure are examples of physiological variables.

The question of the power of the placebo is controversial. The controversy can be illustrated by two papers, one early and one late, each reviewing clinical trial data where there was a physiological outcome. In his paper 'The powerful placebo' Beecher (1955) provided an estimate of the effectiveness of 35% of active treatment. A more recent paper entitled 'Is the placebo powerless?' (Hróbjartsson and Gøtzsche, 2001) suggested the effect of placebo was minimal. Both papers have had a considerable impact. Both have flaws and have been widely criticised.

The question 'how effective?' indicates the need for a metric. To answer the question there must be some way of quantifying the effects of placebos. Quantitative estimates of the effectiveness of the placebo are commonly derived in one of three ways.

Comparison with biological treatments

First, it is possible to estimate the proportion of clinical effect that is psychologically mediated versus biologically mediated. For example,

Kirsch (2009) estimated that 80% of the effect of SSRIs for the treatment of depression is placebo mediated (see above). By contrast, 50% of the effect of analgesics for pain is estimated as being due to placebo (Benedetti *et al.*, 2003; Kirsch, 2009). Both depression and pain are psychological variables, and estimates are based on long-term clinical trials comparing active treatments with placebo. By contrast, research into the placebo effects of asthma inhalers (bronchodilators) are laboratory based and researchers measure the response to a placebo in a laboratory situation where the response time is a matter of minutes. A review of this research shows considerable variability in research findings, but suggests that the placebo effect of the inhaler is at most only 30% as effective as the inhaler containing the active treatment (Sodergren and Hyland, 1999). Proportional estimates of effectiveness of this kind have the advantage that they express the power of the placebo in terms of real clinical practice. Additionally, this metric provides a way of comparing the power of a treatment that is specific with one that is not. The disadvantage of this form of estimation is that value obtained depends on the effectiveness of the biological treatment – the proportion that the placebo contributes to the treatment of depression would be far less if antidepressants were more efficacious. By contrast, bronchodilator asthma medication is highly efficacious. Although the power of the placebo is confounded with the power of the biological treatment, this type of estimation is nevertheless useful because it provides an estimate of clinical relevance of the placebo in terms of current practice.

Effect size
The second way of estimating the power of the placebo is in terms of a statistic called *effect size*. There are several statistics for effect size, but a common one is the standardised mean difference between the placebo follow-up and baseline (i.e., mean difference divided by the standard deviation). Measures of effect size between baseline and follow-up provide a useful estimate of the power of the placebo in clinical trials, but only for diseases that do not change spontaneously and that are therefore unaffected by natural history. For diseases where natural history is assumed to be constant, a meta-analysis (Meissner *et al.*, 2007) of the effectiveness of the placebo suggests that the pooled effect size across several physical measures of disease severity (e.g., those relating to asthma, hypertension, prostatic hyperplasia) was 0.34, whereas that for biochemical markers of disease severity (e.g., those relating to diabetes mellitus, chronic hepatitis C and hypercholesterolaemia) was 0.03. Thus, the effect size for placebos is somewhere between small and moderate for physical markers of disease, whereas it is near zero for

Box 8.7 Effect size convention

Cohen's d is a measure of effect size where the mean difference between baseline and follow-up is divided by the pooled standard deviation of baseline and follow-up. By convention, any effect size of about 0.2 or less is considered small, those about 0.4 are moderate and those above 0.8 are considered large.

biochemical markers. Note that this meta-analysis is based on clinical trials and therefore provides an estimate of the long-term effectiveness of placebos in terms of physiological outcomes. A comparison of the meta-analysis of Meissner *et al.* (2007) with that of antidepressant use in clinical trials (Kirsch, 2009) shows that the effect size of placebo response for (some) psychological outcomes is much greater – at least of the order of 0.8. Note that a figure of 0.8 as an effect size is also that given for psychotherapy (Wampold, 2001); one might be tempted to conclude that the effect size of any psychologically mediated therapeutic effect is about 0.8 for psychological outcomes. Thus effect sizes for psychological symptoms can be large, whereas those for physiological outcomes are at best moderate.

Percentage improving

A final way to estimate the power of the placebo is in terms of the percentage of those improving. Walach and Maidhof (1999) provide a meta-analysis of the results from clinical trials in several disease areas where the percentage improving in the active treatment is compared with that of placebo. The results are shown in Table 8.3.

Table 8.3 shows that the placebo response for dementia is small compared with that of affective disorder, indicating that the placebo effect varies with the disease. However, percentage improvement as a metric should be treated with caution as, owing to measurement error, some people improve and some deteriorate on any outcome measure. One way of detecting and hence accounting for such variation is to measure the degree to which people deteriorate as well as improve during a placebo treatment. Studies (e.g., Hyland and Whalley, 2008) in which people received a placebo treatment for mood indicate that about 50% improve, 40% remain the same and 10% deteriorate. If those deteriorating are subtracted from those that improve, then the figure of improving reduces to 40%. Note that this correction would imply that there is no placebo response in dementia – a conclusion also drawn by Walach and Maidhof (1999).

Table 8.3 *Percentage improvement across different types of disease treatment (adapted from Walach and Maidhof, 1999, p. 328)*

Disorder	Percentage improved	
	Active treatment	Placebo
Affective disorder	65	46
Panic disorder	49	23
Personality disorder	65	35
Dementia	32	10
Pain	37	33
Cancer	37	33

Whatever the method of assessing the power of the placebo, the results indicate that the placebo is more effective for psychological than for physiological outcomes, and that for some diseases or physiological variables there is no placebo effect at all. There are two points of theoretical interest that emerge from the examination of placebos in clinical trials. The first is a curious finding reported by Kirsch (2009) that, across different studies of depression, there is a correlation of about 0.9 between the effect size in the active treatment of the study and the effect size in the placebo treatment. This finding suggests that much of the active treatment is caused by placebo. However, it also shows that the placebo response in clinical trials is variable in a way that is consistent across different clinical trials. That is, the placebo response is not something that is the same in every clinical trial, but, rather, the placebo response is affected by something that is varying between clinical trials. In multi-centre clinical trials, it is not unusual for there to be significant differences in placebo response between centres (Zajicek *et al.*, 2003). Something happens in a clinical trial that contributes to the placebo, and that something varies between centres and between trials. The second point of theoretical interest comes from the meta-analysis of Walach and Maidhof (1999). The authors found little evidence for the placebo response decreasing over time. Thus, it seems reasonable to assume that the placebos are having long-term therapeutic effects – but these effects vary between different centres carrying out the study.

The problem of trial effects

One of the difficulties in inferring the power of placebo effects from clinical trials is that placebo effects can be confounded by trial effects.

A good way of explaining a trial effect is to use an example. Clinical trials of asthma medication commonly show improvement on the placebo arm. The improvement in the placebo arm can come about for two reasons: (a) a psychologically mediated route (i.e., what is normally referred to as placebo) or (b) a biological route (i.e., a trial effect). It is easy to miss the biologically mediated effects of placebo treatments.

Biological effects in the placebo arm. Most people with asthma and hence those entered into clinical trials are prescribed regular inhaled steroids. It is considered unethical to deprive people of their regular inhaled steroids during a clinical trial, as to do so would put them at risk of an asthma attack. Many asthma clinical trials, therefore, have the following design. Patients are randomised to *either* take their regular steroid inhaler plus an additional inhaler containing an active drug *or* take their regular steroid inhaler plus an additional inhaler containing placebo. Thus, the active drug has a placebo control, but patients are safe because even those in the control arm are taking regular steroids – or should be, as in clinical practice about 50% of those prescribed regular steroids do not take them regularly.

The effect of being in a clinical trial is likely to alter patients' behaviour. One possible change is that they become more mindful of their regular inhaler and take it more regularly. i.e., become more adherent to the treatment regimen. Becoming mindful of the regular inhaler can come about for a variety of reasons – increased attention to therapy leading to better adherence or better satisfaction with treatment leading to adherence. Better doctor–patient communication is associated with better adherence (Gross *et al.*, 2003). The result of better adherence will be better lung function because better adherence with the regular inhaled steroid will reduce inflammation and so lead to less bronchoconstriction. Thus, the improvement in the placebo arm is biologically mediated (due to greater adherence to medicine) rather than psychologically mediated. Many other clinical trials have a similar design; patients with chronic diseases cannot be deprived of their regular medication. It is generally accepted that a clinical trial provides patients with better care than clinical practice. Placebo arms of clinical trials are good places to be!

The above shows how difficult it is to provide any fair estimate of the power of the placebo from the placebo arm of clinical trials. It is certainly possible that the estimates given above are overestimates due to confusion with trial effects. One of the main areas of uncertainty concerns the extent to which placebos can have long-term physiological effects. The question of psychological effects on physical outcomes can be examined with another type of study, namely psychotherapeutic interventions for major illness. Several studies have examined the effect of psychological interventions on morbidity and mortality in major illness. Several meta-analyses exist for psychological treatments for cancer and heart disease, and these are reviewed in the next section.

Psychotherapy for major illness

There is ample evidence that psychotherapy for major illness has a substantial effect on well-being. Such a finding is not surprising. Psychotherapy improves psychological outcomes, and there is no reason for there being an exception in the case of people with major illness. The more contentious issue is whether psychotherapy affects morbidity (i.e., physiological measures of disease severity) or mortality (i.e., length of survival).

Psychological interventions for physical illness are commonly predicated on research suggesting that diseases such as cancer and heart disease have *specific* psychological antecedents (see Chapter 3). According to this view, Type A behaviour causes heart disease and Type C (emotional repression and depression) causes cancer. Psychosocial interventions for heart disease commonly aim to reduce the Type A behaviour pattern. Those that are designed for cancer commonly address emotional suppression and depression. Chapter 3 reviewed conclusions that (a) there is little evidence of specificity, though there does appear to be a disease-prone personality, and (b) the relationship between personality and the development of either cancer or heart disease is contentious at best. Thus, the very basis of these interventions can be questioned. Nevertheless, although psychosocial interventions for major disease may be predicated on possibly unsupported theories, the evidence shows that psychotherapy does not always work through the mechanisms assumed by researchers. Thus, it makes sense to review the research on psychosocial interventions for heart disease and cancer without predicating this research on the lack of evidence indicating specificity of a psychosocial cause.

In the case of heart disease, an early meta-analysis showed that psychosocial interventions improve both morbidity and mortality (Linden *et al.*, 1996), at least for the first two years after treatment for heart disease. Following other inconsistent findings, a more recent meta-analysis showed a reduction in mortality following psychological treatment, but only for men (Linden *et al.*, 2007). In both cases, however, the effects are comparatively small. A yet more recent meta-analysis (Whalley *et al.*, 2011) shows that a reduction in mortality following treatment fails to reach statistical significance. The difference between the two most recent meta-analyses is due to the studies selected for inclusion: that by Whalley *et al.* (2001) excluded studies where follow-up was 6 months or less; that by Linden *et al.* (2007) did not. Finally, exercise with or without a psychoeducational intervention *has* been shown to reduce cardiac deaths, but it remains unclear whether the presence of the psychoeducational component makes a difference (Jolliffe *et al.*, 2001). If it is the behavioural component of the psychological intervention produces the benefit, then it may be the physical effect of exercise that improves outcome rather than the psychological effect of therapy. If a psychologically mediated effect did occur, some of the benefit could be mediated through the effect of psychosocial interventions on blood pressure. Whereas negative emotions tend to increase blood pressure, positive ones decrease blood pressure (Ostir *et al.*, 2006). In addition, there is evidence that depression is a risk factor for mortality following heart attack (Barth *et al.*, 2004), so psychosocial interventions may be effective through reducing depression.

Whether psychosocial interventions improve cancer survival and reduce morbidity is also controversial: while some meta-analyses and reviews note that results from different studies are inconsistent, some conclude that there is an effect and others that there is not (Coyne *et al.*, 2007, 2009; Fawzy, 1999; Kraemer *et al.*, 2009; Ross *et al.*, 2002). As it is possible for rational people to disagree, the conclusion to draw is that if there is psychosocial effect on morbidity and mortality for cancer, it is likely to be small. A recent study showing that palliative care reduces mortality for lung cancer compared with normal treatment (Temel *et al.*, 2010) suggests a possible alternative interpretation for the inconsistency of research findings. Psychosocial interventions for cancer are compared with a control group where patients receive normal care. That normal care will involve varying degrees of psychosocial support in the form of good care and attention. It may be that it is not the psychological technique that matters (see 'explanations for the dodo bird effect' earlier in this chapter) but rather the emotional support provided in the clinical setting. Studies where psychosocial interventions seem to work best may be those where normal psychosocial care is poor.

Of course, a meta-analysis is only as good as the data on which it is based. There are several reasons why the conclusions from these meta-analyses should be treated with caution. First, the meta-analyses aggregate over a range of very different studies with different kinds of intervention. There may be interventions that are better than others – or therapists that are better than others (the latter is more likely given the data on psychotherapy outcome). Second, the aggregation fails to distinguish between a small effect that occurs with many patients and a large effect that occurs but rarely. Anecdotal report suggests that exceptional survivors exist, but they are few in number. Finally, meta-analysis of psychological interventions fails to take into account the possibility that psychological factors affect outcome independently of any treatment. There is evidence that when faced with a major illness some patients interpret the illness as a positive event and adjust their lives accordingly (Sodergren and Hyland, 2000; Sodergren *et al.*, 2004). Furthermore, psychological adjustment is reported by patients who are exceptional survivors of cancer (Roud, 1987). Positive psychological adjustment is cited as a predictor of long-term survival for heart disease (Croog and Levine, 1982) and cancer (LeShan, 1994), and is also a factor in recovery from the dysregulatory disease of chronic fatigue syndrome (Hyland *et al.*, 2006b). Thus, it may be that psychological factors do affect survival for cancer and heart disease – but not the factors that are the focus of attention in psychological interventions. Patients may find therapeutic benefits outside of the formally provided psychological intervention.

Conclusions

The research reviewed above leads to the following conclusions:

- Psychological interventions improve psychological outcomes for many but not all patients suffering from mental health problems.
- Although therapists support their particular type of psychotherapy, the evidence suggests that all therapies are effective.
- The reason therapies are effective is uncertain, but it may be due to factors that are common across all therapies.
- The reason complementary and alternative medicine (CAM) is effective is controversial, but it may also involve factors that are common across all therapies.
- The efficacy of antidepressant medication is poor – most of the clinical benefit of antidepressants is caused by placebo effects. The placebo arms of clinical trials have features in common with psychotherapy – and CAM.
- The distinction between placebos and psychotherapy is somewhat artificial – both terms are used for psychologically mediated benefit.
- Psychologically mediated treatments can have non-specific benefits, e.g., benefits beyond those intended.
- The benefits of psychologically mediated treatments (including placebos) can be substantial for psychological outcomes but are less effective for physiological outcomes.

- The size of effect of psychological interventions on physiological outcomes varies. Short-term benefits can be demonstrated in laboratory placebo analogue studies. However, whether psychological interventions have long-term effects on morbidity and mortality is controversial. The effectiveness of these interventions appears to depend on the physiological measure investigated and on the disease.
- If the aim of therapy is to improve health, then there is no clear dividing line between therapy and lifestyle choice.
- In the case of medicine and CAM, the 'other part' of therapy is a psychological input provided by the therapist. However, in the case of psychotherapy, the concept of the 'other part' of therapy – or specific versus non-specific components – is not helpful. Patients, not therapists, may be the primary factor in determining the mechanisms of therapeutic benefit. The client is not concerned about whether the mechanism is labelled specific or not!

Some readers will find the above conclusions antithetical to their own firmly held beliefs. Those who believe in the superiority of pharmaceutical treatment of mental illness will be uncomfortable with the poor efficacy of antidepressant medication. CAM practitioners will be uncomfortable with the suggestion that their effects are psychologically mediated, and psychotherapists will be uncomfortable with the suggestion that their therapy is in principle no different from placebo. Finally, those who were encouraged by the clear relationship between the mind and immune system (see Chapter 2) will be disappointed by the weak evidence that psychological factors can help cure major illness. It is important to emphasise, however, that none of these ideas is presented in this book for the first time. They are all based on meta-analyses carried out by other researchers (don't complain to me, complain to them!). The only novelty of this chapter is to put all these ideas together. When these parts of the jigsaw are put together, as has been done in this chapter, the following conclusion emerges. The psychological component of therapeutic rituals has a non-specific, self-healing effect on the body. That effect is more noticeable for dysregulatory disease than it is for measures of morbidity in specific disease.

9 Therapeutic mechanisms

Introduction

Research concerning placebos in medicine, psychotherapy, and complementary and alternative medicine (CAM) was reviewed in the previous chapter. A possible conclusion from this research is that all these different therapies achieve therapeutic benefit through a common mechanism or set of mechanisms. That mechanism is psychologically mediated. The evidence presented in the previous chapter is inconsistent with the alternative hypothesis that there are unique psychological mechanisms associated with placebos in medicine, psychotherapy and CAM, even though particular therapies may be more likely to elicit a particular mechanism. This chapter examines the psychologically mediated mechanisms that lead to therapeutic benefit, and shows how these mechanisms are linked to the different therapies.

The mechanisms examined in this chapter fall into two categories. First, there are those that occur in short-term, laboratory analogue placebo studies. Second, there are those mechanisms that occur in long-term contexts, namely the placebo arm of clinical trials, psychotherapy and complementary medicine. The evidence that different mechanisms occur in short-term and long-term placebo paradigms is presented towards the end of this chapter.

In previous chapters a distinction was drawn between two types of infornet mechanism. In one, the infornet resolves into a particular state based on its existing inputs. In the second, the infornet changes its beliefs using network learning rules. When the infornet resolves into a particular state – for example, infornet alarm – the response is rapid as the infornet is solving the problem of how best to alter homeodynamic control loops in order to meet the demands of the current situation. When the infornet changes its beliefs – for example, to the belief that *the general situation is bad* – this change is slow as network learning necessarily requires change to be slow. Self-organisational change is slower than problem solving. Changes that occur in short-term, laboratory placebo studies involve the infornet resolving into particular states, whereas the changes that occur in long-term placebo studies and in therapy involve a change in infornet belief. Nevertheless, the two types of mechanism are linked: the infornet resolves into a particular state on the basis of infornet beliefs.

The first part of the chapter focuses on the mechanisms that occur in short-term laboratory studies and the second part on mechanisms responsible for long-term therapeutic outcomes.

Short-term placebo mechanisms

According to infornet theory, the effects observed in short-term placebo studies occur because the infornet resolves itself into a particular state in response to its current inputs. Two related psychological theories provide an explanation of what those current inputs might be: response expectancy theory and conditioning theory. The theory advanced here is based on a combination of response expectancy theory, conditioning theory and infornet theory. A brief description of response expectancy theory and conditioning theory will be presented first.

Response expectancy theory

Response expectancy theory proposes that psychological and physio-logical states tend towards those that are expected (Kirsch 1985). Mental states tend to follow the expectancy of that mental state. So, for example, if a person expects not to be anxious then they will no longer be anxious. If they expect not to be depressed they will not be depressed. In addition to having an effect on mental state, expectancies also influence physiological response. If a person expects blood pressure to rise, then it should rise. The author of response expectancy theory (Kirsch, 1985) suggested that the effect of expectancies on physiological states was directly mediated. In terms of mind–body theory, 'directly mediated' means that the mental state of expectancy is directly linked to the mental state and directly linked to the physiological response. For example, although anxiety reduction could lead to physiological effects, Kirsch suggests that the effect of positive expectancies is not mediated via affect. Instead, expectancy has a direct effect such that affect is not a necessary part of the causal sequence. The evidence in support of the direct mediation hypothesis comes from the observation that only this theory can explain placebo effects in healthy and unhealthy individuals, as well as beneficial effects and harmful effects (called nocebos) of negative placebo suggestion (Kirsch, 1997).

There is a substantial body of research showing that expectancy determines outcome in placebo laboratory studies, and that experimental manipulations that increase expectancy increase the placebo response. For example, expectancies and placebo effects can be enhanced by the colour or size of the pill (the bigger the better), and stronger placebo effects are achieved with more convincing experimenters (Moerman, 2002). Additionally, short-term placebo responses can be enhanced when people have goals that are consistent with their expectations (Geers et al., 2005b). Not only do placebo effects vary with expectancy, but so do nocebo effects (i.e., negative symptoms). Nocebo effects are achieved by leading the participant to expect a negative symptom (Hahn, 1999) and can be enhanced by the presence of others demonstrating those negative symptoms. The presence of others acts as a cue that enhances the expectancy that the negative symptom is likely to occur (Mazzoni et al., 2010).

Although most of the research relating to response expectancies, placebos and nocebos is based on situational manipulations that alter expectancies, some has focused on dispositional variables. Geers and colleagues (Geers et al., 2003, 2005a) have shown that optimism correlates with placebo response for positive outcomes, but this correlation occurs only for high-priority outcomes (Geers et al., 2009). These results are explained in terms of response expectancy theory. Optimists are more likely to form positive expectancies, particularly when the outcome is salient. In sum, there is a good deal of research supporting the role of response expectancy in placebo responses for short-term analogue studies.

Conditioning theory and its relation to response expectancy theory.

According to the conditioning theory of placebos, if an active substance is repeatedly associated with a particular response, for example, an analgesic pill leading to pain relief, then over time the pill will become a conditioned stimulus for that response. As a result, an inert pill will also lead to pain relief. The pill becomes the conditioned stimulus and the pain relief the conditioned response. The immune-conditioning phenomenon described in Chapter 2 can be considered an example of a placebo conditioning phenomenon. The association of a flavour with a physiological response (immune suppression) leads to the flavour inducing the immune suppression. Thus, the conditioning theory of placebos can be considered part of the immune-conditioning phenomenon – for which there is evidence in animals and humans (Schedlowski and Pacheco-López, 2010).

If an analgesic is given to a person with pain, and the pill creates pain relief, then two phenomena will occur simultaneously: (a) the person in pain experiences conditioning; and (b) the person will develop an expectancy that the pill will have a beneficial effect. Even if the person is not told that the pill is an analgesic, it is inevitable that the person will notice the effect of the pill, and therefore develop an expectancy of pain relief. Thus, conditioning paradigms tend to induce expectancies, and the results of conditioning placebo effects can therefore be explained in terms of response expectancy. Because conditioning and response expectancy tend to be confounded in clinical practice, several research paradigms have been developed to try to disentangle these two effects. To summarise a large body of data: the results indicate that consciously mediated response expectancies are stronger and tend to override conditioning effects (Montgomery and Kirsch, 1997), but nevertheless non-conscious conditioning of placebos (i.e., conditioning effects without conscious expectancies) is possible (Benedetti *et al.*, 1999).

Although the above research treats conditioning theory and response expectancy as competing theories, Stewart-Williams and Podd (2004) have proposed an integration of these two theories. According to this integration, there are two types of learning: nonconscious learning and conscious expectancy learning. Both forms of learning provide information about contingency of the form 'if – then'. Thus, both can provide information on 'if the pill, then there is a reduction in pain'. The Stewart-Williams and Podd (2004) theory is represented in Figure 9.1.

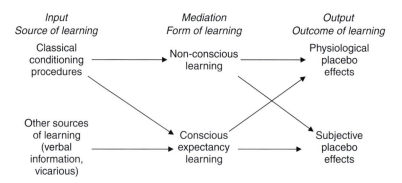

Figure 9.1 The roles of classical conditioning procedures and expectancy procedures in the production of placebo effects, as suggested by Stewart-Williams and Podd (2004).

*Infornet reinterpretation of response expectancy and
conditioning theories*

The Stewart-Williams and Podd (2004) integration proposes that there
are two forms of learning, one mediated by conscious expectancies and
the other mediated via an unconscious form of learning. The former
can be characterised as cognitive learning, the latter as non-cognitive
learning. Infornet theory shows how these two different forms of learning lead to the same output.

The infornet is a network system and therefore capable of pattern
recognition. Pattern recognition can take the form of 'if – then'
contingencies. For example, the infornet recognises that if the pill is
the input, then the output is reduction in pain. The ability to recognise
a particular pattern is due to the activation pattern of the infornet –
i.e., the totality of the activation rules governing the causal connections
between the units that make up the infornet. A change in the activation rules and hence the activation pattern is the consequence of
learning: learning means that the activation pattern has changed. There
are two ways in which this learning can take place.

The first way of changing the infornet activation rules is through
the application of the associative learning rule, namely the rule that
states that connections between contiguously activated units should be
strengthened. The associative learning rule is the rule responsible for
classical conditioning and immune conditioning. The associative learning rule explains the development of placebos through a non-conscious
route. According to this first way of changing the activation rules, it is
direct experience that leads to the change in the activation rules.

Learning theorists distinguish gradual learning from all-or-nothing
learning, also called 'insight learning' or 'cognitive learning'. Much of
human learning is all-or-nothing, or cognitive. If you are told that a
pill will reduce pain, then it is highly likely that you will not need to be
told a second time. To summarise findings from the (very large) topic
of human cognition, the processes underlying human memory follow
very different rules from the form of learning found in classical conditioning. The term *memory* is used rather than *learning* because of the
different mechanisms involved. Although higher cognitive functioning
is a human characteristic, insight learning does occur in some animals,
such as chimpanzees. Humans (and some animals) exhibit gradual learning based on associative learning *as well as* the higher form of insight
learning that is also called memory. There are high-level connectionist models for accounting for this rapid insight or cognitive learning
(Honavar and Uhr, 1993), but these need not concern us. It is merely

necessary to note that the infornet can also be altered through high-level or cognitive inputs in the form of communication from others.

The second way of changing the activation pattern of the infornet is therefore through a cognitive route. That is, changes in the 'if – then' contingencies that lead to the placebo response are mediated via a cognitive input. The cognitive input derives from instructions of others or other forms of externally derived information (e.g., vicarious effects where the behaviour of another is observed). In this second way of changing the activation rules, it is *information from the external environment* rather than experience that creates learning at a high level – i.e., high-level change in activation rules – and that then leads to the changes in the activation rules that concern the 'if – then' contingency of the placebo response. According to infornet theory, the response expectancy mechanism has a greater impact on outcome (Stewart-Williams and Podd, 2004), because the cognitive route is a stronger determinant of the 'if – then' contingencies compared with the associative learning route, at least in the experimental contexts investigated. Furthermore, the idea that information from the external environment (mediated via cognitive appraisal) leads directly to changes in the infornet's activation rules provides a rationale for Kirsch's (1985, 1997) assertion that response expectancies are directly mediated.

Moerman (2002) suggests that a good way of thinking about the placebo response is as a meaning response. Placebo responses are responses to meaning in the external situation. However, as the review by Stewart-Williams and Podd (2004) shows, that meaning need not be consciously mediated even though conscious thoughts appear to be very important. Whether or not the meaning is conscious, the meaning of the external situation is not located in the external situation. The meaning is located in the person who interprets that meaning, and more specifically, it is represented in the activation rules of the brain – which is itself part of the infornet. That meaning can be derived in part from direct experience, which may or not be conscious, but it can also be derived through a consciously mediated route via information from others. Irrespective of *how* the infornet derives meaning about the external situation, that meaning then determines how the infornet responds to that external situation. The infornet interprets what is happening in the external world, using any information that is available – direct experience, verbal instructions from others, and vicariously mediated information – and solves the problem of what to do next on the basis of that meaning.

The infornet model of short-term placebo responses is based on the way the infornet interprets meaning in the external situation. The way this model functions will be illustrated by considering two experimental paradigms: (a) short-term placebo manipulation of pain (i.e., a psychological outcome variable), and (b) short-term placebo manipulation of respiratory function in asthma (i.e., a physiological outcome variable). The aim of these two examples is to show that there is no such thing as a 'placebo mechanism'. Instead, the mechanism underlying the placebo is a commonplace mechanism but one that is being exhibited in an unusual way in placebo paradigms.

Short-term placebo effects of the subjective experience of pain

There are three theories of pain (Horn and Munafo, 1997). The *direct theory* of pain suggests that pain sensation is the consequence of pain receptors in the periphery that send their signals to the brain. The *gate theory* of pain suggests that the pain signal is moderated on its way up to the brain in the dorsal horn of the spinal cord. This moderation takes place at the point of the t-cells (transporter cells) in the dorsal horn and can be achieved in one or both of two ways: by ascending neurons from touch receptors and descending neurons from the brain. The *pattern theory* of pain suggests that pain is a learned response to a pattern of peripheral stimuli. The last two theories show that pain experience is altered by psychological factors, either in the brain itself or through fibres descending to the t-cells. Pain experienced is *increased* by trait negative mood, and *decreased* if attention is focused away from the pain-causing stimulus. These three theories are combined in an integrative model in which information is integrated in a 'neuromatrix' that has multiple inputs, some coming from the periphery including the pain causing event and some from the brain, and where the pattern from this 'neuromatrix' then provides information to the brain about the experience of pain (Loeser and Melzack, 1999).

Consistent with the integrative theory, the infornet interpretation is that pain is a signal from a network system (i.e., a version of the neuromatrix concept) that has multiple inputs (including psychological and biological inputs) and where the experience of pain alters behaviour. The experience of pain is not simply attributable to the external pain stimulus but is moderated by psychological factors as these psychological factors impact on the appropriate behavioural response. Footballers often notice injury only when they leave the field. If you are hunting a mammoth, you don't want to stop to put a plaster on a scratch in the middle of the hunt. The infornet solves the problem of whether or not behaviour needs to be changed. If the decision by the infornet is that behaviour needs to be modified, then there is a sensation of pain. If not, then there is no sensation of pain.

Placebo pain paradigm

Although pain is a naturally occurring experience, it is normally necessary to create pain in order to investigate placebo response to pain stimuli in laboratory settings. Pain can be created in a variety of ways, but a common method is to use a Forgione–Barber strain gauge pain stimulator. The stimulator consists of a bar that presses on the participant's finger, thereby creating pain in the finger, and the pressure of the bar (and hence the level of pain) can be altered with a movable weight. Placebo analgesic cream can be administered to one finger and the difference in pain perception in the treated finger and in an untreated finger (with the same pressure) provides a measure of placebo response. Thus, a common experimental paradigm for placebo pain is one where pain is delivered to two fingers of which one is treated with a placebo cream (Whalley *et al.*, 2008). Participants in such studies are typically students – not people with any particular experience of pain. The students are not hoping to get better – just to complete the study and obtain payment or course credit. Pain perception is measured by a subjective pain scale.

It is now possible to address the fundamental question: why is it that the *expectancy* of pain reduction leads to the *experience* of pain reduction?

From the perspective of the infornet, pain is a signal from the body, namely a signal from a particular part of the body. Pain is the recognition of a particular pattern into which the infornet resolves on the basis of multiple inputs and which leads to a mental signal that is called pain. The pattern and hence the experience of pain can be altered in a variety of ways depending on other inputs to the infornet as well as the current state of the infornet.

Pain research shows that psychological factors alter the pain experience, including mood and attention. Expectancy is simply another input, along with mood and attention into the pain 'neuromatrix' – or in the present theory, the infornet. The expectancy of pain reduction leads to an infornet belief that there is less pain. The infornet's interpretation of its multiple inputs tends towards an infornet belief that *if cream is on the finger, then it is not painful.*

The effect of expectancy on pain perception merely shows that the infornet is an integrated system and that higher cognitive processes have an input like any other. Expectancy is not the only higher cognitive process that alters pain perception; if a person sees blood gushing out of a finger, that person is more likely to interpret the sensation as painful. Similarly, pain research shows that negative interpretation of pain-causing events lead to greater pain perception.

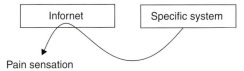

Figure 9.2 Pain is an output from the specific system that is moderated by the infornet

Figure 9.2 shows a causal relationship between pain – which is normally a signal from a specific part of the body – and the infornet. The pain signal from the specific system is moderated by the infornet in order that there is an appropriate response to the event causing the pain. Thus, expectancy is just one of several types of psychologically mediated input to the pain neuromatrix that alters pain perception.

If placebo pain effects are due to the mechanisms of pain perception, then the placebo pain phenomena should involve the same physiological mechanisms as those found in pain perception, namely pattern recognition in the brain and the effect of descending fibres to the t-cells in the spinal cord. Recent research has confirmed that placebo pain does involve both changes in the downward pathways from the brain to the spinal cord (Eippert *et al.*, 2009) and changes in the opioid system (Amanzio *et al.*, 2001; Benedetti *et al.*, 2003). Psychological coping training, namely that involving perceptions of self-efficacy, also involves the opioid system (Bandura *et al.*, 1987). Thus, the placebo pain effects are mediated by the same mechanisms as those that are responsible for other psychologically mediated effects on pain perception.

In sum, the placebo pain response is not some 'special' placebo mechanism, but simply part of a more general mechanism whereby subjective experience of pain can be altered by the current state and inputs into the infornet – or what in pain theory terms is referred to as a 'neuromatrix'. This alteration in symptom perception is not unique to pain: it can be considered as part of the 'symptom reporting and diagnosis bias' described in Chapter 3.

Short-term placebo effects of a physiological outcome:
placebo response to bronchodilator inhalers

Air enters the lungs through small tubes called *bronchioles*. Muscles in the walls of the bronchioles can contract and the contraction of the bronchiole (called *bronchoconstriction*) makes it more difficult for air to flow in and out of the lungs. The bronchiole muscles are homeo dynamically controlled: they are slightly more contracted in the early morning compared with the evening (i.e., they exhibit the kind of diurnal variation that is frequently found in the body's control systems). The muscle tension in the bronchioles is affected by neurological inputs from the vagal nerve. In addition, the bronchiole muscles are sensitive to contaminants in the air. When a person breaths in smoke, the muscles of the bronchioles contract and can cause coughing. Note that these two characteristics are common throughout the body: homeodynamic control is frequently associated with diurnal variation and sensitivity to external events.

The bronchioles of people with poorly controlled asthma differ from the above in three ways. First, the diurnal variation is more pronounced: the bronchioles are much more contracted in the morning but they expand towards the evening. Second, the sensitivity to contaminants is much more pronounced: the airways are 'twitchy' in that they respond with greater vigour to an assault that would normally produce a mild bronchoconstriction. In addition, the airways of people with asthma will respond to allergens that would have minimal effect on those without asthma. Finally, in some people with asthma there is bronchoconstriction in response to psychological stress as well as bronchonstriction to the sight or thought of triggers that have a biological effect on the bronchioles. These psychologically mediated triggers affect the bronchiole muscles via the vagal nerve, which descends directly from the brain.

People with asthma use two different sorts of medication to reduce (a) the inflammation and (b) the twitchiness (bronchoconstriction) of the airways. Bronchodilator inhalers (e.g., salbutamol, trade name Ventolin) relax the bronchial muscles, reverse the bronchoconstriction, work rapidly in less than two minutes and are taken as needed. Many people with asthma carry a bronchodilator inhaler with them at all times and realisation that the inhaler is missing can lead to anxiety and bronchoconstriction. Bronchodilator inhalers are used in asthma placebo research. Bronchoconstriction can be gauged by measurement of respiratory function, such as peak expiratory flow (PEF). PEF is the peak rate at which a person can exhale air – the faster the air can be exhaled, the less the bronchoconstriction.

Placebo asthma paradigm

Asthma inhalers are always clearly labelled and there is a colour convention that bronchodilators are blue. The placebo bronchodilator inhaler appears the same as the real thing but contains an inert gas. In this experimental paradigm, the participant – who must have asthma – breathes in air containing methacholine. Methacholine is a chemical that irritates the lungs and causes bronchoconstriction, but only to any degree in those who have asthma. The bronchonstriction created by methacholine can be prevented by the prior use of a bronchodilator. The bronchoconstriction following breathing of methacholine will be experienced as increased wheeze or breathlessness but is measured quantitatively by a respiratory function test (e.g., peak expiratory flow). In an asthma placebo study, the participant first breathes in methacholine and respiratory function is measured. On a subsequent occasion (e.g., one week later) the participant repeats the procedure but this time inhaling from the placebo bronchodilator inhaler before the methacholine. The difference in respiratory function between the two occasions (i.e., methacholine without placebo versus methacoline with placebo) is a measure of the placebo response to asthma. The placebo response varies between studies but at most is about a third that of the active drug. This methodology is used in some of the studies reviewed by Sodergren and Hyland (1999) and in a more recent study by Kemeny *et al.* (2007).

When triggers elicit bronchoconstriction, the bronchoconstriction can be interpreted as the consequence of an infornet belief that *the airways are being assaulted by a foreign substance*. In the case of the person with asthma, the airways are more prone to the belief that they *are being assaulted by a foreign substance*, and it is for this reason that they are more twitchy. Just as a person high in neuroticism is more prone to see threat in the surrounding situation, so the person with asthma is more prone to interpret otherwise harmless airborne substances as harmful.

Methacholine acts like cigarette smoke: it irritates the airways and, in the person with asthma, the infornet responds by resolving into a state of alarm that then triggers bronchoconstriction. Bronchconstriction is the normal response to infornet alarm of threat to the airway: the response is exaggerated owing to inflammation in the lungs.

Bronchodilators have a relaxing effect on bronchial muscles. If a person uses bronchodilator inhalers on a regular basis, then, either because of expectancy or because of association learning rules, this will lead to the infornet belief *if I use a bronchodilator, then the airways no longer feel as though they are being assaulted by a foreign substance*. Consequently, when a person uses a placebo bronchodilator, this action elicits the same infornet belief as the real medicine, with the result that the airways are less irritated by the methacholine.

Kirsch's (1985) assertion that expectancy effects are directly mediated is consistent with the infornet explanation of physiological responses to a placebo. The infornet integrates biological and psychological information in one single network system. The infornet responds to *any* information so as to resolve itself into a state that is best adapted to deal with the current situation.

An alternative explanation for the asthma placebo effect is that the presence or use of the bronchodilator enhances positive affect. The idea that placebo effects are directly mediated is inconsistent with the alternative explanation that placebo effects are mediated via changes in affect. This alternative explanation is particularly relevant to the case of asthma placebo effects, because respiratory function is affected by mood (Affleck *et al.*, 2000; Ritz *et al.*, 2010). However, in the study by Kememy *et al.* (2007) the placebo inhaler was given either by a researcher who was friendly to the participant or one who was unfriendly. There was no difference in placebo response between the two types of administration. These results suggest that the psychological mechanism for the placebo asthma response is response expectancy, and that the effect of expectancy is not mediated via affect.

Box 9.1 Possible explanations for findings in asthma placebo research

There are several possible explanations why mood influences respiratory function, but there was no effect of the friendly versus unfriendly researcher in the study by Kememy *et al.* (2007). One possibility is that the friendly versus unfriendly researcher did not create change in affect. An alternative explanation follows from the observation that mood changes are associated with change in inflammation in the lung, and it is this change in inflammation that then leads to changes in lung function (Kullowatz *et al.*, 2008). Changes in lung function due to bronchonstriction are faster than changes caused by increased inflammation. Consequently, changes in mood created by the friendly–unfriendly researcher may not have been achieved within the time scale of the experiment.

Commentary on short-term placebo effects

A basic principle of infornet theory is that the infornet uses biopsychosocial information in order resolve into a state that creates optimal management of the internal and external environments. Part of that optimal management involves altering levels in homeodynamically controlled physiological parameters (i.e., altering reference criteria and gain of the control loop). For example, smoky air is an external factor that should lead to a protective response of bronchoconstriction. Additionally, expectancies about either external challenge or protection also affect bronchoconstriction. However, if the external environment is irrelevant to the optimum level of that parameter, then information about the external environment will not provide useful information for managing the level of that parameter. In the case of homeostatic control loops, parameters in the external environment are *not* used to alter the reference criterion. For example, the optimum level of blood sugar is constant, irrespective of external events. The 'ideal pattern' for blood sugar is homeostatic rather than homeodynamic, and any deviation is a reflection of inadequate control rather than a strategy for managing the external environment. Consequently, expectancies relating to the external environment should also be irrelevant to blood sugar level. The infornet ignores external information for the control of blood sugar level, and therefore placebos are ineffective. The above rationale leads to a simple prediction:

Short-term physiological placebo responses occur only for those physiological parameters that, under normal circumstances, are adjusted according to external conditions.

Meissner *et al.* (2007) provide evidence that biochemical parameters – such as blood sugar – do not exhibit placebo responses in long-term clinical trials. Investigation will reveal whether, as predicted here, it is a characteristic of homeostatic parameters that they are not susceptible to short-term placebo effects.

The placebo effect is sometimes considered a puzzling phenomenon. There is no puzzle. The mind is part of the body. However, short-term placebo effects do illustrate something that is theoretically interesting. Short-term placebo effects show that beliefs that are consciously represented – i.e., the normal sort of belief – are linked to beliefs of the infornet. Although infornet beliefs are not accessible to conscious inspection, they are not entirely separate from conscious beliefs. Conscious beliefs, i.e., cognitions, can lead to the infornet having beliefs concordant with those cognitions – at least, as far as short-term placebo manipulations are concerned.

In sum, placebos show that although infornet beliefs and conscious beliefs are different, conscious beliefs can affect infornet beliefs. The mind is therefore a possible route into altering the network system that is responsible for health and dysregulatory diseases. Previous chapters have shown how stressful situations lead to the infornet belief that *the general situation is bad*. It is therefore theoretically possible that positive situations will be therapeutic as they lead to the infornet belief that *the general situation is good*.

Long-term therapeutic effects

According to infornet theory, infornet dysregulation is the distal cause of both specific and dysregulatory diseases. General infornet dysregulation occurs across a range of different diseases. In the case of general infornet dysregulation there is a persistent infornet belief that *the general situation is bad*. This negative infornet belief can be associated with other lower-level infornet beliefs that determine particular forms of general infornet dysregulation. These lower-level infornet beliefs and their associated consequences were discussed in Chapter 3 and are shown below.

I am achieving the wrong sort of goals: Depression
I am achieving goals through the wrong behavioural patterns: Fatigue
The external world is full of threat: Anxiety and HPA axis activation
There is threat of infection: Inflammatory response system activation

These various lower-level infornet beliefs and their consequences tend to correlate because negative infornet beliefs are interconnected, and there is a general factor represented by the infornet belief that *the general situation is bad*.

Therapy alters infornet beliefs. In the case of short-term placebo effects, the infornet beliefs that are altered are in relation to specific aspects of the situation – such as a cream or an inhaler. In such cases, although these infornet beliefs lead to a positive interpretation of the current situation (i.e., lack of infornet alarm) they are context specific. Consequently, they do not alter the more widespread belief that *the general situation is bad*, or any of the other infornet beliefs described above. They do not lead to persisting changes in infornet beliefs. Therapeutic interventions that have long-term therapeutic effects must therefore change the more widespread infornet beliefs, for example, by changing the infornet belief that *the general situation is bad* to *the general situation is good*.

In their classic book *Persuasion and Healing*, Frank and Frank (1991) suggested that there are four characteristics that are common to all psychotherapies as well as shamanistic therapies found in undeveloped parts of the world. These are:

1. an emotionally charged, confiding relationship with a helping person;
2. a healing setting;
3. a rationale, conceptual scheme, or myth that provides a plausible explanation for the patient's symptoms and prescribes a ritual or procedure for resolving them; and
4. a ritual or procedure that requires the active participation of both patient and therapist and that is believed by both to be the means of restoring the patient's health.

These authors suggest that the primary problem when people have mental health problems is that of demoralisation. According to these authors, *all* therapies are effective because they remoralise the individual, irrespective of whether the therapy is psychotherapy, some form of complementary therapy or treatment by conventional Western medicine.

Infornet interpretation of long-term therapeutic effects: overview

Frank and Frank's (1991) clinical observation of remoralisation is consistent with the infornet interpretation of therapy. The psychological component of all therapies, whether medical treatment, psychotherapy or complementary therapy, provides the patient with the interpretation that they are being cared for and helped. Being cared for and helped is a particular characteristic of the external situation that is interpreted by the infornet. The infornet belief associated with being cared for and helped is *the general situation is good*. All effective therapy provides the patient with the belief that they are being helped by someone else. The very fact that they are being helped will influence infornet beliefs towards better self-regulation.

Infornet theory shows that there are several different routes into general infornet dysregulation (see Chapters 5–7). In the same way, there are several different routes that reverse the effects of dysregulation and create a well-regulated infornet. These different routes sometimes involve a therapist and sometimes they do not. Therapist effects are, however, important, as humans are social animals and therefore particularly influenced by the behaviour of others. Before considering specific routes into well-regulation, several points can be made at this general level.

Unconditional positive regard. Being ill is bad, irrespective of whether the illness is mental or physical. If a person experiences illness, then illness contributes to the general infornet belief that *the general situation is bad*. Although the therapist may not help sort out other problems in the person's life, the therapist is someone who is helping change one aspect of the currently bad situation into a good one. In a situation where demoralised patients feel they have to struggle on alone, the therapist acts as a champion, someone who is on the patient's side, someone who is going to make the situation better. Roger's theory of client-oriented therapy (Rogers, 1951) suggests that unconditional positive regard is crucial in helping the patient self-heal. Unconditional positive regard indicates to the patient that the patient is being supported, and that the patient is no longer in a situation of threat where others are critical judges of the patient's behaviour.

It is a curious observation that when patients are able to talk about themselves in front of an attentive practitioner, they feel more satisfied with the encounter than if they receive treatment without the ability to express themselves (Friedlr *et al.*, 1997). Listening skills are important to good psychotherapeutic outcome (Burnard, 2005). By just caring for the patient, the therapist provides the patient's infornet with information that the patient is now in a situation of safety. When patients talk about themselves in front of a caring professional, they experience a situation that contributes to the infornet belief, *the general situation is good*.

Therapeutic intent. The concept of therapeutic intent is found in the literature on homeopathy, although it is a minority idea in this literature (Hyland, 2005; Lewith *et al.*, 2005). Therapeutic intent refers to the effect the homeopath has on the patient merely by intending the patient to get better, and is based on the clinical observation by practising homeopaths that the intention of healing the patient is important to outcome. Therapeutic intent can be communicated to the patient by verbal and non-verbal signals. If the homeopath convinces the patient that the patient will get better, then the patient is now in a new situation. The patient is being made better by a powerful and clever therapist who really knows what is wrong with the patient. Therapeutic intent, like unconditional positive regard, provides information to the infornet that *the general situation is good* because now there is a powerful 'other' on the side of the patient who can help get the patient better. In the previous chapter I suggested that there is little evidence to show what makes a good psychotherapist. Perhaps the reason is that researchers have been looking at the wrong variables – it may be that it is not how the therapist deals with the problem or the therapeutic bond with the patient that matters so much as to extent to which the therapist can 'sell' the idea that the therapist is a powerful person who can effect a cure. To be good at the art of medicine, it may be necessary to convince the patient of the effectiveness of modern medicine. Attractive, up to date and 'powerful' hospitals have their role to play in the art of medicine.

The general practitioner and the art of medicine. Research shows that effective doctor–patient communication can lead to a reduction in medically unexplained symptoms (Thomas, 1987). When a patient visits their general practitioner (GP) with medically unexplained symptoms, there are several things the GP can do that will tend towards the infornet belief that *the general situation is good*. First, the GP takes the patient seriously. The GP validates the patient's concerns with statements such as 'I'm glad you have come to see me' and provides an indication that help is being provided – 'Let's try and see what is happening'. The GP then gives the patient a series of tests 'to rule out anything serious' and, as the tests come back (typically, negative), the doctor is able to reassure the patient that nothing is seriously wrong. Thus, the patient who has been worrying that there is something seriously wrong – and hence *the general situation is bad* – is now presented with the information that nothing is seriously wrong – and hence *the general situation is good*. To some extent, the art of the GP is to provide the patient with support during times of dysregulation so that the infonet can sort itself out, given the context provided by the GP.

Therapeutic pampering. The concept of therapeutic pampering is found in the nursing literature, and is based on the idea that intelligent pampering of patients leads not only to better satisfaction and adherence but also better outcome (MacStravic, 1986). Therapeutic pampering is consistent with the basic premise of infonet theory that situations improve regulation of the infonet to the extent that they provide information that *the general situation is good*. The idea of therapeutic pampering raises the issue of the relationship of therapy to lifestyle. Spa treatments improve symptoms for dysregulatory diseases such as fibromyalgia (Zijlistra *et al.*, 2005) and lower back pain (Constant *et al.*, 1995), as well as reducing symptoms and morbidity for specific diseases such as rheumatoid arthritis and osteoarthritis (Elkayam *et al.*, 1991; Franke *et al.*, 2000; Nguyen *et al.*, 1997). Spa treatment involves a variety of (often water-based) treatments over a 2- to 3-week 'holiday' and commonly provides clients with a safe, secure and pleasurable environment where they feel cared for (Bender *et al.*, 2004). According to infonet theory, there is no dividing line between spa treatments where staff help clients feel safe and secure and therapy where trained health professionals help patients feel that their problems are being sorted. Both types of intervention help develop the infonet belief that *the general situation is good*.

The above sections show how the context of therapy and the context of positive lifestyle interventions – such as a health spa – promote infonet beliefs that run contrary to those that are formed during the process that leads to infonet dysregulation. The following sections show how therapies counteract some of the routes into general infonet dysregulation that were described in Chapter 5. The following routes to well-regulation will be considered:

- changing negative cognitions and affect;
- changing positive cognitions and affect;

- therapy as lifestyle change and the attainment of important goals;
- therapy as a disinhibitor; and
- relaxation.

Changing negative cognitions and affect

Cognitions refer to the beliefs people have about themselves and the world in which they live. Affect refers to a person's mood. Cognitions and mood are closely connected outputs from the same infonet belief system, namely stability–unstability beliefs (see Chapter 3). If negative cognitions are reduced, then negative affect will reduce. If negative affect is reduced, then negative cognitions are reduced.

Cognitive behaviour therapy (CBT) is predicated on the need to change the patients negative cognitions, thereby creating less negative affect (e.g., less depression and anxiety). However, most therapies have the effect of changing the patient's cognitions. In the case of CBT, therapists are trained to deliver techniques that alter the negative beliefs that are troubling the patient. So for example, if the patient believes that other people think the patient is ugly (body dissatisfaction or dysmorphia), the therapist will find ways of helping the patient to challenge those beliefs, often by providing a series of exercises that the patient can practise between therapy sessions. In other therapies, changes in cognition can be incidental to the therapy being provided. Existential psychotherapies (Yalom, 1980) help clients focus on meaning in their lives, and can therefore lead to changes in cognitions simply because cognitions are involved in self-perceptions of meaning. A homeopathic consultation normally requires patients to focus on their likes and dislikes and patterns of behaviour. Such self-focus can also have an effect of reframing the illness, and allows patients to see themselves in a new light. In a shamanic session, the patient is helped to (mentally) enter the underworld and bring back something from that world that is going to help in this world, again leading to a more positive interpretation of cognitions. In addition to the complementary practices that tend to alter belief systems, many complementary medicines provide the patient with an opportunity to reframe away from the belief 'I am helpless, no one knows what is causing my problem, and I don't know to do' to a belief 'I know what is causing my problem, I can now do something about it, and I am going to get well'.

The above shows that changes in cognitions and affect often occur in therapy when the therapy involves some form of mental activity. The question that now needs to be answered is 'How do these changes lead to better regulation of the infonet?'. The reason is that, just as cognitions and affect are outputs from the infornet, they can also be considered 'levers' that act as inputs to the infornet. Techniques that reduce negative cognitions and affect therefore change the infornet beliefs towards one that consists of:

It is a wonderful world. Things go right. There is no punishment. There are no threats, things are going as well as I want them to go.

Any manipulation of the cognitive and affective levers in a way that changes the infornet's beliefs from unstability to stability will therefore contribute to a reduction in general infornet dysregulation. The cognitive and affective levers change the infornet beliefs away from *the general situation is bad* to *the general situation is good*.

Changing positive cognitions and affect

Chapters 2 and 3 provided evidence that positive and negative affect vary independently. From the perspective of infornet theory, the reason for this empirical finding is that these different types of affect are outputs from different clusters of infornet beliefs. Negative affect is an output from stability–unstability beliefs, and positive affect from Plasticity–nonplasticity beliefs. As with negative affect, changes in positive cognitions tend to change positive affect and vice versa.

The perspective of modern Western medicine is that therapy should attempt to correct something that is wrong, which in terms of psychological symptoms is typically depression, fatigue and anxiety. Lack of positive affect is seldom reported as a problem. Nevertheless, there is an alternative approach to therapy that focuses on enhancing positive affect rather than dealing with the negative affect. This alternative may be important as there is evidence that positivity rather than negativity predicts mortality (Xu and Roberts, 2010).

The idea of focusing on the positive has a long history in psychology, dating at least from the humanistic psychology developed by Rogers (1951) and Maslow (1954). Nevertheless, the focus on promoting positivity has been particularly prominent in psychology during the last 10 years under the heading of positive psychology (Seligman *et al.*, 2005). There are several different kinds of positive psychology intervention. A meta-analysis by Sin and Lyubomirsky (2009) includes mindfulness, positive writing, hope therapy, positive reminiscence, life review and gratitude therapy. Of the various therapies, gratitude therapy is one that is commonly represented. There are several types of gratitude therapy, but they all involve mental exercises that cultivate a sense of gratitude (Geraghty *et al.*, 2010a, 2010b). The cultivation of positive states is not limited to positive psychology, as it also features in complementary and alternative medicine (CAM). Mindfulness is a form of meditation: meditation is commonly classified as a CAM. CAMs can involve visualisation techniques and something called affirmation. In an affirmation the patient states out loud a positive statement, such as 'I am now a strong and healthy person'. Émile Coué (1857–1926) was a French psychologist who believed that health and happiness could be achieved by repeating the mantra that one was getting better and better every day. Laughter therapy (Cousins, 1983) is used in the West (Beckman *et al.*, 2007) as well as featuring in the Eastern tradition in the context of yoga laughter (Robbins, 2006). Thus, therapeutic techniques that enhance positive cognitions and affect occur in a wide range of contexts, but are recently most prominent under the heading of positive psychology.

According to infornet theory, the cultivation of positive mood states and cognitions will change non-plasticity infornet beliefs towards plasticity infornet beliefs. That is, there will be shift towards the belief that

There are rewarding opportunities in the external situation. There are plenty of opportunities out there. Let's go out and seek new worlds and boldly go where no one has gone before. Let's explore and do try out new ways of making the world a better place. Rewards are out there – I just need to go and get them.

As Non-plasticity beliefs contribute to general infornet dysregulation, a change towards Plasticity beliefs will contribute to the infornet belief that *the general situation is good*.

Infornet theory leads to the following prediction: If positive affect is due to variation in plasticity–nonplasticity beliefs, then one of the best ways of increasing positivity is by giving the person a sense of success and achievement. The experience of success will lead to the infornet belief that the person is capable of achieving rewards in novel situations. Thus, positivity is particularly enhanced by manipulations that increase perceived efficacy.

Therapy as lifestyle change and the attainment of important goals

The above two sections describe ways in which therapy alters the perception of the world in which we live, so that these changed perceptions then lead to changes in infornet beliefs. However, therapy can also act as a change in lifestyle. That lifestyle change can lead to satisfaction of otherwise unattained goals. Research shows that goal attainment has psychological and physiological consequences. Performing goal-attaining activities leads to better mood and lowers cortisol levels (Hoppmann and Klumb, 2006).

Therapy involves a behaviour on the part of the patient. The change in behaviour created by therapy has a number of effects, in particular that of providing opportunities for goal satisfaction. Moerman (2002) refers to the placebo response as a meaning response. The behaviour of therapeutic rituals has meaning. A good of way of illustrating the rich meaning in therapeutic rituals is to consider the meaning of a clinical trial. In a clinical trial patients are invited to take part in a new treatment, let us suppose a treatment for a new drug, and they are told they will receive either the real drug or a placebo. Some possible meanings of taking part in a clinical trial are:

- There are nice people who care about me and are kind to me.
- I expect to get better.
- I am helping the clever and powerful doctors with their research.
- I respect the people in this hospital.
- I am helping find a cure for others who, like me, have my problem.
- It is a pleasant day out and a change from routine.
- I am valued as a person and they are interested in me.

The meaning of a clinical trial is not just expectancy – it involves a therapeutic bond with those who are running the study, it involves taking part in a new activity, it involves helping others and it involves being an important person.

Actors and other theatre personnel refer to the objects on stage as 'props'. The inert substance or placebo is merely the 'prop' in the ritual

Box 9.2 Example of contextual richness of clinical trials

I was responsible for outcome assessment in a placebo-controlled study of adult growth hormone replacement (growth hormone versus placebo) in people who had lost the ability to produce growth hormone. The outcome assessments were carried out by a young and dedicated psychology research assistant under my supervision. It soon became clear that the research assistant was doing more than collecting outcome data. Patients would telephone her if there was a problem with collecting their medicine or with appointments with the doctor. They would provide far more information than she asked for, and they would talk about problems they were experiencing that were entirely unrelated to the clinical trial. Moreover, not only were the patients developing a strong relationship with the research assistant, but also the research assistant, as a genuinely caring person, was developing a relationship with the patients. It was clear that in this clinical trial, the therapeutic ritual had far more meaning than the mere expectancy of improvement.

that the person engages in. The prop of the inert substance contributes to the meaning of the ritual, but it is often only a very small part. In the theatre it is the story that matters, and the props are there to support the story. The meaning of taking part in a clinical trial can affect infornet beliefs in several ways. The presence of caring others leads to a change in the infornet belief *life is a punishment* to *it is a wonderful world, things go right, there is no punishment*. In addition, the clinical trial is a new experience for the patient, and a new experience that is rewarding because of the way others react to the patient. Hence there is a change in the infornet belief that *everything is OK as long as I do nothing new* to *there are rewarding opportunities in the external situation*. In sum, the behaviour of taking part in a clinical trial alters both Stability–unstability and Plasticity-nonplasticity infornet beliefs.

Failure to achieve important goals leads to negative affect, and in particular to depression (Carver and Scheier, 1998; Deci and Ryan, 2000; Hyland, 1987). The theoretical rationale for this relationship is that persistent failure to achieve important goals leads to the activation of behavioural inhibition, and therefore elicits symptoms associated with behavioural inhibition (fatigue and depression) and contributes to general infornet dysregulation (the infornet belief that *the general situation is bad*). The implication is that if the therapeutic ritual satisfies important goals, this will lead to an improvement in infornet regulation. In Chapter 3, goals were categorised in two categories. First, there are those goals pertaining to all people, namely the goals indentified in self-determination theory. According to self-determination theory, there are three basic goals: competence, autonomy and relatedness, which when satisfied lead to better health and well-being (Deci and Ryan, 1985, Ryan and Deci, 2000). Second, there are goals that vary between people, namely the goals identified in theories of self-actualisation (Maslow, 1954) and represented in theories of human values (Schwartz and Boehnke, 2004).

A caring therapist can help patients satisfy their need for relatedness. A substantial body of research shows that variables with labels such as relatedness, social support and love are associated with better mental and physiological health, although several causal routes are involved (Schwarzer and Leppin, 1991). Additionally the therapeutic bond is a central part of psychotherapy and predicts outcome (Martin *et al.*, 2000). In addition to helping satisfy the goal of relatedness, some therapeutic interactions help satisfy goals of competence and autonomy.

According to infornet theory, the therapeutic bond should be particularly effective at increasing Stability beliefs (i.e., reducing negative affect), whereas competence and autonomy should be particularly effective at increasing Plasticity beliefs (i.e., increasing positive affect). This prediction is yet to be tested.

The above shows how goals that are common to all people can be satisfied during therapy. However, therapy also provides the opportunity for self-actualisation through goals that are specific to the person. Motivational concordance theory (Hyland and Whalley, 2008) is based on the assumption that people are intrinsically motivated to achieve particular self-defining goals, which are also labelled values. In addition, each therapeutic ritual expresses a particular value and provides an opportunity for satisfying that particular value. People gain most benefit when their own values are concordant with that of therapy. This theory is confirmed by data showing that people high in the value of spirituality compared with those low in spirituality achieve better outcomes on spiritually contextualised therapies (Hyland *et al.*, 2006a), but *only* on spiritually contextualised therapies (Hyland and Whalley, 2008). In addition, people high in dispositional gratitude have better outcomes on gratitude therapy (Hyland *et al.*, 2007). Motivational concordance theory is also supported by research showing that people rate as most effective those therapies that are consistent with their own goals (Whalley and Hyland, 2008). Thus, research into motivational concordance shows that intrinsically motivating therapy produces benefit. From the perspective of infornet theory, intrinsically motivating therapies provide a lifestyle intervention that helps satisfy important goals, and therefore encourages the infornet belief that *it is a wonderful world, things go right*.

Therapy as a disinhibitor

In addition to helping satisfy goals, many therapies involve a change of routine, just as taking part in a clinical trial involves a change of routine. Many work environments require long periods of repetitive activity and so have the potential lead to ignored reactive inhibition. For reasons outlined in Chapter 6, ignored reactive inhibition should lead to a potentiation of fatigue and hence general infornet dysregulation. Any therapeutic encounter is therefore likely to act as a disinhibitor of reactive inhibition.

In sum, there are several routes that lead to a change in infornet beliefs: (a) mental exercises devised by the therapist, such as CBT and positive psychology; (b) mental activities that are part of therapy, such as homeopathy; (c) the behaviour of therapy, which includes the therapeutic bond, competence, autonomy and reactive disinhibition.

In addition, the context of therapy is one in which the patient has a caring therapist who is making a bad situation good, and this alters the high-level infornet belief that *the general situation is bad* to *the general situation is good*.

Relaxation

The idea that relaxation is therapeutic has a long history – the rest cure was proposed during the nineteenth century as part of medical treatment. The relaxation response was made popular during the second part of the twentieth century by the pioneering work of Herbert Benson (Benson, 1979, 1983). Relaxation features in many twenty-first-century therapies, including transcendental meditation (mentally repeating a mantra over and over again). Mindfulness meditation (Kabat-Zinn, 1994) involves focusing on the present, focusing on the experience of breathing. Although each of these therapies induces relaxation in different ways, and there are claims for specific benefits of particular types of relaxation, they all produce an effect that is the opposite of stress: the patient is in an 'unstressed' state during the therapy. Meditation or relaxation techniques have been shown to have a large number of psychological and physiological benefits. A meta-analysis of mindfulness meditation across various conditions showed it to be effective, with effect sizes of 0.5 for mental health and 0.42 for physical health (Grossman *et al.*, 2004). A meta-analysis of transcendental meditation for hypertension showed it to have clinically significant effects (Anderson *et al.*, 2008).

Many CAMs involve rest and relaxation even though rest is ancillary to the primary purpose of the therapy. For example, Swedish massage is deeply relaxing; acupuncture sessions can last for about

Box 9.3 Alexander technique

The Alexander technique is based on the idea that there is feedback from muscles to the mind. If muscles normally used to responding to stress are used constantly, then the mind interprets the situation as being one of constant stress. Problems arise in particular when static posture is maintained by muscles that are designed for movement. Alexander developed his technique by observing himself in a mirror. He had developed problems with public speaking and observed that his posture was that of preparedness for attack. The idea that proprioceptive feedback provides information is consistent with the hypothesis of the network presented here. The network responds to any information, including information from the muscles.

half an hour during which the patient lies on a couch doing nothing; healing involves similar or longer periods of inactivity. The Alexander technique involves focusing attention on the position of the body. The proprioceptive awareness that is created by the Alexander technique provides a state of mindfulness in which the person is aware of what they are doing.

Other techniques that increase mindfulness or a state of being include Tai Chi, in which there is a focus on movement. Dance therapy has similarities with these more traditional therapies, as dance can involve focus on position. Sometimes therapies create a state of mindfulness simply because they place the patient in a relaxed state. For example, massage therapy, reflexology and Reiki all create a relaxing environment that enhances states of being. Massage therapists report that these are most effective when their client does not speak – the person will not enter a state of mindfulness if conversation is maintained.

Why is rest so important for health? One possibility is that relaxation is a message to the infornet that the external situation is safe – people do not relax when they feel threatened. However, there is another aspect to relaxation that, although speculative, is worth considering. Supervised networks function in two modes. The first mode is where the network provides a solution to its inputs. According to infornet theory, the infornet resolves into a particular state in order to solve the problem, 'What are the best parameters for the body's control systems to deal with the internal and external environment?' The second mode is when the network self-organises so as to best meet the criterion set by the supervisor. In infornet theory, the infornet self-organises according to supervised and associative learning rules. When networks are trained, they are either in one mode (the test mode) or the other (the training mode). It therefore seems plausible, that the body also operates in two modes: one when it is solving the problem of how to deal with the current situation, and the other when it is self-organising to ensure that the solutions provided are correct. The hypothesis that sleep/rest versus activity represent two modes of functioning is consistent with the observation that the body operates according to the principle of temporal specialisation (see Chapter 2): the body tends to carry out particular functions at particular times.

This infornet explanation for sleep and rest comes with a corollary: that the infornet needs to keep self-organising in order to remain healthy. That is, it is not the case that infornet pro-regulation is a state that can be achieved and then the body 'locks in' to this healthy state, but rather that the body needs to continually self-organise so as to achieve health, or at least it needs to self-organise on a regular basis.

The infornet needs sleep and rest so it can engage in the continual process of sorting itself out. It is interesting to note that in the case of CFS, overactivity leads to increased fatigue the following day. Thus, if sleep is the time for infornet self-organisation, the harmful effects of over-activity are realised only after the occurrence of sleep allows the infornet to move towards greater dysregulation.

Infornet theory is based on an assumption that the body is in a constant state of self-organisation so as to promote health. This assumption is consistent with Antonovsky's (1996) idea of salutogenic orientation, that is, the natural tendency of the body to seek health. It also consistent with the idea that networks are capable of breaking the second law of thermodynamics – by extracting negative entropy from their environment. The extraction of negative entropy is not the something that can be achieved and then locked away: it needs to happen constantly. Life is a state of constant striving after health – rather than the state of health itself.

Summary of infornet beliefs that are therapeutic

The above sections describe ways in which the infornet can be shifted from a dysregulated to a well-regulated state. In Chapter 3, Figure 3.9 showed the hierarchical relationship between infornet beliefs that create dysregulation. There is a mirror image of these dysregulatory infornet beliefs, namely those that contributed to well-regulation. This mirror image of infornet beliefs is summarised in Figure 9.3. All the above mechanisms that contribute to well-regulation can be interpreted as supporting one or more of the beliefs shown in Figure 9.3.

Short-term versus long-term mechanisms: the evidence

This chapter has been based on the assumption that the mechanisms underlying short-term placebo effects are different from those involving long-term placebo effects. Specifically, there is an assumption that the mechanisms that occur in laboratory analogue studies where healthy student participants are recruited are different from those in clinical trials where patients are motivated for health improvement. This section presents the evidence that short-term placebo effects are due to response expectancy, whereas long-term placebo effects are due to the motivational and affective mechanisms described above, in particular, motivational concordance or the affective gain that is achieved through the satisfaction of important goals.

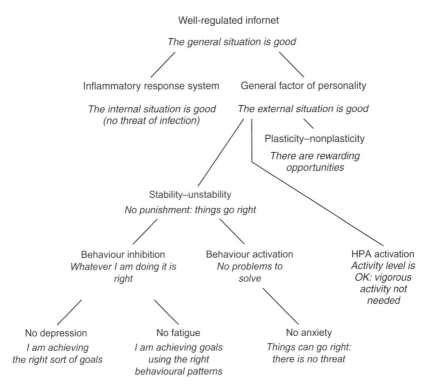

Figure 9.3 Structure of infornet beliefs, showing *in italic type* infornet beliefs at the different levels and in standard type the system to which the beliefs apply

Empirical comparison between motivational concordance and response expectancy theory is made complex by the fact that therapies that are perceived to be intrinsically attractive (because they are concordant with a person's motivations) are also perceived as being more effective (Whalley and Hyland, 2009). Thus, expectancy of benefit from a therapy correlates with the intrinsic value of the therapy. If a person enjoys a therapy, that therapy is perceived to be more effective than one that is not enjoyed. Correlations between expectancy and outcome in long-term studies may therefore be attributable to a third factor, namely the intrinsic value of performing the therapeutic task. The independent effects of expectancy and intrinsic value can be investigated using multiple regression. Where this is done for long-term therapeutic studies, the evidence shows that expectancy does not have an independent effect. The correlation between outcome and expectancy can be explained entirely in terms of motivational factors (Hyland *et al.*,

2006a, 2007; Hyland and Whalley, 2008). Thus, although expectancy correlates with outcome in many long-term studies, response expectancy does not appear to be the underlying mechanism.

Several other pieces of evidence suggest that the mechanisms responsible for short-term effects in laboratory analogue studies do not occur in long-term, clinically relevant placebo studies. First, whereas optimism correlates with outcome in short-term placebo studies (Geers *et al.*, 2005a), it does not in long-term studies (Hyland *et al.*, 2007; Hyland and Whalley, 2008). Second, whereas opioid mechanisms are implicated in short-term placebo studies (Amanzio *et al.*, 2001; Benedetti *et al.*, 2003) and other psychologically mediated pain effects (Bandura *et al.*, 1987), they are not involved in long-term therapeutic effects of pain in irritable bowel syndrome patients (Vase *et al.*, 2005). Third, the rate of change of psychological state in long-term placebo studies is slow – and asymptotes only after about 7 days (Hyland and Whalley, 2008). This finding contrasts with the rapid change that occurs in laboratory studies.

Other findings suggest that effects that are observed in long-term studies do not occur in short-term placebo studies. Although the effect of the therapeutic bond is an important part of long-term change, it does not influence placebo bronchodilator effects (Kemeny *et al.*, 2007). By contrast, in a long-term study on symptom relief in patients with medically unexplained symptoms, a friendly therapist was found to be more effective than an unfriendly one, but whether or not the patient was treated made no difference (Thomas, 1987). As treatment is associated with expectancy of improvement, this study provides additional evidence that response expectancy is not the underlying mechanism of long-term change.

In sum, these different types of data lead to the conclusion that whereas short-term placebo effects may be the consequence of cognitions (i.e., response expectancy theory), long-term placebos or long-term psychologically medicated effects are the consequence of a different kind of mechanism, namely the lifestyle-changing effect of taking part in an intrinsically rewarding therapeutic ritual. Response expectancy is an input to the way the infornet resolves to the current situation. Long-term change, however, involves changes to the infornet beliefs that the *general situation is good*.

Unknowns

Much of the recent research in psychotherapy consists of randomised controlled trials in which a particular psychotherapy is compared with something else – either natural history, another bona fide psychotherapy or something in between that is given the label of placebo. This research is motivated by one objective: to show the superiority of a particular type of psychotherapy. Despite meta-analyses demonstrating the dodo bird effect and despite the findings from component studies (see Chapter 7), the objective of this research is to show that 'my therapy is better than yours'.

Unfortunately, this research provides little information about underlying mechanisms Furthermore, as Cronbach and Mowrer (1953) suggested some fifty years ago, the important practical question is not 'Which therapy is best?' but 'Which therapy is best for whom?' There are several unanswered questions about mechanisms that arise from infornet theory.

First, are the therapeutic routes that lead to reduction in negative affect the same as or different from those that lead to an increase in positive affect? Infornet theory suggests that negative affect should be reduced in particular by goal satisfaction and signals of safety, namely factors that influence stability–unstability infornet beliefs. By contrast, positive affect should be increased by factors that signal that the person is successful (competent and autonomous) at achieving new rewards, namely factors that influence plasticity–nonplasticity beliefs.

Second, are some mechanisms more important than others in leading to therapeutic benefit? Infornet theory suggests that the particular form of general infornet dysregulation depends on the route into dysregulation. It is possible that the most effective therapy is that which elicits mechanisms that counteract the original route into dysregulation. For example, if a patient's problems stem from inadequate personal relationships, then the relationship with the therapist is the important factor in effecting change in infornet beliefs. On the other hand, if the patient's problems stem from over-activity and failure to respond to reactive inhibition, then therapies involving rest and relaxation may be most effective. Investigation of this hypothesis will contribute to an understanding of whether patients rather than therapists determine the mechanism of therapeutic benefit.

Long-term change in physiological outcome

Earlier sections of this chapter suggested a mechanism underlying short-term placebo (psychologically mediated) effects for psychological and physiological outcomes. The infornet resolves into a particular state depending on its inputs, which include psychological inputs. Long-term changes for psychological outcomes have also been examined. Changes in infornet beliefs towards the belief that *the general situation is good* lead to better psychological outcomes. This section examines the mechanism underlying long-term psychologically mediated effects for physiological outcomes. It considers how psychological factors can have an impact on major disease, that is, diseases with a specific pathophysiology.

Meta-analyses of long-term placebo studies (i.e., the placebo arm of a randomised controlled clinical trial), reviewed in Chapter 7, show that psychologically mediated improvement of physiological outcome varies from zero to a moderate improvement. Conclusions from these meta-analyses should be treated with caution owing to the possibility of trial effects (see Chapter 8). Meta-analyses of psychological interventions for cancer and heart disease suggest either a small or zero improvement. Again, conclusions should be treated with caution, but in this case because psychologically mediated improvement may occur independently of interventions. Finally, depression is a predictor of poor prognosis for cancer and chronic obstructive pulmonary disease (see Chapter 3), though this may be because activation of the inflammatory response system leads to both systemic inflammation and depression. Any explanation of psychologically mediated effects of mortality and morbidity must therefore be consistent with these various, sometimes equivocal, conclusions.

The infornet explanation for the effect of psychological treatment morbidity and mortality of specific disease is based on an understanding of disease processes. Dysregulation of the infornet, whether specific or general, is a precursor to specific disease. However, the dysregulation is only a precursor: something else is needed for the specific disease to occur. It is this 'something else' that will determine the extent to which psychological inputs can alter morbidity and mortality.

In Chapter 7, two mechanisms were suggested whereby infornet dysregulation leads to specific disease. One was that the infornet promotes the expression of disease-causing genes. The other was that infornet alters the balance between disease-forming and disease-preventing processes in the specific system. The extent to which the infornet can have a therapeutic effect can be seen in the light of these two processes.

Consider first the case of a specific disease that is controlled by the expression of a particular gene. If that gene can be switched off, then the disease is cured. If the disease is not switched off, then the disease remains. Thus, the extent to which psychological factors can cure a specific disease depends on (a) the extent to which infornet is responsible for gene expression, and (b) the extent to which a well-regulated infornet alters that gene expression.

In the case of diseases that are maintained by disease-forming processes in the specific system, then the extent to which psychological factors can cure the disease will depend on (a) the extent to which the infornet can alter the disease-forming or disease-preventing processes, and (b) the extent to which the disease-forming processes are self-perpetuating.

The conclusion of the above is that one would expect some diseases to be self-perpetuating, for genetic or other reasons, and hence once the disease is formed, a well-regulated infornet will have little effect. For other diseases, the tendency towards self-perpetuation is less and so the well-regulated infornet has some potential for curing the disease. So, some specific diseases should act as a 'one-way ticket' so that the disease is always progressive irrespective of the state of the infornet. Non-reversible diseases should exhibit no natural remission and they are sometimes fatal even with aggressive specific treatment. Several diseases exhibit this pattern of presentation, including some cancers and chronic obstructive pulmonary disease. By contrast, other diseases are reversible, either because they exhibit spontaneous remission or because treatment leads to a permanent cure. In reversible diseases, either the disease-causing gene can be switched off or the balance of disease-forming and disease-preventing processes is altered in a favourable direction. Diseases that spontaneously remit are those that are reversible and include Crohn's disease. For example, a meta-analysis by Su *et al.* (2004) of Crohn's disease gives a spontaneous rate of remission in the placebo arms of clinical trials as about 18% of cases. This meta-analysis shows that factors predicting remission are also those predicting placebo response – which is about 19% of cases. Another example of reversibility is that of childhood asthma – some children 'grow out of' asthma, indicating that the underlying specific pathology remits (Strachan, 1985).

There is a simple theoretical prediction: psychologically mediated therapies should affect morbidity and mortality only for reversible diseases (i.e., those exhibiting spontaneous remission, or cure through treatment), but not for non-reversible diseases. Psychologically mediated effects on the infornet should be unable to help 'one-way-ticket' diseases, but could help those diseases where there is evidence of spontaneous remission.

The above provides a rationale for the somewhat equivocal results pertaining to psychological therapy as a way of reducing morbidity and mortality in cancer and heart disease (see Chapter 8). The term cancer refers to a heterogeneous group of diseases, some of which (breast cancer) respond well to specific treatments such as surgery, chemotherapy and radiotherapy. In other types of cancer (e.g., lung cancer) the outcome is commonly fatal despite treatment. In such cases it would seem likely that the disease is non-reversible. Thus, the question of whether psychological inputs have a beneficial effect on cancer may depend on the type of cancer and the extent to which it is reversible. Psychological intervention may help some types of cancer, but not others, perhaps depending on the interplay between the infornet and gene expression. However, there is a clear theoretical prediction: the effectiveness of psychologically mediated effects for reversible specific disease depends crucially on the management of the disease in the specific system. Specific diseases require specific management. Psychological management should be an addition to effective specific treatment.

Infornet theory suggests that psychological interventions help diseases such as cancer only to the extent that infornet beliefs are changed, and specifically the belief that *the general situation is bad* to *the general situation is good*. The extent to which this change takes place will depend in part on therapy but also on the patient. Patients do not need a therapist to re-evaluate their lives in a more positive way. Future research into the effect of psychological treatment for specific disease should take into account (a) the reversibility of the specific disease and (b) the extent to which the patient's infornet beliefs can be moved to seeing the general situation as good – which is far from easy in the case of major illness. Rather than focus on psychological therapy, future research should also include therapies that pamper the patient (e.g., aromatherapy).

Predictions

Infornet theory provides the following predictions about the therapeutic effects of psychologically mediated interventions:

- Short-term placebo effects should occur for psychological variables, but only for those physiological variables that are controlled by homeodynamic (not homeostatic) control systems.
- Long-term psychologically mediated effects should be most effective for dysregulatory diseases and those where the primary symptom is psychological compared with specific diseases where there is a consistent pathophysiology.
- Long-term psychologically mediated effects should be greater for those specific diseases that exhibit spontaneous remission, but should have little effect on those where there is no remission or where the disease is fatal.

- Psychologically mediated therapies should be effective to the extent that the psychological input provides the patient with positive information about their general situation. Such benefit should not be limited to therapies provided by psychologists.

The above predictions are consistent with existing data on the effect of psychologically mediated effects. However, these data also provide novel predictions that can act as a guide for further primary research and meta-analysis of existing studies.

10   Finding the pattern: health in modern society

Introduction

Infornet theory proposes that the body self-organises to achieve the state defined by the genome. As a result, people should be healthiest (i.e., with a well-regulated infornet) when their lifestyle corresponds to the pattern that is specified in their genome. This hypothesis leads to the following questions: What is that pattern specified in the genome? How do our genes expect us to live?

A simple application of evolutionary theory and genetics suggests that humans are healthiest when their pattern of living corresponds most closely to the circumstances under which they evolved. Anatomically, modern humans have evolved over long period of time but they existed in their present form some 100,000 years ago. Humans evolved in an environment that was different in a number of respects from the modern environment. According to the simple view, the genetic determinants of a modern healthy lifestyle can be understood in terms of a Palaeolithic lifestyle some one hundred thousand to ten thousand years ago. The Upper Palaeolithic ('old stone age') occurred during the last ice age, and the Upper Palaeolithic people lived a life of hunter-gatherers. By contrast the Neolithic people ('new stone age') lived after the end of the last ice age and were farmers. The growing of crops and domestication of animals developed simultaneously in several parts of the world from about 10,000 years ago onwards. The Neolithic lifestyle was different in two important ways from the Upper Palaeolithic people: diet and psychological aspects of lifestyle resulting from differences in social organisation.

The Palaeolithic diet comprised a mixture of meat and vegetables, with proportions varying widely depending on the particular environment in which people lived. As a general rule, the diet was highly varied. The Neolithic diet was less varied and had a large component of carbohydrate-rich grains – for example, wheat in the Middle East, rice in the Far East and maize in the Americas. The modern diet is similar to the Neolithic diet to the extent that it is a carbohydrate-rich diet.

Box 10.1 The concept of property and land ownership

'What is this you call property? It cannot be the earth, for the land is our mother, nourishing all her children, beasts, birds, fish and all men. The woods, the streams, everything on it belongs to everybody and is for the use of all. How can one man say it belongs only to him?' – attributed to the Indian chief, Massasoit Sachem (c.1581–1661), who made peace with the early settlers in North America.

Differences in social organisation (and hence psychological aspects of lifestyle) between Palaeolithic and Neolithic groups can be inferred from characteristics of modern hunter–gatherers. There are three main differences.

First, hunter-gatherers do not, as a general rule, have a hierarchical society. That is, there is no leader or king. The society tends to be egalitarian, with all contributing to decision making, though respect is often accorded to elders because of knowledge accumulated over a lifetime.

Second, in hunger-gatherer groups, there is no ownership of land and seldom ownership of property. Property ownership is a logical consequence of farming. People feel that they own the carrots they have grown in their fields or allotments. They don't own the blackberries they pick from the hedgerows. When the early Australian aboriginals were given clothes by white settlers (who disapproved of nakedness), these indigenous people did not perceive that they owned the clothes they were given – they saw the gift as being given to the whole tribe. The same type of reasoning applied to the provision of social housing – when given a house to live in, the family perceived it as a gift to the tribe, and so invited all their relatives, much to the consternation of those providing the benefit.

Third, population density was lower in the Palaeolithic compared with the Neolithic. Palaeolithic groups would have numbered about 35 people; Neolithic villages would have numbered at least a few hundred people and population density has increased ever since. Population density is important in that the larger the density and the more people in an area, the greater chance there is of meeting someone who is unfamiliar, and hence a stranger.

There are two reasons for supposing that the Upper Palaeolithic people were generally a healthy group of people, and certainly more healthy than the later Neolithic people. First, body size is an indicator of health: poor diet and stress lead to poor health and lower body size. The body mass, cranial capacity and brain mass of the Upper Palaeolithic people were not only larger than those of the Neolithic people, but also slightly larger than the average of modern people today (Ruff *et al.*, 1997). Second, examination of the skeletal remains of the Upper Palaeolithic people shows little evidence of inflammatory diseases such as arthritis, and much less than those of the Neolithic people (Wittwer-Backofen and Tomo, 2008).

It is commonly assumed that the poorer health of the Neolithic people, and the improvement in health that has occurred since that time, are due to changes in diet. Indeed, the Palaeolithic diet has been recommended by a variety of writers (the Atkins diet is a variant on the Palaeolithic diet). Nevertheless, there are two reasons for looking for either an addition or an alternative to the dietary explanation. First, modern people appear to be perfectly healthy eating carbohydrates, or at least most people do not suffer from problems from carbohydrates. There are exceptions (e.g., coeliac disease), but these do not alter the main facts that neither bread- potato- nor rice-eating have been shown by scientific methods to be a danger to health. Second, although lack of green vegetables is associated with increased risk for several diseases (see Chapters 6 and 7), the evidence suggests that early farming communities (and modern farming communities in less developed parts of the world) had an adequate diet of fruit and vegetables (Brothwell and Brothwell, 1998).

The idea that health is compromised by the modern use of carbohydrate-rich food fails to take into account a distinctive feature of human evolution. Humans evolved under conditions of environmental change (Gribbin and Gribbin, 1990). During the last 5 million years there have been a series of ice ages (glacials) followed by interglacials when the temperature was substantially higher. The ice ages last on average about 100,000 years and the interglacials on average 10,000 years – the current interglacial has lasted about 10,000 years. Each shift from glacial to interglacial led to changes in available food and physical environment. Humans evolved the capacity to survive in multiple environments. Although anatomically modern humans evolved in Africa some one hundred thousand years ago, they were able to colonise almost all parts of the world from about 40,000 years ago, with colonisation ranging from the freezing conditions in the north down to Australia. Humans survived in a changing environment because they were adapted to managing change. Although humans evolved to eat foods low in carbohydrates, the ability to eat food such as bread and potatoes reflects a genetically conferred ability to adapt. Humans survived and spread *because* they evolved to be adapted to varied environments.

Although the physical environment was changeable during human evolution, the psychological environment seems to have been fairly constant, namely small hunter-gatherer groups. Thus, the genetically defined pattern that leads to good health must include the psychological environment and not just the physical environment (e.g., what we eat). Support for the idea that psychological aspects of lifestyle affect health outcome comes from a variety of sources reviewed in this book.

This chapter examines the hypothesis that modern living creates health problems not because it is physically dissimilar to the Palaeolithic environment, but because it is psychologically different. Health does not require people to live exactly as our ancestors did. Hunting and gathering in the suburbs is not the answer. However, it may be necessary to take into account the psychological features of the environment in which humans evolved.

The psychology of people living during the Palaeolithic

People evolved to live in small hunter-gatherer groups (about 20–50 persons). Although modern and recent hunter-gatherers are often marginalised groups and may therefore differ from our hunter-gatherer ancestors, the archaeological and anthropological evidence suggests that the psychological environment of our Upper Palaeolithic ancestors was as follows (Geist, 1978).

- *Social support*. Hunter-gatherer groups are socially supportive, with high levels of caring between group members, and there is less evidence of interpersonal conflict compared with other forms of social organisation.
- *Care for the sick*. Modern hunter-gatherers care for the sick, often with ritualistic group activities (e.g., forming a ring round the sick person and chanting and drumming). Shamans provide prehistorical evidence of healing. Evidence of healed broken bones in both Neanderthals and anatomically modern people indicates that our ancestors cared for the sick: our ancestors were caring people.
- *Cooperation and trust*. It is possible to hunt large, dangerous animals only if people cooperate and trust each other when hunting. The hunting of large dangerous animals occurs only with *Homo sapiens*, not (to any extent) with the earlier *Homo erectus*.
- *Achievement of goals*. Human survival during the ice ages was difficult and dangerous. To survive in the challenging environment of an ice age, it is necessary to attain a variety of goals, including hunting, gathering, maintaining the camp, moving to different locations and education of the young.
- *Self-determination*. Hunter-gatherer groups tend to be non-hierarchical in that they do not have a leader or king. Leadership is a feature of

the Neolithic and later periods where *command* authority accrues to people by virtue of birth or strength. In non-hierarchical societies, individuals are able to set their own goals or, in group decision making, contribute to the setting of goals. In non-hierarchical societies, some individuals have *expert* authority by virtue of their greater knowledge. Direction by expert authority leads to greater intrinsic motivation compared with command authority. In the Palaeolithic period, people would have experienced greater self-determination of goals and greater control over their lives compared with later hierarchical societies.

- *Variety of activities.* Hunter-gatherers engage in a variety of activities, which are not limited to attaining and storing food and managing the camp. Cave paintings, pre-historical sculptures (e.g., fertility symbols), as well as a wealth of modern hunter-gatherer rituals show that our ancestors engaged in ritualistic behaviour. Hunter-gatherers often travel large distances and some are nomadic, with winter and summer hunting grounds.

- *Variety of individual characteristics.* Groups of people survive in a complex and challenging environment only if there is some form of specialisation of function within the group. Some specialisation results from gender (only women give birth to children and it is common only for men to hunt animals), but far more specialisation is needed for effective group functioning. Anatomically, modern humans are the first hominid species to provide evidence of the three-generation family, suggesting that older people had a specific function, most likely that of educating the young and being a repository of knowledge. Individual variation within a group is needed if the group is adapted to manage new and unexpected challenges. People are not identical.

- *Rest and relaxation.* A good deal of time in a hunter-gatherer group is spent doing very little – either resting or talking. It has been estimated that the average working week of a hunter-gatherer (work consisting of hunting, gathering, storing food and making and moving camp) is about 22 hours per week.

Some of the psychological characteristics of the Palaeolithic lifestyle have parallels with self-determination theory. The goals of autonomy, competence and relatedness (Deci and Ryan, 1985; Ryan and Deci, 2000) all characterise a society in which there is high mutual dependence and lack of command authority. The goal of relatedness may seem a pale reflection of the strong emotional bond between members of hunter–gatherer groups, but the choice of words reflects the tendency of psychologists to use non-emotive language.

Happiness and pleasure as signals that you are getting it right – most of the time

A basic principle of infornet theory is that chronic mental states such as depression, fatigue and anxiety are signals of general infornet dysregulation. It is therefore to be expected that there should also be signals that the infornet is well-regulated. There should be signals that the lifestyle is 'right' rather than 'wrong'. Happiness and pleasure are signals that something is 'right'. Happiness indicates that the infornet is well regulated; pleasure indicates that the current behaviour is contributing to a well-regulated infornet.

Philosophers and psychologists distinguish happiness from pleasure (Waterman, 1993), and there is a common theme that people should pursue happiness rather than pleasure. Happiness and pleasure are both positive mental states. The difference between them can be understood in terms of the *level* at which goals are being satisfied.

A person experiences pleasure from a good meal, from beating an opponent at a game of tennis or from chatting with friends. The pleasures of life are the consequence of satisfying lower-level goals in a hierarchy of goals, and typically, from specific behaviours. A person experiences happiness from the satisfaction of higher-level goals. For example, a person experiences happiness if they are self-actualising, if they are satisfied with their lives and have high self-esteem. From a psychological perspective, there is no arbitrary cut-off point between the goals that lead to happiness and those that lead to pleasure – there is a continuum in the level of goals a person experiences.

Figure 10.1 shows a diagrammatic summary of how high-level or self-defining goals are each achieved by lower levels. This figure combines four theoretical ideas. The first is that goal attainment is hierarchically organised, where lower-level goals satisfy higher-level goals (Carver and Scheier, 1998; Hyland, 1988). The second is that high-level goals include autonomy, competence and relatedness (Deci and Ryan, 1985; Ryan and Deci, 2000). The third is that the three goals of self-determination theory do not provide a complete picture: there are other goals, such as spirituality and health, which in certain individuals give rise to self-actualisation (Schwartz and Beohnke, 2004). The fourth is that self-actualisation is individualised and that different individuals can self-actualise in different ways (Maslow, 1954).

Figure 10.1 shows that whereas satisfaction of the lower-level goals leads to pleasure (or at least the feeling of a job well done), it is the higher goals that lead to self-actualisation and hence happiness. Note that people can achieve happiness in different ways, as people differ in their

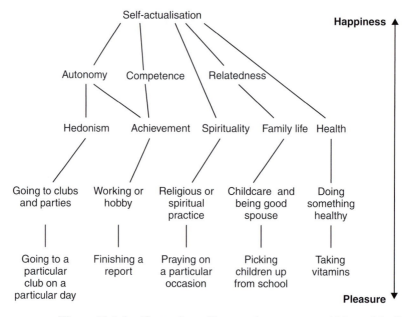

Figure 10.1 An illustration of how goals are arranged hierarchically

high-level goals. In addition, high-level goals can describe not only end states (e.g., being happily married) but also rate of progress to high-end states (e.g., making sufficient progress in a career). From the perspective of infornet theory, self-actualisation can be interpreted as finding the particular pattern for which the person is genetically designed. This self-actualising pattern will include goals that are common to all people (Deci and Ryan, 1985; Ryan and Deci, 2000), namely the goals identified in self-determination theory of relatedness, autonomy and competence, but also goals that are unique to the individual (Maslow, 1954).

According to infornet theory, pleasure and happiness are both 'good' because they indicate that the person is behaving in a way that is consistent with the genome. A counter-argument to that hypothesis that pleasure and happiness are 'good' comes from the observation that some pleasures are harmful. For example, people enjoy sweet and fatty food and can therefore eat an excess of this type of food, leading to obesity and a variety of health problems. Additionally, people enjoy smoking, gambling and other addictive behaviours that are not health promoting. According to this counter-argument, whereas happiness may always be 'good', pleasure often is not. Indeed, the idea that pleasure can be bad (e.g., the sins of the flesh) is behind philosophical and religious arguments against pleasure as an end state.

Box 10.2 Pleasure as the ultimate good

Epicurus was a Greek philosopher who believed that the best way of living was to maximise pleasure. Epicurus' name is used in the word 'epicurean', meaning someone who enjoys food. In fact, Epicurus believed that the eating of rich food led to indigestion and so led to displeasure rather than pleasure. He and his followers had a very simple diet, primarily bread, with cheese on festival days.

The explanation for the existence of unhealthy pleasures is that the genome is tricked into thinking something is healthy when it is not. Non-healthy pleasurable behaviours arise because of a divergence between the Palaeolithic and modern lifestyles. People evolved to enjoy sweetness because sweetness is a feature of vegetables and fruit, particularly when they are freshly gathered. Freshly picked cabbage, for example, is considerably sweeter than supermarket cabbage that is more than 24 hours old. In a Palaeolithic environment, sweetness would have been a sign of healthy food. Similarly, people evolved to enjoy fats because they are part of meat. People evolved as meat eaters because meat provides the rich source of protein necessary to enable time for other non-food-gathering activities (cows eat throughout the day, humans do not). The problem with the modern lifestyle is that foods can be made far sweeter than those found in the Palaeolithic, and similarly a range of foods, not just meat, can be high in fat. Modern foods create exaggerated taste signals. Food enhancers and other additives create a heightened sense of pleasure that is unrelated to the biological features of the food to which they are added.

Modern humans like unhealthy foods because these unhealthy foods provide exaggerated signals that that they are actually healthy. Addictive behaviours all involve positive mood state from something that would not have been available to our hunter-gatherer ancestors. Our ancestors did not have gambling casinos or bars of chocolate. In sum, pleasure evolved as a way of encouraging people to engage in healthy behaviours, but under the specific environmental conditions of modern living, it can do the reverse.

A healthy lifestyle: general orientation and the importance of wealth

General dysregulation is characterised by the infornet belief that *the general situation is bad*. The well-regulated infornet is characterised by the infornet belief that *the general situation is good*. There are several

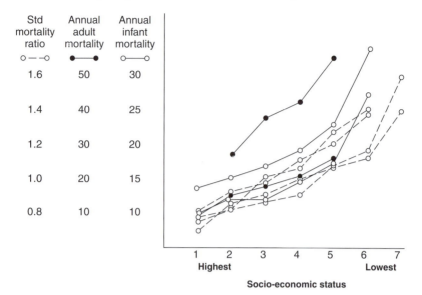

Figure 10.2 Mortality rates and social class, results combined from several studies. Note: On the *y*-axis, mortality rate varies between 10 and 50 per 1,000 adults for adult mortality and between 10 and 30 per 1,000 live births for infant mortality (from Adler *et al.*, 1994).

general ways of indicating to the infornet that the external situation is a good one, and these include wealth and social status – the two tend to correlate in Western society. Wealth is one of the strongest predictors of health status.

The health gradient (Adler *et al.*, 1994) is a term used to describe the gradual improvement in all health indicators, including life expectancy, as social class improves (see Figure 10.2). Some of the differences in health between social class can be explained in terms of biological factors, namely the *unhealthy factors external environment* referred to in Chapter 3. People from lower social classes tend to smoke more and they tend to have a poorer diet, because poorly nutritious convenience foods are often cheap. However, the difference between social class cannot be attributed only to biological factors. The reason is that social class 1 (e.g., lawyers, doctors, university lecturers, company directors) has better health than social class 2 (e.g., teachers, nurses, office workers). Social classes 1 and 2 are both sufficiently affluent to buy healthy food and there is little difference in health-harming behaviours such as smoking.

Box 10.3 Lifestyle difference conferred by wealth

- better self-determination at work and less instruction from others;
- a more varied work activity;
- greater work satisfaction;
- less stress at work;
- job security;
- better control over events at home due to better financial security;
- greater number of holidays, and the ability to have different kinds of holidays on a regular basis; and
- enjoyment of activities in which you are cared for by others: spa treatments, luxurious hotels, complementary medicine.

Consequently, the difference between social classes 1 and 2 in terms of health outcomes would appear to be due to psychological differences in lifestyle, not to biological differences. The world is a better place if you are rich. There is an old saying that 'money doesn't bring happiness, but if you are unhappy, then money helps a lot!' Although there are few data comparing the relative importance of biological inputs (for example, food) versus psychological inputs (for example, psychological stress) in determining health, one study has indicated that psychological differences in work practice accounted for more variance in reported health than material differences arising from the different lifestyles of wealthier and poorer people (Borrell *et al.* 2004).

Although wealth is a strong predictor of health, the relationship is moderated by other factors, as illustrated by research that compares international differences in happiness. As suggested above, happiness is an approximate, surrogate measure of general infornet dysregulation versus well-regulation.

Figure 10.3 is taken is from a large 2004 survey of life satisfaction across nations (Veenhoven, 2009). International comparisons of disease statistics (i.e., measures of the specific disease system) are influenced by the quality of health care as well as biological differences in health practices between different countries. By contrast, measures of happiness provide an insight into the level of infornet dysregulation that is less influenced by health care systems.

Figure 10.3 shows that (at the time of measurement) wealthy countries (Iceland, Denmark and Switzerland) were among some of the happiest, but so were the less wealthy countries of Columbia and Mexico. Examination of the least happy countries shows that great poverty is associated with poor life satisfaction. However, wealth does not necessarily confer happiness, as shown by the comparison of countries.

Top-ranking countries	Comparison countries	Middle-ranking countries	Lowest-ranking countries
8.5 Iceland	7.7 Australia	6.3 Phillippines	4.2 Chad
8.4 Denmark	7.2 Germany	6.3 China	4.1 Togo
8.1 Colombia	7.1 UK	6.0 Iran	4.0 Angola
8.1 Switzerland	7.0 USA	5.9 India	3.3 Zimbabwe
8.0 Mexico	6.5 France	5.9 South Korea	3.2 Tanzania

Figure 10.3 Average rating (as at 2004) of the extent to which people enjoy their life-as-a whole, on a scale of 0 to 10

The research on international differences of happiness shows that:

- In order to be healthy and happy it is necessary to have a basic level of wealth, otherwise biological needs are not satisfied.
- Wealth is no guarantee of happiness, but wealth certainly helps.
- Some societies are better than others at creating happiness and health.
- The reason some societies are better at creating happiness and health is an important topic for future research.

A healthy lifestyle: lifestyle choices

Circumstances, both situational and personal, prevent many people from being wealthy. Additionally, in order to become wealthy it may be necessary to adopt a lifestyle that contributes to infornet dysregulation – for example, by working long hours. Trying to become wealthy may be counterproductive. It is important to emphasise that despite the wealth–health gradient it is by no means necessary to be wealthy in order for the infornet to develop the belief that *the general situation is good*. Irrespective of level of wealth, good health can be achieved by:

- avoiding those patterns of lifestyle that lead to general infornet dysregulation (Chapters 5 to 7); and
- engaging in patterns of lifestyle that are therapeutic (Chapters 8 and 9).

The patterns of living that lead to a well-regulated infornet are those that affect mechanisms indentified in previous chapters. These mechanisms will be reviewed again under the following six topic headings, where the headings are organised by the way society affects infornet dysregulation.

1. Positive social interactions: the goal of relatedness, being loved and cared for by others and loving and caring.
2. Quality and nature of goal attainment: autonomy, competence, learned helplessness theory, chronic stress, individualised goal achievement.
3. Rest and relaxation.
4. Conflict resulting from simultaneous completion of incompatible activities, including simultaneous immune and external challenge.
5. Too much of a good thing: the problem of reactive inhibition.
6. Developmental origins of health: the fetal environment and early childhood.

Positive social interactions: the goal of relatedness, being loved and cared for by others and loving and caring

Humans evolved in groups where survival of the group depended on good interpersonal relationships. Under these circumstances, it is to be expected that people have evolved so they have needs to feel loved, cared for and appreciated by others. There is a very large body of research evidence on the harmful effects of loneliness and the beneficial effects of social support (Taylor and Repettie, 1997). The majority of this research shows the beneficial effect of participants receiving social support and positive regard from others. However, studies also show that caring for others can have health benefits for the carer. For example, depression is reduced when grandparents massage their grandchildren (Field, 1998). Whereas part of the research on social interactions and health focuses on positive interpersonal relations, another body of research focuses on poor personal relations. Again there is a large body of evidence that hostility and conflict leads to a range of poor health outcomes. Additionally, the personality characteristic of hostility is associated with poor health, because hostile people are more likely to have negative, conflicting relations with others (see Chapter 3).

Given the nature of the hunter-gatherer lifestyle, it would seem reasonable that affectionate relations with others is a lifestyle pattern that is genetically specified for all people. Failure to achieve that lifestyle pattern leads to dysregulation as the network self-organises to try to achieve that pattern. The dysregulation leads to behavioural inhibition, so as to prevent continuation of the existing unsatisfactory form of lifestyle. Thus, the lonely person becomes depressed, because the signal of loneliness indicates that the existing behavioural pattern differs from the genetically specified pattern. Additionally, the dysregulation leads to activation of the inflammatory response system, which then contributes to specific pathology.

The modern lifestyle is one in which families often live far apart and in which people can feel isolated owing to circumstances beyond their (easy) control. The increased geographical mobility and high population density of modern society are very different from the close, small personal groups under which humans evolved. Of course, it is possible to find and maintain close, small personal groups today – through either work colleagues or family. One of the advantages of modern technology (such as the Internet) is that it enables communication and contact between family members who are geographically separate.

The therapeutic bond (see Chapter 8) is an important part of all therapeutic encounters. When a client has an hour-long interview with a homeopath, the homeopath will ask questions about the client's life that probably no one has asked about before. The homeopath is interested in the client. The client feels cared for because the homeopath is trying to improve the health of the client. Similarly, when a client is treated by massage therapy, the client experiences the undivided and positive attention of another person. In both cases, the client feels cared for by the therapist. In training psychotherapists, Rogers (1951) suggests that it is the attitude of caring that is most important for good therapeutic outcome. The feeling of being cared for is part of the therapeutic alliance, and the therapeutic alliance predicts outcome in psychotherapy (Martin *et al.*, 2000). The therapeutic bond has therapeutic benefits because it provides an experience that is not sufficiently frequent in a person's life: the experience of being cared for by another human being.

In hunter-gatherer groups, one individual, often called a shaman, specialises in providing medical care. However, other group members can also take part in ritualistic behaviours that help a sick person get better. The modern doctor is the psychological equivalent to the shaman – a powerful, wise person who provides the caring relation that is so important for healing. The doctor, psychotherapist, complementary practitioner or nurse can all take on the role of someone who is able to heal and, by providing a psychological pattern consistent with the genome, help the network self-organise towards a state of pro-regulation. Therapy is a form of lifestyle intervention that works in part because it provides a remedy for a lifestyle bereft of caring. Modern society contributes to health to the extent that it provides people with an opportunity to be cared for and to care for others.

Quality and nature of goal attainment: autonomy,
competence, learned helplessness theory, chronic stress,
individualised goal achievement

Humans evolved in an environment in which survival depended on external goals being realised. Goal satisfaction, whether success at work or in success at a hobby, leads to positive affect and better health. Happiness, which results from the satisfaction of high-level goals, is associated with better health. There is considerable evidence that satisfaction of high-level goals is associated with better health, and particularly with parameters associated with general network dysregulation–well-regulation (Antonovsky, 1996). For example, high levels of self-esteem are associated with lower levels of inflammatory response to acute stress (O'Donnell *et al.*, 2008).

Because Palaeolithic society was non-hierarchical, the pattern of goal attainment specified by the genome is one where goals are self-determined, rather than determined by a leader or boss. Self-determination theory (Deci and Ryan, 1985; Ryan and Deci, 2000) shows that the greatest satisfaction is achieved from attaining those goals that are intrinsically valued and that people decide for themselves what they wish to attain. The healthy pattern of living is one of achievement, but where achievement is self-directed rather than directed by others. People are happier when they feel in control of their lives, rather than being controlled by others. Lack of control of outcomes is the reverse of self-determination. Learned helplessness theory provides an account of the negative health consequences of being unable to control outcomes (Abramson *et al.*, 1978). Learned helplessness leads to depression, inhibition of motivated activities and a decline in cognitive ability. Depression and inhibition of behaviour are both indicators of behavioural inhibition. Thus, when people achieve their self-determined goals, they do more of the same. When they are controlled by others and their outcomes are independent of what they do, then the infornet inhibits them from the pattern of behaviour that leads to this particular type of outcome.

Lack of control in the achievement of goals is stressful, and so uncontrollable work situations are likely to lead to poor health. However, there are many other factors that can make goal attainment a stressful experience. These other factors include time pressure (i.e., insufficient time to achieve the desired end state), conflicting goals that need to be achieved at the same time, and interruption of goal-seeking activity by external demands. Applying infornet theory to the above leads to the following conclusions: satisfaction of important goals gradually contributes to general infornet well-regulation. However,

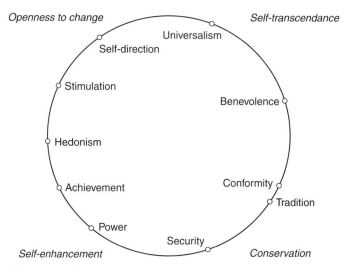

Figure 10.4 Circumplex model, adapted from Schwartz and Boehnke (2004)

stress in the attainment of those goals gradually contributes to general infornet dysregulation. The satisfaction of important goals is healthy; but if the process of attaining those goals leads to stress, then that is unhealthy.

Although people have many goals in common, they also have goals that are unique to the individual or a group of individuals. Satisfaction of these individual goals is also important. Schwartz identified ten values (i.e., high-level goals) that were consistent across cultures and that could be mapped, using multidimensional scaling, onto a two-dimensional space. The ten values are arranged round a circle in this two-dimensional space, so the values are described as forming a circumplex. The position of these values and the labels of the two dimensions are shown in Figure 10.4.

Living a lifestyle that is inconsistent with one's personal values will contribute to general infornet dysregulation. Many of the values in modern working practice involve achievement, power and security (i.e., just a small part of the value circumplex). Achievement-oriented, power-oriented and security-oriented work practices will suit only those for whom these values are important. For others, to achieve a well-regulated infornet it is necessary to satisfy their values in some other way, perhaps through therapy. People prefer therapies that are consistent with their values (Whalley and Hyland, 2009) and, in particular, spiritually contextualised therapies are helpful for those who are oriented towards self-transcendent values (Hyland and Whalley, 2008). People high in spirituality are more likely to use complementary medicine (Petry and Finkel, 2004). However, if a person's spiritual goals are satisfied through some other lifestyle activity (such as religion) then it should not be necessary to have a spiritually contextualised therapy.

Therapies that empower the patient are particularly beneficial because they counteract the discouragement that many patients experience (Frank and Frank, 1991). However, if people live lifestyles that do not lead to discouragement and that provide them with the opportunity to satisfy not only those goals that are common to all people but also those unique to themselves, then they will not need therapy.

Stress is commonplace in modern life, not because people seek stress but because people perceive that is only through stressful activities (such as work) that they can achieve their important goals, whether they be shared goals or goals that are unique to the individual. However, the option of downsizing and adopting 'the good life' is not open to everyone. Social obligations mean that people can be locked into a lifestyle where (a) they do not enjoy the work they are doing because they find it stressful and (b) they do not satisfy their own individual goals.

Rest and relaxation

The working week of a hunter-gatherer was of shorter duration than in modern society. Hunter-gatherers spend a good deal of time doing nothing, as indeed do other animals. People with pets will be aware that cats and dogs spend time being inactive. Fromm (1976) distinguishes two states of awareness: *having* and *being*. *Having* is the normal state of modern life, where people are engaged in goal-oriented pursuits. *Being* is a state in which people are aware of themselves but are not trying to achieve anything. Fromm suggests that people would be happier – and society better – if people spent more time in the being mode than in the having mode.

Compared with our Palaeolithic ancestors, people in modern society have less opportunity for rest and relaxation and, specifically, for entering states of being. People will watch a television 'in order to relax', but the television is not relaxing. The television maintains mental activity, and many television programmes are exciting (i.e., create positive states of arousal). In particular, watching the television does not encourage the person to enter the state of being that Fromm recommends, in which one is aware of oneself and awareness is limited to the experience of oneself.

Box 10.4 Mindfulness in Eastern philosophy

Mindfulness mediation (Kabat-Zinn, 1994) has its roots in Buddhist philosophy and is part of traditional Eastern cultures. A friend of the author was taught judo by a Japanese person who was originally trained as a Samurai. As a child he was taught never to run but to walk from one place to the next, constantly being aware of everything around him. Running would distract from the awareness of the present and so place him at risk of a surprise attack.

The importance of rest and, in particular, mental relaxation is part of a well-established therapeutic approach in psychology as well as complementary and alternative medicine (see Chapter 9. However, relaxation can be part of lifestyle rather than a therapy. Mindfulness meditation (Kabat-Zinn, 1994) is not just a meditative technique but also a prescription for living – to live in a mindful way means being aware of where you are and who you are all the time. When walking or driving by themselves, many people have imaginary conversations with themselves (watch the lips of other drivers who are in a car by themselves). Mindfulness involves stopping these imaginary conversations to live in the here and now.

Complementary medicine is sometimes used as a lifestyle choice rather than to cure an illness (Chapter 8). Health spas are often used as lifestyle choice. The use of complementary medicine or health spas in this way has three theoretically important features: (a) it allows a period of relaxation, (b) it provides a pleasant experience (and pleasure is healthy), and (c) there is the experience of being cared for by someone else. In hunter-gatherer groups, relaxation is part of everyday living. In modern society, relaxation often has to be built into a busy schedule.

Box 10.5 Insight from childhood

From *Winnie the Pooh*, by A. A. Milne:
Sometimes I sits and thinks, and sometimes I just sits.

Conflict resulting from simultaneous completion of incompatible activity, including simultaneous immune and external challenge

The above account of 'a psychologically health lifestyle' is well supported by data: positive relations are good, hostility is bad. Goal attainment is good, stress is bad. Relaxation is good. The following two sections are more speculative and result from the ideas of infornet theory developed earlier in this book. They are dysregulation resulting from conflict and dysregulation resulting from ignored reactive inhibition.

The early psychosomatic researchers (see Chapter 3) believed that psychogenic illness arose from conflict between simultaneous activation of parasympathetic and sympathetic activity. They interpreted this conflict within a psychoanalytic framework and suggested that there was specificity between type of conflict and type of disease. The psychoanalytic interpretation is no longer considered helpful, and the evidence does not support the idea of specificity between psychological state and disease. Nevertheless, the idea of internal conflict presented by these early researchers is important, and this insight can be applied to modern psychological and biological concepts.

Conflict can take a variety of forms. One type involves the conflict between activities that are a normal part of living but which the body is not designed to deal with simultaneously. People commonly get ill with colds and other minor infections, and the body has a way of signalling via pro-inflammatory cytokines that it is time to rest. At the same time, occasional stressful activity is also part of the pattern of normal living, and under particular circumstances occasional stressful activity can be pleasurable and exciting. In each case the infornet resolves into a state appropriate for the infection or the excitement. However, people are not designed for a combination of illness with excitement, as this combination leads, via the compensation rule, to the dysregulatory changes outlined in Chapter 6. I have suggested that the repeated combination of stress and immune challenge was one of the routes into general infornet dysregulation and hence a cause of chronic fatigue syndrome. Taking part in an arousing activity when ill contributes to infornet dysregulation. Thus, it is not just working when ill that is bad (to the extent that work is arousing) but other leisure activities that are exciting are also bad. To be healthy it is necessary to rest when ill – not go out on the town and have a good time.

A second type of conflict is that between exciting (positive affect plus arousal) or stressful (negative affect plus arousal) activity and eating – what one might characterise as the excitement of hunting a mammoth versus the relaxation of eating the mammoth after it has been cooked. This form of conflict, according to infornet theory, is the basis for the associative learning of food intolerance and other gastric problems. The body is designed for periods of *internal maintenance* when it is concerned with eating, healing and self-regulating and of *external maintenance* when it is concerned with managing the external environment. But it is not designed for doing both at the same time. The body is not designed to hunt and eat mammoths at the same time.

If one considers the evolutionary environment of early humans, there would be no need for simultaneous parasympathetic and sympathetic activity, as planning and group support would make it unnecessary. There is evidence from healed bones that early Palaeolithic people helped those who were sick. Indeed, helping the less able members of the community is a feature of the mutually supportive hunter-gatherer lifestyle in which humans evolved. Thus, if one makes inferences from the recent anthropological data, a hunter-gatherer group would plan to engage in exciting activity or relaxing activity, and those who were unable owing to sickness or injury to engage in exciting activity would have been supported by others and enabled to rest.

It is interesting to note that modern pharmaceuticals provide plenty of opportunities to ignore the body's signals and so enable conflicting activities to be carried out simultaneously. Many people come to work despite being ill and take one or more of a range of medicines to suppress their symptoms. People eat 'on the go' and take indigestion tablets rather than slowing down and eating only in a relaxed state. The reason people engage in these conflicting activities is in part that they respond to the expectations of others, but also that people are genuinely unaware that such behaviour may, over time, be harmful. The implication for a healthy lifestyle is simple: enjoy your food and rest after eating (the traditional French eating style of long, lazy lunches is to be recommended) and do not go to work when ill. Employers will not thank me for this recommendation. Businesses thrive on those who overwork. Many people eat their lunch in front of a computer screen. They do not go home and have a good lunch followed by a rest.

Too much of a good thing: the problem of reactive inhibition

Rats that are reinforced for turning right in a T-maze eventually will turn left. Reactive inhibition refers to the inhibitory effect that behaviour has on itself. Reactive inhibition has an evolutionary advantage in that in induces people to explore and find new places to live and new sources of food. Chapter 6 presented the hypothesis that ignored reactive inhibition was one of the potential routes into chronic fatigue syndrome.

There are several reasons why a person will engage in a repetitive activity for long periods of time. First, people working on production lines do so because of extrinsic rewards – they are paid to do so, and would not engage in such boring and repetitive work otherwise. If the idea of the health-harming effects of reactive inhibition is correct, then working on a production line should be less healthy than less repetitive forms of factory work. Hunter-gatherers do not work for eight hours at a stretch. Hunter–gatherers are not subject to the tyranny of the clock.

However, there is a second reason, which is more insidious. People can engage in repetitive activities because they find the activity to be intrinsically rewarding. A child will play on a computer play station for long periods of time, not because they are paid but because the play station provides an exciting (and hence positive) experience. Similarly, people with intrinsically motivated jobs will work very long hours. The musician will practise for hours, the artist will ignore hunger so as to be able to complete a picture, and the writer will sit writing without a break. According to infornet theory, the harmful effects of ignoring reactive inhibition occur irrespective of whether it is intrinsically or extrinsically motivated. Although satisfaction of important goals leads to pro-regulation, if that satisfaction involves too much repetition, then the consequence is dysregulation.

People living during the Palaeolithic had a varied existence, sometimes moving from summer to winter quarters. Hunter-gatherers as a group are great travellers. Among Australian Aborigines, 'going walk-about' is part of their culture. In a modern society, the psychological equivalent of 'going walk-about' is to go on holiday. A holiday 'makes a change' and is therefore pro-regulatory so long as it is not highly stressful. However, there are many ways in people can create variety in their lives. There are many ways in which people can have a change. Change allows reactive inhibition to dissipate, just as rest does.

Complex groups function best if they contain a variety of people. Tolerance to repetitive activity is a dispositional characteristic. Some people, namely those high in extraversion and openness to new experiences (i.e., high in the higher-order factor of plasticity) are more prone to suffer the negative effects of repetition. Such individual variation could be expected to occur in hunter-gatherer groups. Some people in a hunter-gatherer group will be more inclined to explore, others less inclined. Thus, there are group members who ensure continuity as well group members who can explore and find new opportunities. Left to their own devices, people choose the level of novelty and change that suits them best.

Where work is repetitive, it might be helpful to build in short rest periods or periods when the person can 'turn left' in the maze. In most offices, cigarette smokers are required to go outside or to a specially designated room for a smoke. Doing this has the advantage of providing an interruption in the pattern of work activity. Outside work, holidays, hobbies, going for a walk and therapy sessions all provide an opportunity to do something different. Of course, the activities that

Box 10.6 Dilettante and dilettantism

The word *dilettante* is used to disparage someone who dabbles in lots of different forms of art but without specialising or become an expert in any. When aged 16, I overheard my art teacher saying to my music teacher that I was a dilettante. As an adult I have stopped being a dilettante and this change has certainly been injurious to my health. I have every intention of being a dilettante when I retire.

create variety in life depend on what one normally does. Therapies such as dance therapy, music therapy and art therapy are therapeutic for those whose lives are not filled with dance, music and art, respectively. Musicians are unlikely to benefit from music therapy. Therapies that involve behavioural engagement are therapeutic because they provide an activity that the person does not normally engage in. They provide an opportunity to 'turn left' in the T-maze.

The sayings 'variety is the spice of life' and 'change is as good as a rest' both reflect the underlying assumption presented here that life is healthiest when it involves variety. Variety prevents the build-up of reactive inhibition, and therefore prevents the development of general infornet dysregulation that creates not only dysphoric psychological states but also the inflammatory changes that reduce life expectancy. However, the extent to which a person needs variety for good health will vary.

Although therapy, by its very nature, tends to introduce a change in a person's life, the idea of designing a therapy specifically to overcome reactive inhibition is not part of any major therapy. Reactive disinhibition therapy is based on the idea that when people are dysregulated, as occurs with chronic fatigue syndrome (CFS), then tolerance for reactive inhibition decreases. In order to help dissipate this tendency to reactive inhibition, the patient should engage in a lifestyle that involves short periods of pleasant activity, where 'short' means initially no more than ten minutes at a time. Short, varied activity is consistent with the patient-derived idea of *pacing*. Pacing is a therapeutic procedure that has been developed through the experience of CFS patients and those who help them on their journey to recovery. Pacing means not doing too much at a time; a common recommendation is to carry out no more than 50% of what you feel you can do. Reactive disinhibition therapy is formalisation of pacing, but with the additional components of variety of activity and a short time period per activity.

The implication of the above is that people would be happier and healthier if their lives were more varied and the work periods were of shorter duration. It is perhaps worth noting how the variety of life of

Box 10.7 The problem of modern society

The reason people become dysregulated is not that they are perverse. It is that modern society no longer provides the natural guide to health-promoting behaviours that was provided by Palaeolithic society. Addiction, obesity and other health problems are the result of misinterpretation of signals. In the same way, overworking and stress at work are created by a world where there is no limit on achievement. In the Palaeolithic, it made sense only to store a certain number of carcasses over winter because if too many were stored they would thaw and go to waste in the spring. There was a natural limit to ambition. In the modern worker, there is always the potential for doing more. Poor health can be a response to society – but a society created by humans.

a hunter-gatherer was replaced by the prolonged labour of the agricultural worker, and is now replaced by the office worker spending hours in front of a computer monitor.

Developmental origins of health: the fetal environment and early childhood

Stress during fetal development and early childhood leads to a greater likelihood of disease development in later life (Chapter 5). The importance of pregnancy in modern society is recognised in the form of maternity benefit – mothers are not expected to work up to the time they give birth. However, such benefit is far from what would be ideal. The ideal would be that pregnant women, particular in the first trimester, are protected from stress and provided with free access to spa treatment and other forms of activity that lead to psychologically mediated improvement in infornet regulation. Although Utopia is unattainable, the research on maternal stress does indicate a serious lack in public health provision. Dysregulated mothers live dysregulated lives and produce dysregulated children. The way to prevent such vicious cycles developing is to recognise the crucial importance of child production and child rearing in modern society. It may be that, in four hundred years time, people look back in horror at the barbarism of the twenty-first century when mothers and children were so poorly cared for.

Infornet theory and lifestyle: an interactive perspective

Modern health education emphasises the importance of diet and exercise. This book has reviewed evidence to show that psychological aspects of lifestyle are also important. However, the infornet is a

Eating too much food → Obesity → Health problems

Figure 10.5 Conventional model of obesity

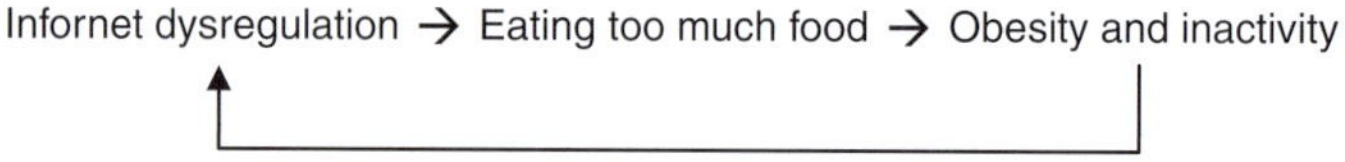

Infornet dysregulation → Eating too much food → Obesity and inactivity

Figure 10.6 An alternative perspective on obesity

network and not a sequential processing theory, and therefore provides a different and interactive perspective on the effects of lifestyle on health. This interactional perspective will be illustrated with the example of obesity.

Obesity is recognised as a common modern health problem. The conventional model is that obesity causes health problems and that obesity is caused by eating too much of the wrong sort of food – i.e., fattening foods (see Figure 10.5).

The cure for obesity, according to this conventional model, is to eat less food. However, the problem, as many dieters find out, is that dieting can lead to hunger. Hunger is an aversive state. From the perspective of infornet theory, hunger is not a good state – it is an indication (like pain) that something is wrong. Moreover, dietary restraint is a predictor of abnormal eating patterns, such as anorexia (Johnson and Wardle, 2005). Furthermore, there is evidence of an 'activitystat', that is, that there is a biologically determined preferred level of activity (Wilkin et al., 2006)

The alternative model is to treat obesity as both a cause and a consequence of poor health (see Figure 10.6). According to the interactional model, people become obese because of infornet dysregulation, which induces a tendency to live a dysregulated lifestyle, which includes overeating. It is interesting to note that low birth weight (for example, caused by poor fetal nutrition) leads to greater adult weight (see Chapter 5). If the infornet is dysregulated by stress, then its response is to protect against stress by eating. As a result, the reason for overeating is itself a consequence of infornet dysregulation, and the overeating therefore leads to further infornet dysregulation. The implication of this hypothesis is that obesity is best managed by a lifestyle that promotes infornet well-regulation, that is, a lifestyle that promotes health using any of the different 'levers' that alter infornet beliefs.

Box 10.8 Obesity and inflammation

The body has two kinds of fat. Brown fat tends to be deposited in the abdomen, and hence makes a body shape that looks like an apple. White fat tends to be deposited elsewhere, but in particular on the hips, and so makes a body shape that looks like a pear. Brown fat is inflammatory, white fat is not. It is far healthier to look like a pear than an apple – for example, apple-shaped people are more likely to develop asthma (de Winter-de Groot *et al.*, 2004) than pear-shaped people of similar weight, because of the pro-inflammatory effects of brown fat. Consistent with the hypothesis that inflammation is associated with behavioural inhibition, there is also evidence that brown fat is associated with depression (Rivenes *et al.*, 2009). Thus, the depressed person has more brown fat, which tends to produce more inflammation, which is associated with depression.

The interactional perspective of lifestyle and health suggests that health is not just a consequence of lifestyle. Rather, lifestyle and health are both part of the same system, and their deterioration or improvement is mutually reinforcing.

Summary

This chapter has examined the ways in which society affects psychological state, and hence health. One conclusion to be drawn is that there are several aspects of modern society that contribute towards infornet dysregulation, ranging from work practice to the treatment of pregnant women. Despite the constraints of society, people have lifestyle choices and, when correctly made, these lifestyle choices can contribute towards better health. However, many people when faced with the question of 'how to be healthy' think only about diet and exercise. Psychological aspects of lifestyle would appear to at least equally important. To be healthy one needs to enjoy life – so long as the enjoyment does not rely excessively on pleasures from the exaggerated signals that the modern world has been able to create. There is a lack of meta-analyses comparing the effect of psychological contributions to health versus the contributions of diet and exercise.

11   Infornet theory in perspective

Infornet theory is a theory that proposes a new type of disease concept: that of dysregulatory disease. Dysregulatory disease can be contrasted with the specific diseases that are familiar to modern Western medicine. Specific diseases have a unique pathophysiology. Dysregulatory diseases do not. Dysregulatory diseases have a biological basis but one that does not appear in terms of gross pathophysiology. Instead, dysregulatory diseases have unique activation patterns within a network system. Unlike specific diseases, dysregulatory diseases vary continuously along several dimensions.

Infornet theory can be seen as an extension of other, earlier ideas. The concept of 'embodied cognitions' is based on the proposition that bodies need minds, and the mind functions to interact with the environment. Cognitions are therefore embodied not just in the brain, but in the way the body interacts with its environment (Wilson, 2002). Although infornet theory shares this perspective, it goes beyond it in one significant way. In the case of embodied cognition, the meaning that is investigated is the meaning familiar to psychologists, and in many cases available to consciousness. By contrast, infornet theory suggests that meaning is encoded within the body that may not be accessible to consciousness. That is, there is another form of meaning that exists in the body, a meaning that occurs because the body is in part a network system and that drives health processes. Infornet beliefs are not part of an unconscious mind – they are a different type of concept entirely.

The idea that information is encoded in biological systems is also not new (Kardos, 1984). After all, the genome is a repository of biological information. However, infornet theory treats this biological information differently. Specifically, the theory suggests that meaning encoded biologically within the body is capable of change and, crucially, has 'higher meaning' that is more familiar within the domain of psychology. An early version of the theory was published under the title 'The intelligent body' in order to draw attention to the high-level meaning that is encoded in the body (Hyland, 2002).

Infornet theory combines network theory with psychoneuroimmun-ology in the explanation of phenomena that are otherwise difficult to explain. Infornet theory proposes a new way of thinking about disease, which is neither 'mental' nor 'physical' but incorporates both these ideas. The theory provides an explanation for the biopsychosocial inter-action suggested many years ago by Engel (1977), which was merely a recognition that psychological factors are important to disease. The theory suggests how this interaction takes place – it takes place in a network structure.

Given the above differences between infornet theory and previous theories, it is possible to question how infornet theory relates, as a theory, to theories found in conventional Western medicine. Does it, for example, represent a paradigm shift?

Thomas Kuhn in 1962 suggested suggested that science proceeds by episodes of *normal science* followed by *scientific revolutions* leading to a *paradigm shift* and a new period of normal science (Kuhn 1970). Each type of normal science represents a different paradigm. There are several examples in the history of science of such paradigm shifts. The develop-ment of modern medicine and rejection of Hippocratic medicine is one such example. Another is the development of quantum physics and the realisation that classical physics is only an approximation of events that occur when objects are neither very large nor very small. Kuhn's con-cept of a paradigm has been criticised as being insufficiently precise. However, it is clear that infornet theory is *not* a paradigm shift, at least not in the sense of the two examples given above. Infornet theory does not reject modern Western medicine. On the contrary, infornet theory is a theory that simply adds something to an existing paradigm, that of scientifically based medicine. Infornet theory is an addition to, not a replacement of, modern Western medicine.

Rather than think of infornet theory in terms of paradigms, a better way of conceptualising it is in terms of a *research programme*. The idea of a research programme was developed by Imre Lakatos (1978), who suggested that theories undergo a process of modification within a domain of enquiry, called a research programme. A research pro-gramme consists of a *positive heuristic*, and a *negative heuristic*, namely a set of theoretical ideas and assumptions that are never tested as they are assumed to be correct. Negative heuristics prevent the programme from straying outside a particular set of assumptions; positive heuristics provide a guide to further theory development. Disease specificity is both a positive and negative heuristic for research programmes in mod-ern Western medicine. The assumption of disease specificity has helped developed the science, but at the same time constrains it. The positive and negative heuristics of infornet theory are that the body acts like a network and that meaning is represented in that network.

Lakatos distinguishes research programmes in which theory development precedes data collection from those in which data collection precedes theory development. Using examples from the history of science, Lakatos shows that programmes in which theory precedes data tend to progress faster, and so he refers to these as having a *progressive problem shift*. Those programmes in which data precedes theory development tend to progress more slowly and so these are described as having a *degenerating problem shift*. A similar approach is taken by Royce (1978, 1985), who suggests that sciences go through three stages of development: programmatic, descriptive and explanatory. Theory is poorly developed in programmatic sciences, and is used only as a way of making sense of existing data in descriptive sciences. By contrast, in explanatory sciences, theories make strong (easily falsifiable) predictions, often of a quantitative nature. According to both authors, the sign of a mature, successful science is a focus on theory development and theory testing by empirical data.

Physics is cited by these and other philosophers of science as an example of a mature and theory-driven science. Physics provides many examples of research programmes with progressive problem shifts. In some cases the theory precedes its empirical verification by decades (quantum entanglement was demonstrated some 30 years after it was proposed). In theory-driven sciences, when data fail to confirm existing theory, then new, speculative theories are developed. For example, the standard model of the universe is that it originated from a Big Bang some 13.5 billion years ago. The model predicts that the rate of expansion of the universe should be slowing and that matter should be unevenly distributed through the universe. The finding that neither prediction is observed (the rate of expansion of the universe is actually accelerating) has led physicists to develop theories about dark matter and dark energy. These theories are in the process of being investigated, but they are currently only speculative. The construction of large and very expensive particle accelerators is driven by theoretical speculation.

What is significant about the discipline of physics is that physicists are intolerant of unexplained phenomena. For example, physicists do not take comfort in the fact that the Big Bang theory explains some but not all of the astronomical data. Instead, physicists operate in the way suggested by Karl Popper: if any datum is inconsistent with the theory then the theory cannot be complete and has been falsified (Popper 1963).

By contrast, neither medicine nor psychology can claim to be theory-driven sciences in the sense that physics is, and are classified by Royce (1978, 1985) as primarily descriptive sciences. In both these sciences, priority is given to data, not to theory. Thus, when data are inconsistent with existing theory, the focus is on collecting more data, not on developing speculative new theory. Tolerance of unexplained phenomena is high. Examples have been given throughout this book of phenomena for which the data are inconsistent with existing theory. These examples include medically unexplained symptoms, the reason why psychotherapy is effective and doubts about the serotonin explanation of depression. Indeed, speculation in the absence of data can be frowned on by journal referees and editors in psychology and medicine.

Two responses are made within medicine and psychology to unexplained phenomena. One is to provide the phenomenon with a label. So, for example, the term medically unexplained symptom or the term functional disease provide the appearance of understanding, when the reality is that these labels are merely redescriptions of the data. Elsewhere such redescriptions are called explanatory fictions (Skinner, 1971) (see also Chapter 1). A second response is to ignore the data on the basis that they may not be quite right and that it is therefore sufficient to focus on the data that support the theory. This second kind of response is not unusual in psychology. The theory that underlies cognitive behaviour therapy (CBT) is supported by some data. CBT theory predicts that people get better from CBT and that is exactly what happens. However, CBT theory is inconsistent with other data – such as the component studies (see Chapter 8). The question then becomes what to do with the other data. Because psychological studies tend to have lower replicability compared with physics, an easy way out is to assume the data are in some sense wrong. Where physics on the one hand and medicine and psychology on the other differ is that in the former the existence of data inconsistent with theory is the key stimulus to new research. It is through the existence of inconsistent data that the advances are made. Thus, the unexplained data that were described at the beginning of Chapter 1 should be considered not as an inconvenience but as the basis for further research.

Infornet theory is a speculative theory. One might therefore expect the theory to struggle to find recognition or influence in the two empirically driven disciplines of medicine and psychology. If that is the case, this book and this theory will have little impact. However, both medicine and psychology are pragmatic disciplines and infornet theory provides an interpretation of symptoms and their treatment that, with current theory, creates problems for clinical treatment. It is possible, therefore that the success of infornet theory in stimulating research within a research programme will depend on the extent to which practical applications of the theory are found helpful – for example, the extent to which reactive disinhibition therapy is found helpful for chronic fatigue syndrome. The short-term value of theory will be determined by the extent to which this new perspective proves helpful for treating patients who have challenging medical conditions.

The weakness of infornet theory is that it is incomplete and is almost certainly wrong in places. If the theory acts as a stimulus for future research, then this weakness will become irrelevant. If this book is considered successful, it will not be because infornet theory as represented here has been shown to be correct, but rather because the present version of the theory is wrong and has been revised through empirically based research.

Summary of infornet theory

1. The body is organised as both a sequential processing system and a parallel processing system.
2. Error in the sequential processing system causes diseases with a specific pathophysiology (i.e., pathophysiology that uniquely identifies the disease). Such diseases include asthma, cancer and heart disease.
3. Error in the parallel processing system leads to dysregulatory diseases (i.e., diseases with no unique pathophysiology) and acts as a precursor to error in the sequential processing system. Dyseregulatory diseases include medically unexplained systems, repetitive strain injury and chronic fatigue syndrome.
4. The parallel processing system is a psychoneuroimmunoendocrine information network, abbreviated to infornet.
5. The infornet controls the reference criteria and gain of the body's homeodynamic control systems, including those that control behaviour.
6. Dysregulation of the infornet creates dysregulatory diseases.
7. Psychologically mediated therapies act by reducing dysregulation of the infornet.
8. Mental states provide information about (a) the external environment and (b) the infornet (i.e., internal environment) and are part of a communication system that enables the body simultaneously to manage the external and internal environment.

9. Mood states of depression and fatigue are outputs from a behavioural inhibition system whose function is to inhibit behaviour. Anxiety is an output from a behavioural activation system whose function is to increase behaviour.

10. Emotions such as fear and anger are interpretations of the external environment and are used by the infornet to alter the reference criteria and gain of the body's homeodynamic control systems.

11. Emotions that signal threat activate the HPA axis and inflammatory response systems.

12. The infornet is a network system with problem-solving capacity. The infornet solves the problem of how best to alter the body's control systems (so as to manage the internal and external environments) by integrating information from the external environment (i.e., psychogenic inputs) with information from the internal environment (e.g., immunogenic inputs). The infornet resolves into a state that provides the solution to its inputs.

13. When presented with an external threat, the infornet calculates to what extent the threat is likely to lead to physical damage, and hence the need for immune protection versus the requirement for enhanced physical activity.

14. The hypothesis of internal–external balance suggests that the solution to the relative need for immune protection versus physical activity leads to the relative activation of the HPA axis versus inflammatory response system.

15. As HPA axis activation leads to suppression of inflammation (via the action of cortisol), the relative activation of the HPA axis versus the inflammatory response system leads to the varying pattern of immune and endocrine responses to stressors.

16. Because it is a network system, the infornet is capable of self-organising, and does so in order to achieve better self-regulation. Sleep may be a period of enhanced infornet self-organisation.

17. As it is a network system, the infornet is capable of encoding meaning. The meaning encoded by the infornet is described as *infornet beliefs*. The infornet beliefs include assessments about the external and internal environments and, in particular, the extent to which these environments present a challenge.

18. Infornet beliefs are changed in response to lifestyle patterns through the application of network learning rules.

19. Infornet theory suggests that two network learning rules affect health: associative learning and supervised learning.

20. Associative learning is the basis for classical conditioning effects (including immune conditioning) and habit formation.

21. Supervised learning is the basis for pattern recognition devices.

22. The genome is the supervisor in the supervised learning of the infornet. Supervised learning enables the infornet to attain the patterns specified by the genome.

23. Infornet dysregulation is caused by network learning rules that normally improve self-regulation, but under particular circumstances lead the infornet to resolve into states that are maladaptive for external circumstances.

24. A dysregulated infornet can be characterised as having a particular set of infornet beliefs, for example, that *the general situation is bad*.

25. The infornet belief that *the general situation is bad* leads to mental signals (such as depression, fatigue and anxiety) and physiological changes (such as raised HPA axis activation and inflammatory response system activation).

26. Infornet beliefs are organised, such that the infornet belief that *the external situation is bad* and *the internal situation is bad* are components of the more general belief that *the general situation is bad* – but with the former leading to more HPA axis activation and the latter to more inflammatory response system activation.

27. Associative learning explains (a) the phenomenon of immune conditioning, (b) food intolerance without a physiological explanation, (c) why repeated stress (i.e., chronic stress) leads to long-term changes including HPA and inflammatory response system activation, and (d) why fetal stress leads to long-term changes in disease incidence (fetal programming of later disease).

28. The infornet is particularly plastic when the organism is young. Inputs signalling that *the general situation is bad* when young therefore tend to persist throughout the organism's life.

29. Early and later experiences of stress lead to the infornet forming a persistent belief that *the general situation is bad*, leading to an enhancement of inflammatory processes, a raised HPA axis profile and negative psychological states.

30. Supervised learning (the compensation rule) explains (a) repetitive strain injury, (b) attention deficit/hyperactivity disorder, (c) chronic fatigue syndrome and (d) depression.

31. Chronic fatigue syndrome, depression and repetitive strain injury are all instances where the infornet is inhibiting behaviour, but in different ways. Attention deficit/hyperactivity disorder provides an example of potentiation of activity levels.

32. The compensation rule suggests that the infornet self-organises so as to compensate for deviations from the pattern specified by the

genome. Because of this rule, particular patterns of living lead to the potentiation of signals of fatigue, pain and activity level.

33. The symptoms of dysregulatory diseases vary continuously, with fuzzy boundaries, and the particular type of dysregulatory disease depends on the particular set of infornet beliefs.

34. Infornet beliefs include specific beliefs such as *there is a parasite in the lung*. Such beliefs act as a precursor to specific disease, in this case, asthma.

35. Dysregulation in the infornet predisposes to asthma through three mechanisms: systemic inflammation, atopy and asthma-specific potentiation of immune response.

36. Psychologically mediated therapy works by changing infornet beliefs. One of the main ways it does this is by changing the infornet belief that *the general situation is bad* to *the general situation is good*.

37. There are several mechanisms by which psychologically mediated therapy leads to the infornet belief that *the general situation is good*. These mechanisms are shared by (a) the art of medicine (e.g., placebo effects), (b) psychotherapy and (c) complementary and alternative medicine.

38. The particular mechanism of therapeutic benefit may be determined by the patient from the context provided by the therapist – rather than by what the therapist believes is therapeutic.

39. Psychologically mediated therapy counteracts the effect of a lifestyle that is incompatible, in terms of psychological features, with the environment in which humans and hence the genome evolved.

40. Therapeutic change in infornet beliefs leads to a reduction in symptoms associated with dysregulatory diseases. The effect on diseases with specific pathology is smaller, and depends on the extent to which disease processes in the sequential processing system (i.e., the specific system) are reversible.

41. Infornet theory is an addition to conventional theories of disease: it proposes a new category of disease for phenomena that are difficult to explain.

42. Infornet theory is not a paradigm shift but may contribute to a new, theory-led research programme.

References

Abramson, L. Y., Seligman, M. E. P. and Teasdale, J. D. (1978). Learned helplessness in humans: Critique and reformulation. *Journal of Abnormal Psychology*, 87, 49–74.

Addington, A. M., Gallo, J. J., Ford, D. E. and Eaton, W. W. (2001). Epidemiology of unexplained fatigue and major depression in the community: The Baltimore ECA follow-up, 1981–1994. *Psychological Medicine*, 31, 1037–44.

Ader, R. and Cohen, N. (1975). Behaviorally conditioned immunosuppression. *Psychosomatic Medicine*, 37, 333–40.

Ader, R., Cohen, N. and Felton, D. (1995). Psychoneuroimmunology: interactions between the nervous system and immune system. *Lancet*, 345, 99–103.

Adler, N. E., Boyce, T., Chesney, M. A. *et al.* (1994). Socioeconomic status and health: The challenge of the gradient. *American Psychologist*, 49, 15–24.

Adshead, G. (2000). Psychological therapies for post-traumatic stress disorder. *The British Journal of Psychiatry*, 177, 144–8.

Affleck, G., Apter, A., Tennen, H. *et al.* (2000). Mood states associated with transitory changes in asthma symptoms and peak expiratory flow. *Psychosomatic Medicine*, 62, 61–8.

Ahn H. and Wampold, B.E. (2001). Where oh where are the specific ingredients?: a meta-analysis of component studies in counselling and psychotherapy. *Journal of Counseling Psychology*, 48, 251–7.

Alexander, F. (1950). *Psychosomatic Medicine: Its Principles and Applications*. New York, NY: Norton and Co.

Alloy, L. B. and Abramson, L. Y. (1979). Judgment of contingency in depressed and nondepressed students: sadder but wiser? *Journal of Experimental Psychology: General*, 108, 441–85.

Amanzio, M., Pollo, A., Maggi, G. and Benedetti, F. (2001). Response variability to analgesics: a role for non-specific activation of endogenous opioids. *Pain*, 90, 205–15.

Anderson, J. W., Liu, C. and Kryscio, R. L. (2008). Blood pressure response to transcendental meditation: a meta-analysis. *American Journal of Hypertension*, 21, 310–16.

Anisman, H., Merali, Z., Poulter, M. O. and Hayley, S. (2005). Cytokines as a precipitant of depressive illness: animal and human studies. *Current Pharmaceutical Designs*, 11, 963–72.

312

Antonovsky, A. (1996). The salutogenic model as a theory to guide health promotion. *Health Promotion International*, 11, 11–18.

Appels, A. (1997). Why do imminent victims of a cardiac event feel so tired? *International Journal of Clinical Practice*, 51, 447–50.

Appleton, K. M., Hayward, R. C., Gunnell, D. *et al.* (2006). Effects of n–3 long-chain polyunsaturated fatty acids on depressed mood: systematic review of published trials. *American Journal of Clinical Nutrition*, 84, 1308–16.

Astin J.A., Harkness E. and Ernst E. (2000). The efficacy of 'distant healing': a systematic review of randomized trials. *Annals of Internal Medicine*, 132, 903–10.

Baines. K. J., Simpson, J.L., Bowden, N.A., Scott, R.J. and Gibson, P.G. (2010). Differential gene expression and cytokine production from neutrophils in asthma phenotypes. *European Respiratory Journal*, 35, 522–31.

Bakker, R. J., van de Putte, E. M., Kuis, W. and Sinnema, G. (2009). Risk factors for persistent fatigue with significant school absence in children and adolescents. *Pediatrics* 124: e89–e95.

Bandura, A., O'Leary, A., Taylor, C.B., Gauthier, J. and Gossard, D. (1987). Perceived self-efficacy and pain control: opioid and nonopioid mechanisms. *Journal of Personality and Social Psychology*, 53, 563–71.

Barker, D. J. P. (1992). The fetal origins of disease. *Journal of Hypertension*, 10(Suppl. 7): S39–S44.

(2007). Introduction: the window of opportunity. *Journal of Nutrition*, 137, 1058–9.

Barker, D. J. P., Osmond, C., Kajantie, E. and Eriksson, J. G. (2009). Growth and chronic disease: findings of the Helsinki birth cohort. *Annals of Human Biology*, 36, 445–58.

Barnes, P. M, Bloom, B., and Nahin, R. L. (2008). Complementary and alternative medicine use among adults and children: United States, 2007. National health statistics reports; no 12. Hyattsville, MD: National Center for Health Statistics.

Barth, J., Schumacher, M. and Herrmann-Lingen, C. (2004). Depression as a risk factor for mortality in patients with coronary heart disease: a meta-analysis. *Psychosomatic Medicine*, 66, 802–13.

Bates, D. W., Schmitt, W., Buchwald, D. *et al.* (1993). Prevalence of fatigue and chronic fatigue syndrome in a primary care practice. *Archives of Internal Medicine*, 153, 2759–65.

Bechtel, W. and Abrahamsen, A. (1991). *Connectionism and the Mind: An Introduction to Parallel Processing in Networks*. Cambridge, MA: Basil Blackwell.

Beck, A.T. (1967). *Depression: Clinical, Experimental, and Theoretical Aspects*. New York: Hoeber. (Republished as *Depression: Causes and Treatment*. Philadelphia: University of Pennsylvania Press.)

Beckman, H., Regier, N. and Young, J. (2007). Effect of workplace laughter groups on personal efficacy beliefs. *Journal of Primary Prevention*, 38, 167–82

Bedau, M. A. (1998). Philosophical content and method of artificial life. In: T. W. Bynam and J. H. Moor, eds. *The Digital Phoenix: How Computers Are Changing Philosophy*. Oxford: Basil Blackwell, pp. 135–52.

Beecher, H. K. (1955). The powerful placebo. *Journal of the American Medical Association*, 159, 1602–3.

Beekman, A. T. F., Penninx, B. W. J. H., Deeg, D. J. H., Ormel, J., Braam, A. W. and van Tilburg, W. (1997). Depression and physical health in later life: results from the longitudinal aging study Amsterdam (LASA). *Journal of Affective Disorders*, 46, 219–31.

Bender, T., Karagülle, Z., Bálint, G. P. *et al.* (2004). Hydrotherapy, balneotherapy, and spa treatment in pain management. *Rheumatology International*, 25, 220–24.

Benedetti, F., Amanzio, M., Baldi, S., Casadio, C. and Maggi, G. (1999). Inducing placebo respiratory depressant responses in humans via opioid receptors. *European Journal of Neuroscience*, 11, 625–31.

Benedetti, F., Pollo, A., Lopiano, L. *et al.* (2003). Conscious expectation and unconscious conditioning in analgesic, motor, and hormonal placebo/nocebo responses. *The Journal of Neuroscience*, 23, 4315–23.

Benson, H. (1979). *The Mind/Body Effect*. New York: Simon and Schuster.
  (1983). The relaxation response: its subjective and objective historical precedents and physiology. *Trends in Neuroscience*, 6, 281–4.

Bieling, P. J., Israeli, A. L. and Antony, M. M. (2004). Is perfectionism good, bad, or both? Examining models of the perfectionism construct. *Personality and Individual Differences*, 36, 1373–85.

Bilchick, K. C. and Berger, R. D. (2006). Heart rate variability. *Journal of Cardiovascular Electrophysiology*, 17, 691–4.

Bjorksten, B. (1999). The intrauterine and postnatal environments. *Journal of Allergy and Clinical Immunology*, 104, 1119–27.

Bleiker, E. M. A., Hendriks, J. H. C. L., Otten, J. D. M., Verbeek, A. L. M. and Van Der Ploeg, H. M. (2008). Personality factors and breast cancer risk: a 13-year follow-up. *Journal of the National Cancer Institute*, 100, 213–18.

Boffetta, P., Couto, E., Wichmann, J. *et al.* (2010). Fruit and vegetable intake and overall cancer risk in the European Prospective Investigation Into Cancer and Nutrition (EPIC). *Journal of the National Cancer Institute*, 102, 1–9.

Borrell, C., Muntaner, C, Benach, J. and Artazcoz, L (2004). Social class and self-reported health status among men and women: what is the role of work organisation, household material standards and household labour? *Social Science and Medicine*, 58, 1869–87.

Brosschot, J. F., Verkuil, B. and Thayer, J. F. (2010). Conscious and unconscious perseverative cognition: is a large part of prolonged physiological activity due to unconscious stress? *Journal of Psychosomatic Research* 69, 407–16.

Brostoff, J. and Challacombe, S. J. (2002). *Food Allergy and Intolerance*. Philadelphia: Saunders.

Brostoff, J. and Gamlin, L. (1998). *The Complete Guide to Food Allergy and Intolerance*. Leicester, UK: Blitz.

Brothwell, D. R. and Brothwell, P. (1998). *Food in Antiquity: A Survey of the Diet of Early Peoples*. Baltimore, MD: Johns Hopkins University Press.

Brown, K. W. and Moskowitz, D. S. (1997). Does unhappiness make you sick? The role of affect and neuroticism in the experience of common physical symptoms. *Journal of Personality and Social Psychology*, 72, 907–17.

Bucknall, C. E., Slack, R., Godley, C. C., Mackay, T. W. and Wright, S. C. (1999) Scottish Confidential Inquiry into Asthma Deaths (SCIAD), 1994–6. *Thorax*, 1999, 54, 978–84.

Burnard, P. (2005). *Counselling Skills for Health Professionals*. Cheltenham, UK: Nelson Thomas.

Camargo, C. A., Weiss, S. T., Zhang, S., Willet, W. C. and Speizer, F. E. (1999). Prospective study of body mass index, weight change, and risk of adult-onset asthma in women. *Archives of Internal Medicine*, 159, 2582–8.

Carlens, C., Jacobsson, L., Brandt, L., Cnattingius, S., Stephansson, O. and Askling, J. (2009). Perinatal characteristics, early life infections and later risk of rheumatoid arthritis and juvenile idiopathic arthritis. *Annals of Rheumatic Disease*, 68, 1159–64.

Carruthers, B. M., Jain, A. K., De Meirleir, K. L. *et al.* (2003). Myalgic encephalomyelitis/chronic fatigue syndrome: clinical working case definition, diagnostic and treatment protocols. *Journal of Chronic Fatigue Syndrome*, 11, 7–97.

Carson, A. J., Best, S., Postma, K. *et al.* (2003). The outcome of neurology outpatients with medically unexplained symptoms: a prospective cohort study. *Journal of Neurology, Neurosurgery, and Psychiatry*, 74, 897–900.

Carver, C. S. and Scheier, M. F. (1982). Control theory: a useful conceptual framework for personality-social, clinical, and health psychology. *Psychological Bulletin*, 92, 111–35.

Carver, C.S. and Scheier, M.F. (1990). Origins and functions of positive and negative affect: a control-process view. *Psychological Review*, 97, 19–35.

Carver, C. S. and Scheier, M. F. (1998). *On the Self-Regulation of Behavior*. New York: Cambridge University Press.

Carver, C. S., Scheier, M. F. and Weintraub, J. K. (1989). Assessing coping strategies: a theoretically based approach. *Journal of Personality and Social Psychology*, 56, 267–83.

Caspi, A., Roberts, B. W. and Shiner, R. L. (2005). Personality development: stability and change. *Annual Review of Psychology*, 56, 453–84.

Catt, S., Fallowfield, L. and Langridge, C. (2006). What non-prescription treatments do UK women with breast cancer use? *European Journal of Cancer Care*, 15, 279–85.

Chen, E., Strunk, R. C. Bacharier, L. B., Chan, M. and Miller, G. E. (2010). Socioeconomic status associated with exhaled nitric oxide responses to acute stress in children with asthma. *Brain, Behavior, and Immunity* 24, 444–50.

Chida, Y. and Steptoe, A. (2009). The association of anger and hostility with future coronary heart disease: a meta-analytic review of prospective evidence. *Journal of the American College of Cardiology*, 53, 936–46.

Christakis, D. A., Zimmerman, F. J., DiGiuseppe, D. L. and McCarty, C. A. (2004). Early television exposure and subsequent attentional problems in children. *Pediatrics*. 113, 708–13.

Connor T. J. and Leonard, B. E. (1998). Depression, stress and immunological activation: the role of cytokines in depressive disorders. *Life Sciences*, 62, 583–606.

Consedine, N. S. and Moskowitz, J. T. (2007). The role of discrete emotions in health outcomes: a critical review. *Applied and Preventive Psychology*, 12, 59–75.

Constant, F., Collin, J. F., Guillemin, F. and Boulange, M. (1995). Effectiveness of spa therapy in chronic low back pain: a randomized clinical trial. *Journal of Rheumatology*, 22, 1315–20.

Corr, P. J. (2008). *The Reinforcement Sensitivity Theory of Personality.* Cambridge: Cambridge University Press.

Cortese, S., Angriman, M., Maffeis, C. *et al.* (2008). Attention-deficit/hyper-activity disorder (ADHD) and obesity: a systematic review of the literature. *Critical Reviews in Food Science and Nutrition*, 48, 524–37.

Cousins, N. (1983). *The Healing Heart : Antidotes to Panic and Helplessness.* New York: Norton.

Coussons-Read, M. E., Okun, M. L. and Netles, C. D. (2007). Psychosocial stress increases inflammatory markers and alters cytokine production across pregnancy. *Brain, Behavior, and Immunity*, 21, 343–50.

Coyne, J. C., Stefanek, M. and Palmer, S. C. (2007). Psychotherapy and survival in cancer: the conflict between hope and evidence. *Psychological Bulletin*, 133, 367–94.

Coyne, J. C., Thombs, B. D., Stefanek, M. and Palmer, S. C. (2009). Time to let go of the illusion that psychotherapy extends the survival of cancer patients: reply to Kraemer, Kuchler, and Spiegel (2009). *Psychological Bulletin*, 135, 179–82.

Cramer, A., Waldorp, L. J., van der Maas, H. L. J. and Borsboom, D. (2010). Comorbidity: a network perspective. *Behavioral and Brain Sciences*, 33, 137–50; discussion 150–93.

Crawford, C. C., Sparber, A. G. and Jonas, W. B. (2004). A systematic review of the quality of research on hands-on and distance healing: clinical and laboratory studies. *Alternative Therapies in Health and Medicine*, 9: A96–A104.

Crawford, J. R. and Henry, J. D. (2004). The positive and negative affect schedule (PANAS): construct validity, measurement properties and normative data in a large non-clinical sample. *British Journal of Clinical Psychology*, 43, 245–65.

Cronbach, L. J. and Mowrer, O. H. (1953). Correlations between persons as a research tool. In: *Psychotherapy: Theory and Research.* Oxford, UK: Ronald Press, pp. 376–88.

Croog, S. and Levine, S. (1982). *Life After a Heart Attack: Social and Psychological Factors Eight Years Later.* New York: Human Sciences Press.

Crum, A. J. and Langer, E. J. (2007). Mind-set matters: exercise and the placebo effect. *Psychological Science*, 18, 165–71.

Cullinan, P., Harris, J.M., Newman Taylor, A.J. *et al.* (2003). Can early infection explain the sibling effect in adult atopy?. *European Respiratory Journal*, 22, 956–61.

D'Amato, G. (2000). Urban air pollution and plant-derived respiratory allergy. *Clinical and Experimental Allergy*, 30, 628–36.

Dantzer, R. and Kelley, K. W. (2007). Twenty years of research on cytokine-induced sickness behaviour. *Brain, Behavior, and Immunity*, 21, 153–60.

Davenport, G., McDonald, I. and Moss-Gibbons, C. (eds.) (2001). *The Royal College of Physicians and Its Collections: an Illustrated History*. London: James and James.

Deale, A., Chalder, T., Marks, I. and Wessely, S. (1997). Cognitive behaviour therapy for chronic fatigue syndrome: a randomized controlled trial. *American Journal of Psychiatry*, 154, 408–14.

Deary, V. and Chalder, T. (2010). Personality and perfectionism in chronic fatigue syndrome: a closer look. *Psychology & Health*, 25, 465–75.

Deci, E. L. and Ryan, R. M. (1985). *Intrinsic Motivation and Self-Determination in Human Behavior*. New York: Plenum Press.

(2000). The 'what' and 'why' of goal pursuits: human needs and the self-determination of behaviour. *Psychological Inquiry*, 11, 227–68.

De Craen, A. J. M., Ketchup, T. J., Ijssel, H. G. P. and Kalinin, J. (1999). Placebos and the placebo effects in medicine: historical overview. *Journal of the Royal Society of Medicine*, 92, 511–15

DeGrandpre, R. J. (1999). *Ritalin Nation*. London: Norton.

Dembroski, T. M., MacDougall, J. M., Costa, P. T. and Grandits, G. A. (1989). Components of hostility as predictors of sudden death and myocardial infarction in the Multiple Risk Factor Intervention Trial. *Psychosomatic Medicine*, 51, 514–22.

Demitrack, M. A., Cale, J. K., Straus, S. E., Laue, L., Listwak, S.J. and Kruesi, M.J.P. (1991). Evidence for impaired activation of the hypothalamic-pituitary-adrenal axis in patients with chronic fatigue syndrome. *Journal of Clinical Endocrinology and Metabolism*, 73, 1224–34.

Demitrack, M. A. and Crofford, L. J. (1998). Evidence for and pathophysiologic implications of hypothalamic-pituitary-adrenal axis dysregulation in fibromyalgia and chronic fatigue syndrome. *Annals of the New York Academy of Sciences*, 840, 684–97.

Denollet, J. (1998). Personality and coronary heart disease: the type-D scale-16 (DS16). *Annals of Behavioral Medicine*, 20, 209–15.

Denson, T. F., Spanovic, M. and Miller, N. (2009). Cognitive appraisals and emotions predict cortisole and immune responses: a meta-analysis of acute laboratory social stressors and emotion inductions. *Psychological Bulletin*, 135, 823–53.

de Winter-de Groot, K. M., van der Ent, C. K., Prins, I., Tersmette, J. M. and Uiterwaal, C. S. P. M. (2004). Exhaled nitric oxide: the missing link between asthma and obesity? *Journal of Allergy and Clinical Immunology*, 115, 419–20.

DeYoung, C. G. (2006). Higher-order factors of the Big Five in a multi-informant format. *Journal of Personality and Social Psychology*, 91, 1138–51.

DeYoung, C. G., Peterson, J. B. and Higgins, D. A. (2002). Higher-order factors of the Big Five predict conformity: are there neuroses of health? *Personality and Individual Differences*, 33, 533–52.

Diehl, H. S., Baker, A B. and Cowan, D. W. (1938). Cold vaccines: an evaluation based on a controlled study. *Journal of the American Medical Association*, 111, 1168–73.

Digman, J. M. (1997). Higher-order factors of the Big Five. *Journal of Personality and Social Psychology*, 73, 1246–56.

Di Marco, F., Verga, M., Reggente, M. *et al.* (2006). Anxiety and depression in COPD patients: The roles of gender and disease severity. *Respiratory Medicine*, 100, 1767–74.

Dinos, S., Khoshaba, B., Ashby, D. *et al.* (2009). A systematic review of chronic fatigue, its syndromes and ethnicity: prevalence, severity, co-morbidity and coping. *International Journal of Epidemiology*, 38: 1554–70.

Diwaker, H. N. and Stothard, J. (1993). What do doctors mean by tenosynovitis and repetitive strain injury? *Occupational Medicine*, 45, 97–104.

Domjan, M. and Wilson, N. E. (1972). Specificity of cue to consequence in aversion learning in the rat. *Psychonomic Science*, 26, 143–5.

Duhme, H., Weiland, S. K., Keil, U. *et al.* (1996). The association between self-reported symptoms of asthma and allergic rhinitis and self-reported traffic density on street of residence in adolescents. *Epidemiology*, 7, 578–82

Eippert, F., Bingel, U., Schoell, E. D. *et al.* (2009). Activation of the opioidergic descending pain control system underlies placebo analgesia. *Neuron*, 63, 533–43.

Eisenberger, N. O., Inagaki, T. K., Mashal, N. M. and Irwin, M. R. (2010). Inflammation and social experience: An inflammatory challenge induces feelings of social disconnection in addition to depressed mood. *Brain, Behavior, and Immunity*, 24, 558–63.

Elkayam, O., Wigler, I., Tischler, M. *et al.* (1991). Effect of spa therapy in Tiberias on patients with rheumatoid arthritis and osteoarthritis. *Journal of Rheumatology*, 18, 1799–803.

Ellis, R. and Humphries, G. W. (1999). *Connectionist Psychology*. Hove, UK: Psychology Press.

Emmons, R. A. (1991). Personal strivings, daily life events, and psychological and physical well-being. *Journal of Personality*, 59, 453–72.

Engel, G. L. (1977). The need for a new medical model: a challenge for biomedicine. *Science*, 196, 129–36.

Ernst, E. (2002). A systematic review of systematic reviews of homeopathy. *British Journal of Clinical Pharmacology*, 54, 577–82.

Ernst, E. and Canter, P. H. (2006). A systematic review of systematic reviews of spinal manipulation. *Journal of the Royal Society of Medicine*, 99, 192–6.

Esmaillzadeh, A., Kimiagar, M., Mehrabi, Y., Azadbakht, L., Hu, F.B. and Willett, W.C. (2007.) Dietary patterns and markers of systemic inflammation among Iranian women. *Journal of Nutrition*, 137, 992–8.

Evans, J. St. B. T. (2007). *Hypothetical thinking: Dual Processes in Reasoning and Judgement*. Hove, UK: Psychology Press.

Eysenck, H. J. (1967). *The Biological Basis of Personality*. Springfield, IL: Charles Thomas.

Fakuda, K., Strauss, S., Hickie, I., Sharpe, M., Dobbins, J. and Komaroff, A. (1994). The chronic fatigue syndrome: a comprehensive approach to its definition and study. *Annals of Internal Medicine*, 121, 953–9.

Fava, G. A. and Sonino, N. (2008). The biopsychosocial model thirty years later. *Psychotherapy and Psychosomatics*, 77, 1–2.

Fawzy, F. I. (1999). Psychosocial interventions for patients with cancer: what works and what doesn't. *European Journal of Cancer*, 35, 1559–64.

Feldman, R. H. and Laura, R. (2004). The use of complementary and alternative medicine practices among Australian university students. *Complementary Health Practice Review*. 9, 173–9.

Field, T. M. (1998). Massage therapy effects. *American Psychologist*, 53, 1270–81.

Fleisher, W., Staley, D., Krawetz, D., Pillay, N., Arnett, J. L. and Maher, J. (2002). Comparative study of trauma-related phenomena in subjects with pseudoseizures and subjects with epilepsy. *American Journal of Psychiatry*, 159, 660–3.

Forsythe, P., Sudo, N., Dinan, T., Taylor, V. H. and Bienenstock, J. (2010). Mood and gut feelings. *Brain, Behaviour and Immunity*, 24, 9–16.

Frank, J. D. and Frank, J. B. (1991) *Persuasion and Healing: A Comparative Study of Psychotherapy*, 3rd edn. Baltimore, MD: Johns Hopkins University Press.

Franke, A., Reiner, L., Pratzel, H. G., Franke, T. and Resch, K. L. (2000). Long-term efficacy of random spa therapy in rheumatoid arthritis – a randomized sham-controlled study and follow-up. *Rheumatology (Oxford)*, 39, 894–902.

Freud, S. (1910). The origin and development of psychoanalysis. *American Journal of Psychology*, 21, 181–218.

Friedlr, K., King, M., Lloyd, M. and Horder, J. (1997) Randomised controlled assessment of non-directive psychotherapy versus routine general-practitioner care. *The Lancet*, 350, 1662–5

Friedman, H. S. and Booth-Kewley S. (1987). The 'disease-prone personality': a meta-analytic view of the construct. *American Psychologist*, 42, 539–55.

Friedman, M. and Rosenman, R. H. (1974). *Type A Behavior and Your Heart*. New York: Alfred A Knopf.

Fromm, E. (1976). *To Have Or To Be?* London: Jonathan Cape.

Fry, A. M. and Martin, M. (1996). Fatigue in the chronic fatigue syndrome: a cognitive phenomenon? *Journal of Psychosomatic Research*, 42, 415–26.

Fulcher, K. Y. and White, P. D. (1997). A randomised controlled trial of graded exercise therapy in patients with chronic fatigue syndrome. *British Medical Journal*, 314, 1646–52.

Fuller-Thomson, E. and Brennenstuhl, S. (2009). Making a link between childhood physical abuse and cancer: Results from a regional representative survey. *Cancer* 115, 3341–50.

Fuller-Thomson, E., Stefanyk, M. and Brennenstuhl, S. (2009). The robust association between childhood physical abuse and osteoarthritis in adulthood: findings from a representative community sample. *Arthritis Care and Research*, 61, 1554–62.

Furnham, A. (2003). The psychology of complementary and orthodox medicine. *Evidence Based Integrative Medicine*, 1, 57–64.

Gallacher, J. E. J., Sweetnam, P. M., Yarnell, J. W. G., Elwood, P. C. and Stansfeld, S. A. (2003). Is Type A behavior pattern really a trigger for coronary heart disease events? *Journal of Psychosomatic Research*, 65, 339–46.

Garcon, F. C. and Rodriguez, A. G. (2009). Where is cognitive science heading? *Minds and Machines*, 19, 301–18

Garfield, S. L. (1995). *Psychotherapy: An Eclectic-Integrative Approach*, 2nd edn. New York: Wiley.

Geers A.L., Handley I.M. and McLarney, A.R. (2003). Discerning the role of optimism in persuasion: the valence-enhancement hypothesis. *Journal of Personality and Social Psychology*, 85, 554–65.

Geers, A.L., Helfer, S.G., Kosbab, K., Weiland, P.E. and Landry, S.J. (2005a). Reconsidering the role of personality in placebo effects: dispositional optimism, situational expectations, and the placebo response. *Journal of Psychosomatic Research*, 58, 121–7.

Geers, A. L, Weiland, P. E., Kosbab, K., Landry, S. J. and Helfer, S. G. (2005b). Goal activation, expectations, and the placebo effect. *Journal of Personality and Social Psychology*. 89, 143–59.

Geers, A. L., Wellman, J. A. and Lassiter, G. D. (2009). Dispositional optimism and engagement: the moderating influence of goal prioritization. *Journal of Personality and Social Psychology*, 96, 913–32.

Geist, V. (1978). *Life Strategies, Human Evolution, Environmental Design: Toward a Biological Theory of Health*. New York: Springer.

Geraghty, A. W. A., Wood, A. M and Hyland, M. E. (2010a) Dissociating the facets of hope: agency and pathways predict dropout from unguided self-help therapy in opposite directions. *Journal of Research in Personality*, 44, 155–8.

(2010b) Attrition from self-directed interventions: investigating the relationship between psychological predictors, intervention content and dropout from a body dissatisfaction intervention. *Social Science and Medicine*, 71, 30–7.

Gilbody, S., Whitty, P, Grimshaw, J. and Thomas, R. (2003). Improving the detection and management of depression in primary care. *Quality and Safety in Health Care*, 12, 149–55.

Gilliland, F.D., Berhane, K., Islam, T. *et al.* (2003). Obesity and the risk of newly diagnosed asthma in school-age children. *American Journal of Epidemiology*, 158, 406–15.

Goebel, M. U., Trebst, A. F., Steiner, J. *et al.* (2002). Behavioral conditioning of immunosuppression is possible in humans. *FASEB Journal*, 16, 1869–73.

Gray, J. A. (1987). *The Psychology of Fear and Stress*. Cambridge: Cambridge University Press.

Gribbin, J. and Gribbin, M. (1990). *Children of the Ice: Climate and Human Origins*. Oxford, UK: Blackwell.

Gross, R., Tabenkin, H., Porath, A. *et al.* (2003). The relationship between primary care physicians' adherence to guidelines for the treatment of diabetes and patient satisfaction: findings from a pilot study. *Family Practice*, 20, 563–9.

Grossberg, S. (1987). Competitive learning: from interactive activation to adaptive resonance. *Cognitive Science*, 11, 23–63.

Grosset, K. A. and Grosset D. G. (2004). Prescribed drugs and neurological complications. *Journal of Neurology, Neurosurgery, and Psychiatry*, 75(Suppl. 3), 2–8.

Grossman, P., Niemann, L., Schmidt, S. and Walach, H. (2004) Mindfulness-based stress reduction and health benefits: a meta-analysis. *Journal of Psychosomatic Research*, 57, 35–43.

Grouzet, F. M. E., Kasser, T., Ahuvia, A. *et al.* (2005). The structure of goal contents across 15 cultures. *Journal of Personality and Social Psychology*, 89, 800–16.

Guerra, S., Wright, A. L., Morgan, W. J., Sherrill, D. L., Holberg, C. J. and Martinez, F. D (2004). Persistence of asthma symptoms during adolescence: role of obesity and age at the onset of puberty. *American Journal of Respiratory Critical Care Medicine*, 170, 78–85.

Hahn, R. A. (1999). Expectations of sickness: concept and evidence of the nocebo phenomenon. In: I. Kirsch, ed. *How Expectancies Shape Experience*. Washington, DC: American Psychological Association, pp. 333–56.

Hahnemann, S. (1999). *The Organon of Medicine*, 6th edn., translated by W Boericke. New Delhi: Jain.

Hakkarainen, R., Partonen, T., Haukka, J., Virtamo, J., Albanes, D. and Lönnqvist, J. (2004). Is low dietary intake of omega-3 fatty acids associated with depression? *American Journal of Psychiatry*, 161, 567–9.

Hamer, M., Stamatakis, E. and Mishra, G. (2009). Psychological distress, television viewing, and physical activity in children aged 4 to 12 years. *Pediatrics*, 123, 1263–8.

Harvey, S. B., Wadsworth, M., Wessely, S. and Hotopf, M. (2008). Etiology of chronic fatigue syndrome: testing popular hypotheses using a national birth cohort study. *Psychosomatic Medicine*, 70, 488–95.

Hebb, D. O. (1949). *The Organisation of Behavior*. New York: Wiley.

Heim, C., Nater, U. M., Maloney, E. Roumiana, B., Jones, J. F. and Reeves, W. C. (2009). Childhood trauma and risk for chronic fatigue syndrome: association with neuroendocrine dysfunction. *Archives of General Psychiatry*, 66, 72–80.

Heim, C., Wagner, D., Maloney, E. *et al.* (2006). Early adverse experience and risk for chronic fatigue syndrome. *Archives of General Psychiatry*, 63, 1258–66.

Herman, J. L. (1992). Complex PTSD: a syndrome in survivors of prolonged and repeated trauma, *Journal of Traumatic Stress*, 1, 377–91.

Holroyd, K. A., Tkachuk, G., O'Donnell, F. and Cordingley G. E. (2006). Blindness and bias in a trial of antidepressant medication for chronic tension-type headache. *Cephalalgia*, 26, 973–82.

Honavar, V. and Uhr, L. (1993). Generative learning structures and processes for generalized connectionist networks. *Information Sciences*, 70, 75–108.

Hoppmann, C.A. and Klumb, P.L. (2006). Daily goal pursuits predict cortisol secretion and mood states in employed parents with preschool children. *Psychosomatic Medicine*, 68, 887–94.

Horn, S. and Munafo, M. (1997). *Pain: Theory, Research and Intervention*. Buckingham, UK: Open University Press.

House of Lords Select Committee on Science and Technology Sixth Report. (2000). *Complementary and Alternative Medicine*. http://www.parliament. the-stationery-office.co.uk/pa/ld199900/ldselect/ldsctech/123/12301.htm

Hróbjartsson, A. and Gøtzsche, P. C. (2001). Is the placebo powerless? An analysis of clinical trials comparing placebo with no treatment. *The New England Journal of Medicine*, 344, 1594–602.

Hughes. C. H. and Baumer, J. H. (1995). Moving house: a risk factor for the development of childhood asthma. *British Medical Journal*, 311, 1069–70.

Huibers, M. J. H., Bleijenberg, G., van Amelsvoort, L. G. P. M. *et al.* (2004). Predictors of outcome in fatigued employees on sick leave – results from a randomised trial. *Journal of Psychosomatic Research*, 57, 443–9.

Hung, H.C., Joshipura, K.J., Jiang, R. *et al.* (2004). Fruit and vegetable intake and risk of major chronic disease. *Journal of the National Cancer Institute*, 96, 1577–84.

Hyland, M. E. (1981). *Introduction to Theoretical Psychology*. London: Macmillan.

(1985). Do person variables exist in different ways? *American Psychologist*, 40, 1003–10.

(1987). A control theory interpretation of psychological mechanisms of depression: comparison and integration of several theories. *Psychological Bulletin*, 102, 109–21.

(1988). Motivational control theory: an integrative framework. *Journal of Personality and Social Psychology*, 55, 642–51.

(1992a). The items in quality of life scales: how item selection creates bias and how bias can be prevented. *PharmacoEconomics*, 1, 182–90.

(1992b). A reformulation of quality of life for medical science. *Quality of Life Research*, 1, 267–72.

(1999). A connectionist theory of asthma. *Clinical and Experimental Allergy*. 29, 1467–73.

(2001a). A two-phase network theory of asthma causation: a possible solution to the impact of genes, hygiene and air quality. *Clinical and Experimental Allergy*, 31, 1485–92.

(2001b). Extended network learning error: a new way of conceptualising chronic fatigue syndrome. *Psychology and Health*, 16, 273–87.

(2002). The intelligent body and its discontents. *Journal of Health Psychology* 7, 21–32.

(2005). Entanglement and some heretical thoughts about homeopathy. *Homeopathy*, 94, 105–6

(2010). Networks and the origins of anxiety and depression. *Behavioral and Brain Sciences*, 33, 161–2.

Hyland, M. E., Bott, J., Singh, S. and Kenyon, C. A. P. (1994). Domains, constructs, and the development of the breathing problems questionnaire. *Quality of Life Research*, 3, 245–56.

Hyland, M. E., Geraghty, A. D. W., Joy, O. E. T. and Turner, S. I. (2006a). Spirituality predicts outcome independently of expectancy following flower essence self-treatment *Journal of Psychosomatic Research*, 60, 53–8.

Hyland, M. E., Kenyon, C. A. P., Taylor, M. and Morice, A. H. (1993). Steroid prescribing for asthmatics: relationship with Asthma Symptom Checklist and Living with Asthma Questionnaire. *British Journal of Clinical Psychology*, 32, 505–11.

Hyland, M. E. and Kirsch, I. (1988). Methodological complementarity with and without reductionism. *Journal of Mind and Behavior*, 9, 5–12.

Hyland, M. E. and Lewith, G. T. (2002). Oscillatory effects in a homeopathic clinical trial: an explanation using complexity theory, and implications for clinical practice. *Homeopathy*, 91, 145–9.

Hyland, M. E., Lewith G. T. and Westoby, C. (2003). Developing a measure of attitudes: the holistic complementary and alternative medicine question-naire. *Complementary Therapies in Medicine*, 11, 33–8.

Hyland, M. E., Sodergren, S. C. and Lewith, G. T. (2006). Chronic fatigue syndrome – The role of positivity to illness in chronic fatigue syndrome patients. *Journal of Health Psychology*, 11, 731–41.

Hyland, M. E. and Whalley, B. (2008). Motivational concordance: an import-ant mechanism in self-help therapeutic rituals involving inert (placebo) substances. *Journal of Psychosomatic Research*, 65, 405–41.

Hyland, M. E. Whalley, B. and Geraghty, A. W. A. (2007). Dispositional pre-dictors of placebo responding: a motivational interpretation of flower essence and gratitude therapy. *Journal of Psychosomatic Research*, 62, 331–40.

Irwin, R. R. (2008). Human psychoneuroimmunology: 20 years of discovery. *Brain, Behaviour, and Immunity*, 22, 129–39.

Irwin, R. R. and Miller, A. H. (2007). Depressive disorders and immunity: 20 years of progress and discovery. *Brain, Behavior, and Immunity*, 21, 374–83.

Irwin, R. S. and Richardson, N D. (2006). Patient-focused care – using the right tools. *Chest*, 130(Suppl. 1), 735–825.

Ishigami, T. (1919). The influence of psychic acts on the progress of pulmon-ary tuberculosis. *American Review of Tuberculosis*, 2, 470–84.

James, W. (1899). *Talks to Teachers on Psychology and to Students on Some of Life's Ideals*. New York: Henry Holt.

Jason, L. A., Jordan, K., Miike, T. *et al.* (2006). A pediatric case definition for myalgic encephalomyelitis and chronic fatigue syndrome. *Journal of Chronic Fatigue Syndrome*, 13, 1–44.

Jason, L. A., Jordan, J. M., Richman, J. A. *et al.* (1999). A community-based study of prolonged fatigue and chronic fatigue. *Journal of Health Psychology*, 4, 9–26.

Jensen, P. S., Arnold, L. E., Richter, J. E. *et al.* (1999a). Moderators and mediators of treatment response for children with attention-deficit/hyper-activity disorder. *Archives of General Psychiatry*, 56, 1088–96.

Jensen, P., Arnold, B., Richter, J., Severe, J., Vereen, D. and Vitiello, B. (1999b),. A 14-month randomized clinical trial of treatment strategies for attention-deficit/hyperactivity disorder. *Archives of General Psychiatry*, 56, 1073–86.

Jensen, P.S., Arnold, L. E., Swanson, J. M. *et al.* (2007). 3-Year Follow-up of the NIMH MTA Study, *Journal of the American Academy of Child and Adolescent Psychiatry*, 46, 989–1002.

Johnson, F. and Wardle, J. (2005). Dietary restraint, body dissatisfaction, and psychological distress: a prospective analysis. *Journal of Abnormal Psychology*, 114, 119–25.

Jolliffe, J., Rees, K., Taylor, R.R.S., Thompson, D.R., Oldridge, N. and Ebrahim, S. (2001). Exercise-based rehabilitation for coronary heart disease. *Cochrane Database of Systematic Reviews*, Issue 1, Art. No. CD001800.

Jones J., Lin, J., Maloney, E. *et al.* An evaluation of exclusionary medical/psychiatric conditions in the definition of chronic fatigue syndrome. *BMC Medicine* 7, 57. http://biomedcentral.com/1741–7015/7/57.

Kabat-Zinn, J. (1994). *Mindfulness Meditation*. London: Piatkus Books.

Kardos, L. (1984). *The Origin of Neuropsychological Information*. Budapest: Akademiai Kiado.

Kemeny, M. E., Rosenwasser, L. J., Panettieri, R. A., Rose, R. M., Berg-Smith, S. M. and Kline, J. N. (2007). Placebo response in asthma: a robust and objective phenomenon. *Journal of Allergy and Clinical Immunology*, 119, 1375–81.

Kemeny, M. E. and Schedlowski, M. (2007). Understanding the interaction between psychosocial stress and immune-related diseases: a stepwise progression. *Brain, Behavior, and Immunity*, 21, 1009–18.

Kern, Z. T. (2007). Psychoneuroimmunology – cross-talk between the immune and nervous systems. *Journal of Neurology*, 254(Suppl 2), 8–11.

Kiecolt-Glaser, J. K., Marucha, P. T., Malarkey, W. B., Mercado, A. M. and Glaser, R. (1995). Slowing of wound healing by psychological stress. *Lancet*, 346(8984), 1194–6.

Kiecolt-Glaser, J. K., McGuire. L., Robles, T. F. and Glaser, R. (2002). Psychoneuroimmunology: psychological influences on immune function and health. *Journal of Consulting and Clinical Psychology*, 70, 537–57.

Kirmayer, L. J., Groleau, D, Looper, K. J. and Dao, M. D. (2004). Explaining medically unexplained symptoms. *Canadian Journal of Psychiatry*, 49, 663–72.

Kirsch, I. (1985). Response expectancy as a determinant of experience and behavior. *American Psychologist*, 40, 1189–202.

　(1997). Specifying nonspecifics: psychological mechanisms of placebo effects. In: A. Harrington, ed. *The Placebo Effect: An Interdisciplinary Exploration*. Cambridge, MA: Harvard University Press, pp. 166–8.

　(2005). Placebo psychotherapy: synonym or oxymoron? *Journal of Clinical Psychology*, 61, 791–803.

　(2009). *The Emperor's New Drugs: Exploding the Antidepressant Myth*. London: The Bodley Head.

Kirsch, I., Deacon, B. J., Huedo-Medina, T. B., Scoboria, A., Moore, T. J. and Johnson B. T. (2008). Initial severity and antidepressant benefits: a meta-analysis of data submitted to the Food and Drug Administration. *PLoS Medicine*, 5(2), e45.

Kirsch, I. and Hyland, M. E. (1987). How thoughts affect the body: a meta-theoretical framework. *Journal of Mind and Behavior*, 8, 417–34.

Kirsch I., Moore, T., Scoboria, A. and Nicholls, S. (2002). The emperor's new drugs: an analysis of antidepressant medication data submitted to the U.S. Food and Drug Administration. *Prevention & Treatment*, 5, Art. 23.

Kirsch, I. and Sapirstein, G. (1998). Listening to Prozac but hearing placebo: a meta-analysis of antidepressant medication. *Prevention & Treatment*. 1, Art. 2a. http://journals.apa.org/prevention/volume1/pre0010002a.html.

Knapp, P. H., Levy, E. M., Giorgi, R. G., Black, P. H., Fox, B. H. and Heeren, T. C. (1992). Short-term immunological effects of induced emotion. *Psychosomatic Medicine*, 54, 133–48.

Knibb, R. C., Armstrong, A., Booth, D. A., Platts, R. G., Booth, I. W. and MacDonald, A. (1999). Psychological characteristics of people with food intolerance in a community sample. *Journal of Psychosomatic Research*, 47, 545–54.

Knoop, H., Bleijenberg, G., Gielissen, M. F., van der Meer, J. A. and White, P. D. (2007). Is full recovery possible after cognitive behavioural therapy for chronic fatigue syndrome? *Psychotherapy and Psychosomatics*, 76, 171–6.

Kop, W. J. and Gottdiener, J. S. (2005). The role of immune system parameters in the relationship between depression and coronary artery disease. *Psychosomatic Medicine* 67(Suppl. 1), S37–S41.

Kraemer, J. C., Kuchler, T. and Spiegel, D. (2009). Use and misuse of the CONSORT guidelines to assess research findings: comment on Coyne, Stefanek and Palmer (2007). *Psychological Bulletin*, 135, 173–8.

Kramer, M. S. (2002). Clinical update: Substance P antagonists in patients with major depression. Paper presented at the *11th Association of European Psychiatrists Congress*, Stockholm, Sweden.

Kuhn, T. (1970). *The Structure of Scientific Revolutions*, 2nd edn. Chicago, IL: University of Chicago Press.

Kullowatz, A., Rosenfield, D., Dahme, B., Magnussen, H., Kanniess, F. and Ritz. T. (2008). Stress effects on lung function in asthma are mediated by changes in airway inflammation. *Psychosomatic Medicine*, 70, 468–75.

Kunik, M.E., Roundy, K., Veazey, C. *et al.* (2005) Surprisingly high prevalence of anxiety and depression in chronic breathing disorders. *Chest*, 127, 1205–11.

Kurina, L. M., Goldacre, M. J., Yeates, D. and Gill, L. E. (2001). Depression and anxiety in people with inflammatory bowel disease. *Journal of Epidemiology and Community Health*, 55, 716–20.

Lacasse, J. R. and Leo, J. (2005). Serotonin and depression: a disconnect between the advertisements and the scientific literature. *PLoS Medicine* 2(12), e392. doi:10.1371/journal.pmed.0020392.

Lakatos, I. (1978). *The Methodology of Scientific Research Programmes: Philosophical Papers*, Vol. 1. Cambridge: Cambridge University Press.

Landay, A. L, Jessop, C., Lennette, E. T. and Levy, J. A. (1991). Chronic fatigue syndrome: clinical condition associated with immune activation. *Lancet*, 338, 707–12.

Landhuis, C. E., Poulton, R., Welch, D. and Hancox, R. J. (2007). Does childhood television viewing lead to attention problems in adolescence? Results from a prospective longitudinal study. *Pediatrics*, 120, 532–7.

Langhorst, J., Klose, P., Musial, F., Irnich, D. and Hauser, W. (2010). Efficacy of acupuncture in fibromyalgia syndrome – a systematic review with a meta-analysis of controlled clinical trials. *Rheumatology*, 49, 778–88.

Larson-Freeman, D. (1997). Chaos/complexity science and second language acquisition. *Applied Linguistics*, 18, 141–65.

Lawrie, S., MacHale, S., Power, M. and Goodwin, G. (1997). Is the chronic fatigue syndrome best understood as a primary disturbance of the sense of effort? *Psychological Medicine*, 27, 995–9.

Le Fanu, J. (1999). *The Rise and Fall of Modern Medicine*. London: Little, Brown.

LeShan L. (1994). *Cancer as a Turning Point: A Handbook for People with Cancer, Their Families and Health Professionals*. Bath, UK: Gateway Books.

Lewith, G. T., Brien, S. and Hyland, M. E. (2005). Presentiment or entanglement? An alternative explanation for apparent entanglement in provings. *Homeopathy*, 94, 92–5.

Lewith, G. T., Kenyon, J. N., Brookfield, J., Prescott, P., Goddard, J. and Holgate, S. T. (2001). Is electrodermal testing as effective as skin prick tests for diagnosing allergies? A double blind, randomised block design study. *British Medical Journal*, 322, 131–4.

Lewith, G. T., Watkins, A. D., Hyland, M. E. *et al.* (2002). Use of ultramolecular potencies of allergen to treat asthmatic people allergic to house dust mite: double blind randomised controlled clinical trial. *British Medical Journal*, 324: 520–3.

Lillestøl, K., Berstad, A., Lind, R., Florvaag, E., Lied, G. L. and Tangen, T. (2010). Anxiety and depression in patients with self-reported food hypersensitivity. *General Hospital Psychiatry* 32, 42–8.

Linde, K. Clausius, N., Ramirez, G. *et al.* (1997). Are the clinical effects of homeopathy placebo effects? A meta-analysis of placebo-controlled trials. *Lancet*, 350, 834–43.

Linde, K. and Willich, S.N. (2003). How objective are systematic reviews? Differences between reviews on complementary medicine. *Journal of the Royal Society of Medicine*, 96, 17–22.

Linden, W., Philips, M. J. and Leclerc, J. (2007). Psychological treatment of cardiac patients: a meta-analysis. *European Heart Journal*, 28, 2972–84.

Linden, W., Stossel, C. and Maurice, J. (1996). Psychosocial interventions for patients with coronary artery disease. a meta-analysis. *Archives of Internal Medicine*, 156, 745–52.

Lindsley, O., Skinner, B.F. and Solomon, H.C. (1953). *Studies in Behavior Therapy (Status Report I)*. Waltham, MA: Metropolitan State Hospital.

Lloyd, A., Hickie, I., Wilson, A. and Wakefield, D. (1994). Immune function in chronic fatigue syndrome and depression: implications for understanding these disorders and for therapy. *Clinical Immunotherapeutics*, 2, 84–8.

Loeser, J. D. and Melzack, R. (1999). Pain: an overview. *Lancet*, 353, 1607–9.

Luborsky, L., McClellan, A.T., Diguer, L., Woody, G. and Seligman, D.A. (1997). The psychotherapist matters: comparison of outcomes across twenty-two therapists and even patient samples. *Clinical Psychology: Science and Practice*, 4, 53–65.

Luborsky, L., Rosenthal, R., Diguer, L. *et al.* (2002). The dodo bird verdict is alive and well – mostly. *Clinical Psychology: Science and Practice*, 9, 2–12.

Luborsky, L., Singer, B. and Luborsky, L. (1975). Comparative studies of psychotherapies: is it true that 'Everyone has won and all must have prizes?'. *Archives of General Psychiatry*, 32, 995–1008.

Lüdtke, R. and A. Rutten, A. (2008). The conclusions on the effectiveness of homeopathy highly depend on the set of analyzed trials. *Journal of Clinical Epidemiology*, 61, 1197–204.

Luyten, P., Van Houdenhove, B., Cosyns, N. and Van den Broeck, A.-L. (2006). Are patients with chronic fatigue syndrome perfectionistic – or were they? A case-control study. *Personality and Individual Differences*, 40, 1473–83.

Lydiard, R. B. (2001). Irritable bowel syndrome, anxiety, and depression: what are the links? *Journal of Clinical Psychiatry*, 62(Suppl. 8), 38–45.

Lynch, J. J. (1977). *The Broken Heart: The Medical Consequences of Loneliness.* New York: Basic Books.

MacStravic, R. S. (1986) Therapeutic pampering. *Hospital and Health Services Administration*, 31, 59–69.

Maes, M. (1993). Acute phase protein alterations in major depression: a review. *Reviews in the Neurosciences*, 4, 407–16.

Magnusson, A. E., Nias, D. K. B. and White, P. D. (1996). Is perfectionism associated with fatigue? *Journal of Psychosomatic Research*, 41, 377–83.

Malaspina, D., Corcoran, C., Kleinhaus, K. R. *et al.* (2008). Acute maternal stress in pregnancy and schizophrenia in offspring: a cohort prospective study. *BMC Psychiatry*, 8, 71. Online at http://biomedcentral.com/1471–244X/8/71/.

Manganello, J. A. and Taylor, C. A. (2009). Television exposure as a risk factor for aggressive behavior among 3-year-old children. *Archives of Pediatrics and Adolescent Medicine*, 163, 1037–45.

Manheimer, E., White, A., Berman, B., Forys, K. and Ernst, E. (2005). Meta-analysis: acupuncture for low back pain *Annals of Internal Medicine*, 142, 651–63.

Martin, D. J., Garske, J. P. and Davis, M. K. (2000). Relation of the therapeutic alliance with outcome and other variables: a meta-analytic review. *Journal of Consulting and Clinical Psychology*, 68, 438–50.

Martin, J., Donaldson, A. N., Villarroel, R., Parmar, M. K., Ernst, E. and Higginson I. J. (2002). Efficacy of acupuncture in asthma: systematic review and meta-analysis of published data from 11 randomised controlled trials. *European Respiratory Journal*, 20, 846–52.

Marucha, P. T. and Engeland, C. G. (2007). Stress, neuroendocrine hormones and wound healing: human models. In: R. Ader, ed. *Psychoneuroimmunology*. San Diego, CA: Academic Press, pp. 825–35.

Maslow, A. H. (1954). *Motivation and Personality.* New York: Addison-Wesley.

Masters, K. S., Spielmans, G. I. and Goodson, J. T. (2006). Are there demonstrable effects of distant intercessory prayer? A meta-analytic review. *Annals of Behavioral Medicine*, 32, 21–6.

Mazzoni, G., Hyland, M. E., Foan, L. and Kirsch, I. (2010). The effects of observation and gender on psychogenic symptoms. *Health Psychology*, 29, 181–5.

McCauley, J., Kern, D. E., Kolodner, K. *et al.* (1997). Clinical characteristics of women with a history of childhood abuse: unhealed wounds. *Journal of the American Medical Association*, 277: 1362–8.

McClelland, J. L. and Rumelhart, D. E. (1985). Distributed memory and the representation of general and specific information. *Journal of Experimental Psychology: General*, 114, 159–88.

McCulloch, W. S. and Pitts, W. (1943). A logical calculus of the ideas imminent in nervous activity. *Bulletin of Mathematical Biophysics*, 9, 127–47.

McCullough, M. E. and Willoughby, B. L. B. (2009). Religion, self-regulation, and self-control: associations, explanations, and implications. *Psychological Bulletin*, 135, 69–93.

McDonagh, A., Friedman, M., McHugo, G. *et al.* (2005). Randomized trial of cognitive–behavioral therapy for chronic posttraumatic stress disorder in adult female survivors of childhood sexual abuse *Journal of Consulting and Clinical Psychology*, 73, 515–24

McDougall, W. (1938). *The Riddle of Life*. London: Methuen.

McKay, K. M., Imel, Z. E. and Wampold, B. E. (2006). Psychiatrist effects in the psychopharmacological treatment of depression. *Journal of Affective Disorders*, 92, 287–90.

Meissner, K., Distel, H. and Mitzdorf, U. (2007). Evidence for placebo effects on physical but not biochemical outcome parameters: a review of clinical trials. *BMC Medicine*, 5:3. www.biomedcentral.com/1741–7015/3/3.

Mick, E., Biederman, J. Prince, J. Fischer, M. J. and Faraone, S. V. (2002). Impact of low birth weight on attention-deficit hyperactivity disorder. *Journal of Developmental and Behavioral Pediatrics*, 23, 16–22.

Miller C. J, Marks D. J., Miller S. R. *et al.* (2007). Brief report: Television viewing and risk for attention problems in preschool children. *Journal of Pediatric Psychology*, 32, 448–52.

Miller, G. E. (2009). In search of integrated specificity: comment on Denson, Spanovic, and Miller (2009). *Psychological Bulletin*, 135, 854–6.

Miller, T. Q., Smith, T. W., Turner, C. W., Guijarro, M. L. and Hallet, A. J. (1996). Meta-analytic review of research on hostility and physical health. *Psychological Bulletin*, 119, 322–48.

Miller, T. Q., Turner, C. W., Scott Tindale, R., Posavace, E. J. and Dugoni, B. L. (1991). Reasons for the trend toward null findings in research on type A behavior. *Psychological Bulletin*, 110, 469–85.

Mittra, I. (2009). Why is modern medicine stuck in a rut? *Perspectives in Biology and Medicine*, 52, 500–17.

Moerman D. (2002). *Meaning, Medicine, and the 'Placebo Effect'*. Cambridge: Cambridge University Press.

Montgomery, G. H. and Kirsch, I. (1997). Classical conditioning and the placebo effect. *Pain*, 72, 107–13

Moons, W. G., Eisenberger, N. I. and Taylor, S. E. (2010). Anger and fear responses to stress have different biological profiles. *Brain, Behavior, and Immunity*, 24, 215–19.

Moyer, C.A., Rounds, J. and Hannum, J. W. (2004). A meta-analysis of massage therapy research. *Psychological Bulletin*, 130, 3–18.

Murray, C. J. L. and Lopez, A. D., eds. (1996). *The Global Burden of Disease: A Comprehensive Assessment of Mortality and Disability from Diseases, Injuries and Risk Factors in 1990 and Projected to 2020*. Cambridge, MA: Harvard University Press.

Musek, J. (2007). A general factor of personality: evidence of the Big One in the five-factor model. *Journal of Research in Personality*, 41, 1213–33.

Nelson, M. and Ogden, J. (2008). An exploration of food intolerance in the primary care setting: the general practitioner's experience. *Social Science and Medicine*, 67, 1038–45.

Nguyen, M., Revel, M. and Dougados, M. (1997). Prolonged effects of 3 week therapy in a spa resort on lumbar spine, knee and hip osteoarthritis: follow-up after 6 months. A randomized controlled trial. *Rheumatology (Oxford)*, 36, 77–81.

NICE (2004). *Depression: Management of depression in primary and secondary care*. Clinical Guideline 23. NICE and National Collaborating Centre for Mental Health; December 2004.

Nimnuan, C., Hotoph, M. and Wessely, S. (2001). Medically unexplained symptoms: an epidemiological study in seven specialities. *Journal of Psychosomatic Research*, 51, 361–7.

O'Donnell, K., Brydon, L., Wright, C. E. and Steptoe, A. (2008). Self-esteem levels and cardiovascular and inflammatory responses to acute stress. *Brain, Behavior, and Immunity*, 22, 1241–7.

Okiishi, J., Lambert, M. J., Nielsen, S. L. and Ogles, B. M. (2003). Waiting for supershrink: an empirical analysis of therapist effects. *Clinical Psychology and Psychotherapy*, 10, 361–73.

Ostir, G. V., Berges, I. M., Markides, K. S. and Ottenbacher, K. J. (2006). Hypertension in older adults and the role of positive emotions. *Psychosomatic Medicine*, 68, 727–33.

Pagani, M. and Lucini, D. (1999). Chronic fatigue syndrome: a hypothesis focusing on the autonomic nervous system. *Clinical Science*, 96, 117–25.

Pavlov, I. P (1897). *Work of the Principal Digestive Glands*. St Petersburg, Russia: Kushneroff.

Pavlov, I. P. (1928). *Lectures on Conditioned Reflexes*. New York: Liveright.

Pepper, O. H. P. (1945). A note on the placebo. *American Journal of Pharmacy*, 117, 409–12.

Petry, J. J. and Finkel, R. (2004). Spirituality and choice of health care practitioner. *Journal of Alternative and Complementary Medicine*, 10, 939–45.

Popper K. R. (1963). *Conjectures and Refutations*. London: Routledge and Kegan Paul.

Porter, R. (1996). *The Cambridge Illustrated History of Medicine*. Cambridge: Cambridge University Press.

Powers, W. T. (1978). Quantitative analysis of purposive systems: some spadework at the foundations of scientific psychology. *Psychological Review*, 85, 417–35.

Pressman, S. D. and Cohen, S. (2005). Does positive affect influence health? *Psychological Bulletin*, 131, 925–71.

Prins, J., Bleijenberg, G., Bazelmans, E. *et al.* (2001). Cognitive behaviour therapy for chronic fatigue syndrome: a multicentre randomised controlled trial. *Lancet*, 357, 841–7.

Proctor, M., Hing, W., Johnson, T. C., Murphy, P.A. and Brown J. (2006). Spinal manipulation for dysmenorrhoea. *Cochrane Database of Systematic Reviews*, Issue 3, Art. No.: CD002119.

Rabkin, J. G., Markowitz, J. S., Stewart, J. W. *et al.* (1986). How blind is blind? assessment of patient and doctor medication guesses in a placebo-controlled trial of imipramine and phenelzine. *Psychiatry Research*, 19, 75–86.

Ragland, R. R. and Brand, R. J. (1988). Type A behavior and mortality from coronary heart disease. *New England Journal of Medicine*, 318, 65–9.

Räikkönen, K., Pesonen, A-K., Heinonen, K. *et al.* (2008). Infant growth and hostility in adult life. *Psychosomatic Medicine*, 70, 306–13.

Raison, C. L., Lin, J. M. S. and Reeves, W. C. (2009). Association of peripheral inflammatory markers with chronic fatigue in a population-based sample. *Brain Behavior and Immunity*, 23, 327–37.

Ray, C., Jeffefues, S., Wei, W. *et al.* (1998). Making sense of chronic fatigue syndrome: patients' accounts of onset. *Psychology and Health*, 13, 99–109.

Reichenberg, A., Yirmi, R., Schuld, A. *et al.* (2001). Cytokine-associated emotional and cognitive disturbances in humans. *Archives of General Psychiatry*, 58, 445–52.

Ridsdale, L., Godfrey, E. and Chalder, T. (2001). Chronic fatigue in general practice: is counselling as good as cognitive behaviour therapy? A UK randomised trial. *British Journal of General Practice*, 51, 19–24.

Rietveld, S., Van Beest, I. and Kamphuis, J. H. (2007). Stress-induced muscle effort as a cause of repetitive strain injury? *Ergonomics*, 50, 2049–58.

Rimes, K. A., Goodman, R., Hotopf, M., Wessely, S., Meltzer, H. and Chalder, T. (2007). Incidence, prognosis, and risk factors for fatigue and chronic fatigue syndrome in adolescents: a prospective community study. *Pediatrics* 119: e603–9.

Rivenes, A. C., Harvey, S. B. and Mykletun, M. (2009). The relationship between abdominal fat, obesity, and common mental disorders: Results from the HUNT Study. *Journal of Psychosomatic Research*, 66, 269–75.

Ritz, T., Rosenfield, D., DeWilde, S. and Steptoe, A. (2010) Daily mood, shortness of breath, and lung function in asthma: concurrent and prospective associations. *Journal of Psychosomatic Research*, 69, 341–51.

Robbins, L. (2006). Yoga of laughter. *Yoga Therapy Today*, 2, 13.

Roelofs, K. and Spinhoven, P. (2007). Trauma and medically unexplained symptoms: towards an integration of cognitive and neuro-biological accounts. *Clinical Psychology Review*, 27, 798–820.

Rogers, C. R. (1951). *Client-centered Therapy: Its Current Practice, Implications, and Theory*. Boston, MA: Houghton-Mifflin.

Romieu, I., Varraso, R., Avenel, V. *et al.* (2006). Fruit and vegetable intakes and asthma in the E3N study. *Thorax*, 61, 209–15.

Rosenkranz, M. A. (2007). Substance P at the nexus of mind and body in chronic inflammation and affective disorders. *Psychological Bulletin*, 135, 1007–37.

Rosenman, R. H., Brand, R. J., Sholtz, R. I. and Friedman, M. (1976). Multivariate prediction of coronary heart disease during 8.5 year follow-up in the Western Collaborative Group Study. *American Journal of Cardiology*, 37, 903–10.

Rosenzweig, S. (1936). Some implicit common factors in diverse methods of psychotherapy: 'At last the Dodo said, "*Everybody* has won and *all* must have prizes"'. *American Journal of Orthopsychiatry*, 6, 412–15.

Ross, L., Boesen, E. H., Dalton, S. O. and Johansen, C. (2002). Mind and cancer: does psychosocial intervention improve survival and psychological well-being? *European Journal of Cancer*, 38, 1447–57.

Roud, P. C. (1987). Psychosocial variables associated with the exceptional survival of patients with advanced malignant disease. *Natural Medical Association*, 79, 97–102.

Rowland, A. S., Lesesne, C. A. and Abramowitz, A. J. (2002). The epidemiology of attention-deficit/hyperactivity disorder (ADHD): a public health view. *Mental Retardation and Developmental Disabilities Research and Reviews*, 8, 162–70.

Royce, J. R. (1978). How can we best advance the construction of theory in psychology? *Canadian Psychological Review*, 19, 259–76.

(1985). The problem of theoretical pluralism in psychology. In: K. B. Madsen and L. P. Mos, eds. *Annals of Theoretical Psychology*, Vol. 3. New York: Plenum Press, pp. 297–316.

Ruff, C. B., Trinkaus, E. and Holliday, T. W. (1997). Body mass and encephalization in Pleistocene *Homo*. *Nature*, 387, 173–6.

Rupniak, N. M. and Kramer, M. S. (1999). Discovery of anti-depressant and anti-emetic efficacy of substance P receptor (NK1) antagonists. *Trends in Pharmacological Sciences*, 20, 485–90.

Rushton, J. P. and Irwing, P. (2008). A general factor of personality (GFP) from two meta-analyses of the Big Five: Digman (1997) and Mount, Barrick, Sullen and Rounds (2005). *Personality and Individual Differences*, 45, 679–83.

Ryan, R. M. and Deci, E. L. (2000). Self-determination theory and the facilitation of intrinsic motivation, social development, and well-being. *American Psychologist*, 55, 68–78.

Saboonchi, F. and Lundh, L. G. (2003). Perfectionism, anger, somatic health, and positive affect. *Personality and Individual Differences*, 37, 1585–99.

Sandel, M. and Wright, R. J. (2006). When home is where the stress is: expanding the dimensions of housing that influence asthma morbidity. *Archives of Disease in Childhood*, 91: 942–8.

Schachter, S. (1971). *Emotion, Obesity, and Crime*. New York: Academic Press.

Schedlowski, M. and Pacheco-López, G. (2010). The learned immune response: Pavlov and beyond. *Brain, Behavior, and Immunity*, 24, 176–85.

Schlotz, W. and Phillips, D. I. W. (2009). Fetal origins of mental health: evidence and mechanisms. *Brain, Behaviour, and Immunity*, 23, 905–16.

Schwarzer, R. and Leppin, A, (1991). Social support and health: a theoretical and empirical overview. *Journal of Social and Personal Relationships*, 8, 99–127.

Schwartz, S. H. and Boehnke, K. (2004). Evaluating the structure of human values with confirmatory factor analysis. *Journal of Personality*, 38, 230–255.

Scott, L. V., Medbak, S. and Dinan, T.G. (1998). Blunted adrenocorticotropin and cortisol responses to corticotropin-releasing hormone stimulation in chronic fatigue syndrome. *Acta Psychiatrica Scandinavica*, 97, 450–7.

Segerstrom, S. C. and Miller, G. E. (2004). Psychological stress and the human immune system: a meta-analytic study of 30 years of inquiry. *Psychological Bulletin*, 130, 601–30.

Seligman, M. E. P., Steen, T. A., Park, N. and Peterson, C. (2005). Positive psychology progress: empirical validation of interventions. *American Psychologist*, 60, 410–21.

Shang, A., Huwiler-Müntener, K., Nartey, L. *et al.* (2005). Are the clinical effects of homoeopathy placebo effects? Comparative study of placebo-controlled trials of homoeopathy and allopathy *Lancet*, 366, 726–32.

Shankardass, K., McConnell, R., Jerrett, M., Milam, J., Richardson, J. and Berhane, K. (2009). Parental stress increases the effect of traffic-related air pollution on childhood asthma incidence. *Proceedings of the National Academy of Science of the United States of America*, 106, 12406–11.

Shanks, N. and Lightman, S. (2001). The maternal–neonatal neuro-immune interface: are there long-term implications for inflammatory or stress-related disease?. *Journal of Clinical Investigation*, 108, 1567–73.

Shannahoff-Khalsa, D. S. (2004). An introduction to Kundalini Yoga meditation techniques that are specific for the treatment of psychiatric disorders. *Journal of Alternative and Complementary Medicine*, 10, 91–101.

Sharpe, M. (1997). Cognitive behavior therapy for functional somatic complaints: the example of chronic fatigue syndrome. *Psychosomatics*, 38, 356–62.

Sharpe, M., Archard, L. C. and Banatvala, J. E. (1991). A report – chronic fatigue syndrome: guidelines for research. *Journal of the Royal Society of Medicine*, 84, 118–21.

Shastri, L. and Ajjanagadde, V. (1993). From simple associations to systematic reasoning: A connectionist representation of rules, variables, and dynamic bindings using temporal synchrony. *Behavioral and Brain Sciences*, 16, 417–94.

Sheldon, K. M. and Elliot, A. J. (1999). Goal striving, need satisfaction, and longitudinal well-being: the self-concordance model. *Journal of Personality and Social Psychology*, 76, 482–97.

Shepherd, C. (2001). Pacing and exercise in chronic fatigue syndrome. *Physiotherapy*, 87, 395–6.

Sherman, R. and Hickner, J. (2008). Academic physicians use placebos in clinical practice and believe in the mind–body connection. *Journal of General Internal Medicine*, 23, 7–10.

Sigurs, N., Bjarnason, R., Sigurbergsson, F. and Kjellman, B. (2000). Respiratory syncytial virus bronchiolitis in infancy is an important risk factor for asthma and allergy at age 7. *American Journal of Respiratory Critical Care Medicine*, 161, 1501–7.

Sin, N. L. and Lyubomirsky, S. (2009). Enhancing well-being and alleviating depressive symptoms with positive psychology interventions: a practice-friendly meta-analysis. *Journal of Clinical Psychology*, 65, 467–87.

Skinner, B. F. (1971). *Beyond Freedom and Dignity*. Indianapolis, IN: Hackett.

Smolensky, P. (1988) On the proper treatment of connectionism. *Behavioral and Brain Sciences*, 11, 1–74.

Smith, C. A., Hay, P. P. MacPherson, H. (2010). Acupuncture for depression. *Cochrane Database of Systematic Reviews*, Issue 1, Art. No. CD004046.

Smith, M. L. and Glass, G. V. (1977). Meta-analysis of psychotherapy outcome studies. *American Psychologist*, 32, 752–60.

Sodergren S. C. and Hyland M. E. (1999). Expectancy and asthma. In: I Kirsch, ed. *Expectancy, Experience and Behavior,*. Washington DC: APA Books, pp. 97–212.

Sodergren, S. C. and Hyland, M. E. (2000). What are the positive consequences of illness? *Psychology and Health*, 15, 85–97.

Sodergren, S. C., Hyland, M. E., Crawford, A. and Partridge, M. R. (2004). Positivity in illness: self-delusion or existential growth? *British Journal of Health Psychology*, 9, 163–74.

Sointu, E. (2006). The search for well-being in complementary and alternative health practices. *Sociology of Health and Illness*, 28, 330–49.

Sok, S. R., Erlen, J. A. and Kim, K. B. (2003). Effects of acupuncture therapy on insomnia. *Journal of Advanced Nursing*, 44, 375–84.

Sorensen, H. J., Mortensen, E. L., Reinisch, J. M. and Mednick, S. A. (2009). Association between prenatal exposure to bacterial infection and risk of schizophrenia. *Schizophrenia Bulletin*, 35, 631–7.

Spiegel, D. and Giese-Davis, J. (2003). Depression and cancer: mechanisms and disease progression. *Biological Psychiatry*, 54, 269–82.

Starkie, R., Ostrowski, S. R., Jauffred, S., Febbraio, M. and Pedersen, B. K. (2003). Exercise and IL-6 infusion inhibit endotoxin-induced TNF-α production in humans. *The FASEB Journal*, 17, 884–6.

Stathopoulou, G., Powers, M. B., Berry, A. C., Smits, J.A. J. and Otto, M. W. (2006). Exercise interventions for mental health: a quantitative and qualitative review. *Clinical Psychology Science and Practice*, 13, 179–93.

Steinmetz, K. A. and Potter, J. D. (1991). Vegetables, fruit, and cancer. I. Epidemiology. *Cancer Causes and Control*, 2, 325–57.

Steptoe, A., Dockray, S. and Wardle, J. (2009). Positive affect and psychobiological processes relevant to health. *Journal of Personality*, 77, 1747–75.

Stevens, T. and Mulsow, M. (2006). There is no meaningful relationship between television exposure and symptoms of attention-deficit/hyperactivity disorder. *Pediatrics*, 117, 665–72.

Stewart-Williams, S. and Podd, J. (2004). The placebo effect: dissolving the expectancy versus conditioning debate. *Psychological Bulletin*, 130, 324–40.

Strachan, D. P. (1985). Wheezing presenting in general practice. *Archives of Disease in Childhood*, 60, 457–60.

Straub, R. H. and Männel, D. N. (1999). *Nature Medicine*, 5, 877–9.

Stunkard, A. J. Faith, M. S. and Allison, K. C. (2003). Depression and obesity. *Biological Psychiatry*, 54, 330–7.

Sturdy, P. M., Victor, C. R., Anderson, H. R. *et al.* (2002). Psychological, social and health behaviour risk factors for deaths certified as asthma: a national case-control study. *Thorax*, 57, 1034–9.

Su, C., Lichtenstein, G. R., Krok, K., Brensinger, C. M. and Lewis, J. D. (2004). A meta-analysis of the placebo rates of remission and response in clinical trials of active Crohn's disease. *Gastroenterology*, 126, 1257–69.

Subramanian, S.V., Ackerson, L. K., Subramanyam, M. A. and Wright, R. J. (2007). Domestic violence is associated with adult and childhood asthma prevalence in India. *International Journal of Epidemiology*, 36, 569–79.

Sul, J. and Bunde, J. (2005). Anger, anxiety, and depression as risk factors for cardiovascular disease: the problems and implications of overlapping affective dispositions. *Psychological Bulletin*, 131, 260–300.

Svartengren, M., Strand, V., Bylin, G., Jarup, L. and Pershagen, G. (2000). Short-term exposure to air pollution in a road tunnel enhances the asthmatic response to allergen. *European Respiratory Journal*, 37, 219–32.

Swanson, J. M., Elliott, G. R., Greenhill, L. L. *et al.* (2007). Effects of stimulant medication on growth rates across 3 years in the MTA follow-up. *Journal of the American Academy of Child and Adolescent Psychiatry*, 46, 1015–27.

Swenson, C. R., Sanderson, C., Dulit, R. A. and Linehan, M. M. (2001). The application of dialectical behavior therapy for patients with borderline personality disorder on inpatient units. *Psychiatric Quarterly*, 72, 307–24.

Tashman, L.S., Tenenbaum, G. and Eklund, R. (2010). The effect of perceived stress on the relationship between perfectionism and burnout in coaches *Anxiety, Stress and Coping*, 23, 195–212.

Taylor, S. E. and Repettie, R. L., (1997). Health psychology: what is an unhealthy environment and how does it get under the skin. *Annual Review of Psychology*, 48, 411–47.

Teasdale, J. D., Segal, Z V., Williams, J. M. G., Ridgeway, V. A., Soulsby, J. M. and Lau, M. A. (2000). Prevention of relapse/recurrence in major depression by mindfulness-based cognitive therapy. *Journal of Consulting and Clinical Psychology*, 68, 615–23.

Temel, J. S., Greer, J. A. and Muzikansky, A. (2010). Early palliative care for patients with metastatic non-small-cell lung cancer. *New England Journal of Medicine*, 363, 733–42.

Temoshok, L. (1987). Personality, coping style, emotion and cancer: towards an integrative model. *Cancer Surveys*, 6, 545–67.

Ternent, M. A. and Garshelis, D. L. (1999). Taste-aversion conditioning to reduce nuisance activity by black bears in a Minnesota military reservation. *Wildlife Society Bulletin*, 27, 720–8.

ter Wolbeek, M., van Doornen, L. J. P., Kavelaars, A. and Heijnen, C. J. (2008). Predictors of persistent and new-onset fatigue in adolescent girls. *Pediatrics*, 121, e449–57.

Thomas, K. B. (1987). General practice consultations: is there any point in being positive? *British Medical Journal*, 294, 1200–2.

Thomas, K., Nicholl, P. and Coleman, P. (2001). Use and expenditure on complementary medicine in England. *Complementary Therapies in Medicine*, 9, 2–11.

Thorndike, E. L. (1911). *Animal Intelligence*. New York: Macmillan.

Tirelli, U., Marotta, G., Improta, S. and Pinto, A. (1994). Immunological abnormalities in patients with chronic fatigue syndrome. *Scandinavian Journal of Immunology*, 40, 601–8.

Tryon, W. W. (2009). Cognitive processes in cognitive and pharmacological therapies. *Cognitive Therapy and Research*, 33, 570–84.

van Kuppeveld, F. J., de Jong, A. S., Lanke, K. H. *et al.* (2010). Prevalence of xenotropic murine leukaemia virus-related virus in patients with chronic fatigue syndrome in the Netherlands: retrospective analysis of samples from an established cohort. *British Medical Journal*, 340, c1018.

van Ravenswaaij-Arts, C. M. A., Kollee, L. A. A., Hopman, J. C. W., Stoelinga, G. B. A. and van Geijin, H. P. (1993). Heart rate variability. *Annals of Internal Medicine*, 118, 436–47.

van West, D., Claes, S. and Deboutte, D. (2009). Differences in hypothalamic–pituitary–adrenal axis functioning among children with ADHD predominantly inattentive and combined types. *European Child and Adolescent Psychiatry*, 18, 543–53.

Varela, F. J. and Coutinho A. (1991) Second generation immune networks. *Immunology Today*, 12, 159–66.

Vase, L., Robinson, M.E., Verne, G.N. and Price, D.D. (2005). Increased placebo analgesia over time in irritable bowel syndrome (IBS) patients is associated with desire and expectation but not endogenous opioid mechanisms. *Pain*, 115, 338–47.

Veenhoven, R., (2009). *World Database of Happiness, Distributional Findings in Nations*. Rotterdam, Netherlands: Erasmus University. Available at: http://worlddatabaseofhappiness.eur.nl.

Vickers, A., Ohlsson, A., Lacy, J. and Horsley, A. (2004). Massage for promoting growth and development of preterm and/or low birth-weight infants. *Cochrane Database of Systematic Reviews*, Issue 2, Art. No. CD000390.

Viner, R. and Hotopf, M. (2004). Childhood predictors of self reported fatigue syndrome/myalgic encephalomyelitis in adults: national birth cohort study. *British Medical Journal*, 329, 928–9.

Viner, R. M., Clark, C., Taylor, S. J. C. *et al.* (2008). Longitudinal risk factors for persistent fatigue in adolescents. *Archives of Pediatric and Adolescent Medicine* 162, 469–75.

VollmerConna U., Lloyd, A., Hickie, I. and Wakefield, D. (1998). Chronic fatigue syndrome: an immunological perspective. *Australian and New Zealand Journal of Psychiatry*, 32, 523–7.

Vonk, J. M., Postma, D. S., Boezen, H. M. *et al.* (2004) Childhood factors associated with asthma remission after 30 year follow up. *Thorax*, 59, 925–9.

Walach, H. and Maidhof, C. (1999). Is the placebo effect dependent on time? A meta-analysis. In: I. Kirsch, ed. *How Expectancies Shape Experience*. Washington, DC: APA, pp. 321–32.

Walach, H., Rilling, C. and Engelke, U. (2001). Efficacy of Bach-flower remedies in test anxiety: a double-blind, placebo-controlled, randomized trial with partial crossover. *Journal of Anxiety Disorders*, 15, 359–66.

Wampold, B.E. (2001). *The Great Psychotherapy Debate: Models, Methods, and Findings*. Mahwah, NJ: Lawrence Erlbaum.

Wampold, B. E., Mondin, G. W., Moody, M., Stich, F., Benson, K. and Ahn, H. (1997). A meta-analysis of outcome studies comparing bona fide psychotherapies: empirically, 'All must have prizes'. *Psychological Bulletin*, 122, 204–15.

Waterman, A. S. (1993). Two conceptions of happiness: contrasts of personal expressiveness (eudaimonia) and hedonic enjoyment. *Journal of Personality and Social Psychology*, 64, 678–91.

Watson, D. (1988). Intraindividual and interindividual analyses of positive and negative affect: Their relation to health complaints, perceived stress, and daily activities. *Journal of Personality and Social Psychology*, 54, 1020–30.

Watson, D., Clark, L. A. and Tellegen, A. (1988). Development and validation of brief measures of positive and negative affect: The PANAS scales. *Journal of Personality and Social Psychology*, 54, 1063–70.

Watson, D. and Pennebaker, J. W. (1989). Health complaints, stress, and distress: Exploring the central role of negative affectivity. *Psychological Review*, 96, 234–54.

Watt, T., Groenvold, M., Bjorner, J. B., Noerholm, V., Rasmussen, N.-A. and Bech, P. (2000). Fatigue in the Danish general population. Influence of sociodemographic factors and disease. *Journal of Epidemiology and Community Health*, 54, 827–33.

Welton, N. J., Caldwell, D. M., Adamopoulos, E. and Vedhara, K. (2009). Mixed treatment comparison meta-analysis of complex interventions: psychological interventions in coronary heart disease. *American Journal of Epidemiology*, 169, 1158–65.

Weiner, J. (2002). Studies comparing homeopathy and placebo are unhelpful. *British Medical Journal*, 325, 41.

Weiss, S. J., Wilson, P. and Morrison, D. (2004). Maternal tactile stimulation and the neurodevelopment of low birth weight infants. *Infancy*, 5, 85–107.

Wessely, S., Hotopf, M. and Sharpe, M. (1998). *Chronic Fatigue and Its Syndromes*. New York: Oxford University Press.

Wetherell, M. A., Hyland M. E. and Harris, J. E. (2004). Secretary immunoglobulin A reactivity to acute and cumulative multi-tasking stress: relationships between reactivity and perceived workload. *Biological Psychology*, 66, 257–70.

Whalley, B., Bennett, P., Ebrahim, S. *et al.* (2011). Psychological interventions for coronary heart disease. *Cochrane Database of Systematic Reviews*, Issue 3., Art. No. CD002902.

Whalley, B. and Hyland, M. E. (2009). One size does not fit all: motivational predictors of contextual benefits of therapy. *Psychology and Psychotherapy: Theory, Research and Practice*, 82, 291–303.

Whalley, B., Hyland, M. E. and Kirsch, I. (2008). Placebo consistency and placebo responders. *Journal of Psychosomatic Research*, 64, 537–41.

Wheeler, P. and Hyland, M. E. (2008). Dispositional predictors of complementary medicine and vitamin use in students. *Journal of Health Psychology*, 13, 516–19.

WHO (1948). Preamble to the Constitution of the World Health Organization as adopted by the International Health Conference, New York, 19–22 June, 1946; signed on 22 July 1946 by the representatives of 61 States (*Official Records of the World Health Organization*, No. 2, pp. 100) and entered into force on 7 April 1948.

Wilkin T. J., Mallam, K., Metcalf, B. S., Jeffery, A. N. and Voss L. D. (2006). Variation in physical activity lies with the child, not his environment: evidence for an 'activitystat' in young children (EarlyBird 16). *International Journal of Obesity*, 30, 1050–5.

Wilson, M. (2002). Six views of embodied cognition. *Psychonomic Bulletin and Review*, 9, 625–36.

Wittwer-Backofen, U. and Tomo, N. (2008). From health to civilization stress? In search for traces of a health transition during the Early Neolithic in Europe. In: J. P. Bocquet-Appel and O. Bar-Yosef, eds. *The Neolithic Demographic Transition and its Consequences*. Dordrecht, Netherlands: Springer Netherlands, 501–38.

Wood, J. D. (2006). Integrative functions of enteric nervous system. In: L. R. Johnson and K. E. Barrett, eds. *Physiology of the Gastrointestinal Tract*. New York: Academic Press, pp. 665–84.

Wright, R. J., Cohen, S., Carey, S. T. and Gold, D. R. (2002). Parental stress as a predictor of wheezing in infancy: a prospective birth-cohort study. *American Journal of Respiratory Critical Care Medicine*, 165, 358–65.

Wright, R. J., Rodriguez, M. and Cohen, S. (1998). Review of psychosocial stress and asthma: an integrated biopsychosocial approach. *Thorax*, 53, 1066–74.

Xu, J. and Roberts, J. E. (2010). The power of positive emotions: it's a matter of life or death—subjective well-being and longevity over 28 years in a general population. *Health Psychology*, 29, 9–19.

Yalom, I. D. (1980). *Existential Psychotherapy*. New York: Basic Books.

Yazdanbakhsh, M., Kremsner, P. G. and van Ree, R. (2002). Allergy, parasites, and the hygiene hypothesis. *Science*, 296, 490–4.

Yehud, R. (2003). Hypothalamic–pituitary–adrenal alterations in PTSD: are they relevant to understanding cortisol alterations in cancer? *Brain, Behavior, and Immunity*, 17(Suppl. 1), 73–83.

Young, E., Stoneham, M. D., Petruckevitch, A., Barton, J. and Rona, R. (1994). A population study of food intolerance. *Lancet*, 343, 1127–30.

Zajicek, J., Fox, P., Sanders, H. *et al.* (2003). Cannabinoids for treatment of spasticity and other symptoms related to multiple sclerosis (CAMS study): multicentre randomised placebo-controlled trial. *Lancet*, 362, 1517–26.

Zeaman, D. and House, B. J. (1951).The growth and decay of reactive inhibition as measured by alternation behavior. *Journal of Experimental Psychology*, 41, 177–86.

Zijlstra T. R., van de Laar M. A., Bernelot Moens H. J., Taal E., Zakraoui L. and Rasker J. J. (2005). Spa treatment for primary fibromyalgia syndrome: a combination of thalassotherapy, exercise and patient education improves symptoms and quality of life. *Rheumatology*, 44, 539–46.

Zopf, Y., Baenkler, H. W., Silermann, A., Hahn, E. G. and Raithel, M. (2009). The differential diagnosis of food intolerance. *Deutsches Arzteblatt International*, 106, 359–70.

Index